MYTHS and REALITIES

MYTHS and REALITIES

✦

Conflicting Currents of Culture and Science

John Whedbee

iUniverse, Inc.
New York Lincoln Shanghai

MYTHS and REALITIES
Conflicting Currents of Culture and Science

Copyright © 2005 by John Whedbee

iUniverse books may be ordered through booksellers or by contacting:

iUniverse
2021 Pine Lake Road, Suite 100
Lincoln, NE 68512
www.iuniverse.com
1-800-Authors (1-800-288-4677)

ISBN-13: 978-0-595-36239-4 (pbk)
ISBN-13: 978-0-595-67356-8 (cloth)
ISBN-13: 978-0-595-80684-3 (ebk)
ISBN-10: 0-595-36239-7 (pbk)
ISBN-10: 0-595-67356-2 (cloth)
ISBN-10: 0-595-80684-8 (ebk)

Printed in the United States of America

Contents

INTRODUCTION

This book is primarily about human life and culture. It is also an attempt to place human beings into the wider context of which they are a part. Without this larger picture, much of the behavior of Homo sapiens makes little sense. So we will look at mankind's place among other living creatures; then at the larger context of the earth, the solar system and the galaxy; finally at the vast expanses of the cosmos.

Some of man's principal activities will be examined: the cultures that he has created, his beliefs and his gods. Also his intellectual achievements: science, technology, art, literature and philosophy. And some of his more obvious shortcomings: war, cruelty, intolerance, greed, and inhumanity towards his fellow man.

A human being is an "intelligent animal," unique among all other creatures in this regard, but his intelligence struggles against his innate instincts, which are an inseparable part of him, due to his origin on the ladder of evolution. In many ways he is like a puppet attached to strings, but the strings stretch back a billion years and more. Only when looked at from this point of view does the apparent senselessness of much of human behavior become more intelligible.

Although our first non-human ancestors appeared on earth more than three billion years ago, our presence as Homo sapiens goes back only some 150,000 years. However, truly modern man, Homo sapiens sapiens, appeared only about 30,000 years ago. But for the most part, even modern man has been no more than dimly aware of the context in which he lives. In fact, really detailed knowledge of the cosmos and its history has only begun to register on human consciousness in the past 50-100 years.

From the time of Copernicus in the sixteenth century, modern science has developed at an accelerating pace, and we will look more closely at these developments in chapter 9. Recent advances have led to the expansion of our knowledge in two opposing directions: into the microscopic on the one hand, and the macroscopic on the other. Both ends of these twin probes have paid impressive dividends in the past few decades.

Culture, science, religion and war will constitute the main elements of our story. These will be examined on a generalized basis. It is obviously not possible to go into very much detail, given the scope of the subject, although from time to time certain topics will be discussed more thoroughly. The selection of these topics is necessarily somewhat arbitrary, but I have tried to select those that will shed the most light on the overall picture. In general, I have tended to omit or summarize those parts of the story that are already well known, while concentrating on important aspects that are often overlooked.

To integrate the various topics, the narrative has been divided into two parts. The first is mainly historical, and traces the way that the various cultures have arisen and interacted with one another. The building of larger states lead to the establishment of empires, which were able to exert control over large and disparate populations. The advancement of science and technology eventually lead to the Industrial Revolution, which had the effect of dividing the world into developed and under-developed regions. But the process of globalization is now beginning to blur the distinction between these two segments of the world community.

The second part examines further aspects of the human scene, including man's place in the physical universe, with its origin in the Big Bang. After this bigger picture has been sketched out, we will again look at selected subjects that will hopefully provide further insight into the nature of man and society. This time there will be less emphasis on history, and more on man's physical and cultural environment. For instance, the relationship between the material universe and its description by the physical sciences will be looked at from several points of view. And various facets of human behavior will be examined more closely, including especially the phenomenon of war.

The part relating to culture is obviously the core of the book, and again, with a topic as broad as this, selections have had to be made. A general knowledge of world history is desirable but not essential. Since I wish to make comparisons and cross-references between different eras and cultures, this can be more effective if the context is already reasonably well known. However, if in a few cases the subject is unfamiliar, this should not adversely affect the overall picture.

Topics such as mind, consciousness, and the nature of physical laws will be discussed in some detail, because they relate directly to the human condition. Evolution and its consequences are naturally of prime importance in the human drama, so this will occupy a central place in the story.

Only the major religions: Christianity, Islam, Buddhism, Hinduism and Judaism will be examined in any detail, since they have had the greatest influence on the world stage. But religion itself is part of the larger topic of beliefs in general, which stem from the most powerful and distinctive human attribute, namely the imagination. The imagination is responsible for the myths that have always been an indivisible part of our diverse cultures. My main purpose is to try and separate these myths from the underlying reality.

Western culture will occupy center stage, not necessarily because it is superior, but because it has played a dominant role in the creation of the modern world. However, to get an accurate picture of our present situation, it is essential that the development of the other major cultures and religions should also be taken into account. Only in this way can we get an accurate idea of how the West fits into the wider global context. And besides, if past history is any guide, the ascendancy of the West may well be fleeting. It seems likely, however, that the different cultures will slowly coalesce into something more rational and universal—that is if we survive, as a species, to see such things.

Subjects such as art, architecture, philosophy and law are included in order to give the picture a broader perspective. Human institutions have been extremely important in shaping human history, and these will be looked at in the general context of cultural development.

New discoveries regarding the nervous system and the brain are providing major insights into our overall understanding of human nature, so I have sketched out some of the avenues of research that are now being followed. The prospect that man may soon be able to create "intelligent machines" has tremendous implications for the future, and one must assume that the day is rapidly approaching when this will become a reality. No one can predict the consequences, but big surprises are undoubtedly in store.

Many subjects have been covered about which my knowledge is clearly limited, and I apologize to the specialists in these fields for my lack of expertise. But the intention has been to integrate all these subjects together, so as to present an overall perspective. I feel strongly that we cannot hope to understand the world in which we live unless we are prepared to look at the big picture, which includes all aspects of human nature and human endeavor.

Obviously the book relies heavily on other people's knowledge and ideas, so in most cases I have allowed the experts to speak for themselves. However, it was inevitable that a few of my own ideas and opinions should be included. Hopefully this will not seriously detract from the overall objectivity that I have tried to maintain.

One further point should be mentioned at the start. The use of the masculine pronoun throughout is done solely to increase clarity and not to express any preference for the male gender. If we constantly have to say "him or her," or "man and woman," the narrative becomes unnecessarily cumbersome. So please excuse this relic from our male chauvinist past, and understand that "man" in fact stands for both genders and implies no preference for either.

So on with the dance. Leave all prejudices and preconceived notions at the door. It's just possible that you will gain some new insight into your world, and a greater appreciation of its amazing complexity and awesome extent.

PART I
HISTORICAL PERSPECTIVES

o o o o o o o o o o o o o o o o o o o o o o o o o o o o o o o o

It has often and confidently been asserted, that man's origin can never be known: but ignorance more frequently begets confidence than does knowledge: it is those who know little, and not those who know much, who so positively assert that this or that problem will never be solved by science.

—*Charles Darwin*
The Descent of Man

1

CULTURAL ORIGINS

○ ○
Man is a rope stretched between the animal
and the Superman—a rope over an abyss.

—*Friedrich Nietzsche*
Thus Spoke Zarathustra

IN THE BEGINNING

The age of the universe is around 15 billion years, and this seems to be approximately the time it takes to make an intelligent being! It took about 10 billion years to produce something like our solar system—give or take a billion years or so. The initial appearance of life and the development of complex life forms have taken about half that time again. So it would not have been possible for us to arrive in our earthly home much earlier than we actually did.

For a long time after the Big Bang, hydrogen and helium were the only elements that existed. These were not sufficiently complex to form the basis for any kind of life. In fact several further stages of cosmic development were necessary before life became possible. The first galaxies were formed about a billion years after the Big Bang. But their constituent stars would have had no planetary systems. Only after several generations of stars had come and gone, did the heavier elements necessary to produce life finally appear—from supernova explosions in dying stars. "Stardust" from these explosions formed "seeds" from which new stars were born. Some of these stars had planetary systems like our sun—this meant that for the first time the potential for life existed in the universe.[1]

Exactly how life first arose is still obscure, but the fog is finally beginning to lift. For a while the scientific community favored the idea that "complexity" might hold the key to the origin of life. It was thought that if a sufficient number of different molecules were allowed to come together in an environment that allowed them to interact freely, self-replicating molecules could be spontaneously produced.[2] Once self-replication is established, the essential mechanism of life is in place and further development logically follows with the help of natural selection. But although it provides us with a simple explanation for life's origin, this scenario has serious difficulties. It implies that life can be produced relatively easily, whereas this does not appear to be the case, because, as far as we know, life has only arisen once in our entire solar system. Furthermore, we are yet to discover life anywhere else in the universe. So although complexity is surely *part* of the answer, it's not the whole story. (This topic is discussed further in chapter 10.)

The point I want to emphasize is that the question of life's origin is now in the realm of science, and the answer will eventually be found. It had previously been relegated to the realm of myth, which, for countless millennia, was the sole source of information on this important subject.

What exactly *is* life anyway? The easy answer is that it is an electro-chemical process. But this sounds too much like reductionism, and so we naturally seek a more satisfactory definition. In truth, like many other important things, life is very hard to define. Even though one knows instinctively what it is, it's difficult to come up with an accurate definition. The best thing is to look at it from several different viewpoints.

A concept known as "vitalism" used to be popular. It postulates some kind of life force, or "vital principle" within living creatures, but it is no longer taken seriously. Another way of looking at life is as a means to escape the consequences of the second law of thermodynamics. This is the law relating to entropy, which says that any system tends to move into a less organized state—one of greater entropy.[3] Living things are able to (locally) reverse this natural process and create *more* order, thus counteracting the natural process of decay. Following this line of reasoning, a living organism takes in energy—ultimately from the sun—and uses it to preserve and enhance the organization of its body, which would otherwise decay into its constituent parts. Living organisms take in food, from which they create order and structure. Having extracted the order from the food, the waste is eliminated. On balance, however, the organism has to consume more order than it creates, so as not to violate the second law. In addition to this, living organisms must be capable of reproducing themselves, because the second law cannot be held in abeyance for more than a limited amount of time. So the cycle of life and death becomes the hallmark of all living things.

Just how organic matter differs from inorganic substances has also been mulled over by the "experts" for millennia.[4] Molecular Microbiologist JohnJoe McFadden asserts that, "at its most fundamental level, life is a quantum phenomenon."[5] This idea will be considered more carefully in chapter 10 (*Aspects of Evolution*).

The progression from the most primitive single-celled creatures to the first multi-celled organisms, or eucarya, took more than a billion and a half years. After that, it took about an equal amount of time before more complex creatures began to develop. This happened during the Cambrian period, about 500-550 million years ago. At this time there was an "explosion" of different kinds of animal species, many of which were considerably more complex than those that had gone before. This period marked a watershed between the primitive life that had existed up until that time, and the more advanced forms, which ultimately developed into those that we see today.[6]

We now fast-forward to the demise of the dinosaurs, which occurred when a large asteroid or meteorite crashed into the Yucatan peninsula some 65 million years ago.[7] This is one of those theories that was pooh-poohed when it was first proposed, but it is now widely accepted by the scientific community. It seems that the removal of the dinosaurs allowed the primates the breathing room they needed to increase and multiply.

The primate line split in two some 55 million years ago, one branch leading to the prosimians and the other to the anthropoids, ancestors of monkeys, apes and humans. The first division of the anthropoids occurred some 30 million years ago: one part leading to the Old World monkeys and another to the Dryopithecines, ancestors of both hominids and chimpanzees, the latter splitting off some 6-7 million years ago. The first hominids to appear in the fossil record were the Australopithecines, ancestors of Homo sapiens.

The first member of the genus Homo to be found outside Africa was Homo erectus, who left Africa about two million years ago. Peking Man, discovered in the 1920's, is a member of this species, which had inhabited East Asia for nearly a million years before the modern form of Homo sapiens appeared in China, around 40,000 years ago. There is no evidence of interbreeding between Homo erectus and Homo sapiens, so the former probably died out long before modern man arrived. The most likely cause is the deteriorating climate.[8]

The Neanderthals were present in Europe some 250,000 years ago. DNA studies show that they are not ancestors of modern man. The split from the hominid line must have occurred about 500,000 years ago. Their fossils have been found in Europe and the Middle East, and they definitely showed signs of primitive culture. But they became extinct about the time that modern man first appeared, so Homo sapiens may have exterminated them. DNA studies show no signs of interbreeding between the two groups.[9]

Cro-Magnon man, named from the rock shelter in southern France where some of his remains were found, was an early form of modern man that succeeded the Neanderthals. Paleolithic cave paintings created by the Cro-Magnons have been found in the region. As paleontologist Richard Fortey writes:

> If you dressed Cro-Magnon man in a suit and tidied him up a little he might have been a suitable tea-table guest for Lady Smith Woodward. His language would have been unfamiliar, but there would have been no doubt about his species. His appearance would have been acceptable in society. He was proficient in another manifestation of humanity: he could paint.[10]

So Cro-Magnon man can be considered as an early example of truly modern man—Homo sapiens sapiens—who came onto the scene some 30,000 years ago. A recent study, using DNA analysis, has traced the migrations of some of his forebears from their origins in Africa. This analysis uses the fact that mitochondrial DNA is passed on only through the female line, and is not subject to generational shuffling of the genes; also that the Y-chromosome is passed from father to son, its sequence also being shielded from mixing. The mutations that occur in these sections of the DNA provide "markers," which can be traced from continent to continent by analyzing blood samples taken from the present inhabitants. By examining these DNA patterns, scientists can trace lineages back to sons and daughters of a genetic "Adam and Eve." The patterns have been traced back to the San Bushmen of the Kalahari, who represent the oldest existing African bloodline.[11]

Geneticist Spencer Wells has studied the migrations from Africa using the Y-chromosome lineages. His findings are reported in his book *The Journey of Man*. He traces the human migrations from Africa starting from about 60,000 years ago. One branch probably journeyed from northeast Africa along a coastal route via India, all the way to Southeast Asia and Australia. The Australian aborigines may have arrived there as long as 60,000 years ago. Other groups spread via the Middle East to Asia and Europe. Many of the migrants must have been able to survive the last ice age, which was well advanced by the time they set out, and which ended about 10,000 years ago. They probably spent much of the glacial period in Central Asia, before moving west into Europe and east into Asia and the Americas. As Wells puts it: "If Africa was the cradle of modern man, Central Asia was the nursery." He says the trunk and the main body of modern man's family tree can be found in Africa. Only the higher branches moved out to spread their foliage around the world. The roots of the tree were probably planted about 150,000 years ago. It took a long time for our ancestors to leave the cradle and step out into the wider world.

The dispersion of the genus Homo from its original home in Africa stands in stark contrast to the history of our nearest "relatives," the chimpanzees. As Ann and David Premack write, in *Original Intelligence*:

> The limited causal reasoning of the chimpanzee has made it impossible for it to develop technologies on which migration depends, and thus has confined it to a small corner of Africa for over five million years.[12]

We find evidence of tool-making going back to the earliest hominids in Africa, more than two million years ago. We also find evidence of spoken language. This is revealed through indentations on the interior of the skull, in the part of the brain now known to relate to language. But significant evidence of cultural development does not arise until the appearance of modern man. It is only with the first signs of art that we start to recognize creatures truly akin to ourselves.

The cave paintings at Lascaux, and also at sites in Spain, dating from about 14,000 B.C., give the first definitive evidence of human cultural expression. Many of these paintings depict the hunting of reindeer, the primary source of food for the Magdalenians, who preyed on the migratory herds. This was before the climate grew warmer and the herds moved northwards.[13]

The existence of art is a sure sign of the development of the imagination, which of course is intimately connected with consciousness. Here is where we encounter the true essence of the human being, which differentiates him from his fellow animals. Art and religion both stem from the imagination, and true culture can hardly exist without them.

The earliest settlements were those of the so-called hunter-gatherers, which made up the basic form of human society for many millennia. About 8,000 years ago, before the advent of larger agricultural communities, small villages that lived by hunting and cultivating various cereals began to appear, principally in Southwest Asia. These were neighborhood or family settlements, which eventually spread across the globe wherever human beings were to be found. Historians J. R. and William McNeill describe this process in *The Human Web*:

By about two millennia after their emergence, agricultural villages had spread like a rash across Eurasia, Africa, and the Americas and became the frame within which the majority of mankind lived and died. The overwhelming majority of our predecessors continued to reside in such villages until very recently.[14]

These communities certainly had a rudimentary form of culture, and the presence of art and precious objects, as well as burials, bears witness to its development. There is also evidence that they were interested in religion, this being mostly of the shamanistic variety. But lack of written records makes these societies difficult to assess in a precise manner, and in spite of valiant efforts by the archaeologists, they will probably remain shrouded in the mists of prehistory.

So in order to construct an accurate picture of past communities, we have to confine ourselves to those that created larger settlements—towns or cities—based on agriculture, and that left some kind of written record. This type of settlement arose in six different locations. These were, in order of their appearance: Mesopotamia, Egypt, the Indus River Valley, the Yellow River in China, and finally Central and South America.

We will look briefly at each of these, with the intention of discovering both their similarities and their differences.

MESOPOTAMIA

This early culture arose between the Tigris and Euphrates rivers in what is now Iraq. Here we find the practice of agriculture well established, and also the domestication of sheep and goats. During the Neolithic period, between 7000 and 4500 B.C., there is evidence of the first real towns. The advent of towns was made possible by the creation of an agricultural surplus by those who worked to produce the food crops. They were able to produce more food than they themselves needed, and this made possible the creation of a central community or town, where the surplus food could be stored, and where the leaders of the community and their attendants took up residence.

By 4000 B.C. there were a number of such towns in Mesopotamia, which were often surrounded by villages and hamlets. Uruk, for example, covered about 25 acres in 4000 B.C. Nine centuries later the town covered 200 acres, and may have had 10,000 inhabitants. Over the next 200 years the population swelled to 20,000.[15] Uruk also had sanctuaries, or temples, reflecting the early importance of religion in the society.

The first writing, consisting of pictograms and other markings, comes from this period. In time the cuneiform method of writing was developed, with wedge-shaped marks incised on clay tablets. These were initially used for accounting purposes.

Uruk was in Sumer, roughly the area around Basra in present-day Iraq. It was an example of what has come to be known as a city-state, and many of these eventually arose in the Fertile Crescent. This was the name given to the area bounded by the Mediterranean to the west, the Taurus mountains to the north, the Zagros mountains to the east and the Arabian desert to the south. City-states often acquired satellites in the form of smaller cities or towns in the surrounding area, with an overlord, or king, established in the central city, where monumental architecture could also be found. The latter consisted of elaborate buildings for the use of the king and his attendants, and also religious structures, the chief example of which was the ziggurat, or stepped pyramid, which was often the distinguishing landmark of the main population center.

Compared to the small agricultural villages, the towns created a much more stratified society. There was a sharp division between the leadership elite and the servants and laborers, which had not existed in the rural settlements. In addition to this, there was the dichotomy between urban and agricultural life. This characteristic of towns and cities has persisted to the present day, with extreme riches and poverty existing side by side. Sad to say, the advance of civilization has generally brought neither justice nor equality. Instead it has increased the disparity between the strong and the weak, the rich and the poor.

There was much competition and almost continual strife between the city-states. Most had their own gods, and if the king was defeated in battle, it was taken as a sign that the gods were not powerful enough, in which case they were replaced, together with their attendant priests. Uruk was one of several city-states that rose to prominence in Sumer during the period 2900-2371 B.C. The latter date marks the end of Uruk's last period of prominence and its defeat by the Akkadians. As historian Jack Finegan writes:

> The Sumerian King List describes the transition from the Third Dynasty of Uruk to the Dynasty of Akkad in the usual fashion, by saying that Uruk was defeated and its kingship carried off to Akkad, then lists the kings and the lengths of their reign.... The capital city of Akkad has not been located, but was probably somewhere in the vicinity of the later Babylon; at any rate, the region of Akkad was the narrow northern plain of Lower Mesopotamia...[16]

The first ruler of Akkad was the famous king Sargon, who reigned for fifty-six years. His many conquests are recorded in the Legend of Sargon.

In 2004 B.C. the ascendancy passed to Babylon, where Hammurabi created his famous Law Code. The city of Babylon was eventually destroyed by the Assyrian king Sennacherib in 689. However, it was rebuilt by Nebuchadnezzar II (605-563 B.C.), who constructed a great palace complex that included the famous hanging gardens.

Babylon fell to the Persians in 539 B.C. One result of this was the release of the Jews, who had been carried off to captivity in Babylon by Nebuchadnezzar in 586.

EGYPT

Egyptian culture developed a little later than that of Mesopotamia. The First Egyptian Dynasty (3100-2890 B.C.) was established at Memphis by King Menes, who united the two kingdoms of Upper and Lower Egypt. The chronology of the early kings and dynasties has been reliably established from the Palermo Stone, which was engraved in the Fifth Dynasty, and also from tablets found in the royal tombs at Abydos and Saqqara. The hieroglyphic writing is more elaborate than contemporary writing from Mesopotamia, and we find monumental architecture dating from very early times.[17]

The form of the Egyptian pyramid developed from that of the mastaba, a block-like rectangular tomb, with burial chambers excavated below. As time went by, this form developed first into the stepped pyramid, as seen in examples at Saqqara, and finally into the fully developed pyramids at Giza, which were built in the Fourth Dynasty (2680-2565 B.C.). There were also elaborate temples constructed at Luxor, Karnak and elsewhere. The quality of the art and architecture was mostly superior to that found in Mesopotamia, and the construction of these monuments represents a stupendous technical and artistic achievement. The actual method whereby the stones were raised and set in place is still not fully understood.

Towns arose along the Nile, and although a few, such as Memphis, Heliopolis and Thebes, developed into what we might call cities, these could not really be described as city-states like those in Mesopotamia, because the whole kingdom was united under one pharaoh. The capital city, or seat of the pharaoh, was changed several times. For instance, during the Ninth and Tenth Dynasties the capital was at Heracleopolis, and during the Eleventh it was at Thebes.

There was an invasion of the Egyptian kingdom by the Hyksos in 1786 B.C. These invaders, the so-called shepherd people from Syria, took over the kingdom and installed their own pharaohs. This usurpation lasted until 1570 when the Hyksos were finally expelled.

Egyptian art, although excessively stylized, was of an extremely high quality, and became more sophisticated with the passage of time. It maintained an underlying continuity through the long series of dynasties, and this gave the Egyptian culture its special character. The intricate nature of the hieroglyphic writing precluded the development of any kind of real literature, and the number system did not lend itself to the advancement of science. Even so the Egyptians did much pioneering work in geometry, which was later expanded and improved upon by the Greeks.

Gold was quite plentiful in Egypt, so the metal was not considered as precious as we deem it to be today. What *was* precious was iron. Most of the known iron ore was in Anatolia, so if there was any precious metal in Egypt it was iron rather than gold.

THE INDUS VALLEY

The next example of a cultural emergence occurred in the Indus Valley during the second half of the third millennium B.C. This covered a large area in what is now Pakistan. Although examples of writing have been discovered, the script has not yet been deciphered. This makes the history of the culture difficult to reconstruct. However, the remains of two cities, Mohenjo-daro and Harappa, have been excavated, and archaeologists have found the remains of other cities in Baluchistan, and also in the desert to the south. Many other smaller towns and villages have been found, and the total area of all these settlements comprises more than 400,000 square miles. In Mohenjo-daro there is a large rectangular platform, or citadel, in the center of the city, and also a granary, assembly hall and religious buildings nearby. The streets of the city are laid out on a grid pattern, and the whole comprises some 240 acres. It probably had a population in excess of 30,000 at its height around 2200 B.C.[18]

Unlike the Mesopotamian and Egyptian cultures, the Indus Valley seems to have suffered a sudden demise, probably as a result of the Aryan invasions that are thought to have occurred about 1500 B.C. The open landscape of the Indus valley provided little opportunity for defense against an attacking horde, and there are distinct signs that many of the cities had been assaulted and pillaged. This would have been an instance of what came to be a common phenomenon—the attack of a hunting, or nomadic, society upon a settled one. But the Indus Valley culture covered a very large area and so could not have been destroyed all at once. Its probable that the southern regions survived the initial assaults and were gradually assimilated by the invaders, who became part of the permanent population of northern India. The Hindu culture arose as a blend of the Aryan culture and that of the indigenous population.

CHINA

The Yellow River settlements in China are not as well documented historically as those in Mesopotamia and Egypt. Their buildings were not constructed of stone, and so have left few indications as to their exact character.

There is evidence of human settlement in the area of the modern city of Xian that dates back as far as 5000 B.C. An early culture, that of the Lungshan, whose chief characteristic was the writing of omens on charred animal bones, existed in the same area between 2500 and 1850 B.C. But it is not until the emergence of the Shang dynasty (1500-1027 B.C.) that true culture, including the appearance of a real written language, appears on the historical scene. The Shang was followed by the Zhou dynasty (1027-256 B.C.), and this was when the main features of Chinese civilization definitely began to emerge. Metal artifacts that have been unearthed from this period, such as ornamental bells and other ceremonial objects show a high level of sophistication, both in their artistic quality and the methods of their manufacture.

It's likely that there was some interchange of ideas between the Mesopotamian, Egyptian and Indus Valley cultures, but the Chinese were effectively isolated, so their myths and legends were unique unto themselves. Here is an example, given by Yong Yap and Arthur Cotterell:

> A legend of the creation of the universe concerns P'an-ku, primeval man. At the outset the universe was an egg. One day the egg split open. The top half became the sky and the bottom half the earth. P'an-ku, who emerged from the broken egg, grew three metres taller every day, just as the sky became three metres higher and the earth three metres thicker. After eighteen thousand years P'an-ku died. Then, like the original egg, he split into a number of parts. His head formed the sun and moon, his blood the rivers and seas, his hair the forests, his sweat the rain, his breath the wind, his voice the thunder and, last of all, his fleas became the ancestors of mankind."[19]

One characteristic of the early Chinese culture was the elevated status of the scribes, who needed special skills to master the elaborate characters of the Chinese script, and who became the custodians of learning under the Confucian system.

Most of the history of the Shang dynasty is uncertain at best. Its capital at Anyang was only uncovered in 1935. But the first Shang king established an important principle: that the people could rightfully depose an unjust ruler. The idea was that heaven would revoke the legitimacy of an unjust monarch. Apparently there was little or no slavery, a significant difference from the Middle Eastern cultures.

The Shang dynasty eventually fell, either by a popular uprising or through conquest by the kingdom of Zhou, and discrepancies in the historical record suggest that the Zhou then replaced the Shang version of history with its own. At any rate, the first certain date of Chinese chronology is 841 B.C., when there was a rebellion against the Zhou king Li.

The Western Zhou dynasty had its capital in the valley of the river Wei. In 771 B.C. the capital was moved to Loyang, where the Eastern Zhou dynasty was established.

The period from 453 to 256 B.C. is known as the period of the Warring States, during which the territory of the Zhou broke up into warring sections with one or another of them gaining temporary advantage. This period ended with the defeat of the royal house of Zhou by the Ch'in, who soon extended their hegemony to the whole of China.

It was during the period of the Eastern Zhou, in the sixth and fifth centuries B.C., that Confucius established his philosophical system, and the literature that subsequently formed the basis of Chinese education was written.

The semi-barbarian Ch'in dynasty ruled from 256 to 207 B.C. But although this period saw the establishment of a stronger central government, it did not last. The infamous Ch'in Emperor Ch'ih-shih Huang Ti is best remembered for the first recorded instance of book burning (213 B.C.). Like other dictators that were to follow him, he considered intellectuals to be subversive. So he set out to destroy as much of Chinese history and literature as he could. But he also started work on the Great Wall.

The succeeding Han dynasty established a stable rule during what has come to be known as the Chinese imperial age, when the boundaries of the kingdom were extended into Mongolia and Central Asia. Efforts were also made to expand the kingdom to the northeast into Manchuria and Korea.[20]

THE AMERICAS

The final examples of early culture are located in Central and South America. Of course the idea that Columbus "discovered" America is pure Western conceit. Leif Ericson probably made a similar claim, in spite of the fact that they both encountered native peoples.

The *real* Americans arrived sometime between 35,000 and 15,000 years ago, when there was a land bridge across the Bering Strait. Many of these immigrants eventually crossed the Isthmus of Panama and established communities in South America.

The arrival of more advanced culture occurred in the Americas at a somewhat later date than that of the other instances that we have considered. There are extensive remains of early settlements in North America, stretching from the Arctic, through the eastern woodlands, and into the Southwest. However, it was in Central America that the most advanced and most extensive centers were established. A series of cultures arose in this region, starting with the Olmecs, on the Gulf Coast, circa 1200 B.C. These people produced vast sculptures made of basalt, some weighing more than 20 tons. They also erected pyramids and monumental structures at La Venta, San Lorenzo and several other locations. The Olmecs imported a wide range of materials, such as jade, obsidian and basalt from the people of the nearby highlands.

Towards the middle of the first millennium B.C., the centers of culture began to move to the central highlands and large cities eventually arose, first at Monte Alban and then at Teotihuacan. By A.D. 150 the latter had become a major city, with temples and pyramids built on a huge scale. These structures, which are still largely intact, bear a striking resemblance to those of Mesopotamia and Egypt. In fact it was once thought that there must have been some communication between the Middle East and Central America in the distant past, in order to account for these similarities. But such notions are now discounted, and it's clear that the American pyramids arose independently.

The Toltecs, whose capital was at Tula in the north, gained dominance over most of Mesoamerica by about 1000 A.D. However, the Aztecs, who had settled in the Valley of Mexico about 1200 A.D., took over the Valley in 1430 and established their capital at Tenochtitlan, the site of present-day Mexico City. By the eve of the Spanish conquest in 1515 the Aztecs had assumed sole control over most of Mesoamerica, except for the Yukatan and the Guatemalan highlands, where the Mayan culture had developed in relative isolation.[21]

The so-called Pre-classic period of the Mayan culture stretches back before 2000 B.C., and recent archaeological discoveries have given strong indications that this period was far more advanced than previously supposed. The flowering of the Maya in the Classic period, A.D. 250-900, saw the establishment of large cities at Tikal and Palenque, together with many smaller centers, several of which contained elaborate monumental architecture in the form of large pyramids surmounted by temples and adorned with intricate sculpture. The Maya developed a complicated system of writing, which has only recently been deciphered. They also had an elaborate calendar, by means of which the dates of the rulers and major events of their reigns were recorded. For a while it was thought that the Maya were a relatively peace-loving people, unlike the Aztecs, who indulged in human sacrifice and other unpleasant activities. However, recent research has uncovered a history of conflict between the various population centers, accompanied by much bloodletting and cruelty.[22]

The Maya went into a rapid decline after about 900 A.D., and although there was a later revival in northern Yukatan, with the construction of large centers at Chichen Itza and elsewhere, they never regained their former prominence. By the time the Spanish arrived, little remained of the great cities, which were largely swallowed up by the jungle.

Lastly, we consider the rise of culture in South America. As in North America, there is evidence of very early human habitation in this region, going back at least nine thousand years. Most of these settlements were in southern Ecuador, Peru and northern Chile. There seems to have been a pattern of seasonal movement to different locations in order to take advantage of the availability of food, such as fish and other animals, also water and grazing grounds. By the third millennium B.C., settled agricultural communities were established adjacent to the river valleys in Peru and southern Ecuador.

A series of interconnected communities arose over the next two millennia, from Tiahuanaco on Lake Titacaca in the south, to Real Alto in the north. At Chavin de Huanter, in the Mosna Valley in the highlands of northern Peru, a religious cult in which oracles played a prominent role arose circa 1200 B.C. This eventually spread to the surrounding area, especially to the coast of Peru, where there was already a tradition of building large pyramids and other religious structures.

Two large multi-ethnic states emerged in the central Andes between 550 and 750 A.D.: one centered at Tiahuanaco, and the other, the Huari Empire, in northern Peru. However, the latter collapsed in the ninth century, and several smaller successor states then competed for supremacy. By the fifteenth century there were again only two: that of the Incas, centered at Cuzco, and the Empire of Chinor, with its capital at Chanchan on the coast of northern Peru.[23] The Incas eventually succeeded in conquering Chinor, and incorporated its territory into the Inca Empire.

Francisco Pizarro had accompanied Balboa on his historic crossing of the Isthmus of Panama in 1513. He had started to explore the west coast of South America in 1524, but it was not until a later trip, in 1532, that he met with the Incas in significant numbers.

The Incas had initially looked upon the small band of conquistadors as little more than a curiosity. But this was a serious mistake on their part. By guile, deceit and treachery Pizarro and his men contrived to ambush and capture the Inca Emperor, Atahualpa, at Cajamarca and to massacre thousands of his followers.

A vast quantity of gold was paid for Atahualpa's ransom, but although the ransom was paid, this did not prevent his murder by the Spaniards. He was told before his death that if he became a Christian his body would not be burnt. But even though he agreed to be baptized, his body was burnt nonetheless.

The taking of Atahualpa had a precedent in Tenochtitlan (Mexico City). As Hugh Thomson writes: "Pizarro would never have seized Atahualpa in the main square of Cajamarca and thereby held a nation hostage if Cortés had not done precisely the same with Moctezuma in the previous decade."[24] The priceless gold treasures, brought by the Incas to ransom their Emperor, were taken back to Spain and melted down to pay for the purchase of more cannon.

Several years later the Incas rose in revolt, but they were defeated by the superior arms and ruthless tactics of the conquistadors. Some continued to resist from their mountain hideouts, but they were hunted down and defeated by the Spanish forces.[25]

The Incas had no written language. The only means of communication that has been found is the *quipu*, which was somewhat like an abacus, made of knotted cords, which was presumably used to designate numbers, or types of goods, etc. The Incas did not make use of the wheel, although they had an extensive system of roads, which included many suspension bridges made of tropical vines that spanned the Andean gorges and canyons over which the roads had to cross.[26] The mountain city of Machu Picchu, together with many other ruins of Inca settlements, sited spectacularly in the mountains of Peru, as well as the capital city of Cuzco, bear witness to the skill of these people in creating monumental architecture, and in the organization of their communities. But like the Spanish who succeeded them, the Incas were cruel and harsh taskmasters. The peoples they conquered were forced to build roads, but were not permitted to use them.

CHARACTERISTICS OF CULTURE

There were many other instances of cultural development outside of the areas that we have considered. For example in Central Asia (the Scythians), Europe (the Celts), Africa (the Bantus), Australia (the Aborigines), and Oceania (the Polynesians). However, we have looked for instances where more advanced cultures have developed more or less independently. The three main characteristics of these societies are: cites, monumental architecture and written language. Belief in gods as well as some kind of religion have been just about universal in all human societies, both primitive and advanced, so these cannot be used as distinguishing characteristics. The same can be said of art. But it is the appearance of agriculture and cities that marks the definitive difference between primitive and more advanced cultures. Monumental architecture indicates the presence of a ruling elite, as well as the practice of religion. This is why the Inca culture was included, even though it lacked a written language.

All the societies that we have considered built cities, and four of them: Mesopotamia, Egypt, Central and South America, produced remarkably similar examples of monumental architecture. I am referring of course to the pyramid. As already noted, the Egyptian pyramid evolved from the mastaba, and continued its function as a tomb throughout its history. Its vast size also served to impress on the populace the power and influence of the pharaoh.

Some people have suggested that the form of the Egyptian pyramid may have been taken from the Mesopotamian ziggurat, but this seems unlikely. Even though there must have been some contact between Egypt and Mesopotamia, the ziggurat's function was quite different from that of the pyramid. There was usually a peripheral ramp leading to the top, where a shrine was located. The Mayan and Aztec pyramids had roughly the same function as the ziggurat, with temples or shrines on the top. But there were steps instead of a ramp to reach the summit, and consequently the Central American pyramids were much steeper. A few of the Mayan pyramids also contained tombs, but this was the exception rather than the rule.

Nevertheless, it seems more than coincidental that the appearance of all these structures had a basic similarity, in as much as they all had a pronounced vertical character, with variations on the basic pyramidal shape. In the Indus Valley civilization, the citadel was also a raised structure, which often had religious buildings on it. But there were other buildings located there as well. These structures were essentially raised platforms rather than pyramids.

Only the Egyptians used the pyramid exclusively as a tomb. However, after the sixth Dynasty, few pyramids were built, and not on nearly such a lavish scale. The later pharaohs were buried underground in the Valley of the Kings.

One of the explanations for the pyramid is that it was intended to be a "sacred mountain," and as such it was an attempt to get as near to the gods as possible—the gods presumably being somewhere up in the sky. It is impossible to know what the real intention was, but it seems reasonable to assume that these structures were built to attract the attention of the populace and to impress upon them the power and majesty of both the gods and the ruler. One would therefore be justified in saying that all the various pyramids were in some sense religious structures.

It's worth noting the very strong superficial resemblance between the Mesopotamian and Mesoamerican cultures, in spite of their being separated in time by some two thousand years, in addition to their geographical separation. Not only are their pyramids similar in both form and function, but we also encounter city-states, gods, priesthoods, kings and ruling elites in each instance. The constant strife between population centers is another feature that they had in common.

The monumental structures built by these early cultures were not utilitarian in the ordinary sense. Vast amounts of labor and materials were expended in works that were of little use to the general community. In the case of the Egyptians, huge pyramids were built to accommodate just one person—and he was dead! Other structures, both in Egypt and elsewhere, were often for religious purposes, and served the general population only to a limited extent. There was little of what we now call infrastructure to support the main functions of the state, at least little that has survived. Only when we come to the Greeks and Romans do we find monumental architecture serving a wider segment of the populace. Resources and labor were expended on non-religious structures, which served the whole community: markets, places of entertainment, administrative buildings, roads and engineering works such as aqueducts were given equal priority with monuments, religious buildings and palaces. The older cultures wasted much treasure and human resources on structures having mostly symbolic value, which contributed little to the overall welfare of the community.

We have now described, in rough outline, the early development of human culture. But it is important to bear in mind that the roots of culture go back a very long way. One could say that the first signs of culture appeared with the use of tools. This was more than two million years ago, and so we must not lose sight of the fact that culture was a very long time in the making. So cultural evolution, if we can call it that, started slowly. It was, however, even in its early stages, lightning fast compared to biological evolution, and its speed of development has continued to accelerate with the passage of time. Since the Great Leap Forward—a phrase coined by Jared Diamond—which occurred about 50,000 years ago, when art, tool-making and the exploitation of raw materials and food supplies all advanced markedly, biological evolution has made relatively minor progress.[27] As a consequence, our basic instincts and natural behavior have changed little since we were living in the African bush.

The maintenance of a *civilized* society, with laws and standards of behavior that tend to conflict with our natural desires and instincts, puts considerable stress on both the individual and the society as a whole. The advent of modern culture has tended to increase rather than decrease these tensions. But not all communities have been affected to the same degree. Certain isolated societies are still living more or less in the Stone Age, while the more advanced societies live in a totally different world, where modern technology has transformed life beyond recognition.

The Stone Age societies that still exist today suffer far less internal stress, because the modern world has not yet intruded upon their simpler way of life. In contrast, modern man is not nearly so well adapted to his lifestyle, having progressed so much further from his original roots. Of course the introduction of an alien religion, or a sudden encounter with modern technology—to say nothing of an unfamiliar virus—can often be lethal to our more primitive kin.

Man's modern world of culture is far removed from his remote past. But he still has his old instincts, which he shows no signs of outgrowing. In spite of his many spectacular achievements, his cruelty to his fellow man has not abated. Over the years he has developed ever more lethal weapons, which have allowed him to conduct progressively more destructive wars. His so-called civilization carries the unmistakable marks of his journey from a savage past, when many of his more unpleasant characteristics were needed for mere survival.

But one can look at things in a more positive light. If the human animal—or a good portion of his kind—were not so basically nasty and brutish, he would long ago have become extinct, and so any possibilities for his improvement, and any hopes for his future, would have long since become academic. In other words, if he had been a nice fellow, he would not be around today. "Nice" behavior seldom pays dividends in nature. All sorts of underhand activities are widespread, and justice is nonexistent. This is the world from whence we came, and having now become soft and "civilized," we would find it difficult to survive in our former state—at least without our modern weapons.

Happily there is more than just accelerating violence to the story. If there were not it would scarcely be worth telling. The science and technology that have so often been used to make weapons can also be used for constructive purposes. In addition, both writing and language can be used to acquire and disseminate knowledge, and knowledge is the key that can unlock the door to a brighter future.

A few points should be cleared up regarding our summary of the emergence of culture. We have been considering instances where a more advanced culture has arisen more or less independently. The early Greek culture was just about contemporary with the Shang and Zhou dynasties in China. But whereas the Chinese culture arose independently, the Greek culture was at least partially derived from the Mesopotamian and Egyptian cultures (also to some extent from the Hittites). Even though there is not much geographical distance between Egypt and Mesopotamia, and their cultural beginnings overlapped chronologically, their language, art, architecture, writing and religion differed quite significantly, which shows that they were effectively independent in origin. The development of the Mesoamerican and South American societies was contemporary with that of European culture, but these were totally isolated from one another. The cultural shock that occurred when they finally met led not only to the effective destruction of the American cultures, but to most of the native population as well. As has often been remarked: the triple scourge of guns, disease and Christianity was lethal to the first Americans. In addition to firearms and horses, the Spaniards had immunity from the diseases that they brought with them. They also had bravery and panache, enabling them to escape from many perilous situations.[28]

In their book *The Human Web*, historians J. R. and William McNeill compare the Old World cultures with those of the New World. Although they differ in some respects, there is a great deal of basic similarity between the two. However, one important difference was the dearth of domesticated animals in the New World.

Human history evolved along parallel paths even in the absence of direct contact...There was, nonetheless, a telling difference between the Americas and the Old World. The Americas offered a paltry collection of domesticable animals, making both plowing and pastoralism impossible. This goes far to explain why the wealth and power generated within the American web never approached that created within the Old World Web.[29]

Incidentally, horses had previously been indigenous to the Americas, but had become extinct, like the mammoth and the mastodon, probably due to the depredations of the human population. So the reintroduction of the horse by the Spaniards came as a shock to the Americans, who had long since forgotten that horses had once lived among them. In Europe and Asia, the horse had meanwhile become a major instrument of war.

We have used the word *culture* to describe the characteristics of certain types of society, but although the term is often used when discussing such societies, its use is perhaps somewhat unfortunate. The dictionary definition of culture lists the attributes of refinement and education, as well as *civilization*. Civilization means having advanced beyond the savage state, and carries connotations of taste, manners, sophistication and nice behavior. Well, few if any of those attributes apply to the societies that we have so far considered. The only sophistication that is apparent is in the realm of art—and this is quite considerable. But we must not fall into the trap of assuming that people capable of producing sophisticated art are necessarily civilized in the true sense. On the contrary, all the societies that we have considered behaved in ways that we would consider anything but civilized. The same could be said for most present-day societies. So calling human societies "civilized" is something of a conceit.

What we have been using is the anthropologists' definition of culture, namely that a society is deemed to have arrived at a significant level of culture if it has developed agriculture, has a written language, has produced monumental architecture and has one or more population centers that could reasonably be described as a city. These societies have a hierarchical structure, differentiating them from the "primitive cultures," which are more egalitarian.

The common element in these early cultures, as far as geography is concerned, is that they were situated in or near river valleys. This provided a suitable environment for the introduction of farming, where irrigation systems could be constructed.

What these islands of culture represented were the seeds of human society as we know it today. But just as in the biological world it is the fittest that survive, so with the islands of culture it was only those that grew and developed that were successful. As previously noted, settled societies were vulnerable to attacks by the nomadic or hunting societies (outer barbarians) who were much more mobile.

The first units, or atoms, of culture were the cities. These acquired satellites, or partners, and formed city-states. Then, on a larger scale, groups of city-states were formed, usually with one maintaining a dominant position. There were conflicting forces within each group. Some helped to keep it together, while others tended to break it apart.

THE DIVISION OF EAST AND WEST

The Egyptian and Mesopotamian cultures gave impetus to the development of other cultures, but they were eventually absorbed into those that succeeded them. The Indus valley culture was destroyed by the Aryan invasion. The American cultures survived, but only under the dominance of the Europeans. Only China can be considered as a continuous cultural entity, with its roots stretching all the way back to the Shang, and it has survived with its essential character still intact to the present day. In spite of being invaded by the Mongols in the thirteenth century, who ruled them for over a hundred years, and being subjected to the domination of the Manchus from the seventeenth century on, they have still managed to retain their cultural identity. Even the upheavals of Mao Tse-tung and the communists have not altered their basic culture in any significant manner.

But the fact that the Chinese culture has survived does not mean that it is stronger or more viable than other cultures. The Chinese have often rejected new ideas, especially when they came from foreign lands. They turned inward in the fourteenth century, when they were ahead of the West in technology, and intentionally stifled innovation. Instead of continuing to explore foreign lands, they shut themselves off from the rest of the world and allowed the barbarians of the West to overtake and eventually to dominate them. So too much reverence for tradition and a belief in the superiority of one's own culture can be counterproductive in a world where there are other people who are seeking to expand their knowledge in many directions and to discover better ways of doing things, who are not afraid to change in order to advance themselves, and who have an insatiable curiosity as to the nature of the world in which they live.

When Peking Man was discovered, those most interested in studying his remains were not Chinese but Westerners. As Ivar Lissner writes in *The Living Past:*

> It is significant that Europeans are far more interested in archaeology than Orientals. Europeans want to *know*; Orientals want to *live*. Europeans explore things, destroy and recreate them. Orientals let them go the way of all flesh.[30]

This does not make the Chinese people in any way inferior to those from the West; they just have a different worldview, which in many ways is healthier. Two such different cultural mindsets were bound to clash. But each has learnt a lot from the other.

2

RITUALS OF SACRIFICE

o o o o o o o o o o o o o o o o o o o o o o o o o o o o o o
Man is certainly crazy. He could not make
a mite, and he makes gods by the dozen.

—*Michel Eyquem de Montaigne*
1533-1592

THE POWER OF IMAGINATION

We will temporarily leave our account of the physical aspects of culture and delve into the more psychological or "spiritual" characteristics of the human animal. In seeking to account for certain aspects of human behavior, we must turn our attention to one of mankind's most distinctive qualities, his imagination. It is this quality, perhaps above all else, which distinguishes man from his fellow animals. It is intimately connected with his capacity for language and abstract thought. It is also reflected in his ability to create and appreciate art. Perhaps most importantly, it is responsible for his propensity to believe in all kinds of phenomena that are beyond the reach of his physical senses, but whose existence he accepts in the same way as those that are part of the physical environment. An abstract, or spiritual, world is created, one that is superimposed on his consciousness of the real world and intimately associated with it.

There are therefore two worlds represented in the human mind: the world apprehended by the senses, and the world of the imagination. As constituted in the brain, both are equally real, in that they both consist of patterns of neural pathways and connections that "represent" the features of these two worlds. The only difference is that one set of patterns represents the *real* world and the other represents an *imaginary* world, which exists only as a configuration in the brain.

But this imaginary world can nonetheless have a very strong influence on human behavior.[1]

Our imagination is a very powerful tool, which can help us in a multitude of ways, and without which we would be unable to operate in human society. But it is also something that can cause all sorts of trouble if it strays too far into uncharted waters. The power of the imagination is demonstrated by our ability to transport ourselves "in spirit" even to a distant galaxy, and to create in our minds a picture of what such a far-off world might be like. This ability accounts for the tremendous popularity of science fiction and other fantastic tales. It also accounts for our attraction to all kinds of make-believe. We not only have fairy tales for children, but also fairy tales for adults in the form of books, plays and movies, which depict an idealized or completely fictionalized world that can be experienced only in the imagination.

Whole libraries of books have been written about the so-called "spiritual" world—one that transcends the world of the flesh. But where is this spiritual world—that is if it actually exists at all? Not much thought is necessary to realize that the spiritual world exists entirely in the human brain. It is an important part of the imaginative world that we have just been discussing. But let's not get too far ahead of ourselves.

Closely associated with the spiritual world is the idea of the *soul*. In various forms this concept has occupied a central place in the human mind since the dawn of culture. Undoubtedly one of the principal reasons for this is because it is essential to any conception of life after death.

Since the human body decays when it dies, it cannot be part of any kind of afterlife. For some Christians, this problem is overcome by the resurrection of the body on judgment day, when it is reunited with the soul; but this obviously requires some sort of miraculous occurrence. The Egyptians tried to overcome the problem with mummification, so that the death of the physical body would not prevent it from entering into the hereafter. But to us this seems a little naïve, and anyway, it was only the elite that had access to the process of embalming. The ordinary citizens, like those who labored so hard to build the pyramids, could not look forward to any afterlife.

The soul provides a quick and easy way around the problem of bodily decay. Since the soul incorporates the true essence of the individual, the fact that the body dies is not an impediment to the attainment of an afterlife. And since the body and the soul are separate entities (the basic tenet of dualism), the death of the body does not affect the soul, which allows the individual to live on in a more exalted state. It's like the Cheshire cat's grin in *Alice in Wonderland,* which remains long after the cat is gone.

Not only is the soul a means to an afterlife, it can also be considered as the "true self" of the individual. It confers on a human being a status that transcends the mundane world of the flesh and affirms his spiritual nature. The soul is the seat of the individual's finer qualities, his artistic sensibilities and his ability to appreciate the finer things in life. Compared to the soul, which is unsullied by the crudities of the flesh, the body stands as basically corrupt, the seat of the baser (animal) instincts that are forever trying to divert the individual from the path of virtue. The soul is what differentiates man from the animals, and what makes him special in the eyes of God.

Unfortunately there are serious problems with this scenario. For instance, where is the soul located? Since it is invisible—by definition it is non-material—its location is impossible to pin down. Maybe it's a sort of aura that enshrouds the whole body, or perhaps it's in the head, the seat of the mind (the distinction between mind and brain will be discussed later.) Aristotle thought it was in the heart. But the most serious problem with the idea of the soul, apart from the fact that it tends to devalue the material body, lies in the difference between the material and the immaterial, or spiritual.

If you wish you can call the soul the *character,* or *emergent quality* of the physical body. But now the soul and the body are tied together as essentially a single entity. If the body dies, so does the soul. For the soul to be a genuine spirit it must be totally independent of anything material.

One can of course *imagine* something that is immaterial. It is the *thought* that brings it to life. Whether or not such a thing can exist outside of the imagination is impossible to verify. But the existence of a pure spirit—something that is completely immaterial—seems problematic at best. The notion that a soul, or spirit, could have any effect on, or interaction with, a physical body is not only a logical absurdity but also violates the laws of physics. Only another piece of matter can have any effect on a material body. A physical entity cannot be affected in any way by anything non-material—assuming that such a thing exists. To be so affected, a body has to be acted upon by a force, and such a force cannot be brought to bear by something that is not material.

Newton's third law states that to every action there is an equal and opposite reaction. But anything non-material cannot—*by definition*—exert a physical force on *anything.* Nor can it, again by definition, be acted upon by anything physical—because it is not a physical entity. (You might argue that an electromagnetic wave can affect material bodies, even though it has no mass. But such a wave carries energy and we know that matter and energy are equivalent (E = mc^2). Something that is completely immaterial could not carry energy.)

The argument that since God—assuming a God exists—is all-powerful, he can therefore suspend the laws of physics at will, cannot be entertained by any reasonable person. Our world would quickly collapse if the laws of physics were violated, even in a small way. Admittedly the laws of physics seem to be violated in a black hole, but these are singularities predicted by Einstein's general theory of relativity, and anyway, life as we know it is impossible in a black hole. (Even though the laws of physics have not been *proved*, their validity is a reasonable assumption, since nothing has been shown to contradict them.) Conceivably there are portions of the cosmos, unseen and as yet unknown, where the laws of physics may be different, but here we are talking about *local* suspensions of physical laws. So if God created the universe, there is no way that he can start fiddling with the laws of physics without destroying his own handiwork.[2]

[But what about ghosts, aren't these manifestations of the spirit world? Well, there may be such things as apparitions, but they certainly are not immaterial "spirits"—otherwise you would not be able to see them, and you *do* see them. There are actually two possibilities. If they are really "out there" they must emit some kind of (electromagnetic) wave. It's possible that ghosts are the result of some phenomenon that has not yet been discovered. After all, radio and other kinds of electromagnetic waves were "magic" until we found out what they were and could reproduce them at will.[3] Or, the image of the ghost is not really "out there," but is actually inside your head, and you just project it out there through your own thought processes. This seems by far the most likely explanation. The fact that drugs can cause hallucinations is a strong indication that "ghosts" originate in the brain. Marvin Minsky, an expert on how the mind works, says, "In my view, believing in vibrations and ghosts diminishes our capacities for mental growth by diverting attention from the mind and attributing those abilities to imaginary entities outside ourselves."[4]]

Something that is truly immaterial cannot interact with a material body. And accordingly, if such a "spirit" exists at all, it must inhabit a completely separate world. Feelings, emotions, thoughts, etc., are clearly just bodily functions, and so have a *physical* reality. Thus they could not have any relation at all to something that is immaterial. You can call the soul the *seat* of the emotions as some have done, but the concept is logically meaningless, it is simply a metaphor.

If you try to get around this by saying that the soul is both material *and* spirit, you run into more logical absurdities, and any kind of afterlife becomes impossible. So it seems that if the soul exists at all, it must inhabit a world that cannot have any contact with the world we know, and this defeats its purpose, as conceived in the human imagination.

If such an immaterial thing as the soul were to exist *outside* of the imagination, it would be essentially unknowable. The concept is elusive but it is nonetheless intelligible. It is also a concept that is found in Hinduism: "The supreme Godhead is unknown and unknowable to the finite mind."[5]

[In chapter 10 we will see that the mind is a *function* of the brain. This does not mean that the mind is an immaterial object, because it is not a separate entity from the brain. The *concept* of the mind, however, is a figment of the imagination!]

Of course the fact that the idea of the soul makes no sense does not prevent most people from believing in it. Against all evidence and all reason, it is generally accepted without question. Very few concepts that actually *do* make sense seem to attract such passionate conviction. The reason for this is undoubtedly because the concept of the soul provides answers to a lot of perplexing questions. It also tells us something about the nature of belief. Belief implies the acceptance of something that cannot be verified, but if the desire to believe it is sufficiently strong, the fact that it defies logic is no grounds for its rejection.

According to philosopher Friedrich Nietzsche, the idea of the soul may have originated from our experience of the dream world. When we sleep we seem to enter a different world, which some may have thought was the world of the soul.

> In the ages of crude primeval culture man believed that in dreams he got to know *another real world;* here is the origin of all metaphysics. Without the dream one would have found no occasion for the division of the world. The separation of the body and soul, too, is related to the most ancient concept of the dream; also the assumption of a quasi-body of the soul, which is the origin of all belief in spirits and probably also of belief in gods.[6]

RELIGIOUS BEGINNINGS

Just as with the soul, whole libraries of books have been written about God and religion. Some of them have genuinely shed light on the subject, but most have been little more than the expression of preconceived notions.

Now, at the beginning of the twenty-first century, the fog is beginning to lift concerning the origin of one of the most ancient and elusive aspects of human behavior. Why does religion promote such fanatical beliefs, when these beliefs are clearly figments of the imagination? And why do almost all human societies, both primitive and advanced, make religion a basic part of their culture? We will eventually conclude that this phenomenon is intimately connected with evolution.

The origin of religion is shrouded in the distant past; a past when man was not the all-powerful creature that he is now, when he was not man the hunter, but rather man the hunted. Human kind did not arise full-blown at the top of the food chain. The journey was long and arduous. Humans spent a long time as the prey of other, far stronger, animals, and it was only after a long and titanic struggle, lasting thousands of years, that they finally emerged as the unchallenged masters of all their fellow creatures.

The blood sacrifices of earlier religions, and even some current ones, are almost certainly related to the time when man was emerging as the hunter rather than the hunted. These rituals reflect the trauma of this mighty struggle, which was indeed a struggle to the death. Although the blood and the sacrifice have now become mostly symbolic, the roots of many of the world's religions can be traced back to this earlier time.

There are roughly three stages in the development of religion, although not all major religions have gone through each of them. The earliest stage, a long way into the distant past, when the sacrificial rituals were initiated, is described in Barbara Ehrenreich's book *Blood Rites*. The gist of this is that the sacrifice of a victim, which could be either animal or human, represented an offering to a beast of prey. The original deities that were the object of the sacrifices were in all likelihood these beasts of prey.

Early humans must have been forced to scavenge their food from the kills of larger and more powerful predators, and so it seems natural that these powerful creatures should have been venerated as superior beings. Eventually man became the master of these beasts, but they still retained their divine status. As Barbara Ehrenreich writes:

> The transformation from prey to predator, in which the weak rise up against the strong, is the central "story" in the human narrative. Some residual anxiety seems to draw us back to it again and again. We recount it as myth and reenact it in ritual, as if we could never be sufficiently assured that it has, indeed, occurred. In folktales, lions are defeated by foxes, wolves outwitted by clever monkeys...[7]

In the ancient rituals, the beasts of prey are represented as gods. Another interpretation of the sacrificial victim is that it represents a member of the human group who sacrifices himself in order to protect the others from attack by the predator.

> If the idea of the deity as a predator beast seems preposterous, recall Jehovah's furious appetite for animal offerings…which may have been a substitute for human sacrificial victims. Zeus, too, often seems to take a more predatory than parental interest in his human subjects. He is sometimes known as Zeus Lykaios, the wolf, a rapist and insatiable consumer of blood offerings.[8]

The initial transition from prey to predator may have been connected with the advance in intellectual capacity—the Great Leap Forward—that occurred about 50,000 years ago, and which, according to geneticist Spencer Wells, allowed mankind to colonize the earth.[9] After the Great Leap Forward, excessive hunting by humans almost certainly contributed to the extinction of many of the larger animals that were living in Europe, Asia and the Americas.

The old type of religious ritual must have lasted for many millennia. But with the rise of the more advanced cultures, we encounter the addition of other categories of deity. The pantheon expands to include entities such as the sun and the earth, the sky and the sea, as well as many animals that were not necessarily beasts of prey. Many of these were related more to *agriculture* than to hunting. But, more ominously, we also find gods whose exclusive realm is war. The sacrificial rituals were continued, but the object of the sacrifices was extended to a larger pantheon of gods. This reflected a change in the cultural context from that of the hunter-gatherer to the cultivator of crops.

The third stage in the development of religion started with the adoption of monotheism by the Jews. This changed the main purpose of religion from the realm of ritual sacrifice to the teaching of ethical conduct and the worship of a single all-powerful God, who was the Creator. As Charles Darwin says, "The highest form of religion—the grand idea of God hating sin and loving righteousness—was unknown during primeval times."[10] The concept of sin is Jewish in origin, and it was taken over by the Christians and also the Moslems, with the Christians adding Original Sin to the list. Buddhism has no notion of sin, but Hinduism instructs its adherents to act righteously, although this is not spelled out in such detail as with the Christians, Jews and Moslems. Virtuous Hindus are reborn into a higher caste; the unjust must start their next life at a lower level.

The new type of God still retained many characteristics of the old predator-gods. Judaism continued to preserve many of the old religious practices. Hinduism, however, has never fully reached this later stage, since it still retains its polytheistic character. Buddhism remains the exception among major religions in that it is essentially non-theistic, the concept of God is not really part of its teaching. It is as much a philosophy as it is a religion.

MYTHS AND LEGENDS

In addition to gods and religion, there are other types of belief that are common. Myths, folklore and legends are also essential elements in practically all societies, both primitive and advanced. All reflect the world of the imagination, and all affect human behavior in powerful ways. They are the life-blood of the emotional brotherhood that binds the community together. They can also be the cause of serious conflict between nations. Myth is a phenomenon that can hold an entire people in thrall and mold the whole character of a society.

Myths are usually thought of as the sort of stories that were part of the early Greek culture. Fantastic tales of gods and heroes were spun and re-spun in different versions. Gods and heroes swapped identities constantly. The origins of these fables go back into the dim mists of prehistory. The Romans also had many myths, some of which were adapted, with much poetic license, from those of the Greeks. These were the classic myths. But such things were not confined to the Greeks and Romans. The Norse sagas, the tales of the Nibelungs and the Vedas are further examples. But these are only the best-known "literary" myths. There are "creation myths," which are found in almost all cultures, together with myths of every sort and description relating to the various aspects of the culture.

Modern studies of primitive societies have found that some of their myths are amazingly similar, even though the societies in question are totally isolated from one another. This may reflect the fact many of them are connected to natural phenomena or animals that are common features of the physical environment. But there are often more subtle similarities, such as the association of particular qualities with particular animals, substances or occupations. In *The Jealous Potter*, the anthropologist Claude Levi-Strauss points out the common features and themes of many myths that relate to the clay from which pottery is made, and the relationship of the potter to the clay.

Levi-Strauss spent a lot of time studying these societies and their myths. He says that the structure of a myth is like that of a painting, only that the painting's structure is created by the artist, whereas the myth is created from a pre-existing structure—in the myth-maker's mind. He likens the mythmaker to a *bricoleur*, a word that is difficult to translate into English. It describes someone like an artist who makes sculptures out of odd bits of material that he discovers lying around.

Mythical thought appears to be an intellectual form of *bricolage*—the activity of the *bricoleur*. Levi-Strauss shows that myths are an attempt to construct a correspondence between nature and culture. This is a very powerful concept, to which we will return later on. [11]

The idea that myths were part of more primitive societies but do not affect more modern ones is entirely erroneous. Although they may take different forms, modern myths are just as powerful as the ancient variety. Myth is a tremendously important factor in human societies. It is hard to imagine what life would be like without it. Myths about war are some of the most deep-seated and powerful motivating factors that affect the human imagination. Modern war would hardly be possible without its mythical foundations. As war correspondent Chris Hedges writes:

> The potency of myth is that it allows us to make sense of mayhem and violent death…. It allows us to believe we have achieved our place in society because of a long chain of human endeavors…. It hides from view our own impotence and the ordinariness of our own leaders. [12]

[There seems to be a correlation between myth and great art. The Greeks were the great mythmakers, and their art was superb. Religions, which have a lot in common with myth, also inspire great art. Since it involves powerful use of the imagination, art seems to be the ideal medium to express both myth and religion.]

CHANGING FACES OF GOD

The concept of God has clearly changed from that of the earliest societies. Many of the hunter-gatherer societies had shamans, who were similar to witch doctors, and were supposedly able to achieve mystical union with the spirit world. Shamanism, which seems to have originated among the tribes of Siberia, is based on animism, a belief in an invisible spiritual presence that affects living organisms. The shaman acts as a medium between the spirits and the real world, so as to protect the community from any evil influences that might arise from their presence. He often exhibits strange, trance-like behavior, which is taken as a sign that he is in contact with the spirit world. These trances can be induced by "psychoactive" plants; cannabis being the one most often used to contact the spirits of the animal world.

Some form of animism existed in almost all hunter-gatherer societies prior to the advent of a more organized type of religion. There may be a relationship between some of the "spirits" of shamanism and the predator deities of the early sacrificial rituals.

Once we arrive at the dawn of civilization, and the hunter-gather societies give way to communities based on agriculture, the old type of religion becomes adapted to the new way of life. As the pantheon of gods expanded, some of them were adopted by large groups, and became the official guardians and protectors of the community. The famous Seven Gods of Sumer were examples of these. At the same time, certain individuals, or *priests,* were designated as intermediaries between the people and the gods. Rituals of sacrifice were established whereby the influence of the gods was sought in order to bring benefits to the community, and these sacrificial rituals were quite similar to those of the earlier societies.

The Egyptian, Mesopotamian, Indus and American cultures that we have discussed all had this kind of religion. The early Chinese culture, which was basically feudal, had a pantheon of gods related mainly to agriculture. But they also practiced ancestor-worship, and a form of divination. The latter was related to animal sacrifice, which undoubtedly had its origins in the old hunter-gatherer days. Heat was applied to the bones of sacrificed animals, and when these became cracked, the resulting pattern was read as an omen, just as entrails were read in the western parts of Eurasia at the same time, and tea-leaves are read today. Under the Shang, there was also human sacrifice, but this seems to have been discontinued under the Zhou.[13] There was no tradition of priesthood in China, since the political-military rulers took care of relations with the gods and spirits themselves.

So the religions that existed in these cultures were mostly confined to an inner circle, or priesthood, and did not involve much popular participation, except possibly in the actual rituals. Only when we come to the major, or universal, religions do we find more public participation, and it is these major religions that have had such an important impact on the cultures in which they arose, as well as on those that adopted them.

This increased participation by the people is reflected in the types of religious structures that started to appear. They contained spaces where the people could gather for public ceremonies. In fact they were in a literal sense "houses of worship." Starting with the Jewish temple, and continuing with the Buddhist stupa, then the church and the mosque, these buildings all reflected the growing involvement of the general public in religion, and were in stark contrast to the pyramid and the ziggurat of the older cultures. Those early structures, together with the Greek and Roman temples, and many of the Hindu temples as well, reflected the tendency of the polytheistic religions to restrict the participation in religious ceremonies to a small select group of priests and other dignitaries. The idea of a *congregation* of people, which actually takes part in a religious ceremony, came only with the universal monotheistic religions—and with these we also include Buddhism.

A major change in religious practices came with the adoption of monotheism by the Jewish people. Freud's contention that the Jews got the idea of monotheism from the Egyptian pharaoh Akhenaten (ruled 1375-1358 B.C.), and that Moses could actually have been an Egyptian, may or may not be correct.[14] At any rate, the Egyptians did try monotheism, but after the death of Akhenaten they reverted to the old polytheistic beliefs.

The origins of Judaism, which are recorded in the Old Testament, go back to the shadowy figures of the patriarchs Moses and Abraham. The Old Testament itself, which is part of the Christian Bible, is one of the first pieces of real literature to occur in the Middle East (the Sumerian epic of Gilgamesh is another example of early literature).[15] Although Judaism can be considered as a universal religion, it really belongs to a specific people, rather than to a culture. It doesn't quite fit in with the other major religions, and the Jews have been happy to keep it that way.

The Jews not only stressed the moral aspect of religion, but also the concept of the hereafter, and the whole world of the spirit, which became increasingly real to them.

Another major, or universal, religion that arose at a very early time is Hinduism. This is a synthesis of the religion that was brought into India by the Aryans and the indigenous religions that existed there at that time. Hinduism is composed of innumerable sects, but has no real ecclesiastical structure. Its two most significant features are the caste system and the Vedas. The latter are its sacred writings, which expound the liturgy of sacrifice and culminate in the Upanishads, which are mystical in nature and present the doctrine of Brahman, the absolute reality, or "neuter monistic spirit," which is identified with the individual soul, or *atman*. Hinduism is polytheistic, three of the gods being given special prominence: Brahma, the creator of the world; Vishu its preserver; and Shiva, a god that has many attributes and functions, involving both destruction and reproduction, as well as music and the arts. Somewhat like the Christian Trinity, these gods can descend to earth as *avatars*, or incarnations; for example Rama and

Krishna are *avatars* of Vishnu. In addition, there are countless other gods and goddesses, each having their own particular specialty. After death, entry into Paradise is possible for the just, while the wicked go to Hell. But this is not necessarily permanent, as the soul can be reincarnated into another life. The Hindu comes back into a higher or lower caste depending on the degree of merit he attained in his previous life.

Four major religions arose in the thousand year period from the fifth century B.C. to the seventh century A.D. Zoroastrianism and Buddhism both originated at about the beginning of the period, Christianity in the middle and Islam at the end.

Zoroastrianism is a religion that arose in Persia in the sixth century B.C., founded by Zoroaster, a teacher and prophet who lived c.626-551 B.C. Zoroaster is the Greek form of his Persian name Zarathustra. Originally an expression of the peaceful life of the sedentary people of northern Iran, as opposed to the animistic polytheism of the nomadic horsemen, who were their enemies, Zoroastrianism failed to attract the adherence of the local people. But Zoroaster eventually succeeded in converting the Persian king Hystaspes, father of Darius I, and Zoroastrianism subsequently became the state religion of Persia. As a consequence, its priests had considerable influence on the throne. The Zoroastrian scriptures are contained in the sacred book of the Avesta. At the core of its teaching is the struggle between the good spirits, personified by Ahura Mazda and his attendant deities, and the evil spirits, the daevas, led by Ahriman.

Zoroastrianism subsequently became polytheistic, having incorporated many of the religious practices that it was intended to replace. It lost its privileged status after Alexander conquered Persia in 325 B.C., and for the next 500 years it survived only in the form of Mithraism. But it re-emerged under the Sassenid dynasty in 226 A.D.

Siddhartha Gautama, or the Buddha, was a north Indian prince, born c.483 B.C. Like Christ, he lived in an era of social upheaval, and in both his life and his philosophy he sought the alleviation of human suffering. The essence of the religion that he founded is the attainment of *Nirvana*, or *Great Awakening*.

> The ultimate reality is "void" (sunna) of any psychic (attaniya) essence, and of all the defects that pertain to it; hence the "Void" is synonymous with *Nirvana*.[16]

The aim of Buddhism is the negation of the self. Ideally one should isolate oneself from the world and turn inward. This Siddhartha himself had done. He abandoned his family and became a wandering ascetic, bent on discovering the true nature of things. He tried self-mortification, but when this failed to enlighten him, he decided to sit in meditation under a pipal tree at Bodh Gaya (the Bodhi Tree) until the truth should came to him. This finally resulted in what he termed his Enlightenment, or "release from the overwhelming consciousness of suffering."[17]

As one can imagine, to teach such a method of Enlightenment to his followers was a difficult task. But various schools or sects of Buddhism eventually emerged to point the way towards the attainment of *Nirvana*. The most important of these were the two "vehicles" of Buddhist teaching: the Hinayana (lesser vehicle), and the Mahayana (greater vehicle), which came later. These become the two main branches of Buddhism. Siddhartha did not require belief in a personal god, or for that matter, any god at all.

Hinduism, Buddhism, Islam and Christianity have become the major religions of the world's cultures. They each have different characteristics, which roughly correspond to the different cultures of the East, the Middle East and the West. Christianity, which like Islam originated in the Middle East, spread westwards and eventually became the religion of the West. Islam, even though it has spread throughout the world, has remained essentially a Middle Eastern religion, with its spiritual center in Arabia, especially the city of Mecca. Buddhism and Hinduism both originated in India, and reflect the distinctive nature of Indian culture to a considerable degree.[18]

Islam and Christianity are fairly similar in character. Both of them have been militant and aggressive at certain times in their history. They have involved themselves in politics and military conquest, and have strayed far from the precepts of their founders and sacred books. By contrast, Buddhism is a peaceful religion that has spread, not by conquest, but by proselytizing. The same can be said for Hinduism, although as a religion, it has a totally different character from Buddhism. One thing they all have in common, however, is that they have broken up into many different branches and sects, and as time has gone by this fragmentation has tended to increase. The numbers of these different "branches" are simply staggering. For instance, as of the year 2004, Christianity had 33,820 separate denominations! [19]

Confucianism arose in China about 500 B.C., and Taoism a little later. Confucianism was originally a system of ethical precepts for the management of society, and only later became a moral and religious system. But even then, it was not really similar to a universal religion. In the same way, Taoism was essentially a philosophical system that was derived from the book *Tao-te Ching*—originally ascribed to Lao-tzu, but probably written later. Taoism is a passive philosophy, which holds that the natural world is the transcendent reality, and the individual should submit himself to its all-encompassing power. It condemns war and violence as being contrary to nature. However, Sun Tzu's *The Art of War* is considered as a classic of Taoist thought![20] Sun Tzu stresses the psychological side of warfare, with deception and knowledge of the enemy playing primary roles. According to Master Sun, the ideal strategy is to win without fighting! This seeming paradox is typical of Taoist thought.

> That Sun Tzu calmly teaches the ruthless art of war while condemning war may seem contradictory if this fact is seen outside the context of total understanding of the human mentality fostered by Taoist learning.... The model of the paradox of *The Art of War* can be seen in the *Tao-te Ching*, where both ruthlessness and kindness are part of the Way of the sage.[21]

In the fifth century A.D., Taoism incorporated much of Mahayana Buddhism, and so one can properly call it a religion. But as far as the afterlife is concerned, Taoism and Buddhism were opposites. Taoism taught that immortality was possible for those who followed the prescriptions of the faith, and this entailed the survival of the body. Buddhism, by contrast, sought the dissolution of the self.

In spite of their fundamental differences, Buddhism, Taoism and Confucianism have all combined to create a unique expression of Chinese culture, which developed from the original culture of the Yellow River Valley. In fact, quite unlike the Christian or the Moslem, the individual Chinese is quite happy to practice different types of religion when it suits him. As historian Fernand Braudel describes it:

> Each member of the faithful turned sometimes to the Buddhist priests and sometimes to the Taoists. Both officiated in the same temple; the statue of Buddha stood there, as well as the statue of the local god or the statue of Confucius, himself almost a deity. Offerings were made to all of them.[22]

When the new universal religions of Judaism, Zoroastrianism, Christianity and Islam arose, the old gods went on existing together with the new Gods, but on the whole it was not a happy or productive partnership, and the old gods

tended to be pushed aside. This was because the new Gods had a different character. Christians, Moslems and Jews can accept the fact that the old gods were
mythological, in fact they tend to look down on these "pagan" deities as being
suitable only for primitive people. They consider belief in such gods to be merely
superstition. *Their* God, on the contrary, is not mythological, and the truth of his
existence is revealed in the sacred book. But obviously there cannot be more than
one *true* God.

In communities with many gods, the arrival of another one is usually accepted
in a spirit of accommodation, the newcomer simply being added to the family.
The Hindus are still happy with a lot of gods. But this kind of good will is
entirely absent from a universal monotheistic religion. Theirs is the only true
God; all others are false.

Whether we are talking about pantheons of gods or a single *true* God, they all
originate from the same source. It's not that none of these gods exist. They do
indeed exist—in the human *mind*. Like the soul, these deities exist only in the
imagination.

So if all these Gods and gods are in fact man-made, does this mean that there
can be no God? Could there be a God that exists *outside* of the human imagination? There is no logical reason to reject this, but such a God would be essentially
unknowable. The Hindus, as we have noted, come closest to a possible definition
of God—in spite of their polytheism! But for a Christian, or a Moslem, or a Jew,
this is too abstract a concept; they prefer a *personal* God that they can talk to and
perhaps influence in some way. Unfortunately this kind of God exists only in the
imagination. Just as beauty exists only in the *eye* of the beholder, so also God
exists only in the *mind* of the believer.

But although these Gods exist only in the mind, this does not mean that they
are powerless, or that they cannot give aid and comfort to those who believe in
them. As we will see, their existence is an important part of man's adjustment to
the world of culture.

During the last hundred years or so, several Western thinkers and philosophers have pronounced the "Death of God." They have said that the idea of God
is passé and that man should now free himself from ancient superstitions. Nevertheless, if you ask the average man or woman in the street, you will find that God
is still alive and well, and still very much interested in the welfare of the human
race.

CULTURE AND RELIGION

So why is the necessity to believe in a God so compelling? This is the question that really interests us, and it is only by attempting to answer it that we can begin to make some sort of sense out of the human condition.

We have to go back to Levi-Strauss to get some answers here. Remember his interpretation of primitive myths? He said that they created a correspondence between nature and culture. Once Homo sapiens started to acquire culture, there was an increasing conflict, between his innate instincts, which were fashioned for his survival in a pre-cultural state, and the behavioral requirements of his new way of life. As culture developed, this conflict only intensified. One way to cope with it was to create myths that served to make his relationship to nature more intelligible. His imagination was called upon to help him adjust to the culture that he himself had created. The world of myth allowed him to feel less isolated and alone; it helped to answer some of the important questions that arose with his expanding consciousness. According to Levi-Strauss, the world of myth resulted from a non-scientific, or rather a *pre*-scientific investigation into the nature of the physical world:

> This science of the concrete was necessarily restricted by its essence to results other than those destined to be achieved by the exact natural sciences but it was no less scientific and its results no less genuine. They were secured ten thousand years earlier and still remain at the basis of our civilization.[23]

Man was happy to accept his myths as fact, even though they actually existed only in his imagination. Many of the myths grew out of, or expanded upon, the original idea of the predator gods, which belonged to earlier times when man first emerged from his animal origins. So a belief in something imaginary need not be such a bad thing at all; in fact it may very well serve an important evolutionary purpose.

As culture has developed, the strains on the human psyche have increased. Both religion and myth were successful for a while in alleviating some of this tension. But the modern world has advanced in all forms of knowledge, and these primitive notions do not retain such a hold on the imagination as they once did. Freud, in his *Civilization and Its Discontents,* describes the conflict between modern society and man's basic instincts and passions. To some extent he was right to call religion "the opium of the people." But religion is much more than an opiate. It is an attempt to ease the conflict between an ever more sophisticated culture—with its rapidly increasing acquisition of all kinds of knowledge—and man's roots in the bosom of Mother Nature.

Religion, with its origins in simpler and more primitive times, is just not up to the job any more—if indeed it ever really was. It did, however, serve to strengthen the developing cultures in many ways, and even now continues to function in the same way, albeit to a lesser degree.

But alas, religion has always been a two-edged sword, and the bad features of religion have often outweighed the good, especially in the case of the two youngest world religions. The beneficial side has included the teaching of moral and ethical behavior, and the encouragement of good works. The bad side has fostered strife among nations and ethnic groups. It has also retarded the spread of knowledge to a considerable degree.

The avowed intention of religion is to bring people together in brotherhood, but the actual result has often been to keep them apart. The division between believers and non-believers has led to bigotry, hatred and even war. Another dark side of religion is its tendency to distort reality (of course part of its original function was to do just that). The true believer, of whatever religion, sees the world in a distorted manner, like the images encountered in those fun-house mirrors at circuses and amusement parks. This distortion causes a continuing conflict with the real world, preventing a person from appreciating its true nature. Religion is indeed an escape from reality.

Anthropologist David Wilson takes a scientific approach to the study of religion. In his recent book *Darwin's Cathedral: Evolution, Religion, and the Nature of Society,* he proposes an evolutionary theory of religion. Wilson says that a religion can be treated as an organism, and that it is adaptive at the group level, rather than at the level of the individual. In other words, the adherents of a religion form a living body, in the same way that an ant colony or a beehive can be said to form an organism, which is subject to the principles of natural selection. The book makes interesting reading and is well researched, but I can't help concluding that Wilson is treating what is essentially an analogy as a fact.

Wilson agrees that religion helps mankind adapt to the rigors of culture. But this does not mean that it's an organism, even though it may *behave* like an organism in many ways. Doesn't an organism have to be able to reproduce itself? And surely a religion and its *followers* are two different things. Wilson is equating the religion with the followers. A religion is a *belief,* which is *held* by the followers. To call the followers—or even the followers *plus* the belief—the religion is not strictly accurate in my view. I think a religion is something *apart* from its followers. The followers may think of it as a living thing, but in essence it's an abstraction, it exists in the *minds* of the followers, just as nationalism exists in the minds of the people.

In the early days of religion, the followers were not nearly so important as they are now. Wilson is really only considering religion in its modern guise. But it is an ancient phenomenon that has taken many different forms in many different cultures. One can say that it has adapted to the various cultures, but that hardly justifies calling it an organism.

Religion is best looked at as a *behavioral* phenomenon—an instance of group psychology if you like. It is part of the world of myth. Whatever else it has done, religion has helped us to survive. So we can best define it as a *survival mechanism*. The way it does this is by providing answers to questions that *have* no answer!

One of the outstanding characteristics of the human animal is his capacity to believe in all kinds of strange things. This trait has been of great benefit to him in many ways. He might not have survived in the early days of culture without the comfort of his myths and superstitions. A belief in religion has likewise brought him solace during the trials and tribulations of daily life.

Mankind's readiness to believe in all manner of tall tales is constantly being demonstrated. In the modern economy, commerce and industry would probably grind to a halt if those in the advertising business were not able to convince their fellow citizens of the reality of some non-existent something in their products. But then again, there is a darker side to this kind of thing. The ability of a Hitler or a Lenin to peddle rubbish as the answer to all kinds of social ills, both real and imaginary, can and has led to unspeakable horror and destruction. Strangely enough, it is often easier to persuade a human being to believe in something that is patently false than it is to convince him of something that is true (a successful politician knows this only too well). In order to understand human behavior, one must constantly remind oneself that the human animal will believe practically anything—so long as it makes absolutely *no* sense at all.

Like religion itself, this trait can be considered as a survival mechanism. In ancient times, those who believed in some kind of myth or fantasy were better able to cope with life than those less imaginative souls who had to bear the vicissitudes of their daily existence without some comforting explanation as to why things were the way they were.

3

EMPIRE AND WAR

o o o o o o o o o o o o o o o o o o o o o o o o o o o o o o o o o

A prince, therefore, must have no other object or thought, nor acquire skill in anything, except war, its organization, and its discipline. The art of war is all that is expected of a ruler.

We find that princes who have thought more of their pleasures than of their arms have lost their states.

—*Niccolò Machiavelli*
The Prince, XIV

WELLSPRINGS OF WAR

What we wish to do now is to examine the origins and nature of warfare in rather the same way that we examined the origins of religion.[1]

The first thing that comes to mind when one attempts to account for man's proclivity for war is that he is a naturally aggressive creature that is prone to violence. However, this does not really fit the facts, because, although there are a lot of violent individuals around, there are many more that are quite peaceful and well behaved. Rather than neglecting or maltreating their neighbors, they are inclined to be courteous and to come to the aid of those in need.

An ordinary fight, or what one might call a localized instance of violence, is a far cry from war. Even a riot has little to do with war. War is a different kind of phenomenon altogether. War is *organized* violence. But it can be one-sided, as when one party attacks another without warning, in which case only one side is organized. But it usually takes two sides to make a war.

As far as active participation in war is concerned, women, with a few notable exceptions, have preferred to leave this kind of activity to the men. But it turns out that males, the supposedly more violent members of the human race, are on the whole quite reluctant to go to war. They tend to look for all sorts of dodges and pretexts in order to avoid participation. In fact when it comes to battle, often only the threat of death will deter them from running away—and sometimes even that won't be enough. It's true that there are some individuals that are attracted to the excitement and danger of war, just as a moth is attracted to a flame. But this kind of person is decidedly in the minority. The average man has to be prepared for war. He has to be coaxed into the army by appeals to his patriotism. This of course is much easier if his country has been attacked or if there is an identifiable enemy. But even then, since he is not really a natural killer of his own kind, he has to be trained and regimented, in order that he may be transformed from an ordinary peaceful citizen into a ruthless and efficient killer. Even after all this training, the only thing the average soldier really wants is to survive. The exceptions are those who simply live for war, like Alexander the Great and George Patton.

One must remember that this reluctance to go to war was not so evident in times past, because one of the main objects of war was to obtain booty. The result being that many a poor man was able to become rich from the spoils of war—that is if he managed to survive long enough to enjoy his loot. However, this sort of motivation is largely absent from modern warfare.

As we shall see, man's natural aversion to war can also be overcome by belief in some kind of ideology, such as nationalism or communism. But, contrary to the views of philosophers such as Hegel and Nietzsche, man does not appear to be innately attracted to war. He can, however, be turned into a sadistic killer by the proper kind of indoctrination carried out by an unscrupulous leader.

The whole concept of war turns morality on its head. Killing other people, looting their cities and towns, even raping their women, are *encouraged* in war, whereas such behavior would bring harsh punishment, or even death, to the citizen in his home community. Committing murder and mayhem for God and country is something that is demanded in time of war, and seems perfectly natural and legitimate to those in command. The enemy must be dehumanized. As Chris Hedges writes:

> "A soldier who is able to see the humanity of the enemy makes a troubled and ineffective killer…. We must be transformed into agents of a divinely inspired will, as defined by the state, just as those we fight must be transformed into the personification of unmitigated evil. There is little room for individuality in war.[2]

So we see that war has actually had a morality of its own—or rather a lack thereof. Despite declarations of opposition to war by the various religious authorities, rationalizations have usually been ready at hand to justify it in almost any circumstance.

If one looks far enough back into the past, a picture of how the phenomenon of war first got started begins to take shape. It is at the time when man first achieved superiority over his fellow beasts—when he emerged as the hunter rather than the hunted—that the origins of war can best be discerned. That hunting eventually gave rise to war seems to be agreed upon by most scholars. But exactly how this came about is not entirely clear. However, it seems that after man had achieved his position of superiority, he began to kill large numbers of the mammals against which he had previously been powerless.

About 12,000 years ago, many of these large animals became extinct. No doubt this was partly due to changing climatic conditions, but over-hunting by man must also have been a contributing factor. This meant that some hunter-gatherer societies were in danger of running out of food. One is tempted to surmise that this situation prompted the rise of agriculture. Cultivated cereals and domesticated animals were able to make up for the scarcity of prey for the hunters and the sparseness of wild cereals.

Competition between groups for valuable resources: game, water, land, building materials, etc., was clearly a motive for warfare. Starting with the reduction in the numbers of big game, the motives for war tended to steadily increase. As previously noted, when the agricultural communities first appeared, they presented tempting targets for the nomadic tribes and the remaining hunter-gatherers. So the transition from hunter to warrior seems altogether natural.

But once a man has become a warrior, it is extremely difficult to entice him away from his new occupation. As a warrior, he becomes a member of an elite group, and his prestige is just as high, if not higher, than that of the hunter. He is a "real" man and tends to look down on those without his war-like abilities. The women of the group encourage this kind of thinking, by preferring the he-man warrior types to the more peaceful ones. Of course the warrior could also be a hunter of animals as he had been before. But his prowess as a warrior became his most important asset.

Other societies or groups that became the prey of these warriors had no choice but to produce warriors of their own, simply in order to defend themselves. You can see where this is leading. Before too long we have a situation where there are several communities that exist, either in a state of uneasy peace, or of outright war. Any group that opts out of the game will be immediately overrun, and each group must constantly endeavor to improve the weapons that it possesses, and also to enhance the motivation and physical prowess of its warriors. This is necessary, not only to repel an attack, but also to take revenge against any attacker, so as to deter further aggression.

According to this scenario—and I think in fact that it is quite close to the truth—you can say that war rapidly became a habit, and one that was hopelessly addictive. In actuality, with the availability of increasingly lethal weapons, this cycle has repeated itself to a terrifying degree throughout history. First of all with the spear and the bow and arrow, then with the dagger and the sword; added to this the chariot and the war horse; then again, with the advent of firearms, this increasingly lethal game has played itself out through the centuries. Now, with the addition of tanks, warplanes and battleships, to say nothing of guided missiles, we have reached a level of all-consuming violence, when not just warriors are attacked, but civilians and cities can be bombed and shelled without mercy. Chivalry, which briefly made its appearance on the scene in the Middle Ages, has long since been forgotten on the killing grounds of Europe, Russia and the Pacific, where in 1945 the destruction finally reached a sickening crescendo when atomic bombs were dropped on Hiroshima and Nagasaki.

During the cold war, with the prospect of mutual annihilation, mankind seemed to have, at least temporally, stepped back from the brink of the abyss. But it was an uneasy peace. The balance of terror was achieved with literally thousands of nuclear weapons stockpiled on either side. Each had an arsenal large enough to destroy the other hundreds of times over. The total madness of the situation was reflected in the serious consideration of scenarios in which hundreds, or even thousands, of these weapons would actually be used. Scientists soberly discussed the possibility of a "nuclear winter," wherein all life on earth might be in jeopardy.

Did such talk finally reveal to mankind how far he had traveled down the road towards his own extinction, and impel him finally to step back from the brink? Not at all! Even after the cold war was over, huge stockpiles of nuclear weapons remained in place, and loaded missiles remained pointed at "enemy" cities. As for the rest of the world, rather than trying to persuade the United States and Russia to cease their madness, many countries have sought to develop nuclear weapons of their own!

This dismal story makes clear just how addictive war has become and just how difficult it will be to eliminate it. (We will see later that the military-industrial complex has prevented even the possibility of rational discussion regarding the prevention of war.)

The history of war and the origin of religion are both intimately connected with the fact that man is a carnivore. As previously noted, this fact also means that he has a bigger brain than he would have had as an herbivore. It was his meat-eating nature that impelled him, first to become a scavenger of the prey of other animals, then to become a predator himself. There was nothing unnatural in this. It followed from the fact that we are part of the food chain, like every other animal. This is often lost sight of when we contemplate our past from the security of our "civilized" modern world.

It is tempting to conclude that God put us among the animals as their superior and master. But when we look carefully, we do not really see a superior creature at all. What we do see is an animal whose roots extend back to the evolutionary struggle for survival. We kill other animals for food, just as they do, but we kill *each other* for no valid reason at all.

Our religions and our wars indicate that we are indeed a different kind of animal. But if we are superior at all it is in our intelligence and not in our behavior. We have piously preached morality to each other, but have seldom practiced it. The question now is, Will we be able to harness our intelligence to the task of curbing our destructive behavior before it's too late?

Having made a lightning survey of the phenomenon of war, we will now look at the history of war more closely, and trace the changing nature of armies, weapons and battles up to the time when firearms were first introduced.

SARGON REVISITED

When we left Mesopotamia, it had developed city-states that were constantly competing with one another. The archaeological record has revealed much of this activity, and many of the inscriptions and sculptural works that have been found paint a picture of aggression and conquest. King Sargon of Akkad, who we have met before, conquered the Sumerian city of Uruk in 2371 B.C. But this was not nearly enough to satisfy his ambitions. We read in the Legend of Sargon:

> After establishing himself firmly in Sumer and Akkad, Sargon moved against Amurru in the west, Elam in the east, and Subartu in the north. [He was] vic-

torious in thirty-four campaigns…as far as the Cedar Forest (the Amanus and Lebanon) and the Silver Mountain (the Taurus)."[3]

Even though one may assume that this is written in order to portray the king's record in the most impressive light, it nonetheless sounds like an imposing list of accomplishments. These accounts definitely do not describe minor incidents between neighbors. Everything is on a much larger scale, and one has to conclude that major resources were committed to the assembly of armies and the prosecution of war.

I have selected Sargon as an example to show that the machinery of war, and the practice of aggressive warfare for the purpose of acquiring territory, was already developed on a significant scale, as early as the twenty-fourth century B.C. This pattern has continued throughout the centuries, even to the present day. Historian William McNeill calls Sargon an example of a "macro-parasite," who had a perpetual following of 54,000 men. He maintained these by constant predation on the surrounding countryside:

> But to keep such a force in being also required annual campaigning, devastating one fertile landscape after another in order to keep the soldiers in victuals. Costs to the population at large were obviously very great. Indeed, Sargon's armies can well be compared to an epidemic disease that kills a significant proportion of the host population yet, by its very passage, confers an immunity lasting for several years.[4]

This describes the curse of standing armies. They have to be fed, and they have to have something to do. Unfortunately the only thing that they are trained to do is to kill their fellow men and destroy property. Sargon had almost no choice but to create an empire. If he had not kept his standing army, the king of Uruk, who he had previously defeated, would have attacked him. In fact Uruk did attack Akkad shortly after Sargon's death, when his two sons had inherited the kingdom. And if he had not embarked on the pursuit of empire, his army might very well have laid waste to his kingdom, or worse still, removed the king himself from the throne.

Survivors of a defeated army were frequently brought back to the home territory to perform slave labor, often in the construction of monumental architecture. Over time this created an underclass that was resentful of its inferior status and looked for an opportunity to sever the chains of bondage. The possibility of insurrection was thus ever present, and armed force was needed to make sure that it did not occur. This made the loyalty of the army of even greater importance.

But to keep the army fed and busy was not the only reason for the pursuit of empire. Another reason was to obtain important raw materials that were not available at home. Two of these materials were tin and copper, which were used to made bronze, an alloy which had many uses other than the obvious one of making weapons. Another material much in demand was wood, especially cedar—hence Sargon's foray into Lebanon. This desire to obtain raw materials remained a motivation for empire until well into the twentieth century. But another method of obtaining raw materials and other goods was trade, and this was also a feature of the interaction between city-states from very early times. Trade and war are very different activities, one might say trade is a positive activity and war is a negative one. Robert Wright, in *Nonzero*, uses game theory for his analysis.

> The founders of game theory, John von Neumann and Oskar Morgenstern.... made a basic distinction between "zero-sum" games and "non-zero-sum" games. In zero-sum games, the fortunes of the players are inversely related. In tennis, in chess, in boxing, one contestant's gain is the other's loss. In non-zero-sum games, one player's gain needn't be bad news for the other(s). Indeed, in highly non-zero-sum games the player's interests overlap entirely. In 1970, when the three *Apollo 13* astronauts were trying to figure out how to get their stranded spaceship back to earth, they were playing an utterly non-zero-sum game, because the outcome would be equally good for all of them or equally bad. (It was equally good.) [5]

According to this definition, war is a zero-sum game and trade is close to being a non-zero-sum game—war is a win-lose situation, while trade has a win-win outcome. It is Wright's contention that as culture evolves it tends to select non-zero-sum over zero-sum outcomes—not just with trade vs. war, but in many other situations, which often boil down basically to cooperation over confrontation. His thesis is that the overall trend is in the right direction, in spite of some backsliding along the way. What's more, he thinks there is a built-in tendency towards non-zero-sum activities. He postulates a parallel with biological evolution, in that the "selection" from the various alternatives tends to be favorable to the culture as a whole.

This is an interesting thesis, but I am not totally convinced of its validity. Nonetheless, in analyzing culture from this point of view, one obtains some interesting insights into its structure and development. What Wright seems to be asserting is that the rationality of cooperation will overcome the irrationality of man's more basic instincts, or natural tendencies, which have their roots in biological evolution.

This is going to be a difficult to achieve. Even so, I think Wright is correct when he points out that the non-zero-sum choice of options does seem to win out in many situations. Indeed, between city-states the option of trade did, in most cases, win out over the option of war. A decision had to be made between cooperation and confrontation, and practical considerations often played a decisive part.

Most leaders tend to be forceful characters who are interested basically in maintaining their own positions of power, and who are not loath to use violence to achieve their ambitions. Thus there must be clear advantages to the more peaceful path of cooperation and trade, if it is to be preferred over that of war and conquest. If trade *did* win out over war and conquest in many cases, it was not necessarily because it was the nice thing to do, but rather because conquest was simply impractical. The movement and supply of armies was a large and difficult operation, which was often too burdensome for a state to undertake, when the desired end was simply to obtain certain materials that could be acquired in a far less arduous fashion.

The issue of relationships between states will be taken up again in Part II.

THE BATTLE OF ISSUS

The basic tools of ancient warfare: the spear, the bow and arrow and the dagger, were all more effective when made of metal. The original metal for weapons and armor in the Old World was bronze, an alloy of tin and copper. Bronze was too soft for use in swords, whose manufacture had to await the coming of iron. The Hittites were the first to introduce iron weapons in large quantities, which were made from the extensive deposits of iron ore in western Anatolia. After the collapse of the Hittite Empire c.1200 B.C., iron weapons spread rapidly throughout the rest of the Middle East.

Long before the introduction of firearms, fire itself had been used in warfare. "Greek fire" was the name given to a tar-like substance similar to bitumen, which contained naphtha, sulfur and other flammable materials, probably first introduced by the Persians, who used it in their fire temples.[6] It was later used by the Greeks and the Byzantines, especially in naval warfare. Projectiles soaked in this material and ignited were very effective in early naval battles. They were the precursors of the flame-thrower.

The light and highly mobile war chariot, with spoked wheels, was introduced about 1800 B.C. and was used by the northern steppe dwellers to overrun the civilized lands of the Middle East between 1800 and 1500 B.C. This had the effect of establishing an elite, chariot-owning class, which could exercise decisive military force when needed.[7]

The Hyksos, who invaded Egypt in 1786 B.C., and may originally have been steppe dwellers, introduced chariots into that country, and this substantially increased the mobility of the Egyptian armies after the Hyksos were finally expelled. The chariots usually carried two men: an archer and a driver, and they needed a large number of artisans and craftsmen to supply and maintain all the equipment, weapons and horses.

By the time of Alexander the Great (356-323 B.C.), all these weapons were in use, and in addition, catapults and cavalry had been added to the arsenal. The cavalry used a type of metaled garment to ward off arrows, and they also had larger horses, which were bred in Iran; these had enabled the Assyrians and the Babylonians to repel the steppe people on their smaller horses. The only thing they lacked was stirrups, which were not introduced until much later by the Huns.[8]

The Greeks were the creators of the phalanx, which consisted of closely massed infantry armed with extra long spears, or lances. To be effective the phalanx had to maintain a very tight formation, so that it presented a densely packed concentration of huge iron spikes, giving the effect of a giant hedgehog. The phalanx could be extremely effective, and when properly used, struck fear and confusion into the ranks of an enemy.

In 338 B.C. Philip II of Macedon completed his conquest of Greece and established a federal system to replace of the old configuration of Greek states. But he was killed while preparing to attack Persia, the ancient enemy of the Greeks. However, in 334 B.C. Philip's mission was taken up by Alexander of Macedon, his son and successor, who resolved to seek out and defeat the Persians.

This quixotic quest could easily have been stillborn. The Persians still occupied Anatolia, and were prepared to contest Alexander's advance towards the Persian heartland. Their ranks were swelled with Greek mercenaries, unhappy after the Macedonian conquest of their native land.

After crossing the Hellespont, Alexander had to fight his first major battle at the river Granicus, in northwestern Anatolia. As W. W. Tarn writes:

The Persian leaders had in fact a very gallant plan; they meant if possible to strangle the war at birth by killing Alexander. They massed their cavalry on the steep bank of the lower Granicus, put the Greeks behind them, and waited.

Alexander's army was in what became his regular battle-order; on the left, Parmenion with the Thessalain, Greek, and Thracian horse; then the phalanx, then the hypaspists; on the right, beyond the hypaspists, himself with the Companions, lancers, Paeonians, Agrianians, and Cretans.... The ensuing battle was fought mainly on the right wing. He ordered some cavalry to cross, and then charged through the river himself, conspicuous by the white wings on his helmet. The Persian leaders concentrated on him and threw away their lives freely in a desperate attempt to kill him; at one point they almost succeeded.... Finally the Persians broke; their men, armed only with javelins, were unequally matched with Alexander's heavy cavalry.... The rest of the army had crossed, and Alexander surrounded the Greeks and killed all but 2,000, whom he sent in chains to forced labour in Macedonia as traitors to the League; among them were some Athenians.[9]

[The hypaspists were heavily armed infantry with shields.]

This battle marked an auspicious start to Alexander's campaign, and bore a remarkable similarity to the later battle at Issus. The Macedonian's courage and daring at the Granicus turned what might easily have been a defeat into a resounding victory. Soon afterwards Alexander set off across Anatolia to search out and destroy the army of King Darius III of Persia.

After several battles along the way, Alexander arrived at the town of Issus in 333 B.C., which was located near the coast in the extreme southeastern corner of what is now Turkey. Issus itself lay on a narrow plain running between a coastal mountain range and the sea. Darius was on the other side of the mountains on the Syrian plain of Sochoi, on open ground that was much more favorable for the deployment of his larger army.

There were two routes from Issus into Syria: one directly over the mountains and the other going south along the coast and then turning inland. Alexander, who had been delayed by a few skirmishes along the way, left his wounded at Issus and set off down the coastal route to Myriandros, where he was further delayed by a violent storm.

Meanwhile Darius, with his army of Persians and Greek mercenaries, got tired of waiting, and thinking that maybe Alexander had decided not to engage him, advanced over the mountain route to Issus. There he found Alexander's wounded men and proceeded to put them to death.

Alexander, hearing that Darius was now behind him at Issus, hurried back from Myrandros into the plain of Issus, in order to engage the king in battle. He realized immediately that he would be meeting Darius on much more favorable terms, since the narrow costal plain made it difficult for Darius to maneuver his larger army. The fact that he now had no line of retreat did not deter him.

Darius had no plan to attack Alexander. Instead he took up a defensive position on the north side of a small river, the Pinarus. When he heard that Alexander was approaching, he sent 50,000 cavalry and light troops across the river, to protect his forces from attack while he deployed his main line of hoplites—30,000 Greek mercenaries, and some regiments of Orientals called *Kardakes.* After the main line was formed, the cavalry was withdrawn back across the river and placed on the right wing near the sea.[10]

Due to the narrowness of the plain, a large portion of Darius' army was forced to remain in reserve, behind the main battle line. Historian J. B. Bury describes the battle:

> Alexander advanced, his army drawn up on the usual plan, the phalanx in the centre, the hypaspists on the right. At first he placed the Thessalian as well as the Macedonian cavalry on the right wing...but when he saw that the Persian cavalry was concentrated on the sea side, he was obliged to transfer the Thessalians to their usual position on the left.... As in the engagement on the Granicus, the attack was to be made by the heavy cavalry on the left centre of the enemy's line....
>
> The Persian left did not sustain Alexander's onset at the head of the cavalry. The phalanx followed more slowly, and in crossing the stream and climbing the steep bank the line became dislocated, especially at one spot, and the Greek hoplites pressed him hard on the river-brink. If the phalanx had been driven back, Alexander's victorious right wing would have been exposed on the flank and the battle lost; but the phalangites stood their ground obstinately.... Meanwhile Alexander's attack had been directed upon the spot where the Great King himself stood in his war chariot, surrounded by a guard of Persian nobles. There was a furious [melee], in which Alexander was wounded in the leg. Then Darius turned his chariot and fled, and this was a signal for an universal flight on the left. On the sea side the Persian cavalry crossed the river and carried all before them; but in the midst of their success the cry that the king was fleeing made them waver, and they were soon riding wildly back, pursued by the Thessalians....
>
> Thus was the Persian host, which had come to "trample down" Alexander and his little army, annihilated on the plain of Issus.[11]

Here we have an example of a military genius, aided perhaps by a little luck (but the best always seem to make their own luck), being able to defeat an enemy far more numerous, but with a leader without the qualities needed to exploit its strength. You will note that Alexander went straight for Darius, because he knew that the king himself represented the weakest part of the Persian war machine.

In the days when torture and mutilation were common, only one such incident by Alexander is recorded, that of the torture and execution of Bessus, the satrap of Bactria.[12] His most gratuitous act of vandalism was the burning of Darius' magnificent palace at Persepolis, perhaps in retaliation for the murder of his wounded men at Issus. On the whole, Alexander treated his defeated enemies in a fair and humane manner.

W. W. Tarn, in *Alexander the Great,* asserts that the size of Darius' army has been exaggerated, and that it may not have been much larger than Alexander's force.[13] But the way in which the battle was fought showed the skill and nerve of the Macedonian as being far superior to those of his opponent. He proved his superior generalship, not only at Issus, but also in countless other battles across Asia.

Alexander went on to victory after victory until he finally reached the Indus Valley, where, after some further battles, his army was no longer capable of further conquest, and told him in no uncertain terms that they wished to return home to Macedonia.

Alexander is an example of someone who loved war. He delighted in the ferocity, savagery and danger of combat, and loved to kill his enemies. Personally leading his men into the midst of battle was his greatest thrill. He was the warrior *par excellence.* Completely fearless, he inspired intense loyalty in his men, who would willingly follow him into the jaws of danger and death. He lived only for war.

The war-lover, or warrior, was familiar to the Greeks. Robert Kaplan, in *Warrior Politics,* describes the essence of the war-lover:

> Like Achilles and the ancient Greeks harassing Troy, the thrill of violence substitutes for the joys of domesticity and feasting. Achilles exclaims,
>   You talk of food?
>   I have no taste for food—what I really crave is slaughter and blood and the choking groans of men![14]

Issus was one of history's pivotal battles. If Darius had been victorious, the Middle East would be quite a different place today. What it would actually have been like is impossible to tell, but we can be sure that its make-up would have been totally different from what we see today. Military conflict has been the prime mover on the historical landscape, and individual leaders have made their mark on it in an indelible manner.

CHURCH AND EMPIRE

As we pass into the Christian era, the fledgling Christian Church, true to the principles of its founder, expressed its solidarity with, and support for the humbler members of society, as well as those who felt oppressed by their rulers. It was also opposed to the concept of war.

At the beginning of the fourth century, the Emperor Diocletian effectively abandoned Rome as the capital of the Empire, and divided his domain into four sections. The Emperor moved his imperial capital to Nicomedia, while at the same time appointing three assistant caesars: Maximian, Constantus I and Galerius, who ruled from three subsidiary capitals at Mediolanum (Milan), Treveri (Trier) and Sirmnium (near Belgrade) respectively. Diocletian's successor, Constantine, moved the principal capital to Byzantium, which was renamed Constantinople.

The soldiers in the Roman armies continued to sacrifice to the old gods, whereas the common citizens were more attracted to Christianity, with its promise of eternal bliss for those who remained faithful followers of Christ. The popularity of Christianity alarmed the Roman leaders, and persecution of the Christians became ever more frequent and severe. This situation continued until the fourth century A.D. But with the accession of the Emperor Constantine, everything changed.

The new Emperor solved the problem of the Christians by adopting Christianity as the official religion of the Roman Empire. We do not know what the Emperor's personal feelings about Christianity were, but the fact that he waited until his deathbed to be baptized, indicates that he was not a particularly zealous convert. It suggests that his conversion was in all probability inspired more by politics than religion. He realized that with the growing popularity of Christianity, it was far more expedient to have the Christians on his side than to oppose them.

The adoption of the Christian religion by Constantine had greater consequences for Christianity than it did for the Empire. The Empire was already on the wane, and would soon be beset by barbarian invasions, which eventually led to its extinction in the West and slow decline in the East. As far as Christianity was concerned, its association with the Empire meant the abandonment of many of its founder's teachings, and the eventual loss of its moral authority. Why was this so? The compromising of its commitment to peace was the most obvious casualty. It was impossible to continue to oppose war after having been adopted as the religion of the Roman Empire, which was ruled by military force. Although many of the Roman soldiers continued to worship the old gods, and later in the century the Emperor Julian temporally restored the old pagan rituals, Christianity eventually became the accepted religion of the Empire for military and civilians alike. This lead quickly to the politicization of the Church, and from then on the genuine teachings of Christ—prince of peace and solace of the afflicted—were kept alive mainly by the faithful followers, rather than by the leaders of the Church.

At the end of the fourth century the Empire was formally split into East and West, but this arrangement only lasted for a century, after which Rome finally collapsed from the onslaught of the Visigoths, the Vandals and the Ostrogoths.

This meant that only the eastern section, ruled from Constantinople, remained. However, the Pope in Rome continued to claim primacy over the entire body of Christians, both in what was now the Eastern Roman Empire and also in what had formerly been the Western Empire, where many of the "barbarians" had by then been converted to Christianity. But the Christians in the east gradually became estranged from those in the west, not only because of the geographical separation, but also because of the cultural and political differences between the two geographical areas.

Many of the decisions that were made by the various councils of the Church with respect to dogma, were in fact political decisions rather than theological ones. Delegates from the eastern part of the Church's jurisdiction tended to vote as a block on doctrinal matters, and those from the west usually voted against them. In one particular case the eastern delegates insisted on taking a vote before those from the west had even arrived.

The final breach came in 1054, although by then the two sides had long since gone their separate ways. So the Christian Church was divided into the Western Church, under the Pope in Rome, and the Eastern (Orthodox) Church, under the Patriarch of Constantinople. The Eastern Roman Empire continued to cling to an ever-shrinking piece of territory, until its jurisdiction finally consisted of a small enclave surrounding the city of Constantinople. When the Ottomans captured the city in 1453, the Roman Empire officially came to an end.

In spite of having associated itself with the Roman state, the Christian Church was by no means incapable of making important contributions to Western culture. In fact the Church actually helped to lay the foundations of culture in the West. This it did by preserving and translating many of the classic works of Greek and Roman, as well as Arabic scholarship. Most of this work was done in the monasteries of the West during the Dark Ages, after the barbarians had overrun Western Europe. The Church played a vital role in preserving this priceless heritage.

SWORD OF ISLAM

The advent of the Prophet Mohammed, at the end of the sixth century, marked the establishment of the last major, or universal religion. Mohammed himself was both a merchant and a soldier, and in some ways he was more successful as a soldier than as a religious leader. However, the Koran, the official scripture of Islam, supposedly revealed to Mohammed by the angel Gabriel, established the new religion on a firm basis. After the death of the Prophet, Islam spread rapidly throughout the Middle East and North Africa, and even reached as far as Spain. The Eastern Roman imperial capital of Constantinople only just managed to avoid being overrun by the forces of Allah on two separate occasions, and its situation remained precarious from that time onwards.

Islam soon split up into two competing branches: the Sunnis and the Shiites. The division arose over the selection of the caliph, or spiritual leader. The Shiites, mainly from the Persian section of the Moslem community, insisted that the correct line of descent from the prophet Mohammed was through his cousin and son-in-law Ali. This was disputed by the Sunnis, who accepted the historic succession of the first four followers of Mohammed, and who comprised the majority of the Prophet's followers.

Islamic rule was centralized and bureaucratic, as opposed to the feudalism that was evolving in Europe. Judaism and Christianity were tolerated by Islam because the five prophets of the Old Testament: Adam, Noah, Abraham, Moses and Jesus were accepted by Islam, Mohammed being considered as the sixth and last of the line. Believers in these two religions were required to pay an extra tax but were otherwise left in peace. Other infidels had to convert to Islam or be exterminated—which in practice usually meant that they were forced into exile. Exceptions were later allowed for "people of the book," that is members of any religion that possessed a sacred book or scripture.

Mohammed, unlike Christ, was a temporal ruler, and what he created was an *Islamic* state. So there was no separation between the religion and the state; the religion *was* the state, and vice versa. There was no church in the Christian sense, and no priests, the Moslem clerics are thought of essentially as teachers. But there is really no laity either, because all Moslems are part of the community of Allah. The only law is the *sharia*, which is accepted as being of divine origin.

This mixing of religion with civil government has had unfortunate consequences for Islam throughout the centuries. Since religion tends to distort reality, this has meant that *all* Moslems are inclined to have a more distorted worldview than is customary in other societies and cultures. While the hold that the Christian Church once had over Western society has weakened almost to the vanishing point, in the case of Islam, although there has been some secularization of the society, the religion has retained its influence to a much greater degree. The only major exception to this is modern Turkey, which was secularized by Kemal Atatürk in 1923, after the fall of the Ottoman Empire. By abolishing the caliphate, Atatürk caused considerable anguish in the Moslem world. But in fact the caliphate was an empty shell by them.[15] All the same, the Moslem religion still retains considerable influence in Turkey.

Over the centuries, Islam has produced a very vibrant culture in many areas of endeavor that have little to do with religion. In the first years of Islamic rule there was a great flowering of culture of all kinds: in art, architecture, literature and even science, although the latter was confined mostly to mathematics. It's true that Islam built on the existing Byzantine culture of the Middle East, but what it achieved was far superior to that which had gone before.

Many of the positive aspects of Islam, featuring the rules and recommendations for the functioning of a civil society, have showed themselves to great advantage throughout its history. There is no question that the Moslem culture has made great contributions to the intellectual and artistic life of mankind. While the great majority of Moslems have supported and adhered to the positive traditions of their heritage, there has been a tendency for a small segment of the faithful to distort the Prophet's message, and to engage in fanatical and destructive behavior, which has proved detrimental to the reputation of the Moslem world. The notion of the jihad, originally intended to apply to the individual's struggle against evil, soon became applied to the idea of military conquest. Although it had a lot to do with the early success of Islam, the concept of the jihad has proved to be its Achilles' heel in more modern times. Instead of letting the whole idea die a quiet death, it has been revived in recent years by fringe groups who have engaged in violent and destructive behavior, claiming without foundation that they are following the true teachings of the Prophet. This small minority has tended to become an embarrassment to the larger Moslem community.

Other aspects of Islam that have tended to weaken the social fabric are the exclusive privileges that have been granted to those who are free, male and Moslem. As Bernard Lewis writes:

> The slave, the woman, and the unbeliever were subject to strictly enforced legal, as well as social, disabilities, affecting them in almost every aspect of their daily lives. These disabilities were seen as an inherent part of the struc-

ture of Islam, buttressed by revelation, by the precept and practice of the Prophet, and by the classical and scriptural history of the Islamic community.[16]

This has been a definite flaw in the otherwise egalitarian society of the Moslems. Slavery, which was authorized under Islamic law, was widely practiced up until the end of the nineteenth century. After that it was finally abolished after several foreign countries had exerted pressure on the Moslem community. But the stamp of inferiority that was placed on both women and the infidel has continued to have a negative influence on Moslem society to this day. In spite of several efforts at reform, the conservative establishment has prevented women from taking their rightful place in the society, and foreigners are still looked on as outsiders, or even infidels.

The Moslem armies that set out on the path of conquest after the Prophet's death achieved a series of remarkably easy victories, and this had to do with the nature of the new faith of Islam. Mohammed himself had been a soldier and this helped to impart military zeal in his followers. But it was the religion itself that was a major motivating factor. Rather than an army with an elite leadership, such as the European knights, the Arab armies enjoyed much broader and more popular support. They were motivated by the concept of the holy war, or jihad, the benefits of which accrued to both leaders and common soldiers alike. The individual soldier had several powerful incentives to fight for his leaders and their cause. As a member of Allah's faithful following, he was part of a sacred band, commanded to do the will of Allah and his representatives. On top of this there was also the usual prospect of enrichment through plunder and pillage. But perhaps most important of all, if a soldier died in battle he was assured of eternal bliss in paradise. Thus, instead of the rank and file being dragged unwillingly into combat, they were only too eager to carry out the will of Allah.

There is a parallel here with Napoleon's armies after the French Revolution. The new secular religion of nationalism made the average soldier feel that he was fighting for his new-found liberty rather than for his former aristocratic masters, and this had a powerful effect on the morale of the army and made it into a much more formidable fighting force. The common soldier was far more motivated than he had ever been before. The brotherhood of the new nation became an almost irresistible fighting force.

So we have two cases of nationalism, one religious and one secular. The common thread is that the masses and the elites are united in a common cause. This was the key to the creation of nationalism, as will be discussed in greater detail later on.

The Arabs, at least initially, had a tremendous military advantage, which they exploited to the hilt. Having expanded their territory as far as Spain, they tried to push their way up into northern Europe. But at the epic battle of Tours in 732, Charles Martel and his armored cavalry defeated them. This was another pivotal battle of history. Victory for Islam would almost certainly have meant the Moslem conquest of Europe, and this would have changed history even more than Alexander's defeat at Issus would have done. Europe would have become Moslem rather than Christian. All those magnificent cathedrals would have been beautiful mosques!

[Perhaps the mosques *do* exist in some parallel universe, in which Charles Martel *lost* the battle—if the "many-worlds" interpretation of quantum mechanics is correct. See the discussion of quantum mechanics in chapter 9.]

I have emphasized these climactic battles in order to point out that the history of human culture has not evolved smoothly, but has had violent discontinuities and changes in direction, where the path of history could have taken a radically different course. One should remember how, time and again, the most fundamental beliefs and institutions of a society have been decided, not by rational debate or free choice, but by military force—in combination with various quirks of fate.

KNIGHTS IN ARMOR

Mediaeval Europe saw the introduction of feudalism, and this in turn gave rise to a distinctive military class—the armored knight. These knights were noblemen and landowners, and so they stood out from the ordinary population as a privileged elite. They would fight for the king if required to do so, and in return they were granted income-producing land for their own use and that of their retainers. Each knight required several attendants to look after his weapons, his horses and his armor. He also needed the services of artisans to fashion and repair his equipment when necessary.

The knights prepared for war by competing in tournaments, where they honed their skills by jousting with other knights and competing for the attentions of the ladies. These tournaments constituted a sanitized form of combat, but were nonetheless violent and dangerous, in fact they were actually condemned by the Church.

To the community at large, this kind of activity was relatively harmless, but some of the knights took to bullying the ordinary citizens, attacking innocent people, stealing their property, and generally behaving badly. Sometimes whole villages or towns were held to ransom, and made to pay money or goods in order to avoid being attacked by the knights. Although the vaunted code of chivalry was supposed to protect women and the weak, in practice it did not apply to anyone outside the knightly circle. Ordinary citizens had to be constantly on their guard against their nominal protectors. By the eleventh century the situation had deteriorated to where the people were searching for deliverance.

In the eleventh century, the Seljuk Turks, a group of steppe people from Central Asia, descended on the Middle East and captured Baghdad in 1055. Another epochal battle occurred in 1071 at Manzikert in Asia Minor, when the Seljuk leader Alp Arslan defeated the Byzantine Emperor Romanus IV. The Seljuks then occupied Syria and the Holy Land, which had enjoyed relative tranquility under the rule of the Abbasid caliphate. Although the Seljuks had converted to Islam, the people of the Holy Land now received much harsher treatment from the less civilized people from the steppe.

Pope Urban II ascended the throne of St Peter in 1088. "He was gentle, firm, courteous and peace loving; he hated bloodshed, avoided controversy, and won people's hearts by a combination of forbearance and innate authority...."[17] Urban summoned a council of the Church in 1095, to which he invited ambassadors from the Byzantine Emperor Alexius. The ambassadors told the assembled delegates of the tragic condition of their Christian brothers in the Holy Land, and called upon Western Christians to rally to the defense of their stricken brethren.

It took the gentle Urban some time to decide on a remedy for this sorry state of affairs, but later in 1095, at Clermont, having assembled the bishops of France and the surrounding countries, he informed them about the maltreatment of their fellow Christians by the Seljuk Turks. He told them:

> It was time for Christians in the West to rise up in righteous wrath and march to the rescue; let them stop making war on each other at home and wage a holy war against God's enemies instead. God himself would lead them, and give them the victory, and to all who died in battle he, Pope Urban, promised there and then absolution and remission of all their sins.[18]

The response was "immediate and overwhelming," and it was not long before a motley band of knights, retainers and ordinary citizens was assembled. Fired with the zeal of the holy crusade, they were ready to do God's work.

Long before their arrival in the Holy Land, a debacle was only narrowly avoided. When the crusaders reached Constantinople, Godfrey of Bouillon, one of the more spirited members of the group, refused to swear allegiance to the Emperor Alexius. He ended up attacking the city—during Holy Week—but was driven off by the imperial forces. The crisis was finally ended when Godfrey agreed to swear allegiance to Alexius.

Thus started a series of crusades, which continued off and on for the next two hundred years. The Turks and the Christians each had their victories, and many of the crusading knights acquired land in the Levant, establishing the so-called Crusader States.

Jerusalem was captured in the first crusade, and this was followed by pillage and massacre. The third crusade pitted the two famous war-lovers, Saladin and Richard the Lion Heart against one another. Saladin recaptured Jerusalem from the Christians, but he permitted neither pillage nor massacre.

The fourth crusade, undertaken in 1202, ultimately set the seal on the whole enterprise, when Constantinople was first captured and then sacked by the crusaders on their way to the Holy Land. The crusade never did reach its destination. After that things went slowly down hill, until the Egyptian Mamluks captured Acre in 1291 and the crusades finally petered out.

In the end the Holy Land remained in the hands of the Turks, and the Crusader States simply melted away. The Holy Places remained in Moslem hands until the end of World War I. The only survivors of those bygone campaigns are the ghost-filled ruins of the crusader's castles, which stand as silent reminders of a time when Christian knights took their fighting, if not their chivalry, extremely seriously.

Although it was the intention of the Christians to bring civilization to the Holy Land, the actual result of the crusades was quite different. Far from being the uncivilized brutes pictured by the crusaders, the Moslems were found to possess far greater refinement than those who came to teach them the ways of God and civilization. However, they were not too refined to make war, and once they had recovered from the initial shock, took considerable satisfaction in dispatching the Christian infidels who had so arrogantly invaded their land. Although their standards of chivalry were generally superior to those of the Christians, they too were capable of some gratuitous butchery from time to time.

The Moslem residents of cities such as Damascus and Baghdad were acquainted with luxuries and learning of a kind that was unknown in Europe at the time. In reality, the crusaders had come across a people considerably more civilized than themselves. As a result of this, Moslem fabrics, art, jewelry and other luxuries found their way into Europe with the returning crusaders. Tales of magnificent buildings, exotic foods and other marks of a sophisticated culture began to open European minds to the realities of what lay beyond the boundaries of their world.

The sequel to this story is a cautionary tale, which emphasizes the transient nature of cultural ascendancy. The Moslems failed to maintain their superiority over the Europeans, and within a few centuries they were outflanked and out-gunned by the rising power of the West. They failed to take advantage of their superior learning and science, and, like the Chinese, allowed the Western barbarians to exploit them.

Apart from the usual accidents of geography and history, there were several important reasons for the stagnation of Moslem culture, and some of these will be discussed in later chapters. It was not that the Moslem culture suddenly collapsed, for the Ottomans were to strengthen it for a time at the expense of the Eastern Christians, but its vitality began to erode as conquerors came and went through the Moslems lands, situated precariously at the eastern end of the Mediterranean. Although the crusaders were ultimately repulsed, other invaders followed in their footsteps. Hulagu (grandson of Genghis Kahn) sacked Baghdad in 1253, and it was again attacked and pillaged by Tamerlane in 1400. These assaults marked the start of a slow decline from the earlier days of Moslem cultural ascendancy, when the wellsprings of creativity had produced so much that was of value to the world of art, science and literature.

Now, at the dawn of the twenty-first century, the superiority that the Middle East enjoyed over the West at the time of the crusades has been turned on its head. The culture of the Moslem world is little different from what it was in the thirteenth century. But the West has forged ahead in so many different areas, especially in science. The voice of fanaticism, which is now heard in the Moslem world, is raised primarily against the supposed shortcomings of Western culture. The cohorts of bin Laden and their sympathizers direct their ire against America and the West, but this only tends to obscure the real object of their anger and frustration, which is the failure of their own Moslem society to move beyond its

Golden Age, now more than half a millennium in the past. Starting at the time of the crusades, the West has caught up and surpassed them in practically all fields of endeavor. Until the Islamic society as a whole stops blaming the West for its lack of progress, and begins to recognize the real source of its frustrations, it will surely remain a laggard in the global community.[19]

The crusades temporarily spared Europe from the ravages of the Christian knights. But as they petered out, the same problems started to arise once more. In Italy, many of the cities had built walls and hired mercenaries to provide protection from armed attack. This development coincided with the rise of the mercantile class, who were better able to defend themselves, and so the balance gradually tipped in favor of the townsmen.

In France, however, things were different. The Hundred Years War with England had broken out in 1337 over the claim of England's king Edward III to the French throne. The infamous *chevauchée,* which was practiced by the English, brought devastation to the countryside of English-occupied France. As historian John Lynn writes, "A *chevauchée* was not a ride but a raid, typified by pillage, burning, rape, and murder."[20] Ostensibly to obtain provisions for the army, it laid waste to great swaths of land on either side of the main line of march. Neither churches nor monasteries were spared, and the clergy were subjected to the same horrors as the ordinary people. Whole towns were held for ransom, and forced to pay the infamous *pâtis,* or protection, to avoid being attacked. Vast amounts of treasure were seized and taken back to England, where French booty could be found for sale throughout the land.

This state of affairs dragged on for nearly a century, until in 1428 help for the French finally appeared from a most unlikely quarter. In the words of Winston Churchill:

> There now appeared upon the ravaged scene an Angel of Deliverance, the noblest patriot of France, the most splendid of her heroes, the most beloved of her saints, the most inspiring of all her memories, the peasant Maid, the evershining, ever-glorious Joan of Arc.[21]

But as historian Desmond Seward explains in *The Hundred Years War,* far from driving out the English, Joan of Arc merely checked their advance by reviving the Dauphinists' morale. The English could be forgiven for thinking that Joan was a witch, because for a decade God had apparently blessed the Lancastrian cause with victory after victory.[22] The counter-offensive by the Dauphin's forces was soon arrested and the English were not finally expelled from France until 1453.

Long before the end of the Hundred Years War, the days of the mounted knight were numbered. New weapons that could strike from a distance with sufficient force to stop an armored knight were already appearing. The longbow, used by the English to strike down the flower of French nobility at Crécy in 1346, had given the English their foothold in France.

But there was another weapon used at Crécy, which would eventually change the face of war, and that was the firearm. The "cannon" used by the English at Crécy were as dangerous to those firing them as they were to the enemy, but they would eventually revolutionize warfare. Their story will be taken up later. Now we will look at what was happening on the other side of the world.

CHINA AND THE MONGOLS

The Asian steppe stretches all the way from Eastern Europe to the Pacific. This was the domain of the nomads, or pastoralists. The more settled people, who lived to the south, presented tempting targets for the nomads. Warriors equipped with chariots had descended on the Middle East in the second millennium B.C., and similar incursions into China from Manchuria occurred on the eastern end of the steppe. During the Shang dynasty we find a noble class of charioteers similar to those that arose in Mesopotamia, so it is likely that these also originated on the steppe.[23]

Attacks by these northern people were a continuing problem, and in order to counter them the Great Wall was begun by the Ch'in dynasty in the third century B.C. The Wall was expanded many times, but was largely ineffective in stopping the raids.

The large Iranian horses, which had been used for cavalry in the Middle East, were introduced into China in the first century B.C., but the Chinese did not use them for armored cavalry. Crossbows capable of knocking an armored man off a horse at a hundred yards negated the strength of the horsemen, and besides, the armor at that early date was made of bamboo and wood rather than metal.

Instead of spending money to equip large forces in order to fight off the nomads, the Chinese preferred to hire some of the tribesmen as border guards and use diplomatic gift-payments to the potentates north of the border. This policy of appeasement worked reasonably well, but did not stop the occasional foray from north of the Wall.[24]

By the time of the Sung dynasty in 960 A.D., iron production had greatly increased, and all sorts of new weapons were in use. By the tenth century two border states of steppe people, the Khitan and the Jurchen, had established themselves at the eastern end of the steppe. These had been considerably "sinicized" and they had also become much more formidable fighters, thanks to the warrior tradition of the steppe and the adoption of the skilled tactics of the sedentary peoples.[25]

By 1126 the Jurchen had acquired weapons capable of attacking cities, and they succeeded in taking over the Sung territory north of the Yangtse. However, they were not able to advance into the southern domains, because the Sung had hurriedly built a fleet of ships that were capable of keeping the invaders north of the river.

The Mongols were a confederation of tribes from Central Asia and Mongolia, who had been unified by Genghis Khan into a formidable nation of warrior-horsemen. Their capital was at Karakorum, just to the north of the Gobi desert, and the boundaries of the Mongol domain spread rapidly westward, until it had encompassed the whole expanse of the steppe, all the way from the Pacific to Europe. The Mongols were thus in a position to prey on the settled lands to the south almost at will, using their horses and their crossbows to devastating effect.

After attacking both Afghanistan and Persia, Genghis Khan turned his attention to the Jurchen in northern China. Although his armies overran the Jurchen, he himself was killed in battle in 1227. It took fifty years before his successor, Kublai Khan, was able to conquer the Sung stronghold south of the Yangtse. To do so he had to build a navy of his own. But the Sung put up a brave fight:

> Against Genghiz Khan, the "pacifist" dynasty of the Sung had used the most advanced arsenal of weapons ever developed. Gunpowder, explosive grenades and bombs launched from catapults, rocket-aided arrows and flame throwers, poisonous smoke and a primitive armoured car had held up the Mongol advance for nearly half a century, the stoutest resistance shown to the fierce, mounted horde from the steppe, before the last Sung ruler perished in a sea battle off what is now Hong Kong (1279).[26]

Kublai Khan continued to expand his navy, and even attempted an invasion of Japan in 1281, but this was driven off with severe losses. A typhoon, which arrived providentially for the Japanese, almost destroyed the Mongol navy.

The Mongols were not finally driven out of China until 1368, when the Ming dynasty was proclaimed in Beijing. The insurrection that finally succeeded in expelling the Mongols had caused widespread destruction, and it was some time before the damage to the economy was repaired. But the Ming eventually succeeded in restoring some measure of prosperity, as well as a revival of the basic Chinese culture. In order to facilitate the defense of the northern border, the capital was moved to Beijing and more than a thousand extra miles were added to the Great Wall. But by the thirteenth century, a major portion of the Chinese population had moved from the original homelands north of the Yangtse into the wet, rice-growing areas of the south.

Although the maritime expeditions of the famous eunuch Zheng He (Cheng Ho), between 1405 and 1433, began to open up China to the world at large, these initiatives were not followed up, and China's leadership in technology and shipbuilding was not exploited to the full. One reason for this was attacks on the northern border by the nomads, which caused the Ming regime to concentrate on domestic defense in preference to foreign expansion. But entrepreneurial activity was not encouraged in the same way that it was in the West. As a result, China was eventually caught and overtaken by the Western barbarians in almost all categories of science and technology.

Genghis Khan is another example of someone who lived solely for war—he even admitted as much to his followers. To burn a town and slaughter its inhabitants was his greatest joy. But his military and political prowess should not be underrated.

After Genghis' death, the Khanate of the Golden Horde was established in Russia by his grandson Batu. Another grandson, Hulagu, founded the Khanate of Persia, after sacking Baghdad in 1257. These lands were largely left to pay tribute to the conquerors, while being governed by local surrogates. This was especially true in the case of Russia.

In China, the Mongols eventually became "sinicized," but it was the native Chinese that maintained the culture, not the Mongols. In the long run, this was beneficial to China, because when the Mongols were finally expelled, they left no permanent imprint on the culture and few reminders of their passing.

Although the Mongols are justly renowned for their brutality, their ability to maintain a continuous cultural entity across the vast steppe-land meant that the caravan routes between Europe and Asia were kept open to traders traveling between the two cultures. Their ability to transmit messages by horseback across hundreds of miles of steppe rivaled that of the Romans. Another important reason for their success was their ability to keep their internecine quarrels to a minimum, integrating numerous different tribes into an organization capable of controlling vast amounts of territory. There seemed to be no effective limit to their potential conquests. In fact, but for the untimely death of Ogedei Khan, son of Genghis, in 1241, the whole of Europe could very well have been overrun by the Mongol horde.

But the Mongol Empire did not last. Its internal cohesion was too weak to sustain such a huge and disparate mass of territory. The various parts gradually fell away as the subject peoples rose up against their Mongol overlords.

The Mongols transmitted little of cultural significance to the world. Anything of genuine cultural value was of secondary importance compared to their lust for conquest.

SAMURAI WARRIORS

Although the Chinese produced no parallel to the Western knight, this was not the case in Japan. The warrior class that arose in medieval Japan had many similarities to that which existed in Europe at about the same time.

During the twelfth century, power shifted from the Emperor and his court to the heads of warrior families. These were country squires who had originally been estate managers under the feudal system. Their increasing power allowed them to take control of the land and gather about them a body of armed retainers.

Between 1180 and 1185 there was what amounted to a civil war between two great houses of these country squires: the Taira and the Minamoto. After fierce battles between these adversaries and their allies, the Minamoto were finally victorious.

Whereas the Taira had been involved in the life of the court, the Minamoto, under their ruthless leader Yoritomo, kept aloof from court affairs. This resulted in the rise of the warrior class, or *samurai*, which was separate from the imperial court, and which has had such a strong influence on Japanese culture from that time onwards.

Yoritomo assumed the title of Shogun, or military dictator. The shogunate was a system of military government, separate from the Emperor's court. As historian W. Scott Morton writes:

> The cultural emphasis moved gradually from admiration of the gentleman, the scholar, and the aesthete to a code of fierce loyalty among fighting men

and a worship of honor and the sword.... The actual swords themselves acquired a mystique of their own. In a man's sword resided his honor and he would sooner die than part with it.[27]

This martial spirit, known as *bushido,* "the way of the warrior," was the equivalent of chivalry for the Western knight. The Japanese warrior was also an armored horseman, although the armor consisted of plates of steel or lacquered wood laced together with red silk or cords. Thus the armor was lighter and allowed better mobility than in the West. The armament was also different in that the Japanese warrior was armed with a bow and a sword, rather than a sword and lance.

The behavior of these knights bore a striking similarity to that of their Western counterparts. A *samurai* would often cut down a commoner just for a little sword practice. *Bushido* did not extend beyond the warrior caste. As Ian Buruma writes:

> Samurai ranked from the shogun down to the lowest retainer. Barred from engaging in trade, which was beneath them, the samurai were mostly poorly paid government servants. But they were the only caste allowed to bear arms or to commit ritual suicide.[28]

Confucianism and Buddhism were both introduced into Japan from Korea in the sixth century A. D. The later doctrine of Zen Buddhism was established in the twelfth century. This became popular among the warrior class, probably because of its emphasis on meditation and self-control. Scott Morton explains:

> It is at first surprising that any form of the Buddhist religion, with its gentleness, reverence for all forms of life, and shunning of desire and hate, would be practiced at all by warriors. But Buddhism was so well established and Shinto had so little to offer in the way of coherent philosophy, that those who were in any way religiously inclined had little alternative to some form of Buddhism. And such is the power of human rationalization that they probably were scarcely conscious of any contradiction between faith and conduct.[29]

One difference between chivalry and *bushido* involved the treatment of women. Morton continues:

> As G. B. Sansom has pointed out, the quality of chivalry as consideration for women and weaker persons is entirely lacking in the Oriental code. And the

very idea of tilting for a woman's favor would be shocking to a Japanese. Courtly love and the worship of womanhood were unknown.[30]

When firearms were first introduced into Japan in 1543, the Japanese commenced their own production of guns. But to the *samurai* the gun was an inferior weapon, and besides, it could be used by the common classes just as well as by the nobility. The sword was not only a work of art, but also a class symbol. As Jared Diamond relates:

> Japanese warfare had previously involved single combats between samurai swordsmen, who stood in the open, made ritual speeches, and then took pride in fighting bravely. Such behavior became lethal in the presence of peasant soldiers ungracefully blasting away with guns. In addition, guns were a foreign invention and grew to be despised, as did other things foreign after 1600. The samurai-controlled government began by restricting gun production to a few cities, then introduced a requirement of a government license for producing a gun, then issued licenses only for guns produced for the government, and finally reduced government orders for guns, until Japan was almost without functional guns again.[31]

Once Japan's antipathy to guns was overcome, however, she made up for lost time. When Commander Perry's fleet of warships arrived in 1853, Japan realized just how far she had fallen behind the rest of the world militarily. After considerable internal dissention, which more than once descended into violence, she abolished the title of Shogun, granted to Yoritomo after his assumption of power in 1192, and restored the Emperor to his full powers.[32]

Modernization initially paid rich dividends in the rapid development of Japanese society. But the militarism with which it was accompanied eventually spelled disaster for Japan as well as much of the Far East in the twentieth century. By the beginning of the 1930's the military had effectively destroyed the authority of the civilian government, and all vestiges of liberal thought were crushed. The Emperor had failed to rein in the militarists. As a result, the Japanese went on an orgy of destruction throughout China, Korea and South East Asia, to say nothing of the attack on Pearl Harbor in 1941. Although the Japanese paid heavily for the sins of their leaders, this was small consolation to their victims.

4

ROOTS OF WESTERN CULTURE

Nothing changes more constantly than the past; for the past that influences our lives does not consist of what actually happened, but of what men believe happened.

—Gerald White Johnson
American Heroes and Hero-Worship

GREEK ORIGINS

The development of Greek culture occurred at a time when similar developments were already under way in Mesopotamia and Egypt. I have already indicated why I did not include the Greeks in the original group of nascent cultures. It is of course impossible to fit all the cultural developments into a nice neat picture, where we have several spontaneous cultural births, and then offshoots of culture that grow out of them in a regular way. The picture is much too complex to lend itself to any kind of simple analysis. If even someone like Arnold Toynbee, with all his scholarship, could not quite do it, obviously the task is beyond me. Nevertheless, what we are looking for is overall patterns rather than detailed analyses, and from these it may be possible to draw some general conclusions.

The Greeks might have been included in our original group of six cultures—making it seven. The decision was to a certain extent arbitrary. But there must have been some dissemination of ideas from both Egypt and Mesopotamia into the Greek heartland, even though travel in those days was an arduous business. And besides, the Greek culture arose in a somewhat different manner, which makes it harder to fit in with the others. The six that were selected all arose

70

in fairly localized areas, and close to river valleys, where agriculture could develop easily. But the Greek homeland is poorly suited to agriculture, and in addition, the origins of Greek culture are still rather obscure.

The bridge between the Mesopotamian world and that of Greece was Anatolia, or Asia Minor. There we find the Hittites, "outsiders" who had arrived from the east about 2000 B.C., and who came in contact with the Egyptians during the latter's imperial forays, and also with the Akkadians, the Babylonians and the Assyrians. But the Hittite Empire disintegrated about 1200 B.C.

In order to get a more accurate picture, it seems best to consider the overall context of the eastern Mediterranean, since it is there that we find, not only the cradle of the civilizations of the Middle East and Western Asia, but also the cradle of Western civilization as well. To the north of this area one encounters the habitat of the Asian steppe dwellers and the people of the northern forests; to the south, the nomadic desert tribes of Arabia. These people were constantly infringing on the settled lands, and sometimes overrunning them. To the "civilized" agriculturalists they were barbarians. But sometimes when these barbarians overran a settled area, they themselves would become civilized, and after a while it was difficult to tell the civilized people from the barbarians.

Going hand in hand with this influx of people from outside the settled communities was a growing interchange of peoples between the various areas as a result of trade. Trade grew steadily, first of all in raw materials, then in luxury goods, which were the easiest to transport over large distances, and finally in ordinary merchandise. At first the only trade routes were overland, but before long boats became large enough to navigate the rivers, and finally the Mediterranean itself became a highway for all kinds of commerce.

Not that all journeys were peaceful. As William McNeill puts it in *The Pursuit of Power*, "the choice was between trade and raid." The human animal tends to do what comes naturally, and this seems to be to take other people's property. So along with trade there was plenty of piracy. But the pirate often has to sell his booty, so he is forced to combine some trade with his main occupation. Anyway, in spite of the existence of pirates, powerful trading communities arose in the Mediterranean as early as the third millennium B.C. Of course they too may have indulged in a little piracy on the side, but pirates usually operate as individuals rather than in groups, for reasons having to do with the nature of piracy. Cooperation among pirates is virtually impossible, because no one will trust a pirate, least of all one of his own kind.

The Phoenicians were the outstanding traders of the ancient world, and they possessed colonies all around the Mediterranean, two of which were Tyre and

Sidon, in what was their original homeland of Canaan. The Minoans, on the island of Crete, were a trading and seafaring state, or thalassocracy, as is revealed by the many foreign objects—from Egypt and Greece especially—that have been found in archaeological sites on the island. These people created a sophisticated culture, with art and architecture of a high quality. But there seems to have been a fragile quality to the society. Their palaces had no defenses, and so were vulnerable to attacks by more warlike people, and eventually such attacks were sure to come.

So from very early times a network of trade routes connected the eastern Mediterranean states, and as time went by, these routes expanded to include cities and states that were outside of the region altogether. Soon the whole of the Mediterranean, including Italy, North Africa, Spain, and even parts of southern Europe, were included in this network. By the first century B.C., the famous Silk Road was opened, which reached all the way across the Asian steppe to China. In spite of all the comings and goings of the various nomadic tribes, this route remained open until it was effectively bypassed when the Portuguese opened a sea route to the Orient in the sixteenth century. This route also brought Africa, India and Southeast Asia into contact with the West, and signaled what McNeill, in *The Rise of the West,* calls the "closing of the Ecumene."

Having briefly described the context in which the Greek culture arose, we can now look at it in a little more detail.

Starting in the third millennium B.C., various Greek-speaking peoples settled in the southern end of the Balkan Peninsula and on some of the Aegean islands as well. Exactly where they originated is not known, but it is clear from the archaeological evidence that previous settlers had occupied the land since at least the fourth millennium B.C. These indigenous inhabitants must have acquired the Greek language and become absorbed into the population of the new arrivals.

By the beginning of the second millennium, the Peloponnesus was occupied by the Mycenaeans, an Indo-European, Greek-speaking people, who had come down from the north, and who developed close relations with the Minoans in Crete. It is not clear what the exact connection was with Crete, whether Mycenae was simply a trading partner, or actually became a colony of the Minoans.

The Achaeans were probably Greeks who lived originally in Thessaly to the north, but they may have originated even further north near the Danube. In any case, they took over the Mycenaean homeland about 1400 B.C., and may have destroyed the Minoan palaces on Crete as well. It is the Achaeans that are the main protagonists depicted in Homer's *Iliad,* which describes the Greek war against Troy c.1200 B.C.

Then came the Dorians, from the northwestern mountains. They displaced the Achaeans and went on to establish settlements in Crete and Ionia, on the west coast of Anatolia, where the Hittites had previously held sway. So it is a complex story, and much of it still remains to be filled in.

The ancient city of Troy, on the west coast of Anatolia, has been located and excavated, and so has the city of Mycenae. The archaeological investigations have tended to confirm at least the outlines of Homer's epic story in the *Iliad.* So rather than being basically mythological, as many scholars had previously thought, the *Iliad* may very well be based on fact. But if the bloody battles depicted in the *Iliad* are true accounts, it tells us something of the nature of the ancient Greeks themselves. They were not peace loving pastoral people, but were addicted to warfare and heroic deeds. Their later history has only tended to confirm this image.

As in Mesopotamia, there arose city-states with their own kings and gods. But the different geography of the Aegean and its surrounding lands helped to give the Greek culture its distinctive flavor. Even so, the behavior of these city-states resembled those in Mesopotamia in that they formed alliances and engaged in almost constant warfare with one another.

The Heroic Age, that time of myth and legend so dear to the Greek imagination, which existed long before the Trojan War, depicts men and gods in close communion with one another. The leading families in the various city-states sought to trace their ancestry back to this age. This tended to sharpen the difference between the leadership class and the common citizens, and led to the creation of an aristocratic elite, which was inclined to look down on and to exploit the humbler members of society.

In the 6th and 7th centuries B.C. we find the Greeks creating colonies in Thrace and on the shores of the Black Sea, also in Italy and Sicily, and even in Spain. As historian J. B. Bury points out, the motivation for this expansion was not primarily trade, although trade was involved in many cases.[1] One reason for the colonies was the shortage of land in the Greek homeland, and another lay in the social stratification of the city-states, which kept those outside of the ruling elite in an inferior status, and frustrated any ambitions that they might have had for their own advancement. As a result of this, many an enterprising young man, seeking the freedom to exercise his talents and to better himself socially, set out to create a community in another place, which became in effect an extension of his own city-state, but without the restrictions that he had found so burdensome at home.

The aristocratic elites in the home cities had no objection to the planting of colonies, in fact in many ways they welcomed it, because it provided a safety valve, whereby potential challengers to their authority were removed to a safe distance. Many of these colonies ultimately became independent city-states in their own right. Syracuse, a Corinthian colony in Sicily, is a prime example.

In the long run, the safety valve of colonies proved insufficient to prevent unrest against the aristocrats at home. Many of the city-states came under the rule of tyrants, who would often espouse the interests of the downtrodden in order to obtain power. But this type of government did not sit well with the Greek people, and the tyrants yielded to oligarchies, or in some cases to a species of democracy.

Greek democracy was not the institution that we know today. Slaves and those who did not own property were not considered full citizens, and so it was far from a perfect system. However, compared to what had gone before, it was a great improvement. Athens, the most famous example of early democracy, emerged as the leader of the ten districts of Attica when Cleisthenes became its ruler in 506 B.C. He introduced many democratic reforms, and these helped to establish Athens' position as a leader of the Greek world.

Although Athens again reverted to tyranny, happily this was only a temporary setback. The idea of the polis, or city-state, exemplified a sense of community and citizenship, which tended to offset the natural stratification that normally accompanied an urbanized environment. This gave Greek society its unique character, in contrast to the more hierarchical nature of the Mesopotamian city-states. It was something that the Romans tried to emulate, and was largely responsible for the extraordinary flowering of Greek culture during the classic age (510-338 B.C.). [2] This saw many different schools of philosophy, drama, poetry and other academic pursuits, not only in Athens, but also throughout most of the Greek-speaking world.

After the famous victories against the Persians, at Marathon in 490 B.C., and at Salamis in 480, Athens entered its period of cultural greatness under the leadership of Pericles. This period saw the creation of architecture and sculpture of supreme quality. Buildings like the Parthenon on the Acropolis, which had been destroyed by the Persians, were rebuilt and decorated by the sculptor Phidias.

With the outbreak of the Peloponnesian War in 431 B.C., and the death of Pericles in 429, the golden age of Athens came to an end. The war between Athens and Sparta, which lasted until 404 B.C., resulted in the permanent eclipse of Athens, and marked the beginning of Sparta's decline as well.

The conquest of Greece by Philip of Macedon in 338 B.C., which has already been referred to, and the subsequent invasion by the Romans, brought an end to Greek cultural supremacy. But the legacy of the Greeks lived on, and came to flower again in the Italian Renaissance and the European Enlightenment. Thinkers such as Aristotle and Plato examined questions regarding human nature and human values that are essentially timeless, and are as applicable to the twenty-first century as to the fifth century B.C. The Greeks laid the foundations of the mathematics that underlies our modern science. If only they could have learned to live in peace, they would undoubtedly have been able to achieve a great deal more. But that sentiment applies equally to us in the twenty-first century.

THE LEGEND OF SPARTA

Since Sparta was a city-state without parallel in Greek history, it seems appropriate to look at this unique community in a little more detail. The term Spartan has come down to us as describing its basic character. Also "laconic," from Laconia, the area where Sparta was situated in the Peloponnesus.

As Bertrand Russell explains, there were two separate Spartan city-states: the myth and the reality. It is largely the myth that has come to us in the word Spartan.[3]

Founded by the Dorians in the eighth century B.C., Sparta was originally quite a typical Greek city-state, which encouraged both learning and the arts. But after about 600 B.C. it became essentially an armed camp, given over to all things military. The helots, or serfs, farmed the land for the Spartans, but had no rights and were not considered citizens. In consequence, they were constantly on the verge of insurrection, and the Spartans harassed them continually.

The Spartan administration was unique in several ways. There were two kings, who were basically co-rulers. There was also the Council of Elders, which decided matters of law. Then there was an Assembly of all the people, which could veto laws, but not initiate them. In addition, there were five "ephors," chosen by lot from all the citizens. They acted as a balance to the two kings.

Looked at as a whole, the Spartan regime can best be described as a blend of communism, fascism and militarism. Some have described it as "the scout troop from hell." Spartan boys were given rigorous military training from an early age.[4] Boys and girls did gymnastics together—naked. This was not really unusual, as athletic activities in the nude were a common Greek practice. As far as the girls were concerned, the object was to make them physically tough so that they would produce healthy male offspring—this being their main purpose in life.

After marriage, which was permitted at age twenty, the husband continued to live with the men until he was thirty, while the wife remained with her parents. They saw each other only on the few nights when the husband was permitted to visit. Since they only met in the dark, it's quite possible that many Spartan couples did not know what their spouses actually looked like!

Homosexuality was not just tolerated, but was actively encouraged. Companies consisting entirely of homosexuals were quite common. They were considered some of the best fighters, since they would defend their companions with the utmost fortitude.

Although the Spartans placed great emphasis on military training, they were loath to actually use their armed forces. In normal times, their chief military activity consisted of beating up on the helots. However, when it came to defending the Greek homeland against the Persians, they rose to the occasion magnificently. At Thermopylae (480 B.C.), Leonidas and his 300 Spartans made a heroic stand, refusing to retreat while facing certain death; this saved the day for the rest of the Greeks. And they were chiefly responsible for another historic Persian defeat at Plataea in 479 B.C.

Although the Spartans were victorious in the Peloponnesian war against Athens, they suffered grievous losses and were further weakened by another war with the Persians. Hegemony over Greece eventually passed to Thebes. The coming of the Macedonians, under Philip II, saw the Spartans easily defeated, and they would never again attain their previous position of prominence.

The Spartans have slowly faded from history, but they have left us with their name, exemplifying tough and rigorous discipline, honesty and love of community. However, the myth that has come down to us probably bore little relation to the reality. Aristotle and others painted a very different picture of the Spartans. Far from being pure in body and mind, they were often cruel and avaricious. Their women were frivolous and lovers of luxury. According to Herodotus, bribery was widespread. Of course they may have been biased in their opinions, but other Greek contemporaries tended to agree with these sentiments. So Sparta, like many a human institution after it, was undoubtedly better in theory than in practice. Lycurgus, supposedly the lawgiver of Sparta, was in fact mythical. As Bertrand Russell tells us:

The myth, fully developed, can be found in Plutarch's *Life of Lycurgus;* the ideals that it favours have had a great part in framing the doctrines of Rousseau, Nietzsche, and National Socialism, not mention Dr. Thomas Arnold and the English public schools.[5]

The myth of Sparta also profoundly influenced Plato's *Republic.*

ROMAN POWER

Having defeated king Darius and the Persians, Alexander of Macedon eventually reached India, where he fought several more battles, in one of which elephants were used against him. On another occasion, he was severely wounded and narrowly escaped defeat. Eventually, at the river Beas in the Punjab, his army mutinied and refused to go any further, so he was forced to turn for home. But on reaching Babylon in 323 B.C. he contracted a fever, from which, in his state of exhaustion and with his many wounds, he was unable to recover.

The sudden death of Alexander left his army without a leader. But his closest companions nevertheless tried for a time to keep his empire under a unified command. This proved impossible, and so in 301 B.C. the empire was split up among the five commanders that had been Alexander's immediate companions. Seleucus took the East as far as India; Ptolemy Egypt; Antigonus Anatolia and Syria; Cassander Macedon; and Lysimachus Thrace.

Seventy-year-old Antigonus promptly decided to try and reunite the empire under his sole command, but the others combined against him. This set off a series of internecine wars between Alexander's successors and their respective followers.

After several rounds of fighting and the deaths of the original protagonists, three separate Hellenistic kingdoms were established: the successors of Seleucus in the east; those of Ptolemy in Egypt; and Alexander's original Macedonian kingdom in the west. The extreme eastern-most province in India was ceded to Chandragupta, the founder of the Mauryan dynasty, who was the first ruler to unite the whole northern section of the Indian sub-continent.

Alexander had founded many towns that bore his name, and these were administered as city-states, in imitation of those in the Greek homeland. They essentially became colonies, since Greeks were encouraged to settle in them and they became outposts of Hellenic civilization. As a consequence, Alexander's empire became "hellenized" over time, and a veneer of Greek culture spread from

Macedonia all the way to Persia and Afghanistan. But this culture was mostly restricted to the towns; the countryside was largely unaffected.

The expansion of Greek culture was actually accomplished by the Macedonians, not by Greeks themselves. As historian M. Cary tells us:

> It is the strangest paradox of Greek history that the catastrophe of the Macedonian conquest raised the Greeks to the pinnacle of their power. At the death of Alexander they were the dominant people in each of the three continents, and had a unique opportunity of hellenizing the world. On the other hand, their statecraft was now confronted with immense new problems of imperial administration, and their culture was brought into competition with the deep-rooted civilizations of the Near East. In a word, the Greeks were called upon to play for high stakes, and the Hellenistic age was their supreme testing-time.[6]

But the opportunity was lost, and in the end the Greeks came up against the rising power of Rome, which would soon overwhelm them. Perhaps it was too difficult to organize the individual city-states, as constituted in Greece as independent units, into a larger entity, such as a confederation or a republic. After all, the Roman Empire really consisted of just one city-state, that of Rome itself, although it gained a second one, Constantinople, when the Empire became divided.[7]

[In the Renaissance, the Italians sought to rediscover Roman law, literature and art. But politically they reverted to classical Greece, with its multitude of warring city-states. The unity that Rome had given to the Empire was gone forever. The Athens of the Renaissance was Florence, which became the leader in art and culture. Parallels with ancient Greece can be seen in the governments of the Italian city-states, which started as republican but often reverted to despotism.]

The Romans, having military power but lacking real culture, absorbed that of the Greeks to a remarkable degree. So one can say that the Romans became hellenized in the same way as the territories occupied by Alexander, but the process was inverted, in that the victorious party received the culture from the conquered, rather than vice versa.

After defeating the Carthaginians in the Punic wars, and having absorbed not only Macedonia but considerable portions of Alexander's former empire as well, the Roman Republic was convulsed by a vicious power struggle that played itself out among her leading generals. Julius Caesar, having conquered Gaul, formed a secret alliance with Crassus and Pompey. This, the First Triumvirate, sought to control the military arm of the state, but made no attempt to take over the reins of government.

After Crassus was killed in battle in 53 B.C., Pompey made a bid for supreme power that was fiercely contested by Caesar, who routed his forces at the battle of Pharsalus in 48 B.C.

The saga of Caesar and Cleopatra, of Caesar's murder, Anthony's marriage to Cleopatra and Octavian's victory at Actium are all well known.

The victorious Octavian was now undisputed master of Rome. The Roman people were tired of war and wanted strong leadership to ensure peace and stability. Although Octavian claimed that he was not interested in absolute power, he allowed himself to be made *princeps,* or first citizen, and took the name Augustus. Even though he claimed to have restored the Roman Republic, in fact the Republic was no more. Its place was now taken by the Roman Empire, with Augustus as its first Emperor.

Augustus ruled for forty-one years. Although he kept the old forms of government intact, he created the imperial "household," which effectively ran the Empire, and was drawn mainly from the lower echelons of society.[8]

The immediate successors of Augustus were something of a disappointment. As Edward Gibbon recounts:

> It is almost superfluous to enumerate the unworthy successors of Augustus. Their unparalleled vices, and the splendid theatre on which they were acted have saved them from oblivion. The dark unrelenting Tiberius, the furious Caligula, the feeble Claudius, the profligate and cruel Nero, the beastly Vitellus, and the timid inhuman Domitian, are condemned to everlasting infamy. During fourscore years (excepting only the short and doubtful respite of Vespasian's reign) Rome groaned beneath an unremitting tyranny, which exterminated the ancient families of the republic, and was fatal to almost every virtue and every talent that arose in that unhappy period.[9]

The sickening spectacles of gladiatorial contests and other "blood sports" that took place in the Colosseum—completed by Domitian in 82 A.D.—stand in stark contrast to the Olympic games of the Greeks. The scale and brutality of these "spectacles" is not generally appreciated, since we like to emphasize the more positive aspects of the Empire and its citizens: their legal system, their art, their monumental architecture, their amazing aqueducts, their literature and the efficiency and discipline of their armies. We think of the Pax Romana and the pride of Roman citizenship. But we tend to forget that the only thing that held the Empire together was brute force, that slavery and cruelty were widespread, and that even the limited democracy that had been practiced in the Greek city-states was nowhere to be seen. The hunting of wild animals, enormous numbers of which were slaughtered in the Colosseum for the entertainment of the people, resulted in many of these species becoming largely extinct.

Just how seriously the Romans took their brutality is reflected in the ruins of the Colosseum. Under the arena were two elaborately built levels of chambers and labyrinthine passages, which modern excavations have now exposed to view. These housed the animals, gladiators and supporting personnel that produced and participated in the deadly spectacles. The complex even included elevators, which brought the larger animals, such as lions and elephants, up to the floor of the arena.

After the series of woeful leaders described above by Gibbon, there appeared on the scene a succession of five exceedingly able and competent emperors, start-ing in 96 A.D. These were: Nerva, Trajan, Hadrian, Antoninus Pius and Marcus Aurelius.

The last was a scholar and poet, not at all the sort of person one would expect as a Roman Emperor. In fact the only similar figure that comes to mind is the Mauryan Emperor Ashoka in India, who reigned from 269 to 232 B.C., one of the most enlightened rulers that the sub-continent has produced. But in the fam-ily of emperors, Marcus Aurelius and Ashoka were rare individuals. Such cultured and sensitive human beings are seldom found in positions of supreme power.

According to Machiavelli, Marcus Aurelius was fortunate not to have been overthrown. This was because "the soldiers loved a warlike ruler, and one who was arrogant, cruel, and rapacious."[10] So the cultured Marcus Aurelius was in danger of being deposed by the army. But he had not become emperor with the help of the soldiers, so he owed them nothing. Pertinax and Alexander were not so lucky. As Machiavelli tells us:

> Marcus Aurelius, Pertinax, and Alexander, who all lived unadventurously, who loved justice, hated cruelty, were kind and courteous, all, Marcus apart, had an unhappy end. Marcus alone was held during his life and after in high esteem, because he succeeded to the empire by hereditary right, and did not have to thank either the soldiers or the populace for it.[11]

The decline of the Empire has been ascribed to many causes, but a combina-tion of causes seems the most likely. Commodus, the son of Marcus Aurelius, was one of the worst emperors, so the rot may have started with him. The use of the Goths as mercenaries was probably a major contributing factor, because, as Machiavelli points out, mercenaries are notoriously unreliable and are invariably more trouble than they are worth. However, the reasons are not important to us, only the results.

The Western Empire, centered at Rome, had ceased to exist by the sixth century when the Ostragoths overran Italy. The Franks occupied most of what had been Gaul, and the Visigoths established a kingdom in Spain. But we should not rue the passing of the Western Empire too much. Supposedly more civilized than the "barbarians" that replaced it, the Empire had actually brought to Europe only certain elements of culture—law, administration, public works—from which something completely different would eventually grow. The Romans produced no science of note and their clumsy number system was an impediment to its development. It was only when the decimal system was imported from India that real progress started to be made in this field. The whole edifice of the Empire eventually became so rotten that it was barely preferable to barbarian rule.

THE AWAKENING OF EUROPE

The Visigoths had driven the Romans out of Spain. But it was their turn to be expelled by the armies of Islam in the eighth century, and we have seen how the Frankish leader Charles Martel prevented further Moslem conquests at the battle of Tours in 732.

At the beginning of the ninth century, Charlemagne, a grandson of Charles Martel, aspired to create a new version of the Western Roman Empire, and the Pope crowned him as the first emperor in the year 800.

This revival, known as the Holy Roman Empire, lasted until the time of Napoleon. But it was only a shadow of its former namesake. The usual trouble with the succession occurred when Charlemagne's son and successor Louis I divided up the Empire between his three sons. This partition created the three Kingdoms of Germany, Italy and the Franks.

Lengthy dynastic squabbles, lasting many years, eventually resulted in the Empire being confined mostly to Germany and what is now Austria. The final configuration was a complex patchwork of princedoms that competed endlessly for the imperial crown. Italy, having detached itself from the Empire, became a network of warring city-states, but this did not prevent it from becoming not only the commercial center of the Mediterranean, but also the cradle of the Italian Renaissance. The Kingdom of the Franks was the only part of the original Holy Roman Empire that became united under a single monarchy. Even though its authority was at first quite limited, the fact of a centralized power in France was of considerable importance.

The abbey of Cluny, founded in Burgundy in 910, became the center of the Cluniac order of monks, which made important contributions towards the development of Western Culture. The monks preserved much of the classic Greek literature and philosophical works that had been taken by the Romans, and this proved of great importance when Western learning started to develop significantly in the late Middle Ages. They were also able to preserve much of the mathematics and other science developed by the Arabs, which were obtained through contact with the Moors in Spain.

The assimilation of the Scandinavians, who invaded Normandy at the end of the tenth century, eventually helped to stabilize the nascent Western culture. Descendents of the Viking marauders, the Normans ultimately became civilized and productive citizens.

The Normans invaded England in the eleventh century and defeated the Saxon monarchy. Consequently, the new English ruling class obtained possessions in England in addition to those they already owned in France. This led to conflicts over territory, eventually leading to the Hundred Years War between the two countries.

The twelfth and thirteenth centuries saw considerable economic progress throughout Europe. This period was also notable for the building of many of the great Gothic cathedrals, especially in England, France and Germany. However, the fourteenth century brought not only the catastrophic war between England and France, but also the plague, or Black Death, which decimated the European population.

Yet neither the Black Death nor the squabbles of the English and French could arrest the steady progress of the European continent. For now the development of trade began to herald a long-term improvement in the economic sphere.

Maritime trade had been confined mostly to the Mediterranean, since the ships that were involved could not operate in the open sea, or even in the Black Sea, except in the summer time. But this was soon to change. As William McNeill writes:

A fundamental advance in naval architecture took place between 1280 and 1330, as a result of which larger, stouter, and more maneuverable ships could for the first time sail the seas safely in winter as well as summer.... Bills of exchange facilitated payment across long distances.... Cities of north Italy and a secondary cluster of towns in the Low Countries remained the organizing centers of the whole system of exchanges.

Geographically, waters which had previously been effectively separated from each other became for the first time parts of a single sea room. The Black Sea to the east and the North Sea to the west fell within the extended scope of Italian-based shipping.[12]

This commercial network was extended to the Baltic, through German shipping based in the ports of the Hansa, a league of commercial cities. So Europe had two main commercial centers: one in the Netherlands and one in Italy. The former was connected with the Baltic and Russia, the latter to the old trade routes of the eastern Mediterranean, which now included the Spice Route to India in addition to the Silk Road. The Netherlands had previously been connected to Italy by a combination of land and river routes, but the opening of the shipping route from Italy to the Low Countries represented a vast improvement both in communications and the movement of goods.

Without the central authority of Rome, the rising level of commerce created powerful city-states, especially in northern Italy, where the new mercantile class of citizens lived in uneasy proximity to the old aristocratic social order. Amid the general lawlessness, bands of armed adventurers, or "free companies" would attack and pillage these cities like the English had done in France. In addition, shifting alliances between the cities and with the Pope, who as head of the Papal States assumed the status of a temporal monarch, resulted in a constant state of strife between the various parties.

The merchants eventually found ways of defending themselves, mainly by building walls around the cities and either manning the defenses themselves or hiring mercenaries to do so. Armed townsmen also patrolled the countryside to insure safe passage for their goods.[13] The maritime cities of Genoa and Venice vied for supremacy in the commerce of the Mediterranean. Venice was the most successful, acquiring trading partners in Constantinople and other seaports in the eastern Mediterranean.

Despite the turbulence of the times, the increase in trade and consequent rise in wealth of the merchant class contributed to an extraordinary cultural Renaissance. Not only the arts, but also science began to make the sort of progress that had not been seen since the age of classical Greece. The improved communications with northern Europe allowed this cultural advance to spread rapidly to France, England and Germany. The autonomous university, an institution that arose in Europe in the 12th and 13th centuries, did much to facilitate the advance of scholarly pursuits of all kinds. This, together with the invention of the printing press in 1454, laid the groundwork for the birth of the modern world, ushered in by the likes of Copernicus, Kepler and Galileo.

At the end of the fifteenth century, events at opposite ends of the Mediterranean had a major effect on relations between the Christian and Islamic worlds. In Spain, the Kingdom of Castile, which had been steadily expanding at the expense of the Moors, finally expelled them from their last stronghold at Granada in 1492. But in the east, where the Byzantine Empire had been barely clinging to life, the roles were reversed.

About 1360, the Ottomans, an obscure Turkish clan, had established themselves in northwestern Anatolia, from where they proceeded to expand vigorously both to the east and west, leaving the Byzantines with only a small enclave round Constantinople. The Ottoman Sultan Bayezid, alias the Thunderbolt—another intrepid lover of destruction—defeated the Serbs at Kosovo in 1389 and then turned east to conquer the rest of Anatolia.

Bayezid was about to finish off the Byzantines, when an even more formidable warrior appeared. This was Timur the Lame, or Tamurlane, a Turkish noble who had taken over Turkistan from a descendant of Genghis Khan. Timur led his armies on a series of savage expeditions of pillage and plunder through all the countries within striking distance of his armies—even making a foray into India in 1398. He defeated Bayezid at Ankara in 1402, but failed to press his advantage. The only state he actually established was the Timurid Emirate in Persia. The rest he first plundered, and then abandoned. All the same, his capital at Samarkand reflected a surprisingly sophisticated culture.

Timur's defeat of Bayezid gave Constantinople a temporary reprieve, but the Ottomans soon recovered and re-established their rule in Anatolia and the Balkans.[14]

When the Ottoman Sultan Mehmed the Conqueror finally breached the walls of Constantinople and sacked the city in 1453, the Eastern Roman Empire was finally no more. But not much was left of the once-proud city that had already been sacked by the Christians in the fourth crusade. The magnificent Byzantine church of Hagia Sophia, built in the sixth century, managed to survive the rampage and was turned into a mosque.

The Ottomans went on to expand their empire into Syria, Egypt and northern Africa. Suleiman I, the Magnificent, even laid siege to Vienna in 1529, but the city was finally spared, like Moscow in World War II, by the onset of winter, which left the Sultan and his army shivering in their tents in the bitter cold.[15] In 1565 Suleiman attempted to capture Malta, but was repulsed by the Knights of St John with heavy losses. This was his last attempt at conquest, and his long reign finally came to a close in 1566.

Suleiman's successor, Selim II, suffered a major defeat at Lepanto in 1571. "Here the Crescent met the Cross in the last great naval battle between galley fleets in the history of Europe."[16] Don Juan of Austria, half-brother of King Philip II of Spain, commanded the Christian fleet, which decimated a huge armada of Ottoman galleys in the Gulf of Lepanto, under the command of Ali Pasha. Christian slaves, who manned many of the Ottoman galleys, turned on their captors and slaughtered them as soon as they were freed. This was the climax of the "thirteenth crusade," which is immortalized in G. K. Chesterton's famous poem *The Battle of Lepanto*.

So northern Europe was spared, once again, from invasion by a Moslem army, and any advance into the western Mediterranean was also blocked. But the presence of the Ottomans in the eastern Mediterranean meant that Moslems rather than Christians controlled the major trade routes to the East. These routes encompassed the increasingly important traffic making its way to India and beyond. However, the development of ships that could cross the oceans would soon enable the Europeans to reach India and the Far East without having to go through Moslem-held territory.

Even though the Moslems had been expelled from Spain, this was only a minor setback when looked at from a global perspective. The Moslem faith continued to travel southwards and eastwards from its Middle Eastern homeland. Moslem ports were established on the east coast of Africa, and parts of Malaya and Indonesia also came under Moslem rule. So the overall strategic position of the Moslems *vis á vis* the Christians was little changed.

5

RELIGION AND WAR

o o o o o o o o o o o o o o o o o o o o o o o o o o o o o o o o o
Has God forgotten all I have done for him?

—Louis XIV
After the battle of Malplaquet (1709)

NEW FACES OF WAR

The introduction of firearms gave rise to the next big escalation in organized violence, although it took some time for the effect of this development to be felt on the battlefield. The first firearms appeared more or less simultaneously in China and in Europe, at the end of the twelfth century. It is not known who was the first to introduce them; they may have been developed independently. In any case, the first firearms were of little practical use. They consisted of something like an arrow placed in a kind of jar with a bulb at the bottom containing gunpowder. Accuracy, range and safety left a lot to be desired, so it was the idea that counted more than its immediate application.

Firearms were initially looked down upon as weapons unworthy of a real soldier, who liked to do his fighting face to face with the enemy. The first practical application of firearms in war was with large cannon, which were used in siege warfare. Before the end of the Hundred Years War in 1453 the French were using cannon to expel the English from towns in northern France, and the Ottoman Turks used huge cannon to breach the walls of Constantinople in the same year. The latter were cast on site, as they were too heavy to be transported more than a short distance. The projectiles were huge stones, weighing over 1000lbs.

The introduction of cannon in warfare marked the start of an arms race, which was originally confined to Europe, but eventually spread worldwide. The two metals used for cannon were iron and bronze. Those made of iron consisted of iron bars welded together with hoops placed around them for extra strength. This construction was similar to the way a wooden barrel is made, hence the term "barrel of a gun," which is still in use today. But these iron cannon were crude and unreliable, so the weapon of choice for most countries in the fifteenth century was the bronze cannon, which was made by the method of casting.

Bronze casting was mainly employed in the making of church bells, and the techniques used in this peaceful application were now applied to the production of weapons of war. The French, the Germans and the Dutch were in the vanguard of this new industry, and later the Swedes joined the circle. Many of the Italian cities, especially Venice, produced high quality cannon. The Turks also produced cannon, but they were enamored of the huge unwieldy type, which became less practical as time went on.

The problem with bronze was its high cost, and this proved to be a problem. As vast sums were spent to acquire this new weapon, state coffers became quickly depleted. The English, who had lagged behind in the manufacture of cannon, had large deposits of iron ore in the Ashdown Forest in Sussex. This ore contained phosphorous and was especially suitable for the casting of iron cannon.

In 1541, king Henry VIII appointed William Levett sub-tenant of the royal ironworks at Newbridge. Levett was the parson at the little town of Buxted, and the good cleric, seeing no conflict with his priestly duties, entered into his new appointment with enthusiasm. Before long he had assembled a group of skilled artisans who set about producing cast-iron cannon of good quality.[1]

Although iron was considered inferior to bronze, iron cannon cost only a quarter to a third as much, and once their quality had been sufficiently improved, they rapidly became popular with European military establishments, which had been pouring money into armaments at an ever-increasing rate.

Meanwhile the application of guns to naval vessels had begun to forge ahead, pioneered by the English and the Dutch. In the Mediterranean, the old type of galley, propelled by oars, which was used by the Venetians and other traders, relied on the old method of ramming and boarding for attack, and the crossbow for defense. This was slow to give way to the new type of warship, featuring sails and guns. Some of the galleys were fitted with cannon in the bow, but this restricted the field of fire to the forward direction, and so proved of little value.

In northern Europe the installation of guns on sailing ships proceeded apace. First of all the cannon were located on the top deck or the castles, but they interfered too much with the rigging and also made the ships unstable. So the guns were installed on the main deck, to fire through ports cut into the hull, and this made the ships less top-heavy.

At first the intention was to put as many guns on board as possible, and the bigger the better. But this type of warship was difficult to maneuver. So the galleon, which was more maneuverable and had slightly less firepower, was introduced by the Spanish, and subsequently incorporated into the English and Dutch navies as well. However, many of the Spanish galleons were larger and less maneuverable than those of the English. This proved a handicap when the Spanish Armada reached the English Channel in 1588.

Those who produced guns as well as ships were clearly at an advantage, because those who did not had to acquire what they lacked from abroad. Although the Spanish did produce some guns, the quantity fell far short of that required by Spain's wide-ranging foreign adventures. As soon as gold from the Americas arrived in Spain, much of it was sent abroad to pay for more guns, and the need for more armaments always seemed to be greater than the amount of gold available for their purchase.

The Ottomans concentrated mainly on producing large cannon, and were unable to keep up with the West in the realm of naval warfare. They were still using galleys in the Mediterranean when most of the European powers had converted to guns and sail. In the next leg of the competition, that of the production of lighter transportable field guns, they were to fall even further behind.

The journey of Columbus to the New World marked a bold step in Europe's climb to mastery of the world's oceans. But although it was intended to open a passage to the East Indies, it ended up as being mainly a voyage of discovery. The real age of European dominance was inaugurated with the voyage of the Portuguese navigator Vasco da Gama, who traveled to India via the Cape of Good Hope in 1497-98. This allowed Portugal to obtain great riches from the spice trade.

Portugal subsequently acquired an empire that stretched from Brazil in the west to Asia in the east. According to the treaty of Tordesillas, following a papal bull by Pope Alexander VI, Spain and Portugal were to divide up the non-Christian world between them! The dividing line was to be 370 leagues west and south of the Cape Verde Islands. This left Brazil on the Portuguese side, but the rest of the Americas went to Spain. The fact that the line went south from a point west of the Cape Verde Islands meant that the "northwest passage" to India, sought by England in the sixteenth century, would not have been a violation of the treaty!

The territorial conquests of Islam after the Prophet's death extended all the way from Spain to Afghanistan. But beginning in the eleventh century, the eastern end of the Mediterranean was overrun by a series of Turkish clans that had originated in Central Asia. This culminated in the Ottoman occupation of most of the eastern Mediterranean, which remained part of Islam, even though the original "sons of the Prophet" had been removed from power.

Further to the east, another Turkish clan, the Ghurids, descended into India and established the Delhi Sultanate in 1206. At its height the Sultanate encompassed most of the sub-continent, establishing the Moslem culture as a major influence in India, where it existed in uneasy proximity to the indigenous Hindu and Buddhist faiths. In 1526 the Sultanate was succeeded by the Mughal Empire, which was established by Babur, another Turkish-Moslem warlord and a descendant of Tamurlane. Babur's son Humayum lost the Empire to the Afghan Sher Khan, but it was regained by Humayum's son Akbar, the greatest of the Mughal emperors, who reigned from 1556 to 1605, and whose Empire stretched from Afghanistan to Orissa in eastern India. Akbar's magnificent capital at Fatehpur Sikri, a few miles from Agra, still stands as a superb example of Islamic architecture. Unfortunately it soon became impractical for the Mughal court because of an inadequate water supply.

Vasco da Gama's voyage to India had taken the Turks completely by surprise. They thought that their control of the trade routes to the East was secure, but as it turned out, they had been completely outflanked. Belatedly, they put a fleet together to prevent the Portuguese from entering the Indian Ocean. But although they used sailing ships with guns, their tactics and techniques of naval warfare were no match for the Portuguese, who easily defeated them.[2]

The Portuguese voyages to Brazil and Africa had encountered no meaningful resistance, since the indigenous people did not possess firearms, although the existence of tropical diseases in Africa kept the Portuguese confined to the coast. But to the east, in India and China, it was another story.

Metal guns appeared in China and India in the fourteenth century, about the same time that they did in Europe, and at first their quality was as good as, if not better than, those in the West. But by the fifteenth century, European technology had advanced to a point where it was significantly superior to that of Asia. As historian Carlo Cipolla describes it, by the time the Portuguese arrived

> European artillery was incomparably more powerful than any kind of cannon ever made in Asia, and it is not difficult to find in contemporary texts echoes of the mixture of terror and surprise that arose at the appearance of the European ordnance.[3]

When the Portuguese arrived in Malacca in 1511 they found that the technology of gun making had already been imported from China. And the Chinese were well aware of the superior weapons possessed by the foreign barbarians when the Portuguese finally dropped anchor in Canton harbor in 1517. The Chinese were confronted by an unsettling reality. As Cipolla relates:

> For many a responsible Asian, merchants apart, it was a nightmare. How to deal with the "foreign devils"? To fight them or to ignore them? To copy and adopt their techniques and give up local habits and traditions or to sever all contacts with them and seek refuge in the dream of isolation? To be or not to be? The fog of Hamletic doubt began to pervade the soul of Asia—a doubt that was to plague Asia for centuries, a dilemma that was tragically unanswerable because both alternative solutions implied surrender and the only alternative to surrender was death.[4]

The British and the Dutch, whose warships were just as formidable, soon followed the Portuguese. However, in spite of their superior guns, the foreigners were mostly confined to the coastal harbors, because that was the only place they could bring their cannon into action in case of trouble.

The Chinese made some effort to match the advances of the Europeans, but several factors were working against them. Chinese culture was inherently conservative and dislike of anything foreign was pervasive, especially with the Imperial Court and the scholar-officials. Their adherence to the Confucian philosophy caused them to look down on both the artisan class and the military. The idea of manufacturing guns also seemed to run counter to the precepts of Buddhism and Taoism. All in all it was a struggle to keep up with the proficiency of the barbarians, who had no such inhibitions regarding the production of armaments. Ironically, the Jesuits became an important source of gun technology for the Chinese. They supplied valuable assistance in return for being allowed to set up Christian missions.[5] But the Chinese were never able to achieve parity with the Europeans, and as time went on they fell further and further behind.

The Industrial Revolution might well have occurred in China. But the encouragement of private enterprise and the search for new ideas, whatever their source, together with the spirit of adventure and the lust for power, allowed the West to overshadow the East and to dominate its trade, both internally and with other nations.

The Chinese never built a navy that was up to Western standards. The junk was much admired for its seaworthiness and carrying capacity, and these were amply demonstrated in the voyages of Zheng He, but the Chinese were not able to convert it into a warship in a satisfactory manner. Guns were placed fore and aft on the castles but no gun-ports were added. As a result, the junks were only good for ramming and boarding, and were outmaneuvered and outgunned by the Europeans.

Cannon were used extensively in India, for the defense of forts and as siege guns. But like the Ottomans, from whom they acquired much of their gun-making technology, they concentrated on larger pieces, which were not easily moved around. This lack of mobility would prove to be a serious handicap when the Europeans started to produce lighter and more mobile cannon.

ITALIAN BATTLEGROUNDS

As William McNeill points out in *The Pursuit of Power,* from roughly 1300-1600, Italy was a kind of testing ground for different kinds of weapons and military tactics. In the eleventh century a few hundred Norman knights had conquered the south of Italy and Sicily, and these French possessions were to cause serious problems for the Italians.

As has already been noted, the city-states and the Papal States lived in unstable equilibrium. In addition, outside interference from France and the Holy Roman Emperor in Germany kept things constantly in flux. The seafaring states of Genoa and Venice held territories outside of Italy and were in competition with each other for the maritime trade in the Mediterranean. So Italy was a hive of commercial activity and competition. This is the Italy that Niccolò Machiavelli describes in *The Prince.*

The mercantile class in the cities had succeeded in protecting themselves by building walls and other fortifications, and also by hiring pikemen to take on any hostile knights in the countryside. So an uneasy balance existed until the advent of firearms.

The first firearms to appear were a kind of musket, which had been developed from the early primitive type of firearm, and these did not upset the balance of power to any appreciable degree. Even the introduction of large cannon had only a limited effect, because they were few in number and difficult to move around.

But meanwhile the French and the Burgundians, using new technology developed in the Low Countries, had succeeded in producing powerful mobile cannon. And when these were introduced into Italy, the balance of power began to shift against the cities.

When Charles VIII of France invaded Italy in 1494 to claim the throne of Naples, the once-impregnable cities were almost defenseless against the new cannon. But it was not long before the Italians found an answer to this threat. They discovered that by building earthworks instead of masonry walls, and mounting large numbers of cannon at strategic locations, the new mobile siege guns were effectively neutralized. The *trace italienne,* as this new type of fortification was called, was soon adopted by other European powers, but it was expensive and so could only be installed where considerable resources were available. The *trace italienne* made it impossible for even large states like Spain or France to completely subdue smaller ones, because although they could occupy the open countryside, there remained isolated strong points that could not be reduced by cannon fire, as was previously possible. The only way of capturing these well-fortified positions was by a long siege.

The next development in the Italian testing ground came when Charles V of the house of Hapsburg, through multiple connections of marriage and inheritance, acquired not only the Holy Roman Empire, but the Spanish Empire and the Netherlands as well. Not satisfied with this huge windfall, he set out in 1525 to drive the French out of Italy. (The French had already been thrown out of Italy in 1512 by a coalition including Ferdinand of Spain, but they had since managed to re-establish their presence there.)

Charles succeeded in his mission with the help of another novel military device, the Spanish *tercio*—a mass of pikemen protected by a fringe of musketeers. This proved capable of defeating the French cavalry and infantry formations. In a few years the remaining French strongholds had been eliminated and Italy was effectively under Spanish control. But the other powers, including some of the disaffected German princes, began to combine against the Spanish assault. Although Charles had driven France out of Italy, the French monarchy continued to defy him, and was constantly looking for ways to turn the arms race in its favor.[6]

By the mid-sixteenth century, the days of the armored knight were effectively over, since they were now no match for well-armed infantry. But the tradition of the mounted warrior died hard, and most armies retained cavalry regiments well into the twentieth century, even though they were essentially ceremonial.

The guns that Charles VIII of France had brought to Italy to batter down the city walls were not sufficiently mobile to be used on the battlefield, except in special circumstances. The next big advance in mobility was made by Sweden in 1629, when the royal foundry in Stockholm produced the first 3-pound *rege-*

mentsstycke, an artillery piece weighing 123 kilograms that could fire three shots in the time that a musketeer took to fire one. This was immediately put to use by the Swedish king Gustavus Adolphus (another fine example of a warrior) in his campaigns during the Thirty Years War, and its success caused it to proliferate rapidly among the other European powers.[7]

The widespread use of firearms had greatly increased the "commerce of violence," in that the manufacture of guns became a thriving international business for enterprising gun-founders operating outside of the official command structure. This resulted in the birth of what McNeill calls the "military-commercial complex," which in our time has become the military-industrial complex.

The creation of standing armies, built around a bureaucratic type of military organization, became more and more the norm in Europe. But, as in the days of Sargon, there was always the problem of having armed men sitting around without having enough to do. It was tempting to start a small war in order to keep them busy. The Dutch, however, helped to solve this problem by introducing long hours of drill into the soldier's routine. It was found that this improved their *esprit de corps* and made the army more efficient in battle.[8] This innovation became a permanent feature of most armies, starting in the seventeenth century, and it has been used, with considerable success, to turn ordinary citizens into efficient fighters.

RELIGIOUS UNDERCURRENTS

The influence of religion on war is part of its influence on culture, and since it is of considerable significance, it deserves to be looked at more carefully. Actually, religion and war have been closely related from very early times.

We have already had cause to lament the adoption of Christianity by the Roman Empire, because this meant abandoning the Church's original commitment to peace. But to be realistic, in the world of the Romans, who ruled by military force, any attempt to preach peace and brotherly love would have fallen on deaf ears, and invited the same fate that Christ himself had suffered. So a pact with the devil was probably seen as the best way to influence him, especially after the bloody persecutions that the Christians had endured. So for better or for worse, the Pope became the spiritual head of the Roman Empire as well as the head of the Church.

When the Romans encountered the barbarians on their borders, the Church supported them in their efforts against the heathen invaders. So war was all right, in fact it was encouraged, so long as it was against the heathen. However, many of the heathen, for example the Franks and the Visigoths, eventually became converts to Christianity.

When the western part of the Roman Empire collapsed, the Pope in Rome still claimed to be the spiritual head of the Eastern Christians. But when the Church itself split into eastern and western branches, the Pope deemed the Byzantine Church to be outside of the true Church—though it was not so far outside as to be considered heathen.

Let us now look at the case of Islam. Immediately after the death of the Prophet, the Moslems commenced a series of wars of conquest. But although these were ostensibly holy wars, undertaken to extend the House of Submission, following the prescription of the Koran, they looked suspiciously like wars of conquest by "outsiders"—in this case Arabs from the desert rather than nomads from the steppe—against the "inner" cultivated lands.[9] The conclusion is inevitable that the idea of the holy war was in reality more of a pretext, while the real motivation was plunder, just as it was for the people of the steppe. And just as some of the steppe people had done, the Arabs from the desert subsequently established themselves as a ruling class in the countries that they overran. The only difference was that they brought their own religion with them—as the Aryans had done in their invasion of the Indus Valley—rather than adopting the religion of the "civilized" society. The stated motive was war against the infidel, but there were obviously other, less lofty, motives at work as well.

However, the *idea* of the jihad so galvanized the Arab armies that they became almost invincible in battle. What fighting men need is motivation, and the ablest leaders will find a way to give it to them. The mere prospect of riches, without any further justification, will often be sufficient to inspire the pursuit of conquest, but discipline can easily break down and leaders can be toppled. The appeal to a higher cause works wonders in cementing a body of men together, and the prospect of heaven or paradise, should death perchance be their lot, is a wonderful incentive towards maximum effort and faithful service. Either paradise or riches, what better choice could there be?

Jihad may have originally meant the struggle of the *individual* to do what is right (experts disagree about this). But it soon came to mean the forcible conversion of outsiders, or infidels, to the Moslem faith. The notion of jihad, or holy war, has been an important influence on Islam throughout the centuries.

[Although appeal to lofty principles can produce formidable fighting men, it can also produce great art. At a time when religion had a greater hold on the imagination than it does now, some of the finest artistic creations ever conceived by man were produced. The magnificent cathedrals of Gothic Europe, the sublime mosques of Moslem Persia, the sensuous splendor of the India's Hindu temples and the transcendent majesty of the Buddhist shrines of India, China and Tibet; all produced with a sense of the proximity of some kind of divine presence or superior power.]

To the casual observer, the break up of Islam into the Sunni and Shiite branches, and the division of Christianity into the Eastern and Western Churches, appeared to have quite different causes: the succession of the caliphate in the case of Islam, and doctrinal differences with the separation of the Christian Churches. But if one looks more closely one finds that the causes were essentially political and cultural in nature: the splitting off of the Persian part of the brotherhood in the case of Islam, and the breakaway of the Middle Eastern, or Byzantine section of the Church where Christianity was concerned.

When we come to the Reformation, the split that occurred in the Roman, or Catholic Church was much more than just a political schism. But we must first review the major developments in Christendom after the fall of the Roman Empire in the West.

With the creation of Charlemagne's Holy Roman Empire, the Pope had sought to reunite Western Christendom in a new kind of association, with himself again as its spiritual head. But this eventually proved impossible when Italy and Germany became fragmented into small states, and the Pope himself compounded the problem by stepping out of his role as spiritual leader and becoming head of a Papal State, thus adding one more faction to the warring parties. This left France in a relatively strong position of having a central government—although this was weakened by quarrels with Burgundy, which were not settled until the reign of Louis XI (1461-63).

France and the Pope were constantly drifting in and out of alliances with one another. At one time the Papacy moved to Avignon, where it essentially became a prisoner of the French king. All this had the effect of weakening the spiritual authority of the Church and leading to venality in high places.

What we have been describing, as far as Christianity is concerned, can basically be attributed to too much involvement in politics, which, although unfortunate, was the result of expediency rather than serious malfeasance. But little by little the core of the edifice started to be eroded. Strangely, the selling of indulgences and the immorality of the clergy, which were cited by Martin Luther in his complaints against the Church, did not constitute the most egregious abuses that had actually occurred. The worst betrayal of the teachings of Christ came with the fight against heresy, initiated by Pope Gregory IX in 1233, with the establishment of the Inquisition. This was first applied in France against the Albigensians.

The whole affair of the Albigensians constituted a low point in the history of the Church, since it involved secret trials, torture and burning at the stake—the infamous auto-da-fé—among other horrors. (The ostensible reason that the victims were burnt was because the Church was forbidden to shed blood!) The purpose of the Inquisition may well have been to win back heretics to the faith, but the methods used showed a total disregard for any kind of civilized behavior, or for that matter of the humanity exhibited by the founder of the Church.

The Spanish Inquisition was instigated by the Spanish monarchy, and reluctantly approved by Pope Sixtus IV (1471-84). The latter's only power over the proceedings was the appointment of the Inquisitor General—the most famous example being the notorious Torquemada. "The Spanish Inquisition was much harsher, more highly organized, and far freer with the death penalty than the medieval Inquisition; its *autos-da-fé* became notorious."[10] The primary purpose was to root out Jews who had converted to Christianity in order to avoid being deported or even killed, but who were suspected of still practicing the Jewish faith. But many others were caught in the Inquisition's net. St Ignatius Loyola and St Theresa of Avila were both investigated for heresy. The methods used were uncannily similar to those used by Hitler's Gestapo against the Jews in the twentieth century. It seems that the Gestapo and the Inquisition, as well as the NKVD, the KGB and the Stasi, were all cast from the same mold. In other words the Inquisition provided a blueprint for the modern police state. Indeed, the Spanish version of the Inquisition was not confined to heresy. The monarchy used it to consolidate state power.[11]

The Church continued with its own form of the Inquisition for several hundred years. It was the Inquisition that condemned Galileo for the "heresy" of proclaiming the sun as the center of the solar system. He was lucky to escape the auto-da-fé. However, Giordano Bruno was not so fortunate. He had the temerity to suggest, among other heretical ideas, that there might be planetary systems like our own far out in the universe. He was condemned to death and burnt at the stake in 1600.

Fortunately, the power of the Catholic Church has now diminished considerably, and sanctions against members that go astray are not nearly so extreme, although one can still be excommunicated for heresy. It's worth noting that the Inquisition, with horrors like the auto-da-fé, did not prevent the Church from inspiring great art. But the fire of faith, which conjured up the great Gothic cathedrals, with their soaring spires and intricate tracery, vaulted ceilings and magnificent stained glass, is now gone. As the Church has become more "civilized" it has lost the zeal and passion that it had when Western culture was young. It no longer inspires the creative imagination as it once did.

Looking at the Moslems, we see a similar trend. Today there are the *Islamists*—zealots who still like to kill the infidel and inflict harsh punishments for supposed violations of Islamic law. The militant side of Islam has never been very far from the surface, due to the fact that the Prophet himself was a soldier. The cultural, non-military, aspect of Islam has made significant contributions to civilization. But this aspect of the religion has faded over the centuries, reflecting the weakening of the underlying culture. Part of the problem has been Islam's very success. It has spread to so many different countries and cultures that its original character has inevitably become diluted. The violence of the zealots only tends to emphasize this loss of cultural integrity.

Both the Christians and the Jews also have their share of fundamentalists, and these are intolerant and sometimes violent as well. But they are usually less extreme than the Moslem variety. Even the Hindus are not without their extremists, and they can be just as unpleasant as the rest of them. Although they all claim to have the *true* religion, their most recognizable common trait is intolerance.

When Martin Luther posted his famous theses on the castle door at Wittenburg in 1517, his intention was not only to remedy the abuses of the clergy but also to promote his own interpretation of Scripture, which was at variance with that of the Roman Church. This encouraged others to do the same, and the result was the creation of a whole series of denominations, which were grouped under the designation of Protestant: Lutherans, Calvinists, Methodists, Episcopalians, Anglicans—the last being started by Henry VIII of England because the Pope refused to give him an annulment of his marriage to Catherine of Aragon. In point of fact, England remained Catholic, except that Henry replaced the Pope as head of the Church, and collected the revenues that had previously gone to the Vatican. Most of the Protestant Churches encouraged a more personal type of faith, so they tended to be less authoritarian than the Catholics.

After the Protestant Reformation, several "religious wars" broke out in six-teenth century Europe, but these were of relatively short duration. The Thirty Years War, which occurred in the next century, was much more serious. It devastated large sections of Germany, with its armies laying waste to the countryside in a manner not seen since the Hundred Years War in France two centuries earlier.

The Thirty Years War started when the Holy Roman Emperor Ferdinand II tried to impose Catholicism on Bohemia, which had elected a Calvinist king in 1618. This caused the Protestant countries of Denmark and Sweden, as well as Catholic France, to come to the aid of Bohemia. But the presence of France on the Protestant side should make us suspect that this was not just a religious war, although the French did have their own Protestant minority, the Huguenots. With Spain renewing her old rivalry with the Dutch, and later with the French, we could hardly be blamed for concluding that the religious aspect of the war was really secondary, and that the old motives of power and territorial ambition were still the main incentives.

A reasonable conclusion is that "religious wars" are often religious in name only, with religion providing the pretext rather than the basic motivation. The recent wars in the Balkans seem to support this thesis, because at first glance the religious factor would appear to be the primary motivation for the war, with Moslems, Catholics and Orthodox Christians all at each other's throats. But war correspondent Chris Hedges disagrees:

> Look not to religion and mythology and warped versions of history to find the roots of these conflicts, but to the warlords who dominated the Balkans. It took Milosovic four years of hate propaganda and lies, pumped forth daily over the airways from Belgrade, before he got one Serb to cross the border into Bosnia and begin the murderous rampage that triggered the war. And although the war was painted from afar as a clash of rival civilizations, the pri-mary task of Milosevic in Serbia, Franjo Tudjman in Croatia, and the other ethnic leaderships was to dismantle and silence their own intellectuals and writers of stature and replace them with second-rate, mediocre pawns willing to turn every intellectual and artistic endeavor into a piece of ethnic triumpha-lism and myth.[12]

There you have it in a nutshell. And a similar analysis could be made of the conflict in Northern Ireland. In contrast, the conflict between Israel and the Pal-estinians appears at first glance to be a war primarily over territory. But in fact it is much closer to being a genuine religious war than are the examples that we have previously considered.

Politics and religion should be kept apart as far as possible. Most Western countries seem to have learned this lesson reasonably well, but the Moslems are still wedded to the idea of a theocratic form of government, often with disastrous consequences. The Americans have never quite managed to divorce religion from politics, and this has served to poison the political climate in many ways. The British, even with an established church, do a far better job, as do the French. Their history reminds them of the dire consequences of mixing religion with politics.

SONG OF INDIA

Each of the four major world religions has its own distinctive character. A religion usually reflects the country or region where it originates, but it can change its character if it is transported to other regions. All the major religions have spread well beyond their place of origin. Christianity, although it originated in the Middle East, is now considered to be a Western religion, whereas Islam, although it has spread throughout the world, is still tied to the wellsprings of its inspiration in the Middle East. Nonetheless Islam and Christianity can be considered as culturally similar, at least if one compares them with the two Eastern religions of Buddhism and Hinduism, which reflect the Indian and Eastern cultures in their contrasting ways. Buddhism has been considered as a derivative of Hinduism, but the difference in character between the two religions is too great to sustain this idea. Even so, the Buddha was venerated as one of the *avatars* (incarnations) of Vishnu. This practice may have been promoted in order to attract those who had taken up Buddhism back to the Hindu fold.

When we look at Hinduism, with its many gods and multiple sects, and then at Buddhism, which is basically non-theistic and has fewer different sects, the conclusion is that they are quite separate religions. And besides, Buddhism rejects the caste system, which is basic to Vedic lore.

The character of Indian culture reflects the fact that geography has played a major role in its development. The Indian sub-continent consists of three main regions. First, there is the large northern sector, bounded by the Himalayas, with its exit routes in the northwest corner leading to Afghanistan and Central Asia. Moving south we find the central plateau of the Deccan, running roughly east-to-west between the eastern and western ghats, or coastal ranges. And finally, the southern tip below the Deccan. This is the wet, sub-tropical area, which is in marked contrast to the dry Gangetic plain that comprises much of the northern section.

The southern part of India is home to the old Dravidian culture of the Tamils, which, it is claimed, predates the Aryan invasions. The northern section has seen incursions of neighboring people from Afghanistan (an example being the invasion of Alexander) and from Central Asia; the earliest recorded being that of the Aryans c.1500 B.C. The central plateau has been a buffer zone between north and south, sometimes overrun by powerful states such as the Mauryan and Mughal Empires, and finally by the British Raj. But often it has managed to remain more or less independent.

The culture that eventually emerged after the shock of the Aryan invasions was a mixture of the indigenous culture and that of the Aryans. But the invaders brought with them the language of Sanskrit, and also their own religion, with its pantheon of gods and Books of Knowledge, or Vedas, which were written down after their arrival. They also brought the caste system, headed by the Brahmans, who presided over the sacrificial rites.

The assimilation of the Aryan "barbarians" into the pre-existing culture of the Indus Valley, which had been so violently overthrown by the invaders, took hundreds of years to complete. When a unified state finally emerged under Mauryan rule in 326 B.C., the center of power had shifted from the Indus valley to the plain of the Ganges, with its capital at Pataliputra (modern Patna). The founding monarch was Chandragupta Maurya, who many regard as the father of Hindu civilization, which still lies at the heart of Indian culture.

After the eastern portions of Alexander's Macedonian Empire had been ceded to Chandragupta by Seleucus, one of Alexander's successors, his Empire stretched all the way across the northern section of the sub-continent.

The Mauryan Emperor Ashoka, Chandragupta's grandson, who reigned from 269 to 232 B.C., extended the boundaries of the Empire to include the Deccan, but the southern tip, home to the Cholas and the Pandyas, remained outside his realm. Ashoka was converted to Buddhism, but the religion of the vast majority of Indians remained Hinduism, which was by then a syncretic religion, incorporating that of the Aryans into the indigenous religion of the existing culture. The Aryan part of Hinduism is much easier to recognize because the Aryans brought a written language with them, whereas the indigenous culture had no written language. However, the discipline of yoga is a survival from pre-Aryan times.

Ashoka encouraged the export of Buddhism to China, and it was in China that this religion eventually came to flower, but not before the appearance of the

Mahayana form of Buddhism, at about the time of Christ. As historian Stanley Wolpert explains:

> The central tenet of Mahayana Buddhism is the concept of the *Bodhisattva* ("he who has the essence of Buddhahood"), a compassionate and loving savior who, rather than selfishly abandoning the world, pauses at the threshold of *nirvana* to reach down to help all mankind attain liberation from sorrow and rebirth through his grace. Was the idea of the Bodhisattva inspired by reports of the life of Christ that may have reached India through Persia and Bactria, or was the process of cultural diffusion one that flowed from east to west? Or did such similar concepts emerge totally independent of one another in such distant regions at virtually the same time? [13]

In India, the country of its birth, Buddhism has remained in the shadow of Hinduism, which seems to reflect the many strains of Indian culture, stretching back into its pre-Aryan past, whereas Buddhism has an abstract quality to it, which attracts those who are more inclined towards contemplation. Hinduism is much more down to earth, while Buddhism is "otherworldly" and encourages asceticism with its concepts of nothingness and *nirvana*. Nevertheless Buddhist monasteries thrived in India, as did the religion of Jainism, founded by Mahavira, a contemporary of Siddhartha. (A feature of Jainism is its prohibition against the killing of anything living, including insects.) Even though both Buddhists and Hindus make war on their fellow humans, neither religion contains any concept like that of the jihad or the crusade. When compared to those of the West, the character as well as the record of the Eastern religions is far more peaceful, and also much more tolerant of ethnic and religious differences between human communities.

A period of political fragmentation followed the end of the Maurya sovereignty in 184 B.C., but in spite of this and even in the face of several invasions from the north, notably by the Kushans from Central Asia, there was a general advancement of the culture, especially with respect to trade. This trade extended both to China and countries to the west, including Rome. Incidentally, the Kushan Emperor Kanishka, who reigned for about twenty years around A.D. 100, was converted to the peaceful religion of Buddhism, but this did not deter him from making war.

The reunification of northern India was achieved by Chandra Gupta, whose coronation in Pataliputra in A.D. 320 marked the start of the Gupta Empire, which lasted until A.D. 550. Chandra Gupta had no connection to his namesake who founded the Mauryan Empire.

The rule of the Guptas, together with that of Harsha Vardhana (606-47) is considered to be the classic age of Hindu culture. Chandra Gupta's son Samudra extended his territories to the Punjab in the west and to Bengal in the east, and even to the Deccan in the south. A feature of his reign was the revival of the famous (or infamous) *ashvamedha* or "horse sacrifice," marking the historic revival of royal patronage to Brahmanic ritual.[14]

The high point of Gupta culture was attained during the reign of Samudra's son, Chandra Gupta II (375-415), who encouraged the development of Hindu temple architecture. This had started with quite simple structures, and only later attained its "baroque" virtuosity of sculptural splendor familiar to visitors to Khajuraho, Gwalior and other sites in central India. This period also saw the flowering of Sanskrit literature, personified by the "Indian Shakespeare," Kalidasa, the famous poet and playwright to the Gupta court. His dramas became classics like those of the Greek classical age. His personal life, however, remains a mystery. All that is known about him is that he lived sometime in the fifth century.

According to the Buddhist monk Fa-hsien, the people of north India enjoyed personal freedom and tolerance under the Guptas. He reported that, "the king governs without decapitation or corporal punishments."[15]

Trade with Rome decreased as the balance began to shift heavily in India's favor. Although Indian jewels, spices, ivory, perfumes and cloth were much in demand in Rome, all the Indians wanted was money in the form of coins, and Arabian horses. The Romans, with the Huns at their gates, were sorely lacking in hard currency, so the trade became too one-sided. But to the East, trade grew apace, as the shipping routes to Southeast Asia and China started to supplement the older routes across the steppe. As a result of this Asian trade, Hindu kingdoms arose in South Vietnam, Sumatra and Java.[16]

Incursions into India from the north and west caused the Gupta kingdom to disintegrate by A.D. 550. But the kingdom was restored by Harsha Vardhana (606-47), who moved the capital to Kanauj. He was a poet and a supporter of Buddhism like Ashoka, but not quite so devoted to the principles of peace.

After Harsha Vardhana's reign, India reverted to a patchwork of independent kingdoms, some of which wielded considerable power. For instance, the Chola kingdom in the south had a powerful navy that dominated the Indian Ocean. Chola influence extended as far as Malaya and Southeast Asia.

Six schools of Hindu philosophy emerged in the classical period. They involve all sorts of complicated systems relating life to nature and the "elements" (the material universe is made from combinations of the atoms of earth, water, fire and air). All these things are closely intertwined with the spirit or soul, which somehow has to be freed from the world of suffering. These concepts are analyzed through a complex system of logic called *nayaya,* quite different from that used by the Greeks. The best-known school is that of yoga, whose appeal to Westerners has contributed to its popularity with many sections of the world community. Another school of philosophy is Vedanta (end of the Vedas), which is the most influential school among Indian intellectuals. "Through the monistic principle of Brahman, Vedanta philosophy seeks a reconciliation of all the seeming differences and conflicts in Hindu scripture."[17]

The Indian classical age falls almost midway between the Greek classical age in the fifth century B.C. and the classic age of European Gothic, beginning in the twelfth century. The Indian classical age is barely known to most Westerners, and the resulting lack of historical perspective has been an impediment to better understanding between the two cultures. Modern travel has only remedied this to a limited degree.

Unfortunately the Indian Hindu culture was not allowed to grow old and mellow in peace. Events in far-off places were occurring that would radically change India and its society forever. The rise of Islam and its spread into Persia brought an alien culture with a radically different religion and an aggressive philosophy almost to India's doorstep. Arab trade with India gave the Moslems an idea of the riches that could be found to the east, and Indian attacks on Moslem shipping gave them an excuse to make an incursion into Sind in 711. This was a relatively minor confrontation, but it gave the Indians a taste of what was to come.

In 997 a series of attacks from Afghanistan by Mahmud of Ghazni began to make serious inroads into northern India. The plundering of cities, smashing of Hindu temples and killing of the inhabitants became an annual occurrence for the next seventeen years. And in the years to come other Turkish-Moslem invaders from Afghanistan followed the lead of the Ghaznids.

The Islamic jihad had originally decreed that any infidels that were conquered had to convert to Islam or be exterminated. But this proscription was later rescinded for "people of the book." This meant that believers in some other religion that had a written scripture, like the Jews or Christians, were tolerated if they paid a special tax. The Zoroastrians had originally been forced to flee to India, until it was realized that they too had a scripture, the Avesta. Similarly, the Hindus were initially considered to be ordinary infidels. But the elimination of the Hindus, who showed no inclination to convert to Islam, presented the invaders with a Herculean task. Fortunately, as with the Zoroastrians, it was found that they also had a written scripture, the Vedas, and so were granted a dispensation. But the unfortunate Buddhists were given no such relief, and many of them were forced to flee to Nepal, Tibet or Southeast Asia. As a result of this, Buddhism barely survived in the areas under Moslem rule, which became more extensive as time progressed. Although some of the later Mughal emperors, notably Akbar, were more tolerant of Buddhism, it never fully recovered from the persecution of the early Moslem conquerors.

In Afghanistan, the Ghaznids were replaced by a rival Turkish clan, the Ghurids, about 1170. Muhammad of Ghur and his slave lieutenant Qutb-ud-din Aybak led a raid into India in 1175. He destroyed the Ghaznid garrison at Peshawar in 1179, and in spite of fierce resistance, especially by the Hindu warriors of Rajasthan (the Rajputs), he captured Delhi in 1193.

In 1206 Muhammad of Ghur was assassinated in Lahore and Qutb-ud-din Aybak proclaimed himself sultan of Delhi, establishing a slave dynasty, otherwise known as the Delhi Sultanate. Upon his death in 1210 Qutb-ud-din was succeeded by his son-in-law Iletmish.[18]

After the Hindus had been granted the status of *dhimmis* (people of the book), and many of the local rajas had been permitted to retain control of their domains, Iletmish succeeded in bringing a semblance of peace to the troubled land. He was also able to keep the Mongol hordes of Genghis Khan out of India. This was done by diplomacy rather than force. But the Rajputs continued to resist his rule whenever the opportunity arose.

Several Turko-Afghan dynasties succeeded to the sultanate of Delhi, which continued to control most of northern India, although Bengal declared its independence in 1338. Even though some Indian-born Moslems were eventually admitted into the governing bureaucracy, the Hindus were effectively excluded from all but secondary positions of power. Non-Moslem India was reduced to parts of the Deccan and the territory to the south. Strangers ruled the Hindu heartland in the north.

The uneasy peace was shattered in 1398 by the invasion of Tamurlane, who attacked and sacked Delhi before moving on to other fields of plunder and pillage in the Middle East (his defeat of Bayezid at Ankara is recorded in chapter 4).

Although the Sultanate was severely shaken, two more dynasties were to rule in Delhi, and by the early sixteenth century some blending of Hinduism and Islam had begun to emerge, notably that of the Sikhs. But by that time Vasco da Gama had already landed at Calicut, and Babur was about to found the Mughal dynasty. Vasco da Gama took spices and other luxury goods home to Portugal, where he realized a 3000% profit on his cargo. In addition, the British and the Dutch were just over the horizon. So the European quest for profits from Indian trade was soon under way.

The story of the Europeans on the Indian sub-continent is part of the general subject of colonialism and European expansion, which will be taken up in chapter 7.

6

TRADING EMPIRES AND THE RISE OF NATIONALISM

o o o o o o o o o o o o o o o o o o o o o o o o o o o o o o o o o o o

A nation is a group of people united by a mistaken view about their past and a hatred of their neighbors.

> —*Ernest Renan*
> *1823-1892*

OF WARLORDS AND EMPERORS

Since man is a gregarious creature, human beings have a tendency to gather into groups. In chapter 3 it was shown how the progression to larger and more concentrated groups created tensions between then. For a long time these groups consisted mainly of hunter-gatherers, who moved around from place to place without occupying any fixed geographical area. But with the coming of agriculture this changed dramatically. When a group was able to settle permanently in a particular area, the excess production of foodstuffs allowed for the creation of urban communities, which were capable of supporting a leadership elite as well as a permanent military garrison.

In Mesopotamia, the Indus Valley and the Yellow river in China, several of these settled communities co-existed in uneasy proximity. But the agricultural settlements were exposed to attacks from outside the settled area by hunting peoples who looked on them as easy targets for plunder. These natives of the hinterland, who still retained the traditional lifestyle of the hunter-gatherer, were the bane of the more settled societies, and it was always difficult to organize an effective defense against their incursions. Sometimes a settled group on the periphery would be overrun, or the hunters themselves would settle close to the established communities. In either case there would be what one might call a semi-barbarous group on the fringe of the settled communities.

The traditional category of leadership in the agricultural settlements was that of the king or warlord. And even today, this type of leader is to be found in more isolated or less developed societies, such as Afghanistan, Indonesia, Africa or Central Asia. The warlord makes little pretense of protecting the interests of those over whom he rules, being interested primarily in preserving, and if possible extending, his personal power. There was thus a tendency for the most warlike among them, often the leader of a semi-barbarous group on the periphery, to try and gain control over some, or all of the others. This was the basic process by which larger groups were formed, and if this happened over a large area, the enlarged kingdom was considered to be in a different category altogether. It took on the status of an empire.

According to this scenario, we should not consider someone like king Sargon of Akkad a warlord, but rather an empire-builder. This is because his territory comprised several city-states that had previously been independent. However ruthless he may have been in the pursuit of his enemies, he sought to build a viable kingdom that would serve the interests of at least the more favored members of his realm. And besides, it was to the advantage of the various city-states to engage in trade and to provide for their mutual protection.

The early Chinese culture was seriously afflicted with warlords and the endless conflict between them. The Age of the Warring States, starting in the fifth century B.C., saw one warlord after another gaining hegemony over a particular area of the Chinese heartland, only to be displaced in his turn by a new upstart. The Chinese did eventually develop a more effective central government, first under the Ch'in dynasty in 221 B.C., and then, more permanently, under the Han dynasty, beginning in 202 B.C. But even though the Han succeeded in expanding the Chinese territory, the central authority was not strong enough to prevent the warlords from making trouble. Indeed, throughout its history, one of the weaknesses of Chinese culture has been its inability to unite its various ethnic and linguistic regions under a strong central government. Incidentally, the Ch'in originated as a semi-barbarian state on the western periphery of the Chinese territorial domain, conforming to the general tendency of such peripheral states to take over those in the interior.

When we look elsewhere, there are often similar patterns, although they vary considerably in the details. Larger polities are almost always built up from smaller ones, but binding them together into a larger whole is often difficult. Only those that can effectively unite their separate parts will be successful.

By building a more extensive polity, or empire, undertakings on a larger scale become possible, and more effective defense against external enemies can be organized. But in order to maintain the cohesion of the whole, the leadership must be backed by a powerful and effective military organization. (The rise of nationalism, which will be considered later, made it harder to bind diverse ethnic groups into a single nation.)

The early civilizations of the Middle East created states that can definitely be considered as empires. Sargon's Akkadian Empire, as well as the Assyrian, Babylonian, Hittite and Persian Empires are prime examples. The Greeks created an empire only after they were united under the leadership of Philip II of Macedon, whose kingdom lay on the periphery of the Greek heartland. Until the time of the Macedonian conquest, the territory of the Greeks consisted largely of a group of warring city-states, somewhat analogous to that of the Chinese. The "empires" of Athens and Sparta were actually competing groups of city-states. Not all the rulers of these city-states could be classified as warlords, since some presided over a limited form of democracy. But tyranny or oligarchy rather than democracy was the general rule.

Egypt succeeded in forming an empire by uniting its upper and lower regions under one pharaoh. After the expulsion of the Hyksos in the eighteenth century B.C., the Egyptians extended their sovereignty all the way to Anatolia. But this enlarged territory proved difficult to defend, since it constituted a natural crossroads of peoples and cultures at the eastern end of the Mediterranean.

In India, after the absorption of the Aryan invaders and the establishment of the Mauryan Empire in the fourth century B.C., the northern part of the subcontinent held together reasonably well for more than a millennium. The southern part, below the Deccan, had a different ethnic character, and was never included for long in any of the larger Hindu kingdoms. It is actually surprising that India was united as much as it was, considering the linguistic and ethnic diversity of its people. The arrival of the Moslems tore the northern part of the country apart, and although it was nominally united under the various sultanates, in reality the rajahs, or local potentates, of the different territories became semi-independent warlords. The arrival of the British left this basic configuration in place, but imposed a ruling structure on top of it.

The greatest of the early empires, and perhaps the greatest of all empires was that of Rome. It had several unique features, which gave it its special character, for never before had an empire covered such an enormous area. Many reasons can be given for its amazing success, but one stands out in particular. This concerns its organization, especially military organization, which was the foundation of

Roman power. When one contrasts the Romans and the Greeks, who had a superior culture, but spent much of their time in pointless internecine feuds, one sees that central command and organization were the keys to Roman success. The original Roman Empire was a single city-state, whereas the Greeks were fragmented into many city-states. Even though the Roman Empire finally succumbed to internal and external pressures, this does not detract from the greatness of its organizational structure. But it was above all its *military* organization that gave it a decisive advantage over its challengers. And this can also be said of the British Empire.

The empire of the Mongols rivaled that of Rome in the matter of size, and also in its ability to communicate rapidly over vast distances. Though they were considered as barbarians by the more "civilized" Old World cultures, the military and political prowess of the nomads was formidable. Historian Edward Gibbon writes of Genghis Khan:

> The Catholic inquisitors of Europe, who defended nonsense by cruelty, might have been confounded by the example of a barbarian, who anticipated the lessons of philosophy and established by his laws a system of pure theism and perfect toleration.[1]

As a Shamanist, he was much more tolerant of other religions than either the Christians or the Moslems. Gibbon seems to gloss over the fact that the Mongols were renowned mainly for their brutality.

During the Dark Ages, and much of the Middle Ages as well, the only effective form of power in Europe was that of the warlord. Most of the original territory of the Holy Roman Empire degenerated into warring factions soon after the death of Charlemagne, and its surviving remnant in Germany remained fragmented up until the nineteenth century.

A significant development of the late Middle Ages was the creation of a central authority in both France and England. These two were soon followed by Spain and Portugal, after the expulsion of the Moors in the fifteenth century. It is noteworthy that these four countries, with the addition of the Netherlands, were able to build the European empires that eventually came to dominate the global stage. In addition to a central government, the other important thing that these states had in common was their location on the Atlantic seaboard, which allowed them to become maritime nations. Although central authority was initially weak in all of them, it gradually coalesced into an institution capable of acquiring and supporting an overseas empire.

The British were ultimately the most successful of these five empire-builders, in spite of the fact that the country was one of the smallest. But the British had a slight edge in economic and technological development, which, combined with their position as an island nation, eventually enabled them to outstrip the other colonial powers.

What then is the difference between a warlord and an emperor? Well, the distinction should be apparent in the words themselves. Warlord is more of a pejorative term, whereas emperor implies leadership on a much more exalted plane. A warlord has more of the connotation of a bandit or gangster, whereas an emperor carries the implication of kingship or royalty. But before we separate these two by too great a gulf, we have to concede that their methods of attaining and retaining power are just about the same. In fact we might be tempted to say that an emperor is a warlord in fancy clothing. The fact that the emperor's domain is usually larger than that of the warlord, should not let us forget that they both hold power by the threat or actual use of force.

So when does a warlord actually become an emperor? The simple answer is, When he has got rid of all his challengers. But there is more to the distinction than this. The difference between a warlord's realm and that of an emperor is not only one of size, but it involves the important features of organization and central administration, just the factors that we have been talking about with respect to the Roman Empire and the European maritime powers. There is also another distinguishing factor between a warlord and an emperor, and this is in the matter of status. An important reason why we think of an emperor as being above a warlord is that the emperor has somehow managed to acquire a superior status. Knowing this, some of the Roman Emperors decided that an excellent way of enhancing one's status was by becoming a god. And Charlemagne obtained status by being crowned as Holy Roman Emperor by the Pope in Rome.

So it is eminently possible for a warlord to metamorphose into an emperor. Looking again at the Chinese society, Ch'in Shih Huang-ti (ruled 221-210 B.C.), the founder of the Ch'in dynasty, was definitely a warlord until he raised himself up to the status of emperor. Even then his behavior hardly lived up to his title. His most famous act was the burning of books containing the works of China's intellectual history. (In this he anticipated similar actions by his communist successors more than 2000 years later!) Most historians refer to him as a semi-barbarian. But the Ch'in dynasty only lasted a short time, and was succeeded by that of the Han in 202 B.C. By then the transformation from warlord to emperor had effectively been made, and the leader of the Han naturally took on the status of emperor.

The decline of the Han and Roman Empires occurred at about the same time (200-500 A.D.) and for roughly the same reason—the incursions of the steppe people. The Han Empire was weakened by incursions from the eastern end of the steppe. At the western end, the steppe people were prevented from entering Iran by a warrior class of horsemen, armed with bows and arrows, that arose in the Parthian, and subsequent Sassanian Empires bordering the eastern end of the Roman Empire. This forced the nomads to bypass the Middle East and swing northwards into Europe. As a result of this, the civilized metropolitan regions in the Middle East and India were allowed to develop in peace, while the Chinese and the Romans were both beset by the nomads.

In Southwest Asia, the Parthian (247 B.C.-224 A.D.) and Sassanian (226-651 A.D.) kingdoms each had difficulty in sustaining their empires. A major reason for this was the difficulty they had in controlling those same fierce independent-minded horsemen, who had saved them from being overrun by the nomads! [2] When the Sassanian Empire finally collapsed, Turkic tribesmen from Central Asia overran much of the Middle East.

Examples of empires that have coalesced from a group of competing warlords are found also in the Americas, where the Aztec and Inca empires arose in this fashion. In India, as mentioned above, warlords and emperors periodically exchanged roles, especially after the arrival of the Islamic invaders.

Another significant empire, which became consolidated in the fifteenth century, was that of the Ottomans. By about 1300, several Turkish clans, known as Ghazis, which had originated on the Asian steppe, took advantage of the decline of the Byzantines and set up a number of principalities in Anatolia. These were soon united under a charismatic leader named Osman, and the resulting kingdom of the Ghazis, now known as the Ottomans, gradually ate away at what remained of the Byzantine Empire. The Ottomans finally took Constantinople in 1453.

The empire that the Ottoman's established lasted into the twentieth century and comprised most of the eastern Mediterranean at its height. But the Ottoman Turks had originated on the Asian steppe, and they never really lost their character as "horse people." In spite of their sumptuous palaces and other trappings of Islamic culture, they never quite transcended their lowly origins on the steppe. Expansion through holy war and colonization were what kept the Ottoman Empire going. When further expansion became impossible, the Empire simply rotted from within. The Janissaries, a bureaucratic-military elite recruited from trained slaves, served as guardians for the Ottoman Sultans, who lived in a perpetual state of insecurity. In *History Derailed,* historian Ivan Berend describes the decline of the Ottomans:

> This system was later replaced by open, institutionalized bribery. During the later centuries of the empire, the entire state administration was built on corruption: tax farming became pervasive, and concessions were sold to the highest bidder. Office-holding was considered an investment for high returns.[3]

As with any despotic regime, the loyalty of the citizenry was ever suspect. Any hint of disloyalty was immediately punished by death. The executioner was always on call. Consequently, power could not be delegated to the lower echelons. So the Ottoman Empire never had the same organizational efficiency and technological know-how of the European colonial powers. Even so, it seriously threatened the peace of Europe on more than one occasion.

Another important empire that emerged at the beginning of the seventeenth century was that of Russia. Peter the Great (tsar 1682-1725) was the effective founder of the empire and his reign marked the beginning of Russia's rise to the status of world power. Although Peter sought to integrate Russia into Europe, bringing European technicians and architects to modernize his military forces and help design his new capital of St Petersburg, the vast eastern territories, encompassing much of the old Mongol Empire, gave Russia the aspect of an Asian rather than a European power. This "divided loyalty" has continued to prevent Russia from being fully integrated into either East or West.

Just as there are different kinds of warlord, so there are different kinds of empire. The empires built by the five Atlantic maritime powers were *overseas* empires, built by the expansion of their domains outside of their original spheres of influence. The usual pattern of several territories, each ruled by a warlord, coalescing into an empire ruled by one of them, was now superceded by a second phase, that of overseas expansion.

Actually, these maritime empires were not something entirely new. We have seen that many of the Greek city-states had colonies. The Minoans in Crete, and also the Phoenicians, can both be said to have possessed maritime empires. The Carthaginians were also a maritime power, which forced the Romans to build a fleet in order to defeat them. Later, the city-states of Venice and Genoa, especially the former, created what might be termed maritime empires. But all of these empires were confined to the Mediterranean.

The modern colonial empires were created from states with relatively strong internal cohesion, which had been built up over a considerable period of time. Most of them had coalesced from smaller groups. Britain, for instance, was a mixture of Danes, Celts, Angles, Saxons, Vikings and Romans, among others. But the process of nation building was long and arduous. Power struggles between monarch and nobility were complicated by dynastic quarrels over succession. Into this incendiary mix was added the influence of religion, which could be both a unifying and a divisive force, and was used by those in power in order to further there own ambitions. This resulted in the further political involvement of religion, as well as its secularization.

In Spain, the unification of Aragon and Castile under the joint monarchy of Ferdinand and Isabella in 1469 had started the process of unification, which would eventually lead, with the aid of dynastic intermarriage, to the creation of a huge Spanish Empire.

In England, the centralizing power of the Normans was offset by the ambitions of the barons, and there was a long and bloody progression towards the final creation of a strong central monarchy under the Tudors. Even though the four kingdoms of Ireland, Wales, Scotland and England were never truly united, this did not stop Britain from building an enormous empire.

France, although nominally united under a central monarchy, was in fact split into various dukedoms, the most powerful of which was that of Burgundy. The French people were also further divided by the existence of five separate languages. However, the devastation of the Hundred Years War may have actually served to strengthen the central authority, and after Louis XI conquered Burgundy in 1477, a more stable central government began to emerge with monarchs like Francis I and Henry II. But religious strife, pitting Protestant (Huguenot) against Catholic, rent France until the absolutist monarchy of Louis XIV brought unity through the expulsion of the Huguenots.

Another feature of the proto-colonial powers was their relatively small size. This made for greater internal stability, once the transition to an effective central government had been made. In contrast, China, India, and Russia were all much larger, and it proved difficult for them to maintain an effective centralized power structure. With the advent of modern communications, it is now much easier to keep larger territories under central control, but excessive size can still be a disadvantage.

We will now look more closely at the effect that the five Atlantic maritime powers had on the global scene, for this effect was both far-reaching and permanent.

OVERSEAS EXPANSION

In chapter 5 we showed how the commercialization of violence and the growing bureaucratic nature of military establishments had spread throughout Western Europe by the beginning of the seventeenth century. But this was also the time when capitalism was emerging as well. The new bourgeoisie, as against the old aristocratic elites, became more and more interconnected with the growing military establishments, which came into being in order to support the standing armies that European countries now thought it necessary to maintain. The military-commercial complex had its start in Italy and the Netherlands, where the rise of capitalism saw the emergence of the banking sector, which was essential for the development of commerce and manufacturing. The initial reluctance to engage in this kind of activity stemmed from the Christian Church's opposition to usury, which was associated with any kind of money lending. Since the Christians were thus reluctant to get into the banking business, the Jews, who were less inhibited in this regard, stepped into the breach. Some criticized the Jews for indulging in usury, but this was basically hypocritical, since the lending of money was essential to any commercial enterprise. The Moslems also had a prohibition against lending money at interest, and this put them at some disadvantage in the world of commerce, but they usually found ways to circumvent it.

The availability of private capital was the wellspring of the whole commercial system that contributed to the rise of the merchant class, or bourgeoisie. But the creation of permanent military establishments was intimately connected with the emergence of the banking sector as well.

Up until that time, monarchs had difficulty in procuring the resources necessary to raise an army. Imposing taxes was the usual method, but this tended to stifle private enterprise. However, if the king himself could go to the banking sector and raise money, taxes could remain at a reasonable level, and business could still prosper. This resulted in an *increase* in tax revenues, which in turn enabled the monarch to pay off his loans.[4] It was this system that fueled the rise of the West, for not only did it fuel the economy at large, it also allowed for innovation in the types of weaponry that were then being produced by companies and private individuals. This contributed greatly to the effectiveness of the military establishments. The involvement of private enterprise in arms production would eventually have dire consequences, but this was not yet evident in the seventeenth century.

The Moslem, Indian and Chinese worlds never matched the efficiency of the West, which was built on the strength of the private sector. This was because private enterprise was far less developed in those countries, for reasons having to do with their political and social systems, which differed markedly from those of the West. The Moslems were great traders, but their military establishments lagged behind their Western counterparts, as did those of the Chinese, whose tradition of Confucian opposition to both merchants and the military helped to prevent a more vibrant private sector from emerging. These countries attempted to remedy this situation by importing Western technology and technicians, but they could never offset the advantages of the Western capitalist system.

Militating against the European nations was their disastrous addiction to internecine warfare, the same scourge that had afflicted the city-states of Greece and Mesopotamia, the Chinese kingdoms and the Amerindians in the early days of culture. Contributing to this pathology was the very existence of standing armies and well organized military establishments. These were forever ready to engage in some kind of military adventure.

Intense competition rather than cooperation was the norm among most of the European states, not just the maritime powers. And the fact that many of them possessed powerful military arsenals only increased the likelihood of conflict. There was always the temptation to try out one's new tactics or weaponry on some hapless neighbor, and besides, combat experience was good training for the men. Conflict in the colonial sphere was widespread, but conflict at home was also entered into on a regular basis.

The Protestant Reformation that split Christendom in the sixteenth century provided a wonderful excuse for a little territorial acquisition at the expense of one's separated brethren. The Catholic Counter-Reformation only served to accentuate the divide. As a result, Europe suffered a plague of "religious wars," culminating in the Thirty Years War, which was, as we have already seen, by no means only about religion.

By the time the Thirty Years War (1618-48) had run its course, the Spanish and the Portuguese were ahead in the race for overseas expansion. But the Dutch, the British and the French were not far behind. The Spanish Empire was the most extensive, running from what is now the southwestern United States, through Central America and the Caribbean, and on into western South America. It also included the Philippines in the Pacific. Portugal, who earlier had gained control of the Indian Ocean, increased the number of her trading posts. She also established inland holdings in both East and West Africa, as well as in Brazil. The Dutch had set up trading stations in Africa, Ceylon and Indonesia, and in addition, established several outposts in the Caribbean.

The British, although hindered by the outbreak of civil war, nonetheless had obtained important footholds in North America, the Caribbean, Africa and India. They had initially cooperated with the Dutch in the Spice Islands of Malaysia. But an incident in 1623, when the Dutch massacred some British seamen, caused the British to fall back on India. Ironically this incident was instrumental in laying the foundations of the British Indian Empire. A factory had already been established in 1619 at Surat, on the gulf of Cambay in northwest India, and this became Britain's Indian headquarters, from whence she was soon able to challenge Portuguese supremacy in the Indian Ocean.[5]

The French East India Company established its Indian headquarters at Pondicherry in 1674, and this would eventually lead to hostilities with the British. On the North American continent, French outposts in New France (Canada) and Louisiana also clashed with British interests. These two nations would again cross swords in other theaters of the globe.

On land, the Russians had carried the domain of the tsars half way across Siberia, absorbing the steppe-land of the nomads into what would eventually become a vast empire stretching from Eastern Europe to the Pacific. Russia, with its huge reserves of manpower, was finally recovering from the depredations of the Mongols, which had held her development in check for more than two centuries, and left her at a disadvantage both culturally and militarily in comparison to Europe.

As far as the people with whom the Europeans came into contact were concerned, they were merely there to be exploited. Since they were non-Europeans, what culture that they had was assumed to be inferior. So the idea of treating them as equals was not seriously considered. And besides, the Europeans were far from home, and had to be prepared to meet a hostile reception from native peoples who vastly outnumbered them. Any kind of working relationship had to wait until a firm foothold had been established.

The Portuguese initially treated the people they encountered in India with respect, but this soon changed to ruthless exploitation. The Spanish had treated the native peoples with contempt right from the start, just about exterminating the inhabitants of the Caribbean, and destroying the cultures that they found in

Central and South America. The French, the British and the Dutch exploited and abused their fellow human beings in a similar manner.

The Thirty Years War left all the participants exhausted, and produced a general consensus that religious wars were to be avoided in the future. But there was only a brief pause before other excuses for conflict arose.

In France, the internal disturbances generally known as the Fronde had left her, though victorious in the larger war, in a state of insecurity.[6] Louis XIV, when he came of age in 1659, was determined to strengthen the French military establishment, so as to avoid any repetition of these internal troubles. Louis, full of his own importance, arrogant and intolerant, was ever willing to sacrifice his own countrymen to enhance his personal power. His phrase *l'etat c'ést moi* sums up nicely his attitude towards his own people and also to the rest of the world. His revocation of the Edict of Nantes, which had allowed the Protestant Huguenots freedom of worship, resulted in large numbers of French citizens having to flee the country.

Louis made several attempts to extend his possessions into the Netherlands in the 1690's, but these acts of aggression resulted in a coalition being formed against him, consisting of the Dutch, English and Swedes. This provided sufficient motivation for the French king to withdraw.

But Louis was soon involved in a much wider conflict, the War of the Spanish Succession (1701-1714), the details of which will not concern us. The source of the conflict involved the thrones of France and Spain. Spain's Charles II had left his throne to the grandson of Louis XIV, who would thus have become ruler of both France and Spain upon Louis' death. Louis insisted on keeping Charles' bequest intact, but the Grand Alliance, consisting of most of the rest of Europe, was determined to deny him.

The war went poorly for France at the beginning, but French losses were minimal, and she even gained an ally in Bavaria. However, Marshal Eugene of Savoy and England's Duke of Marlborough delivered the coup de grâce at the battle of Blenheim in 1704, where the French forces were routed. Even though Louis subsequently agreed that his grandson should be excluded from the French succession, the war dragged on until 1713. By this time the French were exhausted and the Sun King, with his sumptuous palace at Versailles, was no longer the envy of Europe.

But as so often happens, the French defeat served as a catalyst towards the further improvement of her armed forces. Jean Maritz, a Swiss engineer and gunfounder, was employed by the French at Lyons in 1734. He developed a new system for the manufacture of artillery, whereby the cannon were cast as a solid unit and the barrel was bored out afterwards. This resulted in far greater uniformity and much more efficient use of the explosive power of the charge. The new method required the development of accurate boring machines, which took time to construct, but once this was done, the advantages became apparent and a new arms race was soon under way.[7]

Although the European states had shown that they could enforce their will in foreign lands, until about 1750, the difference in military organization and manufacturing capacity between Europe and either the Middle East, India or China, had not been of critical importance. Now however, Europe stood at the threshold of a great leap forward, fueled by advances in science, technology and industry, and also by a significant rise in population. These factors placed it in a position where the rest of the world stood at a definite disadvantage.

As far as power was concerned, the main areas of difference between Western Europe and the rest of the world lay in their technological development and in their political systems. As we have seen, the strength of the West derived from the integration of the private sector into the command structure. In the overseas expansion of the European nations, private individuals often carried out the initial operations. In fact many of them started out basically as commercial ventures.

The profit motive was all-important to the success of empire building. In the case of British India, the commercial enterprise, in this instance the East India Company, had what amounted to its own private army, and acted for all intents and purposes like an independent state. The East India Company effectively ruled the British Raj until after the Mutiny of 1857, when the British government took over direct control. The Dutch East India Company operated in a similar manner in Indonesia.

Even though the basis of Western superiority lay in the institution of capitalism, the expansion in overseas trade would not have been possible without superior military power, both in organization and in weaponry. The development of light mobile cannon, which could be used on the battlefield, together with the superior fire-power of their naval vessels, as well as improved discipline and a more efficient command structure, all contributed to the decisive military superiority of the West.

The Ottomans, the Indians and the Chinese had political systems that did not take advantage of the power of individual initiative and did not promote the growth of an entrepreneurial class. This was partly because they ruled by intimidation and the treat of force, and were thus never sure of the loyalty of their own citizens. They could not afford to delegate power, which might be used against them. As a result, their military establishments did not keep up with developments in the West. They failed to create powerful navies like the Europeans, and they failed to produce more effective mobile cannon, instead relying on the old type of heavy cannon, which were really only suitable for siege warfare.

The command structure of the Ottomans was ponderous and adapted to change only with difficulty. Although they engaged in trade with many countries, this was mainly controlled from the highest echelons of the government, rather than developing from the initiatives of the merchant class, as happened in Europe.

Islam had a much tighter grip on the political structure in Moslem countries than Christianity did in Europe—especially after the Reformation. The exceptions here might be Spain and Portugal. Their economic and technological development was held back by the excessive power of the Church in combination with the monarchy, and also by a social structure that was inherently conservative. This tended to discourage any entrepreneurial activity that might threaten the power of the aristocratic elite. Spain's reliance upon the gold of the Americas led to the neglect of her manufacturing capabilities, since many of the necessary goods could simply be purchased from other countries. When the gold supply began to decline, due to the depredations of the English and the fiscal irresponsibility of monarchs such as Philip II, Spain found herself at a distinct disadvantage compared to the rest of Europe.

Countries like England and Holland were able to develop powerful commercial structures that were fully integrated into their political systems, and this was due in no small measure to the waning power of the Church and the introduction of constitutional monarchies. The legal and banking systems of these two nations also provided a firm basis for their development. France, in spite of her absolute monarchy, was not far behind in these areas. Italy, which had helped pioneer the new banking systems, had lost its former dominance, due not only to its lack of unity, but also to the transfer of commercial power to the Atlantic seaboard. Germany, suffering the same lack of unity as Italy, and lacking the trading empires of the other European states, was nonetheless catching up in military organization and weaponry, as well as with the integration of capitalism into the political system.

The Ottoman Empire was the odd-man-out of the Mediterranean countries. It made one final assault on the eastern end of Europe, with another attempt to capture Vienna in 1683. But this was thrown back with heavy losses and the Ottomans never seriously threatened in that quarter again.

In the case of India, the dead weight of the caste system, combined with the alien cultural imposition of the Mughals, tended to keep her at a severe disadvantage in a developing world. Added to this was the increasing presence of the British, who manipulated the whole cultural mix for their own benefit. The inherent richness of India's natural and human resources was to a large extent wasted.

The failure of the Chinese to develop their power in the same manner as the Europeans has been a source of considerable speculation. There seem to be many reasons, none completely convincing. The depredations of the nomads have already been mentioned. But other reasons, inherent in the Chinese system, also came into play: distrust of foreigners, a conservative political system, and the discouragement of the merchant class by the scholar bureaucrats. The Confucian system did not encourage individual initiative, a vital ingredient in the rise of the West. The Chinese also felt that they were somehow superior to the rest of the world, and could get along nicely without them. All these factors helped to prevent the Chinese from reaching their full potential.

From very early on, China had been beset by invasions from the northern steppes, and the building of the Great Wall served to mark the boundary of the Chinese domain. Outside lived the barbarians, who were considered to be culturally inferior. But in reality these barbarians had infiltrated the Chinese culture right from its inception, and had tended to strengthen rather than to weaken it. Nor can one say that the Chinese were inherently less aggressive and more peace loving than the Europeans. The constant internal struggles between various warlords put them squarely in the same category of belligerence as their fellow human beings elsewhere. Sun Tzu's *The Art of War*, is just one of several treatises on war that were written at the time of the Warring States.

It's true, however, that historically the Chinese have liked to think of themselves as more peace loving than warlike. As historian John Lynn writes:

> Those who praise the Chinese are apt to claim that *wen*, civilization and culture, triumphed over *wu*, war and force. Some go so far as to speak of a dominant pacifistic strain in Chinese history, in contrast to the violent history of the war-like West. Such belief in the influence of *wen* over *wu* derives from the written historical record bequeathed by the past to the present. To gauge the objectivity of that record we must ask who wrote it and for what audience it was intended.[8]

But, as Lynn explains, it was the educated elite, rather than military men, that compiled the historical record, so the military aspect was given little emphasis. The peace loving Chinese society was actually more myth than reality.

The Chinese engaged in trade with Southeast Asia and Indonesia, and even with Europe, via the Silk Road. So one has to conclude that they lacked only the intense drive and aggressive self-interest of the Europeans, which propelled the latter to seek riches from all corners of the earth. The necessary technology was available to the Chinese by the fourteenth century, but it seems that the will to exploit it was lacking. Unfortunately for them, it simply was not possible to opt out of the global arms race and the struggle for dominance, without becoming a pawn in the power games of the very barbarians from whom they had sought to isolate themselves.

Japan, in her island enclave, xenophobic and with a false sense of security, managed to remain in her own little world for much longer than the Chinese. But when the spell was finally broken in the middle of the nineteenth century, she put all her energies into making up for lost time, and joined the Asian power game with a vengeance. (More about this in chapter 7, *The Rising Sun*.)

Not only did the European states of the Atlantic coast extend their trading empires into America, Africa, India, Southeast Asia, China and Indonesia, they changed the trading patterns and economic structures—and even to a certain extent, the social systems—of the countries with whom they came into contact. As historian William McNeill writes:

> The really important result of the balance between superior armed force and almost untrammeled commercial self-seeking that characterized European ventures overseas in the eighteenth century was the fact that the daily lives of hundreds of thousands, and by the end of the century of millions, of Asians, Africans, and Americans were transformed by the activity of European entrepreneurs. Market-regulated activity, managed and controlled by a handful of Europeans, began to eat into and break down older social structures in nearly all the parts of the earth that were accessible by sea.[9]

The first three sea-faring nations to come onto the world scene—Portugal, Spain and Holland—were ultimately surpassed by the British and the French. The latter two entered into a spirited rivalry in India, Africa and America, in addition to their home continent of Europe. The British had come out ahead in the War of the Austrian Succession and were again victorious in the Seven Years War. But there were two important events, each involving Britain and France, which followed in quick succession at the end of the eighteenth century.

WAR AND REVOLUTION

The War of the Austrian Succession, which broke out in 1740, after Maria Theresa had been designated by her father, the Emperor Charles VI, as ruler of the Habsburg lands was important mainly because of the involvement of Frederick II (the Great) of Prussia. As a result of this war, Prussia gained Silesia, and would figure prominently in the next round of the conflict between England and France. This was the Seven Years War, which opened in 1756, and pitted England and Prussia against an array of antagonists, including France, Austria, Sweden and Russia.

The Seven Years War was fought in two main theaters: in North America and India between England and France, and in Europe between Prussia—aided by England—and the rest of the belligerents. Few outside observers would have given the Anglo-Prussian side much chance of victory. But through the dogged persistence and superior military tactics of Frederick, combined with the fortuitous withdrawal of the Russians on the accession of the Empress Catherine, the European part of the war went against the odds. The outcome marked the beginning of Prussia's rise to power, and this was to have profound consequences for Europe in the next two hundred years.

In India, the Mughal Empire had collapsed. This left the British and the French to pursue their colonial rivalry. The main sphere of British influence comprised the northern provinces of Oudh and Bengal, while that of the French included Hydrabad, Mysore and Carnactic in the south, with the Hindu Marathas being caught in between. In the end, the British had more trouble with the Marathas than they did with the French.

The British, having been provoked by an attack on Calcutta by the governor of Bengal, replied by sending troops, led by Robert Clive (originally a clerk with the East India Company), who proceeded to win an easy victory at Plassey in 1757. The British then took control of the governorship of Bengal, India's richest and most populous province, and this set them firmly on the path towards eventual domination of the whole sub-continent.

The French were soon ousted from their remaining outposts and they retained no further military presence in India. The subsequent assumption of the governorship of Bengal by Clive marked the birth of the British Raj, which reached its greatest extent with the conquest of the Punjab in 1849.

At sea and in America the French fared no better. After a French fleet had suffered a decisive defeat at Quiberon Bay, off the coast of Brittany, a British expedition sailed up the St Lawrence and took Quebec in 1756. Other expeditions succeeded in dismantling the French overseas empire piece by piece. When Spain came in on the side of the French, the British immediately occupied Havana and Manila, thus establishing Britain as the world's most powerful seafaring nation.[10]

Although Britain had paid for the war against the French in Canada, she decided that the American colonies should start paying for their own defense. So a stamp tax was imposed on legal transactions. But the colonists vigorously opposed this, and the British eventually backed down. However, it was not long before other frictions arose. The famous Boston Tea Party occurred when a tea-importing monopoly was granted to the East India Company, and a boycott was declared by some of the colonists, who dumped a shipload of tea into Boston harbor in 1773. Further trouble between local militias and British troops led to the Declaration of Independence being proclaimed in 1776.

This was the first of the two revolutions that occurred at the end of the eighteenth century. It was a setback for England, in as much as the North American trade was an important part of her economy, and France took advantage of the situation to try and inflict as much further pain on England as possible. But on the worldwide stage, British power was not significantly diminished, and what losses that did occur were soon made good. The American colonies had grown in population and prosperity to the point where their eventual independence was only a matter of time. Even so, Britain retained an American foothold in Canada, which provided a haven for those who had stayed loyal to the British crown.

Unlike the French Revolution of 1789, the American Revolution of 1776 was not really a genuine revolution; it was more like a palace coup. The landowning elite, most of whom owned slaves, did not relinquish their positions of prominence, but merely cut the umbilical cord to the mother country. Even though a democracy was created, the Constitution was written so as to make sure that the common people did not have too much power. Like the Greeks before them, the governing elite—now referred to as the founding fathers—had a congenital fear of the mob. So they made sure that their positions of influence would not be seriously challenged.

The curse of slavery, bequeathed as a legacy from the colonial past, was to make all declarations of equality or of human rights ring hollow, until the Civil War brought some sort of reckoning, but no final solution, to this stain on the nation's honor. But America was free to develop her vast resources in her own way, and for her own benefit. Although she was in no hurry to expand to her full potential, when this finally did occur, the old established European powers, not to mention the other nations of the world, would no longer be able to ignore this young nation, with its ever increasing wealth and its unshakable belief in the power of free enterprise.

The French Revolution, at least initially, was a *real* revolution. Ironically, conditions in France in the 1780's were considerably better than they had been for some time, and Louis XVI showed a concern for the welfare of the ordinary citizen that had been absent during the reigns of his predecessors. However, revolutions are actually more likely to occur after reforms have been initiated. When things start to get a little better, thoughts of insurrection are apt to stir in the minds of the masses, whereas the heavy hand of authority had previously left little hope for deliverance. This was the situation that existed in France on the eve of the revolution.

In *The Old Régime and the French Revolution,* Alexis de Tocqueville explains that the revolution did not suddenly occur over night, but had actually been building for several decades. Many of the "changes" that the revolution supposedly wrought, had actually taken place long before it started. The centralization of power, which manifested itself during the revolution, had been firmly in place since the reign of Louis XIV. Neither the feudal system nor the power of the aristocrats was destroyed by the revolution, since both had long since faded from the scene. The great landed estates had mostly been divided up, so the peasants were no longer landless. However, this meant that they forfeited any protections afforded them under feudalism. With ownership of the land came the exactions of the tax collectors and the necessity of making a living from meager resources. The nobles were exempt from the *taille,* or land tax, so the tax burden fell on those least able to pay. Resentment against the aristocracy naturally mounted. As Tocqueville writes:

> In England during the eighteenth century it was the poor who enjoyed exemption from taxation; in France it was the rich. The English aristocracy voluntar-

ily shouldered the heaviest public burdens so as to be allowed to retain its authority; in France the nobles clung to their exemption from taxation to the very end to console themselves for having lost the right to rule.[11]

The French king was constantly in need of money, and the selling of offices became widespread. These offices were sometimes revoked and then resold! The problem of public finance was clearly a major contributing factor in the revolution. But the inability of the social structure to adapt to the rising power and wealth of the entrepreneurial class, or bourgeoisie, was also an important influence.

In Holland, and even Germany, the power structures were accommodating themselves to the presence of the rising merchant class. But in France, the dead wood at the top of the tree shut out the sunlight from the new growth springing up from below. Too much national treasure had been squandered on the amusements and extravagancies of the high and mighty, who could not see beyond their powdered wigs that the world was rapidly changing, and that their enclave of privilege was no longer secure. Although the advent of the Enlightenment had infused new vigor into France's intellectual life, the king and the court were insufficiently sensitive to the political, ideological and economic currents swirling around them.

Hubris had long since set in, and the eventual reckoning was fast approaching. The increase in population, which occurred in the eighteenth century all over Europe, was certainly an indirect cause. The excess rural population tended to move to the cities, especially major cities like Paris, where it became a source of civic unrest and a receptive audience for agitators.

So the proximate cause of the French Revolution may have been overcrowded cities and lack of bread, but the deeper causes were the suppression of political freedom; the chronic financial irresponsibility of the monarch; and the failure of the power structure to adapt to a changing world. Finally, it was the ideas of the Enlightenment, in which the *philosophes* envisaged a society where logic and reason would replace the myths and superstitions of the Church, and where freedom, equality and brotherhood would be the guiding principles. The writings of the *philosophes* involved only abstract ideals rather than practical directions about how to achieve a better society. But they sparked a fire in the minds of the French people that could not be easily extinguished.

When the revolutionaries sought to apply the principles of the Enlightenment to the world of practical politics, the outcome was not exactly what they had been hoping for. As Tocqueville describes it:

The result was nothing short of disastrous; for what is a merit in the writer may well be a vice in the statesman and the very qualities which go to make great literature can lead to catastrophic revolutions.

Even the politicians' phraseology was borrowed largely from the books they read; it was cluttered up with abstract words, gaudy flowers of speech, sonorous clichés, and literary turns of phrase. Fostered by the political passions that it voiced, this style made its way into all classes, being adopted with remarkable facility even by the lowest.[12]

In 1788 Louis XVI decided to convene the Estates General—consisting of the Church, the nobility and the people—in Versailles. This was done primarily to address the severe fiscal problems that were facing the country. But it was here that the first phase of the revolution occurred when the Third Estate (the people) took over the Estates General and renamed it the National Assembly.

When the Assembly met at Versailles, it soon became a captive of the nobles, the senior clergy and the king. But it refused to disband, and the people of Paris, the *sans-culottes,* rose in support. The king relied on foreign mercenaries to quell the insurrection, but the common French soldiers soon joined the rebels. The taking of the Bastille followed, and the lower classes now joined the revolt, burning and pillaging several chateaux. Alarmed and fearful, the nobles and the clergy renounced their privileges. The Third Estate—the People—joined by a few minor nobles and lower clergy, was in full control.

Suspicions that the king and the aristocrats were planning to seize back power (which were in fact justified) led the Paris mob to march to Versailles and force Louis XVI to come to Paris.

The Assembly then moved to Paris, where it proceeded to institute various reforms and also to write a new constitution, which included the establishment of a constitutional monarchy. It also enacted several measures restricting the power of the clergy.

By 1790, many of the aristocrats had already fled abroad, and some were advocating an invasion of France to restore the monarchy. The new government attempted to stir up revolution in the Netherlands, but this was aborted when the hoped-for revolution failed to materialize.

In the next move on the foreign front Louis, still nominally king, declared war on his old enemy Austria, no doubt hoping that the French would be defeated and he would be restored to full power. In reply, the Austrians and Prussians mounted an invasion of France in 1792, intending to take advantage of the weakened state of the revolutionaries; but the strategy misfired badly.

The invasion was far from the walkover that had been expected. After several towns near the border had capitulated, the resistance stiffened and the Austro-Prussians were soon forced to withdraw. This French success ignited an outbreak of revolutionary fervor in the countryside, and the king eventually decided to flee abroad in 1793. He was apprehended, however, and brought back to Paris as a prisoner.

The second phase of the revolution saw the leadership of the rebels taken over by Maximilien Robespierre, leader of the Jacobins. A student of Rousseau's democratic ideas, he emphasized the concept of civic virtue. He opposed the war proposals of the Girondists, a group of moderate republicans, and this made him unpopular. But his fortunes revived when he was elected to the insurrectionary Commune of Paris in 1792, where he was instrumental in the final suppression of the Girondists. In 1793 Robespierre was elected to the Committee of Public Safety, where he rapidly gained power. He demanded the execution of the king and the rooting out of all those who opposed the Revolution. The actions of the Committee soon degenerated into a Reign of Terror, which resulted in over 40,000 deaths, including that of the king and queen.

Robespierre's name has always been associated with the Terror, although he was in fact a man of intelligence and high principles, hardly fitting the description of a bloodthirsty tyrant.

The ruling elites of Europe looked on in horror as violent and disorderly crowds toppled established authority with apparent ease, and they now feared the spread of the revolution to their own countries. Another French advance into the Netherlands followed, and this, together with the capture of Mainz, caused consternation in the capitals of Europe. The last straw came with the execution of the king and the issuing of a decree by the Convention (called to draw up a new constitution) that offered assistance to all peoples desiring liberty. This resulted in the formation of the First Coalition against France, consisting of Britain, Holland and Spain, who now joined Austria and Prussia.

The "Thermidorian reaction" of July 27th, 1794, brought the death of Robespierre and an end to the Terror. The Thermidorians who came to power were drawn from the old bourgeoisie and the newly rich. This ushered in the third stage of the Revolution, which did away with the violence but soon led to corruption and mismanagement when the five-man Directory was established in 1795.

The fourth and last stage was inaugurated in 1799 with the coup d'etat of 18 Brumaire, which got rid of the Directory and set up a three-man Consulate, one of whom was Napoleon. This lasted until 1804, when Napoleon crowned himself Emperor.

The crowning of Napoleon as Emperor of France led to a series of wars, but the character of these wars gradually changed from that of liberation, or the encouragement of revolutions outside France, to the single-minded pursuit of empire by Napoleon. The latter shrewdly used the revolution to enhance his personal power. He was not only a military genius but also an adventurer, who understood how to manipulate people to his own advantage. He was also a gambler, who played for high stakes and pulled off many remarkable victories. Although he paid lip service to the revolution, his assumption of the title of Emperor made his support of the revolutionary principles suspect.

The history of the Napoleonic wars, the famous battles: Trafalgar, Jena, Austerlitz and Borodino; the retreat from Moscow and the defeat at Leipzig, are all well known. The final acts: return from Elba and defeat at Waterloo, marked the end of Napoleon's reckless adventure. All that remained was his final resignation and exile to St Helena.

Once Napoleon had taken command of the revolutionary army, peace was impossible. War was the only option, and continued to be so right to the very end. The French army had undergone a fundamental change, from an army of soldiers to an army of *citizens*. As historian John Lynn writes, "The French Revolution changed war from an affair of kings to an affair of peoples and transformed men in the ranks from hirelings to citizen soldiers."[13] Every male citizen could now be a soldier, so the size of the army swelled beyond measure. Napoleon channeled all this new energy into the pursuit of glory—for France, and for himself.

The French have never been able to banish Napoleon from their collective consciousness. Conveniently forgetting the bloodshed of his many battles, they like to point to the vaunted Code Napoleon as a progressive measure, generously given by the French to the nations that she conquered. The Code, which owed much to the Enlightenment, certainly influenced the modernization of Western Europe. But it was imposed from above on the conquered territories, and the countries concerned had no choice in the matter.

Although the final result saw the restoration of the monarchy, France, and to a large extent the rest of Europe, would never be the same. The ideals of the Revolution: *Liberté*, *Égalité*, *Fraternité* were all compromised by the pragmatic decisions forced upon the participants, and by their own ambitions and fears. It was revealed that *Liberté* and *Égalité* are basically incompatible; the presence of one erodes the effectiveness of the other. However, on a more psychological level, the Revolution changed forever the way the citizens of Europe, and indeed the people of the world, looked at themselves in relation to those in power. The Declaration of the Rights of Man and of Citizens, influenced strongly by Rousseau, and adopted by the Constituent Assembly in 1789, remains as a permanent legacy of the Revolution. But a more tangible result was the rise of nationalism, which will now be examined in greater detail.

UNLEASHING THE POWER OF NATIONALISM

A good introduction to the concept of nationalism comes from Barbara Ehrenreich's book *Blood Rites*:

> "The nation" is one of the most mysterious categories of modern thought. It is, most citizens of nations would agree, something that people are willing to die for. But anyone seeking a more precise and scientific definition will be plunged into the swamp of turgid scholarship, which gets even more deeply frustrating if the quest is expanded to include the passions inspired by nations, or *nationalism*.[14]

To Isaiah Berlin, nationalism proclaims the inferiority of all other nations and peoples. Just as racism asserts the superiority of a particular race, so nationalism places a nation above all others:

> Nationalism is not consciousness of the reality of national character, nor pride in it. It is a belief in the unique mission of a nation, as being intrinsically superior to the goals or attributes of whatever is outside it; so that if there is a conflict between my nation and other men, I am obliged to fight for my nation no matter at what cost to other men; and if others resist, that is no more than one would expect from beings brought up in an inferior culture, educated by, or born of, inferior persons, who cannot *ex hypothesi* understand the ideals that animate my nation and me.[15]

Nationalism is sometimes thought to have been started by the French Revolution, but it had existed for many centuries before that, albeit in a less extreme form. It is generally defined as attachment to, or love of, a nation-state. But a nation-state exists only in the *minds* of its citizens. It has no material existence of its own.

In the case of France, the revolution created a concept of community, of being *French*, that had only existed before in a much milder form. Under the *ancien régime*, a citizen of France, if he was not of the nobility, was considered as a servant of the king, rather than someone with equal rights, shared by all. The American Revolution, like that of the French, had produced a Constitution, whereby the rights of the people had been spelled out. So these revolutions had certainly strengthened a sense of belonging, which had previously existed only in a much weaker form.

But ultimately nationalism is a state of mind, and so it is intimately connected with the imagination. The influences that give rise to this state of mind are many and varied, so we will try to isolate some of the more important ones.

Collective defense is a concept older than prehistory. Facing an enemy or a predator alone can be terrifying, but facing the same danger as part of a group can be exhilarating. It is this sense of being part of a group, which is somehow stronger than the sum of its individual members that is at the heart of nationalism.

The group is seen as protective of its members, and confers on them a common identity. But when some members of the group are perceived to be more important than others, this sense of group identity starts to fade. Only when the group identity can be seen as a "common cause," and when all citizens are perceived to be on an equal footing, only then can the idea of the nation be fully realized. True nationalism is based on *equality* rather than freedom.

We have seen that religion provided a common cause for the Christians and the Moslems. But something like the French Revolution, with its ideas of liberty and equality, provided an even stronger "cement" to galvanize a group of people into collective action. France, which had been a country divided between the haves and the have-nots, was now united as a *nation* in brotherhood and equality. The fact that much of this was illusory did not matter very much; it was the belief that mattered, and the belief was enough to move armies and to conquer nations.

The entity that we call a nation can actually mean different things in different circumstances. It can be a collection of people that have successfully defended themselves against another group. It can comprise one ethnic type, or it can be multi-ethnic. More often it consists of people with a common language, but it can also be multi-lingual. A common religion is a strong unifier, but nationalism can also transcend religion. A group can also be defined by its history. Wars, and especially pivotal battles, can contribute powerfully to the building of a nation. The strength of British nationalism undoubtedly lies, to a large extent, in the numerous heroic battles that have marked her history: Crécy, Agincourt, Trafalgar, Waterloo, Blenheim and the Battle of Britain. Glory can also come in defeat: the charge of the Light Brigade, or the retreat from Dunkirk. Many other nations have been similarly defined by military actions. The Greeks had Marathon and Salamis, with Thermopylae as a heroic defeat.

When they saw what happened to the French aristocracy, the crowned heads of Europe certainly did not want anything to do with the French type of nationalism. Neither liberty nor equality was something that they sought to encourage. But they found that the force of nationalism could be unleashed in other ways. The key was to find some idea, some concept, which could be used to unify the nation. An appeal to a people's ethnic and cultural roots could be very effective in evoking some of the same feelings that had motivated the French. This suited the aristocracy, since no revolution declaring the equality of all citizens was required.

Another way for an ambitious leader to stir up nationalistic fervor is to create an enemy—a nemesis, an historic foe, or perhaps an evil ideology—that prevents the nation from fulfilling its destiny as a people. In this sense nationalism and romanticism, the literary and artistic movement contemporary with the French Revolution, tended to merge into one another. This was especially true in the countries of Eastern Europe. Romanticism encouraged the mythological side of nationalism.

In the case of Germany, Bismarck used the idea of ethnic and cultural identity to foster German nationalism. As Ian Buruma writes, this had a decidedly martial flavor.

> What made a German feel German was something less political than cultural and ethnic, not citizenship so much as *Kultur*, music, poetry, and race; you belonged if your language was German and you were of German stock.... National unity, under the Prussian kaisers, would be imposed by military discipline and cultural propaganda about national essence and the German spirit. National strength would be forged in iron and fed with blood.[16]

At about the same time, across the world in Meiji Japan, Japanese nationalism was emerging in the same militaristic mode as in Germany. Again quoting Buruma:

> The Meiji oligarchs, despite some opposition even in their own ranks, chose to go the German route. This was partly because the oligarchs had come of age as warriors, for whom the notion of political liberalism or republicanism was alien. They knew that a constitution and the semblance of political representation were necessary accoutrements of a modern state.... They wanted to be modern and invoke ancient traditions at the same time. This was accomplished by grafting German dogmas onto Japanese myths.[17]

So the seeds of militarism were sown in both Germany and Japan at approximately the same time, and this was to have tragic consequences for the future.

In spite of the fact that communism is an international ideology, both Lenin and Mao used it, in their separate ways, to create Russian and Chinese nationalism respectively, and this helped to unite both countries under despotic regimes. Analogous to the French Revolutionary ideal of fraternity was that of comradeship, which supposedly put everyone on the same level and abolished the elites. The international nature of communism did not override, but rather complemented, the nationalism of each individual country.

The fascist dictatorships of Franco and Mussolini were not nearly so successful in creating nationalism in their respective nations, since they did not appeal to the ordinary people in the same way. Nonetheless Mussolini succeeded in creating a kind of nationalism for the Italians. But Franco came to power by means of a civil war, and so he was unable to create a genuinely united nation.

Western nations like Britain, France and Spain had been able to unite disparate groups of people into a nation state, but this was before the age of nationalism. By the nineteenth century, each ethnic group wanted to have its *own* nationality.[18]

America is a special case when it comes to nationalism. She is a mixture of different ethnic groups, but these groups must suppress the nationalism of their country of origin when they become American citizens. A genuine American nationalism has developed only gradually, perhaps because the American emphasis on rugged individualism militates against the unifying force of nationalism. Patriotism, or love of country, has been the dominant unifying force in America for most of its history. But as historian John Lukas explains in his excellent book, *Democracy and Populism,* patriotism gradually gave way to full-blown nationalism, a much stronger and more aggressive ideology, which has propelled the United States to try and Americanize (democratize) the world. Lukas says that as the power of the state (bureaucracy) has declined in America, the power of nationalism has increased.

Some say the nation can actually be treated like an organism. It is quite popular to describe certain accumulations of people or animals—such as cities or anthills—as *organisms* in themselves. But if something does not have life in the biological sense, calling it an organism is just an analogy.[19] A city, an army, a country or a planet can be considered as an organism, and they all may resemble organisms in certain ways, but one has to be careful not to carry the analogy too far. It's only in the *imagination* that something like a nation can become an organism. In chapter 2 we looked at David Wilson's theory that a religion can be treated as an organism, which evolves like a living creature. But treating religion as a living body is nothing more than an analogy, and only tends to confuse the issue.

Obviously nationalism is intimately connected with war, or more accurately, the *mythology* of war, because nationalism is basically myth. But this should be no surprise, since the nation state is the quintessential war machine. According to Fernand Braudel:

> The modern State arose from the new and imperious needs of war: artillery, battle fleets and larger armies, made combat ever more costly. War, the mother of all things—*bellum omnium mater*—also gave birth to the modern world.[20]

The connection with war is also reflected in the martial music of most national anthems, and even more strongly in national symbols, many of which are beasts of prey: the British lion, the Russian bear, the German and American eagles, and so on.[21]

But nationalism is not exclusively related to war. It has many of the characteristics of a religion; we might say that it is actually a secular religion. And just as with the conventional kind, it has a tendency to distort the worldview of its adherents. Its more sinister side can also be considered as a virus, a mutant of the virus of war, or an avatar of the primordial beast, the god of war.

Just as ordinary religion can be used for both constructive and destructive purposes, so nationalism can be used in a similar manner. The fanning of nationalism into flame can cause violent and uncontrollable forces to be released. Once the genie is out of the bottle, it's extremely difficult to put him back inside.

7

THE INDUSTRIALIZATION OF VIOLENCE

o o o o o o o o o o o o o o o o o o o o o o o o o o o o o o o o o o
He who ascends to mountaintops, shall find
The loftiest peaks most wrapt in clouds and snow; He who sur-
passes or subdues mankind
Must look down on the hate of those below.

—*Childe Harold's Pilgrimage, canto III*
George Noel Gordon, Lord Byron

RULE BRITANNIA!

The Industrial Revolution and the French Revolution can be regarded as the twin pillars of the modern world. The first grew out of the scientific revolution of the 16th and 17th centuries, the second from the ideas of the Enlightenment.

The Industrial Revolution should really have occurred in China. But having failed to take place there, it might very well have taken place in Italy, since that country was a pioneer in the development of capitalism. It might also have arisen in the Netherlands, or even France. But in fact it was the British who led the world into the modern age.

The overall strength of Britain had been building, with periodic setbacks, for several centuries. The year 1588 marked the beginning of Britain's emergence as a leader on the world scene, when Spain's attempt to re-establish Catholicism in England went down to defeat with her armada in the English Channel. Before that, England was considered only as a second-rate maritime power. Holland, although it was a small country, had the largest navy of the European powers. But three Anglo-Dutch wars, ending in 1670, broke the naval supremacy of the Dutch. From then on no other country was able to surpass Britain on the high seas, and very few on land.

In addition to the power of Britain's armed forces, the stability of her social structure provided the vital underpinning of her strength. The breakdown of the feudal system and the development of more efficient agriculture, allowed Britain's rapidly rising population to become more prosperous. The Glorious Revolution of 1688 established secure property rights and an economic environment more favorable to private business. The establishment of a thriving mercantile class provided the backbone of this structure, which was further bolstered by a robust legal and banking system. Although Napoleon derisively called Britain "a nation of shopkeepers," he had identified one of her major strengths, that of her mercantile class.

All these things combined to put Britain ahead of the other European nations. Britain's geographical position, as an island on Europe's Atlantic fringe, reduced her vulnerability to attack by other nations, and served as a springboard for her colonial ventures. This relatively small nation was able to exert an influence on the rest of the world far out of proportion to her size and population. The power that the British once wielded is reflected in the widespread use of English as a first or second language by a considerable portion of the world's population.

The development of science had been accelerating throughout Europe from the sixteenth century onwards, and certain important developments in technology, especially those involving both steam and water power, occurred in England around the beginning of the nineteenth century. The transition from human labor to that of the machine had been steadily advancing for some time, but in the first decades of the nineteenth century the pace began to quicken.

In spite of the loss of the American colonies, Britain's worldwide network of trading outposts gave her access to a wide range of raw materials, many of which were not available to other nations. Compared to the French, whose military power remained formidable even after the defeat of Napoleon, Britain was in a position of far greater overall strength, and this was to be the case for some time to come. The battle of Trafalgar in 1805, where Admiral Horatio Nelson defeated a combined French and Spanish fleet, set the seal on British naval supremacy. This was demonstrated when Britain was able to supply her army in Portugal by sea, as contrasted with Napoleon's inability to adequately supply his own troops by land transport, both in Spain and Russia. The failure of the Napoleonic blockade, which was intended to keep the English from trading in Europe, revealed the superiority of the British in the arena of world trade. Britannia really did rule the waves.

The demand for armaments during the Napoleonic Wars had kept the English gun-founders busy, and new coke-fired blast furnaces helped increase the quality as well as the quantity of their products. The construction of canals greatly improved the transportation of goods throughout the country, and the introduction of steam power to run all types of machinery soon started to revolutionize many manufacturing processes. More efficient agriculture allowed many of those who had worked on the land to move into the new factories.

The manufacture of cotton textiles was a key industry, and this was facilitated by several important inventions, including the spinning jenny and the power loom. In fact the manufacture of cotton was the spark that set Britain on the road to industrial power.[1] Profits from the sale of cotton were reinvested to facilitate the manufacture of other products, and the whole process of industrialization was further accelerated with the introduction of the railroad. Soon steam replaced sails in the transportation of goods overseas, and this increased the profits from Britain's trade even more. Large deposits of coal provided her with an enormous reservoir of energy to stoke the fires of industry.

During most of the nineteenth century, Britain, with its worldwide colonial empire, its solid governmental structure and legal system, its ever-increasing industrial might, and above all, its powerful army and navy, had few competitors on the world scene. The American War of Independence had been a setback. But the colonies had been fortunate to catch the British at a difficult time, when her military commitments around the world, especially those relating to her rivalry with France, made it difficult to bring sufficient forces to the defense of the American colonies. It became necessary to hire mercenaries to supplement the British troops, and these proved inadequate to the task. France naturally took advantage of the situation by coming to the aid of the revolutionaries. The poor quality of British leadership in America was also a contributing factor.

Britain may have been the world's leading military power, but this did not mean that she was an example to the rest of the world as far as her treatment of the native peoples with whom she came into contact was concerned. What she visited on the native population of North America can only be described as attempted genocide. The Spanish had exterminated most of the indigenous populations that they encountered in the Caribbean, since they considered them to be of an inferior race. However, many Spanish eventually intermarried with the native inhabitants of the mainland. The British seldom intermarried with the natives of North America, although they used some of them as allies against the French. For the most part the British tried to exterminate those that they could not subdue. Once they realized that the native people were susceptible to diseases like smallpox, they encouraged the spread of these infections by giving the Indians contaminated clothing and other materials. This was one of the first instances of biological warfare. Although the British government did not condone such conduct, little effort was made to prevent it, and after the Revolution the treatment of the Native Americans remained for the most part one of exploitation and abuse.

THE RAJ

In the case of India, the treatment of the native peoples, while callous and cruel, was not as barbaric as in North America, probably because they were considered to have a certain level of culture. But, at least at the outset, the inhabitants of the sub-continent were exploited and cheated to a remarkable degree.

When Robert Clive took over the governorship of Bengal in 1765, he and his fellow agents in the East India Company misappropriated the company's funds on a vast scale. As historian Stanley Wolpert describes the situation:

> By the end of 1769, when the monsoon rains failed, Bengal was left naked, stripped of its surplus wealth and grain. In the wake of British spoliation, famine struck and in 1770 alone took the lives of an estimated one-third of Bengal's peasantry. The company stored enough grain to feed its servants and soldiers, however, and merchant speculators made fortunes on the hunger and terror of less fortunate people, who bought handfuls of rice for treasures and were eventually driven to cannibalism.
>
> What finally roused British parliamentary concern over the state of Bengal was not the plight of India's peasantry, but the company's professed inability to pay a promised annual tax of 400,000 pounds to the company treasury in 1767.[2]

The behavior of British personnel in India improved somewhat after the British government took direct control in 1857, but the administration cared little for the welfare of the ordinary people.

> "Between 1876 and 1892, during the great famines, millions of Indians died of starvation while the British government continued to export food and raw

materials to England. Historical records put the figure between twelve and twenty-nine million people.[3]

That Queen Victoria was able to become Empress of India is truly astonishing. But the British possessed the necessary arrogance, panache, organizational know-how and military discipline to pull it off. To govern this vast multi-ethnic territory needed the flair and imagination that only the English seemed to possess.

At its height, the British Raj comprised most of the Indian sub-continent. The states of Agra and Oudh, with largely Hindu populations, were governed directly by the British after the Mutany of 1857, and became known as the United Provinces in 1877. The remaining third of India consisted of 500 assorted rajas and maharajas, nawabs and nizams. These were initially considered to be corrupt and despotic, and the British intended to replace, or at least to reform them. But after the Mutiny the policy was changed. The 500 suddenly became "autonomous rulers of princely states." Far from being replaced, they were promoted to the top rung of the social ladder.[4] They competed for favor and prestige, and were encouraged to emulate British pageantry and ceremony, while building sumptuous palaces for themselves in the same style as that used by the British for their own residences and administrative buildings. This style was "Indo-Saracenic which, in its exuberant asymmetries and its aura of instant antiquity, was very much the spirit and values of the Gothic Revival transported to India."[5] The 500 princes became extensions of the British aristocracy, and they enjoyed every minute of it. They sent their sons to English public schools and universities, and were accepted into the highest echelons of British society.

The maharajas thus became toothless tigers as far as resistance to the British was concerned, and the native Hindus, a potentially more serious threat, were kept well in hand by the colonial administration headed by the queen's viceroy in Calcutta.

As David Cannadine writes, in his book *Ornamentalism,* the British discriminated on the basis of class, rather than color, status rather than race. The caste system in India was a ready-made hierarchical system that mirrored that which existed in Britain.

Similar methods of creating a "landed aristocracy" were employed in other parts of the British Empire as well, but only where there was an established hierarchy of native leaders. These leaders were left in place, but "advisors" were supplied from London to aid them in their administrative duties. However, in places like Australia and New Zealand, where the native peoples lacked the kind of stratified society that the British considered acceptable, they were driven from their lands and marginalized. The landed aristocracy had to be imported from England.

The mixture of different cultures and ethnic groups that called itself India was pulled together into a rough kind of unity under the British Raj. A postal service—the famous "penny post"—was instituted, and this, in combination with the railroads, which were introduced in the nineteenth century, provided an efficient system of communications. The use of English as the lingua franca of the whole country, with its myriad languages, was also a step toward easier administration, which brought benefits to the Indians that continued after the British had gone, even though Hindi was adopted as the official language after independence. Factories were built for the manufacture of textiles and other goods, and much of the industrialization that had taken place in England was transferred to India. A centralized administration was set up in Calcutta, which was later moved to New Delhi, where a new city arose with its principal buildings designed by the well-known English architects Edward Luytens and Herbert Baker.

The British legacy also included India's law courts and a quasi-free press. So one can say that the British laid the foundations for Indian democracy. Even though the Indians were happy to see the British leave, several reminders of the Raj still linger in India. For instance, the game of cricket—a relatively minor English secular religion—has continued to retain its popularity among the Indians.

In spite of these positive aspects, the relationship between Britain and India was too one-sided to last. If we look once more at the game analogy, the situation was closer to a zero-sum than a non-zero-sum game. Although there was trade, it was almost entirely controlled by the British, and the lion's share of the benefits accrued to them as well. The ultimate factor, which prevented any real cooperation between the parties, was the fact that the relationship was sustained by military force.

The Indians were incapable of producing a united front against Britain because their country had been divided between Hindu and Moslem for the past 800 years. The British were able to use this fact in brilliant fashion, in order to forestall any organized resistance to their rule. The only serious upheaval, the Mutiny of 1857, was largely attributable to the mistakes of the British themselves. The two proximate causes of the Mutiny were the annexation of Oudh and the use of animal fat to grease the cartridges of the native sepoys, who were mercenaries employed by the British. Use of the fat offended their religious sensibilities. All the same, not all of the sepoys rebelled, and only a few of the "princes" joined the rebels. The rebellion itself was mostly confined to Bengal and the Gangetic Plain. Nonetheless, it lasted for more than a year, and atrocities were committed on both sides. Even so, the British were never in any danger of defeat.

Various "reforms," instituted by the British government at the beginning of the twentieth century, which increased the participation of native Indians in the administration of the Raj, had the effect of encouraging Indian nationalism and planted in the minds of the populace the prospect of eventual independence. Mahatma Gandhi and his non-violent movement managed to harness this latent nationalism to a degree that the British had not anticipated.

In point of fact, the writing had been on the wall for some time. Lack of political will at home, and increasing unrest in India had made the British begin to question the wisdom of the whole colonial enterprise. But it was Mahatma Gandhi who finally made independence inevitable. In the end, the British simply packed up and went home, leaving their princely protégés to the wrath of the populace. The ethnic violence precipitated by the departure of the British is estimated to have caused more than a million deaths.

The partition between India and Pakistan, like most partitions, has caused more problems than it has solved. It has not even separated Hindus from Moslems, since a large Moslem minority still remains in India. These Moslems tend to be treated as second-class citizens by the Hindu majority.

After two wars, Pakistan and India remain at daggers drawn. From its foundation, the artificial state of Pakistan has proved to be an open wound, not only in the sub-continent, but also in neighboring Afghanistan, Central Asia and even China. Effectively united under the Raj, India has been left fragmented and at war with itself. Its much-vaunted democracy has failed to close the gap between the haves and the have-nots, and globalization, while bringing benefits to certain sectors of the population, has resulted in more, rather than less inequality.[6]

OF WEAPONS AND ARMIES

The democratization of the French armies during the revolutionary wars, which broke up the entrenched class structure and allowed the promotion of the lower ranks into positions of leadership, was not emulated by the other European powers. They feared that too much power in the hands of the lower classes might lead to the overthrow of the established political structure. So the composition of

European armies remained much the same until the 1840's, and neither was there much improvement in weaponry, due to the inherent conservatism of the military establishments. As William McNeill tells us:

> Despite the new power that revolutionary idealism and the administrative implementation of liberty and equality had conferred upon the French between 1782 and 1815, the rulers and military men of Europe clearly and emphatically preferred the security of their old routines. Consequently, the traditions and patterns of Old Regime armies and navies survived the storm of the revolutionary years essentially intact. Weaponry changed little. Promising innovations met short shrift from conservative minded commanders.[7]

Several developments, which grew out of the Industrial Revolution, were to change all this by the middle of the nineteenth century. Improvements in transportation, involving the use of steam power, were fundamental in this regard. The introduction of the railroads, and the use of steam engines in ships, meant that armies could be moved to battle zones far more rapidly and efficiently than before. At the same time, there occurred important improvements in firearms, both small arms and cannon.

The possibilities of rifling, the placement of helical groves inside the barrel of a gun, had been known for some time. This resulted in a spinning bullet, or missile, which carried further and was more accurate. But in order to take advantage of this improvement, it was essential that the bullet should fit tightly into the barrel. This meant that the shot had to be carefully crafted and correctly loaded in order to ensure the successful operation of the weapon. Because of the fact that it took much longer to load (all the guns were muzzle-loaders) than the standard musket, the rifled weapon had not been used in battle, except in the hands of a few selected sharpshooters. However, the minié bullet, named after Captain Minié of the French army, which had a flanged base that expanded to fit tightly into the barrel when fired, was introduced in 1849. This allowed the rifle to be fired at about the same rate as the musket. The result was that all the European armies scrambled to introduce this innovation. The old muskets could be adapted to the new bullet by re-boring the barrel to incorporate the rifling grooves, a relatively simple process.

Another improvement in armaments came with the introduction of shell shot, meaning that the projectile itself was now equipped with an explosive charge. This development, when combined with rifling, considerably increased the destructive power of cannon. This type of cannon, when mounted on ships, proved so formidable that it was now necessary to protect the hull of naval vessels with iron plate.

These innovations led to a revolution in the design of warships. Since gun-ports in the hull were no longer practical, the guns had to be mounted on the top deck in armored turrets. It took some time before these improvements were adopted on a significant scale, but by the 1860's the leading powers were all hurrying to catch up with their competitors.

The American Civil War was the first truly modern war. Up to that time the Americans had placed very little emphasis on the production of guns, in spite of the myths of gun-toting outlaws from frontier days. However, Samuel Colt made a significant advance in gun manufacture when he produced the pistol named after him in the 1840's. But it was the invention of the Springfield rifle, which had standardized parts that were made on a special milling machine, and could thus be mass-produced, that initiated the large-scale manufacture of guns. This happened just in time for the Civil War. The increasing power and accuracy of small arms, together with the ability to bring large numbers of fighting men and cannon rapidly to the field of battle, combined to produce one of the bloodiest conflicts that had occurred up to that time.

Destroying civilian property became the deliberate policy of Union generals Grant and Sherman, especially the latter, during their marches through the South. These "marches" bore a remarkable resemblance to the *chevauchées,* conducted by the English in the Hundred Years War, and described in Chapter 3.

The invention of the telegraph vastly increased the efficiency of the railroads in bringing the troops to battle. In fact in the very first battle of the war, that of Bull Run, the timely arrival of reinforcements by rail turned the tide in favor of the Confederacy.

Robert E. Lee was offered command of the Union army by Abraham Lincoln, but chose to fight for his native Virginia. Had he accepted, the war would probably have been over, with the same result, in two or three months. Here again we see how certain individuals, and seemingly small quirks of fate, can turn the tide of history. As it was, the war dragged on for over four years, and thousands of America's young men were sacrificed to its folly. The superior generalship of Lee denied the Union its victory until Ulysses Grant finally wore down the Confederates in a battle of attrition. The North's greater reserves of manpower, together with its superior industrial capacity, made victory for the Union inevitable in the long run. The South was prevented from importing the necessary munitions from Europe by the imposition of a blockade, made effective by the superior naval power of the North.

The American Civil War was one of the earliest conflicts to be recorded on film.[8] Photography had been invented shortly before the war, and the horror of the conflict can be felt by anyone looking at the stark images of slaughter. No armor or shields protected the combatants from the powerful new weapons, which were often employed at almost point-blank range. Much of the flower of American manhood was mowed down on the fields of Gettysburg, Antietam, Shiloh, Cold Harbor, Fredricksburg and many others.

[The casualties in the American Civil War were about half a million dead. But this was relatively minor compared to the Taiping rebellion in China at about the same time (1850-64), which cost 20 to 30 million lives.]

SOWING THE SEEDS OF CONFLICT

By the 1850's the French and British armies had been modernized according to the dictates of the new industrial age, and the Prussians were not far behind. The latter had already equipped their army with muskets that could use the new minié bullets, and they had also been experimenting with breech-loading guns for some time. After several setbacks, they produced the "needle gun," the first successful breech-loading rifle, and this was soon to prove effective in battle. Prussia had also taken advantage of the advent of the railways and the telegraph, and these had significantly increased the mobility and efficiency of her army.

In 1848 there had been a series of minor "people's" revolutions in several European countries, including Germany, which had resulted in some liberalization of the various regimes. In France, for instance, the Second Republic was created. These changes set in motion a general tendency among western European nations towards allowing the people a greater voice in government. It was a direct result of the example set by the French Revolution.

So when Wilhelm I became King of Prussia in 1861, he wanted to make sure that this kind of sentiment would not undermine the established power structure, especially since the unification of Italy had recently created an example of the expression of nationalist feeling. He was not opposed to the unification of Germany, but it would have to be on his terms, not those of the people. His first action was to strengthen the armed forces. And here was one instance where Prussia did borrow something from the French. By introducing conscription, and borrowing some of the tactical ideas of the Napoleonic armies, Prussia replaced the aristocratic professional army with something more akin to the citizen's army of France.[9] The spirit of nationalism was thus unleashed, but in the service of the ruling elite, not of the nation as a whole.

Wilhelm had just the right man to help him carry out his policies in the person of Otto von Bismarck. Ambitious and ruthless, knowledgeable in the ways of power politics and willing to use war as a means of obtaining his goals, Bismarck was eminently suitable for the job that Wilhelm wished him to perform.

When the *Landtag* refused to grant money for the army, Wilhelm and Bismarck spent it anyway, and nobody dared to oppose them. There was also a third member of the team, who made sure that the policies were implemented by the military establishment, this was the chief of the General Staff, Helmut von Moltke. All three of these major players were well versed in Clausewitz's theory that war is the extension of politics. Through a combination of deceit, betrayal and intimidation, they relentlessly pursued their primary goal, that of Prussian hegemony over the German Confederation of states.

Prussia had originally consisted of a flat sandy region on the Baltic, which became known as East Prussia. The people were subjected to harsh treatment by a rural nobility of hardy Teutonic estate owners, known as the Junkers, whose land was adjacent to the Slavs of Russia and Poland. In 1701 the Elector of Brandenburg assumed the title of King of Prussia, and it was through the connection with Brandenburg that Prussia came to exert its influence inside the German Confederation. As it turned out, the tail (Prussia) ended up wagging the dog (Brandenburg), but we are getting ahead of the story.

The beginning of Prussia's rise to dominance occurred as a result of the victories of Frederick II, otherwise known as Frederick the Great, in the War of the Austrian Succession (1740-8). At the treaty of Aix-la-Chapelle in 1748, Prussia gained Silesia, which resulted in her emergence as a major European power.

The Napoleonic Wars had seen the demise of the Holy Roman Empire. Its successor was the German Confederation, created in 1815, comprising 39 states. The Confederation was similar to the Holy Roman Empire, but with a diet instead of an Emperor. The diet met at Frankfurt under the chairmanship of Austria and had about as much power as the Holy Roman Emperor had had, which was not very much. Austria and Prussia were the dominant members, but the creation of the Confederation had resulted in Prussia being broken up into two non-contiguous pieces. Historian Geoffrey Barraclough explains the consequences of this in *The History of Modern Germany*:

As in earlier centuries, the fate of Germany was settled, its frontiers drawn, by the princes in league with foreign powers. In this respect also the system of 1815 was a direct continuation of the old system. Like the settlement of 1648 the German settlement of 1815 was part of a European settlement: it was drawn up partly in the interests of the German princes, largely in the interests of the great powers, and not at all in the interests of the German people. Thus it was the English desire for a strong barrier against French aggression, reinforced by the necessity for finding territorial compensations to offset the Russian absorption of nearly the whole of Poland, which led to the acquisition by Prussia of a major accretion of territory on the Rhine—a cardinal change in the political geography of the Prussian state and in the direction of Prussian policy without which its rise to predominance between 1815 and 1871 would scarcely have been thinkable.[10]

With this background we can now relate the moves that were made by Prussia in order to secure hegemony over the German Confederation. The primary motivation for this was to unify the two separate parts of the Prussian state—its original homeland in the east and its newly acquired territory in the west, adjacent to the Rhine.

Prussia's first move involved a short war with Denmark over the sovereignty of Schleswig and Holstein, the details of which will not concern us. Suffice it to say that in 1864 Prussia and Austria combined to remove the two provinces from Danish sovereignty.

Austria and Prussia soon fell out over who should actually rule these two territories. This was all to the good as far as Bismarck was concerned, since he had already decided to remove Austria as the remaining impediment to his taking over the leadership of the German states. All he needed was a pretext to cover his aggression.

A Prussian alliance with Italy was designed to tie up the Austrians on two fronts. Meanwhile the quarrel over who should control Schleswig and Holstein was taken before the diet by Austria, where sides were taken among the various states. Bismarck would have none of such peaceful negotiations and proposed instead a new Confederation under the leadership of Prussia, while at the same time making preparations for war. When his proposal was rejected he proceeded to invade the states that had supported Austria. As historian H. A. L. Fisher writes:

> In the first week of this war north-west Germany was under the Prussian heel: in the third (July 3) the main Austrian army was crushed at Sadowa (König-

grätz), in Bohemia. The fight was stiff. The issue was long in doubt; and the day was won only when the Crown Prince was in a position to attack the enemy right flank; but in proportion as the Austrian resistance had been obstinate, so was the catastrophe of the army, when that resistance was finally broken down, irretrievably complete.[11]

The war lasted for seven weeks until Austria, as was her wont, decided to sue for peace after one lost battle. Bismarck had achieved his aims and wisely called the fighting off. For in truth, after all his meticulous planning, his use of the railways and the telegraph did not result in the type of efficient operation that he had hoped for. The telegraph did not always operate and the trains did not always run on schedule. The needle-gun, however, had definitely proved its worth. And Bismarck learned from his mistakes, so that in the next, and decisive, part of his plan he was much better prepared.

The German Confederation now became the North German Confederation, under the leadership of Prussia. This would soon blossom forth into the German Empire. All that stood in the way was Louis Napoleon's France.

Napoleon III was stunned by the outcome of the Seven Weeks War. Having assumed that Austria was the dominant power in the German Confederation, he realized that he had completely misjudged the situation. It also began to dawn on the rest of Europe that the menace to peace might no longer be France, but instead the rapidly rising power of Prussia. But Bismarck was not even interested in the opinions of the German people, who were largely opposed to his aggressive policies, let alone those of the rest of Europe. So he proceeded to the last phase of his plan. H. A. L. Fisher writes:

> To Bismarck and his military friends it was clear they could not reckon on completing the half-finished fabric of German unity without a violent clash with France. Strenuously, seriously, methodically they pushed on the work of military preparation.[12]

That Bismarck would eventually have his war with France was a foregone conclusion, and the diplomatic shell game carried on with the French in order to bring it about will not concern us. Suffice it to say that Napoleon III was inveigled into declaring war on Prussia, at a time when his forces were completely unprepared for battle.

The war soon went from bad to worse for the French. Mobilization was so slow and muddled that Bismarck was able to seize the initiative. He crossed the border into France and soon had the French in serious trouble. At Sedan, Napoleon III and a large French force were surrounded and forced to surrender.

In France, the Second Empire was now dead, and the Third Republic was born. The Government of National Defense was formed, in order to continue the fight against the Prussians. But it was not long before the latter were at the gates of Paris and much of the rest of the country had fallen into their hands.

A temporary government was set up in Tours, to direct French resistance outside of Paris, but the situation continued to worsen. The Prussians shelled Paris, which continued to hold out stubbornly. Eventually the Parisians agreed to surrender, but stipulated that there must first be an election to create an Assembly, so that peace could be negotiated with the invaders.

The situation then progressed from the unusual to the bizarre. With shades of 1792 and the regime of Robespierre, the Paris Commune was formed, which accused the Third Republic of giving in to the Prussians too easily. The Republican forces that had assembled at Versailles then proceeded to initiate a second siege of Paris, this time by the French themselves! All this went on while the Prussians watched in amazement.

After bitter fighting, every bit as savage as in the revolution of 1789, the Commune was crushed and a humiliating peace with the Prussians was finally signed. The German princes then assembled in the Palace of Versailles to proclaim Wilhelm I as Emperor. As part of the peace treaty, Alsace and Lorraine became part of Germany.

The French had now gone through three revolutions: one in 1789, one in 1848, and another in 1871. She had been invaded by the Prussians in 1792 and again in 1870, and was to be invaded by the Germans on two further occasions during the next 70 years.

SOCIAL CONDITIONS IN BRITAIN, FRANCE AND GERMANY

It is instructive to compare the social conditions of Britain, France and Germany in the 18th and 19th centuries. All three societies consisted of an aristocracy, an emerging middle class, or bourgeoisie, and a working, or peasant class. Friction between these classes, caused by increasing population and also by the advance of industrialization, was absorbed by the British through well-established, though flexible, institutions of government, which permitted the gradual improvement of working class conditions without upsetting the social order. Her trading empire and the effects of the Industrial Revolution served to strengthen the whole structure by increasing overall prosperity and thus minimizing any social disruptions as the economy became modernized.

The French were unable to prevent the pressures from below from eventually undermining the system. The aristocracy saw any liberalization as something that might encourage the masses to revolt. No gradual improvement of working-class conditions was permitted to take place. The whole system was too inflexible to adapt to change, and the pressures of population growth, combined with the restlessness of the bourgeoisie, eventually caused an explosion.

The initial revolution of 1789 was not strong enough to contain the forces of working-class discontent pushing up from below. These were brought to the surface by the example of middle class revolt. The Reign of Terror that was then unleashed set in motion a chain of events that saw the abandonment of revolutionary ideals and the pursuit of military conquest. When the whole process had run its course, the problems of the society had not even been faced, let alone resolved. As historian Alfred Cobban explains:

> France, throughout the nineteenth century, was an oligarchy of wealth, especially landed wealth, and office; but unlike the British governing classes in the same period, the French *elite* was insecure, not only because its internal divisions went much deeper, but also because it did not believe in itself. It had no reason to: it had neither inherited an old tradition of government nor had it evolved any Burkian or Benthamite philosophy to provide a moral basis for its new powers and privileges.[13]

The ruling elite was still fearful of introducing reforms lest their own position of privilege be challenged. The result was that parts of the same cycle were repeated in 1848, and again in 1870.

In Germany there was no tradition of central government, and although there was an aristocracy, it was split up among many different princedoms. Neither the Holy Roman Empire nor the German Confederation provided any real cohesion. The more powerful states, such as Austria and Prussia, were not interested in advancing the welfare of the whole, but only in maintaining their positions of dominance. The ruling aristocrats gave no thought to the welfare of the lower classes, only to the maintenance of their own privileges. But there was a considerable middle class, which was becoming more influential with the spread of the Industrial Revolution. However, they were kept much more subservient to the aristocratic elites than was the case in England.

The Prussian rise to power changed the whole character of Germany. Her leaders were determined not to allow any diminution of their power or privilege through the introduction of popularly elected institutions. As we have seen, the fact that its territory was geographically fragmented led Prussia to seek hegemony over the other states by the only means possible, that of military conquest. This meant ignoring any democratic institutions that existed, and making sure that any others that were formed would be subservient to Prussian leadership. They created what amounted to a military dictatorship, with no accountability to the people over whom it ruled.

In hindsight we can see how the rise of Prussia led, in a seemingly inexorable fashion, to the two world wars of the twentieth century. It is tempting to place most of the blame with Bismarck and Wilhelm I. The fact that they were totally amoral in their diplomatic dealings tends to repel us; they almost seem like incarnations of evil.

But this is not a realistic picture. Any diplomat who was not an accomplished liar would get nowhere in his profession. In point of fact, personal morality and morality between nations are two entirely different things. Or, to put it more bluntly, morality between nations is practically non-existent. Incidentally, even morality between individuals is highly relative, but more of that later. The impotence of any kind of international body has shown how difficult it is to extend any sort of moral or legal code of conduct beyond national boundaries.

Bismarck was a devout Lutheran, and could not be considered amoral in his personal life. Although he may have been feared, he was also much admired for his diplomatic skills. Many European diplomats were envious of his ability to manipulate others, and he himself often boasted of his accomplishments.

It has been suggested that Wilhelm's withered left arm may have driven him to compensate for this infirmity by trying to prove his manhood through excessive attention to military matters. But who is to say that he would not have been attracted to the military in equal fashion even if his arm had been sound? The fact that he believed in the divine right of kings might help explain his antipathy to any kind of democracy. But it's likely that the majority of the princes in the German Confederation felt the same way.

The danger created by the rise of Prussia was the danger of militarism, and it is doubtful if either Bismarck or Wilhelm had the slightest idea of its possible consequences, or even that there *was* such a thing as militarism. Certainly they were ambitious, selfish and greedy. But if we were to exclude such people from positions of leadership, there would be a serious dearth of leaders. Their ever-present willingness to use war to achieve their aims; the shunning of any kind of democratic institution, when other nations were moving in the direction of democracy; their arrogance and lack of human feeling; these were the characteristics which made them dangerous.

The Prussian system of government lacked any kind of mechanism for the expression of the popular will. So these men were able to manipulate it in ways that were ultimately detrimental to the good of the nation.

THE RISING SUN

On the other side of the world, at just about the same time that Prussia had succeeded in establishing herself at the head of the German Confederation, another nation was stirring from a long slumber. In Japan, the Meiji Restoration of 1868 marked a major turning point in the history of that country. The overthrow of the Tokugawa shogunate saw the beginning of Japan's modernization, after centuries of isolation and the rejection of most things foreign. The old *samurai* traditions, although they did not die out, were no longer able to dictate the direction of Japanese society. The restoration of the power of the Emperor, so long subservient to the shogunate, finally allowed Japan to stake out her place among the world's major powers. Although small steps were made towards the establishment of democratic institutions, such as "deliberative assemblies" in the various domains, in fact these were soon discontinued. The main emphasis was on industrialization and a build-up of the military. Education was also a priority.

The method of attaining these goals was "westernization." Japan had traditionally lived in the cultural shadow of China, but now she wished to establish her own cultural identity. To do this, Japan looked to the West. Agents were sent abroad to learn the latest methods of manufacturing and the organizational principles of a modern industrial society. For their armed forces, the Japanese again took their inspiration from abroad. The navy was based on the British model. An Imperial Guard was created, based on that of the French, and the command structure was modeled on the German General Staff.

Universal conscription was introduced whereby all, regardless of social origin, had to serve three years of active duty followed by four years in the reserves. A Ministry of Education was set up in 1871 and the French system was at first adopted, but later more liberal ideas from America were espoused. However, these were later modified. As historian W. Scott Morton tells us:

In the 1880's a further change in educational style took place; a convergence of nationalistic, Confucian and German influences emphasized the supremacy of the state. The highest value was put upon the good of the nation as a whole, while the free development of individual personality through education was accorded a lower place. An Imperial Rescript on Education was issued in 1890 in which harmony and loyalty were stressed above all else. The schools thus became a means of official indoctrination ready to the hand of future governments.[14]

There was considerable distress among the old *samurai* about the direction in which things were going, and the new leaders were for the most part from the same class. But these leaders realized that if Japan was to take her place in the modern world, she must modernize. Failure to do so would mean that she would fall further behind and would be unable to exert any influence on foreign powers. The slogan of the new leaders was *fukoku-kyohei,* "rich country-strong army." Morton tells us further:

> Above all they realized, in contrast to the limited modernizers in China, that a modern war machine required not only arsenals and shipyards but also the whole apparatus of modern industry to undergird it. Their slogan led directly to what is now known as the military-industrial complex, though they would probably not have approved the uses to which their more chauvinistic successors put the military-industrial tool which they so skillfully forged.[15]

The large government expenditures necessary to carry out these programs proved so costly that in the end it was decided to sell many of the government-run factories and enterprises to private buyers. A number of these enterprises were sold at bargain prices to friends of officials in the government ministries, thus creating an oligarchy of businessmen who controlled much of the vital industry of the country.

Westernization would not have been complete without the creation of some sort of representative national body, for it was thought that democracy had had some influence on the success of the Western nations. So the Meiji Constitution, setting up a Diet, with one appointed and one elected body, was introduced in 1889. A peerage had previously been created and from this a House of Peers was formed to act as the senior body, as in the British parliament. In addition, a House of Representatives was to be elected by all males over twenty-five who paid taxes of at least fifteen yen per annum—this turned out to be only one percent of the population. Nevertheless, the supreme power resided with the Emperor, whose sovereignty was "sacred and inviolable." The Emperor was also made supreme commander of the armed forces.[16]

One source of annoyance for the Japanese had been the "unequal treaties," which she had been forced to sign with China and some Western nations. Her leaders felt that by becoming strong militarily, and also acquiring colonies, this kind of humiliation could be avoided in the future.

By the 1890's Japan was feeling strong enough to consider the possibility of overseas expansion. In 1895 war broke out with China over a political dispute involving Korea. The Koreans were traditionally divided between pro-Chinese and pro-Japanese factions. But when the leader of the pro-Japanese faction was assassinated in Shanghai, this lead to war. The Japanese invaded Manchuria, meeting little opposition, and were victorious in two naval engagements, finally bringing the war to a close with the capture of Port Arthur. This quick victory boosted Japanese confidence. The shadow of a more powerful China was no longer threatening. Indeed, Japan now felt herself superior to the Chinese, and this attitude was encouraged in the ultra-nationalistic press.

The war established a foothold for Japan on the Asian mainland and this was to lead to a violent confrontation with Russia in 1905. The Japanese attacked the Russian fleet at Port Arthur in a similar manner to the attack on Pearl Harbor forty years later. The fleet suffered a devastating blow, from which it never recovered. Further losses led to a humiliating Russian defeat, so humiliating that it caused a revolution in Russia. But the Japanese forces also suffered severe losses, so the victory celebration was muted.

Japan had made a remarkably fast transition, from an isolated nation with little power, to one with a modern industrial economy and with armed forces on a par with those of the Western nations. But this success story did not have a happy ending. The process of westernization eventually created a mixture of resentment and envy of the West, and Japan retreated into her old xenophobic ways. By the 1930's militarism had gained the upper hand, and the stage was set for the catastrophe of World War II.

THE MILITARY-INDUSTRIAL COMPLEX

In the last twenty years of the nineteenth century the production of armaments took another quantum leap. New methods of steel production provided the catalyst for development of more powerful guns and for the creation of the modern warship. The Industrial Revolution, initiated in Britain, had been spreading to other countries, most notably the United States, France, Germany and Japan. In fact this second leg of the Industrial Revolution found the British somewhat lagging, because the machinery in her factories was by now almost obsolete, and the newly industrialized nations were equipping themselves with more up-to-date manufacturing facilities. But the process of industrialization had profound effects worldwide, for it tended to divide the family of nations into two unequal parts: those who were industrialized, or were in the process of industrializing, and those who were not. And this division is still with us today.

The Krupps steel works in Germany was using the new steel process to increase the reliability of the German breech-loading weapons, both small arms and artillery. The torpedo was invented in the 1860's, and in 1885 the American naval inventor John Howell fitted it with gyroscopic controls. Another American invention, the Maxim machine gun, became instantly popular in the arms-manufacturing community. The Maxim gun was used with lethal effect by Britain in many of her overseas ventures.

In England there was a transition from the manufacture of armaments in government-owned arsenals to production in factories run by private gun-makers. These private gun manufacturers sold their products not only to the government, but also to other purchasers, including those in foreign countries as well. There had been an international trade in arms for some time, much of which was centered in the Netherlands, but now it was on a much larger scale, and involved much heavier weapons. The introduction of the internal combustion engine in the 1880's made it possible to move heavy equipment much more easily, and so added impetus to the whole process.

Although the British government tried to regulate the export of arms, it was in a weak position in this regard. It needed the private gun-makers to provide it with weapons, but these same gun-makers had to have other customers in order to justify their expenditures on capital equipment. In most cases sales to the government were simply not sufficient to defray the costs. Guns for export were the obvious answer to this need, and the gun-makers were willing to supply anyone who would pay for their lethal wares. Components of large items, such as battleships, were often produced at different facilities before being finally assembled. This required coordination between different companies, as well as the necessary transportation, on a scale not previously encountered.

Such coordinated activities could only be carried out by the industrialized nations. So those countries without the requisite manufacturing capacity, but that nonetheless wanted the latest in armaments, had to purchase them from abroad. This meant that the gap between the power and wealth of the European nations and that of the rest of the world—with the exception of Japan—continued to widen.

Competition in armaments was also brisk among the industrialized powers, since each had to make sure that it did not fall behind in the race for the latest weaponry. Germany was a leader in this regard, and it was the advances made by both Germany and France that sparked the effort in England that led to her extensive use of the private sector for the manufacture of armaments. Designs that were successful were copied almost immediately and a new round of intensive production commenced.

Once this process found its way into politics, and it was inevitable that it should, it soon became self-perpetuating. The government had to raise money to buy or manufacture armaments, and the gun-makers needed the government to buy their products in order to make a profit. You can see where this is going. The politicians were motivated to encourage the manufacture of arms, because government contracts brought money and employment into their districts. All that was needed was a little saber-rattling by a potential foe to get this process going, because each country had to counter any threat, either real or imagined, by increasing its output of armaments.

As far as the British naval command was concerned, everything went swimmingly. The French were extremely co-operative. Gone was the feeling of comradeship bred during the Crimean War. Instead, a wave of anti-British feeling erupted, which expressed itself in jingoistic statements in the press and the increased production of armaments. This produced an invasion scare in England, prompting passage of legislation authorizing vast new expenditures for the navy. McNeill writes:

> With party advantage, national interest, and popular enthusiasm all pulling in the same direction as the special interest of private arms makers and the steel and shipbuilding industries, it is not so surprising that the Admiralty got more money to spend for new ships in 1889 than it had asked for or expected. The effect within British society, clearly, was to confirm and strengthen vested interests in continued, indeed expanded, naval appropriations.[17]

One natural effect of the British build-up of her navy was to encourage other countries to do likewise. Britain had demonstrated that those who ruled the waves were in a position to dominate other nations. The introduction of the British Dreadnought battleships, each with ten 12" guns, encouraged the Germans to produce similar warships. Kaiser Wilhelm II saw that a powerful navy was essential to the maintenance of German hegemony in Europe. In addition to surface ships, he started to produce submarines, and these were employed with deadly effect in the coming World War.

It is arguable that this kind of arms race can get started more easily under democratic governments. The whole process of popular representation lends itself to exploitation by special interests, and without serious efforts to prevent this from occurring, the welfare of the people and the nation can easily be sacrificed to the greed of the few. Even though authoritarian regimes can increase arms production whenever they choose, the imposition of new taxes may cause sufficient unrest to weaken the regime.

So the last part of the nineteenth century saw the birth of the military-industrial complex, and this is still with us today. A mutant of the virus of war, it has taken on a life of its own, and has become a habit that seems almost impossible to break. Vast sums of money and resources are squandered on this destructive merry-go-round. The military-industrial complex is centralized and inherently wasteful. Essentially an alliance between big business and the military, it operates independently from the rest of the economy—without competition, regulation or accountability.

The worldwide armaments industry, seeking to sell its lethal wares anywhere it can, provides weapons to insecure despots who use them against their own people, while at the same time driving their nations' economies into bankruptcy. Little effort to stop this activity is made by the countries that produce the weapons, for it is a valuable source of revenue, which rapidly becomes indispensable.

At the dawn of the twentieth century, the standing army, coupled with the military-industrial complex, stood ready and willing to engage in conflict wherever and whenever a suitable provocation might occur. And such provocations were not long in coming.

8

WINDS OF WAR

INTELLECTUAL VISIONS

The development of science accelerated significantly during the nineteenth century, and some important aspects of this development are related in chapter 9, Darwin's theory of evolution being a primary example. But science was not the only intellectual endeavor that flourished during that era. The nineteenth century saw the rise of the "Romantic Movement," which was a reaction against the Enlightenment and the rising influence of science, with its emphasis on reason over faith, spearheaded by men like Descartes, Leibnitz and Newton. The romanticists were especially active in Germany, where the philosopher Johann Fichte had considerable influence. But artists, poets and historians, as well as philosophers, joined throughout Europe to resist the march of science, which they felt was a dehumanizing and degrading influence on society in general. The movement was in part a reaction against the stultifying influence of classicism, and could also be considered as a revolt against rationalism. Philosophers such as Jean-Jacques Rousseau, who considered civilization a perversion of man's true nature, advocated a return to Nature. The English poets Shelley and Byron exalted the life of the senses over that of the intellect.

Romanticism is an important episode in the history of ideas, and has many facets, involving art, religion and philosophy. Isaiah Berlin, in his book, *The Crooked Timber of Humanity,* gives a detailed account of how Romanticism originated and how it affected the intellectual life of Europe. One of its consequences, according to Berlin, was the rise of the totalitarian ideologies of communism and fascism.

The romanticists maintained that science did not depict the real world; things such as art, emotion and religion were the true expressions of reality. They were only half right about this. Science is an abstraction from reality, not an exact description. But art and religion come straight from the imagination, and while emotion is certainly part of the real world, it can hardly be said to *represent* it. Science helps us to understand the physical world; religion and emotion emphasize the irrational side of human nature.

Social philosophers, such as John Locke and Thomas Hobbes, had considerable influence on political thought prior to the American and French Revolutions. Adam Smith, the eighteenth century economist, with his *Wealth of Nations,* continues to influence economic thought even today. But during the latter half of the nineteenth century, the two most important thinkers in the realm of social and political thought were Herbert Spencer and Karl Marx.

Herbert Spencer, a "social Darwinist," had immense influence on late nineteenth century thought. His simple thesis was that if living organisms evolved, then so did human society, and the basic mechanism was the same, the survival of the fittest. He was an Englishman of unsophisticated mien, an agnostic who was contemptuous of most conventional opinions. Darwin's evolutionary theory allowed him to demolish most of the accepted wisdom regarding civilization and human society. As H. A. L. Fisher says:

> He wrote of the evolution of man, of the evolution of the family, of the evolution of social and ceremonial institutions.... He saw society passing from a military and despotic into an industrial and democratic phase.... Society, becoming industrial, could condemn the unreason and barbarity of war. Government itself, being a deciduous organ and a remnant of the predatory State, would, as civilization advanced, contract its functions.[1]

All this sounded fairly reasonable until one looked at the facts a little more closely. Government, far from getting smaller, was actually expanding, and war was increasing both in ferocity and scope. The tide seemed to be flowing in the opposite direction from that predicted by Spencer. But the part of his theory pertaining to social evolution remained popular for some time, and has even had a kind of renaissance of late, albeit in a slightly different form. As already noted, Robert Wright, in *Nonzero,* subscribes to a kind of cultural evolution.

Karl Marx (1818-83) first appeared on the scene in Germany during the social disturbances of 1848, during which he produced his *Communist Manifesto*. This put forth his ideas regarding the struggle of the proletariat against the bourgeoisie, and advocated nothing less than the violent overthrow of the social order.

After the revolution of 1848 failed in Germany, Marx moved to London, where he spent most of his time in the reading room of the British Museum. There he wrote the work that was to become the bible of the new religion of communism—*Das Kapital*. For anyone brave enough to read this work, it lays out the Marxist doctrine of economics and class struggle that lies at the heart of the communist creed. Again I quote Fisher:

> Marx hated nationality with the rancour of an outcast, despised liberty with the arrogance of a despot, and throughout his life lost no opportunity of assailing the class from which he was himself sprung. The vital division of human society was not, in the view of this fierce cosmopolitan atheist, based on religion or nationality, but upon class. There was no common interest between German employers and German workers, but a common interest among the workers of the world to put an end to the capitalists by whom they were exploited.[2]

Marx understood that capitalism would inevitably lead to liberal democracy. The first capitalists came from England's "yeoman" class, ranging from minor aristocrats to enterprising peasants. They were the first members of the property-owning class, whom Marx called "the owners of the means of production." As Fareed Zakaria writes:

> Marx accurately recognized that this class was the vanguard of political liberalization in Europe. Since its members benefited greatly from capitalism, the rule of law, free markets, and the rise of professionalism and meritocracy, they supported gradual reforms that furthered these trends.[3]

Marx saw that the bourgeoisie were the harbingers of democracy. But since they were the exploiters of the proletariat, democracy would lead only to the enslavement of the masses. Happily his prediction turned out to be false. Although capitalism did cause much hardship, it ultimately led to a better society for all.

Communism was a worldwide religion, transcending national boundaries and seeking to supplant nationalism itself. The wage earners of the world—the proletariat—would unite in order to throw off their chains. The inevitable war with the capitalists would be won by taking over the means of production. Private property was to be removed from the hands of the exploiters and handed back to the people. Government would gradually shrink away, much as in Spencer's theory, and all would be harmony in a People's Paradise.

Much of the inspiration for his creed came from the harsh working conditions in the factories spawned by Britain's Industrial Revolution. However, measures to alleviate these problems were already under way in Marx's adopted country.

During the nineteenth century Britain had gradually, with halting steps and over the determined opposition of the privileged classes, introduced various "reforms" that resulted in considerable liberalization of the structure of British society. The franchise was substantially increased, although universal suffrage was still a long way off. After much resistance, several Reform Bills were passed: the first in 1832; a second, under Disraeli, in 1867; and a third, initiated by Gladstone, in 1884. All these dealt with the extension and reform of the franchise and had the effect of opening up the government to larger sections of the population, including not only shopkeepers and small traders but also some of the workingmen in the towns.

Several Factory Acts were passed, which established better working conditions and limited the hours of work in the factories. The Trade Union Act of 1871 granted legal status to labor unions, which had been banned after the French Revolution for fear that the revolt of the masses might spread to England. The effect of this liberalization was to make possible a peaceful evolution towards a more democratic society, and to make the possibility of a violent upheaval far less likely. The British parliamentary system was flexible enough to allow for a gradual improvement in the lives of the people. And therein lay the true strength of Britain—greater by far than the strength of her armed forces or her Empire. In fact, although this was not realized at the time, the British Empire had already passed its zenith, since other countries were already challenging her monopoly of world trade. Even more important, the rigid class structure on which the Empire was built was being challenged by the rising tide of nationalism. Ironically, Britain's Empire became an anachronism at about the time that it reached its peak! Britain herself was slowly giving way to a more democratic society, and this only served to strengthen rather than to weaken her social fabric. The intellectuals and the rising middle class were generally opposed to the Empire and the class structure on which it was based. But even so, the Empire continued on its course until after the Second World War. It then disintegrated into its constituent parts, with only a "Commonwealth" remaining to remind the British people of the Empire that was once theirs.

It probably did not dawn on Marx, genius though he was, that the country that he had chosen as his refuge, and in which he was to compose his master work, was one of the least likely to serve as a springboard for his proposed revolution. He had not felt welcome in his own country after his initial attempt at revolution had failed in 1848, so he went to England, a country that would tolerate him in spite of his eccentricities and his dangerous ideas, to say nothing of his uncouth appearance. He was constantly short of money, and if it hadn't been for his friend Frederick Engels, he would probably have ended up destitute. The conditions of the workers in England, which aroused so much ire in him, were in fact being slowly ameliorated. The Marxist doctrine of class warfare was completely alien to the British character, even though class distinctions were very strong in England. So Marx's ideas did not fall on fertile ground in his adopted country.

But many people on the Continent did take Marx seriously. As Fisher says:

> In Italy, in France, and above all, in Russia, Marxist doctrines began from the [eighteen] nineties to captivate the imagination of many of the foremost minds of the younger generation. Poets and professors, teachers and artisans, embraced the theory of class struggle, the iron law of wages, and of the coming triumph of the Proletariat.... Within the span of a decade Marx had dethroned Herbert Spencer as the leading oracle of political and economic wisdom among the Italians.... Indeed, the more backward the country, the more likely it was that the influence of the revolutionary thinker would become decisive. In Russia, where the standard of living was unsheltered by trades unions, the teaching of Marx speedily asserted its ascendancy.[4]

The new religion finally found its St Paul in the person of Vladimir Ilyich Ulyanov, alias Lenin, who had the ruthlessness and the iron will necessary to actually carry out the revolution. Compared to Lenin, Bismarck was a boy scout. The Russian Revolution was to show that rule by the proletariat—or rather in the *name* of the proletariat—could be every bit as brutal as the worst abuses of those who believed in the divine right of kings. Although a taste of what *could* happen had already been experienced during the second phase of the French Revolution in 1792, this turned out to be quite mild when compared to what eventually was to come.

In the event, however, Lenin almost missed the boat. He was exiled to Siberia as a troublemaker in 1887, and on his return from exile he left Russia to study Marxist doctrine abroad. In 1903, at a meeting in London, the Russian Social

Democratic Labor Party split into two camps: the Mensheviks and the Bolsheviks, with Lenin becoming the leader of the latter, more radical, section.

Lenin returned to Russia during the 1905 revolution, and the Bolsheviks became part of the Duma in 1907. But it was not long before he again left Russia, and after several temporary sojourns in various European countries, the outbreak of the First World War found him in Switzerland. There he continued to plot revolution, rather like Marx had done in London fifty years before. His two principle items of reading matter were Marx's *Das Capital* and Clausewitz's *On War*. The latter proved extremely useful to him after the Revolution.

Lenin was still in Switzerland when the first uprising, led by the Mensheviks, occurred in Russia in March 1917.[5] This sort of "bourgeois" revolution was not nearly radical enough for him. In October 1917 he made a deal with the Germans, whereby he was transported back to Russia via Finland in a sealed boxcar. The Germans calculated that he would take over the revolution and remove Russia from the war, and it turned out that their surmise was correct. The October Revolution brought Lenin and the Bolsheviks to power, and by the treaty of Brest-Litovsk the Russians withdrew from the war with Germany.

Just as in the French Revolution, the original bourgeois uprising by the Mensheviks was swept away by more radical elements, and a long-drawn-out Reign of Terror commenced. And just as before, the ideals of the cause were soon forgotten, and the pursuit of power became the main purpose of Lenin and the revolutionaries.

This time it would take more than seventy years, and the sacrifice of tens of millions of lives, before reaction finally set in and the cycle was complete. By then Russia had changed forever.

ENTANGLING ALLIANCES

The last quarter of the nineteenth century saw the Industrial Revolution accelerate rapidly, especially in two countries: America and Germany. America, having recovered from the Civil War and completed her expansion into the western reaches of the continent, went about the industrialization of her economy with energy and enthusiasm. Much of the capital that she needed was obtained from England, her erstwhile colonial ruler. Apart from a considerable build-up of her navy, military outlays were relatively minor, as there had been a general demobilization after the Civil War. America did not consider it necessary to retain a standing army, and so military spending was kept within reasonable bounds. As a result, her economy was free to modernize without being weighed down by a military-industrial complex. All this would eventually change, but in the latter part of the nineteenth century it was still some way in the future. Social reforms, such as those that had occurred in England were not as far-reaching, but labor unions were permitted, although they did not enjoy much popularity with the general public.

The new German Empire, created in 1871 after the victory over France, was democratic in name only. The *Reichstag*, or Parliament, although it was elected by universal suffrage, had very little real power. It could debate but not initiate legislation, and had no power of voting or refusing to vote taxes. It had no control over the ministers of the executive, headed by Bismarck, who were solely responsible to the Prussian king, now Emperor of Germany. The Bundesrat, or Federal Council, was composed of representatives from the constituent states. It was dominated by Prussia, who could veto any proposed changes to the constitution. As Geoffrey Barraclough tells us:

> There was no mention in the new constitution of the 'Fundamental Rights of the German People', on which the Frankfurt Parliament of 1848-1849 had spent so much time and toil...the system of government established in 1871 was, in fact, a veiled form of monarchical absolutism vested in the king of Prussia.... The real power of the state was wielded by the Prussian aristocracy: through Bismarck it became the dominant force not only in Prussian but also in German life. The constitution of 1871, fending off the realities of popular self-government, ensured both the preponderance of the Junkers in Prussia and the preponderance of Prussia in the *Reich*.[6]

Bismarck continually harassed the small Social Democratic Party in the *Reichstag*, but to make sure that they did not win over popular sentiment, he instituted the German Insurance Acts, providing compulsory insurance against sickness, accidents and old age. These were in fact models for their time, and predated similar legislation passed in England. However, there was no insurance against unemployment.

Having created the German Empire by means of war, Bismarck spent the next eighteen years trying to keep Germany at peace, while at the same time increasing the strength of the armed forces in case war should come. He hoped that peace could be preserved by means of diplomacy and a series of alliances. France was considered the main enemy, and likely to seek revenge after her humiliating defeat.

The *Dreikaiserbund,* or Treaty of the Three Emperors, formed in 1873 between Germany, Austria and Russia, was the first step in the isolation of France. Neither Austria nor Russia was a particularly stanch ally for Germany, the former still smarting from her defeat in the Austro-Prussian war.

A short war in the Balkans occurred in 1878, in which Russia came to the aid of her Slavic brothers, who had been attacked by the Turks. It was won decisively by Russia, who, as a result of her victory, had thoughts of making serious inroads into the Balkans. This was fiercely opposed by the European powers and was ultimately prevented through the efforts of Bismarck, aided by both the Austrians and the British. Nevertheless, the victory significantly increased Russian influence in the Balkans.

Now the Iron Chancellor saw a potential struggle, not only against France, but also against Pan-Slavism, aided and abetted by Russia. Accordingly, he negotiated a secret treaty with Austria-Hungary behind Russia's back (Austria and Hungary were now united under a dual monarchy). This treaty stipulated that, should Russia attack either party, the other would come to its aid "with the whole strength of their Empire."

Since this agreement was inconsistent with the *Dreikaiserbund,* it had to be kept secret. In hindsight we can see that this was the fuse that would eventually ignite the First World War. All that was needed was a spark to set it off. In 1882 Italy, frustrated with the French occupation of Tunis, was added to the treaty, making the Dual Alliance into the Triple Alliance.

When Wilhelm I died a nonagenarian in 1888, the liberal-minded Crown Prince Frederick succeeded him. But as fate would have it, Frederick was already dying of cancer and his reign lasted only ninety days. His successor, Wilhelm II, thirty-one years old, and anything but a liberal, immediately took the reins of power firmly into his own hands. The clash of egos between Wilhelm and his Chancellor led inevitably to Bismarck's dismissal in 1890, placing the youthful autocrat, of impulsive and unstable character, in sole control of one of the world's most powerful military machines. Again fate had stepped in, to radically change the course of history.

France ended her isolation by signing a treaty with Russia—just what Bismarck had sought to avoid. This enabled the Russians to obtain armaments and finance their new railways, while it gave the French an ally against the German powers. The tsar was now aware of the secret treaty between Germany and Austria, so a secret convention was added to the Franco-Russian treaty, which stipulated that either party would come to the other's assistance in case of a German attack. This latter agreement was the second link in the chain of circumstances that led to the outbreak of war. The Dual Alliance of Russia and France now opposed the Triple Alliance of Germany, Austria-Hungary and Italy.

Meanwhile England sat alone in her island home, unfettered by alliances. Bismarck had wanted an alliance with England, but the latter was not interested in secret treaties. So he endeavored to keep England and France from any *rapprochement*. He envied the English their command of the sea, but despised their form of government, which was constantly changing leaders and so appeared chaotic and unreliable. But his efforts to keep England and France apart were ultimately unsuccessful.

Following the alliance of France and Russia, it seemed that England would remain neutral in the continental power game. Russia was a thorn in England's side with regard to India, and the interests of France and England had recently clashed in Egypt and at Fashoda on the upper Nile, as well as in Tunis. Their partnership in the Crimean War was now all but forgotten.

But cooler heads on both sides of the English Channel saw Germany, with its huge army and unstable leader, its burgeoning pursuit of empire and its increasingly powerful navy, as the real menace to peace. Accordingly, an *entente* was entered into between the two countries, although no formal alliance was signed. This reconciliation between France and England marked a final end to the long history of antagonism and rivalry between the two countries, a history that stretched back to the Hundred Years War in the fourteenth century. The only thing that finally persuaded France and England to bury the hatchet was not any kind of burgeoning friendship or amity, but a mutual fear of the rising power of Germany, under the sinister guidance of Kaiser Wilhelm.

So a rough balance of power was established between Germany, Austria-Hungary and Italy on the one hand, and Russia, France and England on the other. They were all heavily armed, but only Germany was really anxious for war.

It was not just the Kaiser that was the problem, although he was the one that ultimately failed to avert war when the crisis came. The sons of the German Reich were imbued with a martial spirit by their customs and upbringing. Universal conscription had created a nation familiar with military discipline, and the large officer class prided itself on the traditions of the Junkers. As H. A. L. Fisher writes:

> All young Germans expected, many young Germans hoped, that among the experiences which life would offer them would be a war for the Fatherland. Such a war they had been taught to regard, not as a crime against civilization, but as a good and necessary medicine in the moral history of states. Accordingly they did not, as did so many English, dread, detest, and despise war as a

relic of barbarism dishonouring to human nature. Rather they were disposed to welcome it as offering a supreme test of manhood, and the more readily since, judging from recent enterprises, they believed that the next war would be brief, exhilarating, and triumphant.[7]

The events that actually sparked the war are all familiar: the assassination of the Austrian Archduke Ferdinand by a Serbian nationalist; the Austrian ultimatum to Serbia; partial compliance with the ultimatum; and finally the Austrian declaration of war. Although it was still possible that not all the dominoes would fall, in the event a weak tsar Nicolas II could not stand against the sentiments of the people, who demanded that Russia go to the aid of their Slavic brothers. The entry of the Russians precipitated that of the Germans and the French, and after that there was no turning back. The invasion of neutral Belgium, and especially the burning of the library at Louvain, made it impossible for England to remain aloof from the conflict. English sentiment turned from admiration of Germany's culture and achievements, to revulsion against the use of naked force upon an innocent country. They were reminded of the Huns, that ancient Germanic scourge of Europe, and answered the call to arms with patriotic fervor. Ironically, the Kaiser himself had great admiration for the Huns, especially their leader Attila, who he considered a model of manhood and a superb example of military leadership.

WORLDS IN COLLISION

The international network of trade and commerce that had been built up during the years between 1871 and 1914 came to an abrupt halt with the outbreak of World War I. The belligerents cut off all commerce with their enemies and sought cooperation only from their allies, this being mostly in the form of military aid. The process of globalization that had looked so promising was stopped in its tracks, and did not recommence until after World War II. The industrial nations turned their economies almost exclusively to the production of armaments.

The history of the war itself is well known. The submarine, the machine-gun and the airplane had all been added to the arsenal of weapons since the Franco-Prussian war, and the tank was soon to follow. The deadly effect of modern weapons, which now included the use of lethal gas, combined with the horror of trench warfare, soon revealed the true face of war to the citizen soldiers. The acres of silent crosses that mark the battlefields of France, where so many brave men lost their lives, bear witness to the willingness of the high command on both sides to sacrifice the flower of their manhood for a few yards of territory.

In Russia, Lenin's arrival in 1917 meant the signing of a humiliating peace with the Germans, followed by a brutal civil war. This was followed in turn by the Communist Reign of Terror, initiated by Lenin, and intensified by Stalin after Lenin's death in 1925.

The First World War was indeed a war of almost global proportions, and serves as a seminal example in our study of the phenomenon of war. Most of the European powers were involved, as well as the United States, whose entry in 1917 turned the tide in favor of the Allies. In the Asian theater, the Japanese entered the war on the side of the Allies, and proceeded to seize German possessions in Shantung and the Pacific Islands. But Japan was for the most part able to sit out the war, while continuing to build up her armed forces. The Paris Peace Conference in 1919 awarded the former German possessions in China to Japan.

In spite of the terrible suffering inflicted on all sides, nothing seemed to have really been settled. This was the "war to end all wars," but the outcome actually served to make another war more likely.

The Germans, far from gaining the decisive victory that they had expected, were forced to accept a humiliating peace treaty together with payment of vast sums in war reparations. All the sacrifice of her manhood seemed to have been in vain. The German people felt betrayed by their leaders and sought to redeem their honor. They also sought ways to escape from the onerous terms of the Treaty of Versailles.

The war shattered the economic foundations of pre-war Europe and dislocated trade and commerce around the world. The Russian, Ottoman and Austro-Hungarian empires disintegrated. On top of this, there was a global pandemic of influenza, spread by soldiers returning to their home countries from the European battlefields. This caused 40 million deaths, four times the number of those killed in the war.

To make matters worse, the specter of fascism was beginning to raise its ugly head. This was the new religion of the modern military state, which now began to cast its dark shadow not only over Europe, but also the Far East. It was in part a reaction to the dislocations caused by the war, which encouraged countries to become self-sufficient, in order to insulate themselves from the chaos of the international marketplace. Instead of cooperation, they wanted independence. The first to turn to fascism was Mussolini's Italy, but others followed after the collapse of Wall Street in 1929, and the resulting worldwide depression. Spain, Japan,

Germany, and several South American countries would soon experiment with fascism.[8]

The Russian empire had been replaced by the communist state, which comprised much the same territory, but under a regime even more oppressive than that of the tsars. Stalin's Russia, admired and praised by many of Western Europe's intelligentsia as the face of the future, continued behind the scenes to terrorize its own people through mass starvation and murder. The *gulag* became a new word in the chronicles of human misery—the creation of a paranoid dictator, for all who were suspected of posing a challenge to his power. But in spite of Stalin's cruelties, the machinery of Soviet industry marched forward at an amazing pace, and by the 1930's it had gone a long way towards closing the gap between itself and its Western counterparts.

In Spain, after the fall of the monarchy, the Second Republic was created in 1931. This sought to dismantle much of the structure of privilege that existed in Spanish society. It was also anti-militaristic. The Church, the aristocracy and the military opposed the new Republic, and the next five years were marked by political struggles between left and right. A victory by the Popular Front in 1936 sparked a revolt by the right led by General Francisco Franco, and soon the country was plunged into civil war.

Both sides received aid from the outside. Hitler and Mussolini aided Franco, whereas Russia and the famous International Brigade sided with the Republic. Both the fascists and the communists used the war as a proving ground for their military machines, and this was the first conflict that saw the large scale bombing of civilians. In retrospect the Spanish Civil War appears to have acted as a preview of the horrors of World War II.

By 1939 the forces of reaction were victorious and Franco had installed his fascist regime, to the satisfaction of Hitler and Mussolini. But this left the Spanish people still bitterly divided, and many were forced into exile to escape the harsh reprisals carried out against those who had supported the Republic.

On the other side of the world, also in 1931, the so-called Manchurian Incident occurred. Japanese officers used the excuse of an explosion in Mukden, which they themselves had set, to attack Chinese forces there. The military had precipitated the crisis, without the knowledge of the civilian members of the government. But it was a *fait accompli,* and the Japanese went on to set up the puppet state of Manchukuo, pretending that it was with the consent of the Manchurian people. China appealed this illegal seizure to the League of Nations, which appointed an investigating commission. In consequence, Japan was condemned as an aggressor. But when she walked out of the League, no sanctions were imposed, and a disastrous example was set. Historian W. Scott Morton observes:

> There is little doubt that Mussolini in his adventures in Ethiopia (1935) and Hitler in his occupation of the Ruhr and subsequent mounting acts of aggression looked upon Manchuria as a test case which failed to produce anything beyond harmless verbal condemnation. But it was not only the League that was powerless; the Japanese Foreign Ministry and civilian members of the government were able to do little to stem the advance of the fire-eaters among the military.[9]

The ultimate responsibility rested with the Emperor, who was supreme commander of the armed forces under the constitution. He had failed to rein in the military when this was still possible, and the consequences to Japan and to Asia were catastrophic.

So after only twenty years, another war was looming. Well-armed and militant regimes were threatening the peace. Japan, in the grip of an aggressive military clique, was seeking to expand at the expense of Russia, China and Southeast Asia. Germany, ruled by an unstable demagogue, with a military high command itching to avenge the humiliations of 1918, sought ways to expand at the expense of her neighbors. Italy, in the grips of a fascist dictator, sought an empire in the Mediterranean and in Ethiopia, where she had been humiliated in 1896. Meanwhile France, England and the United States saw the darkening clouds but looked for a silver lining. England wanted to believe that Adolph Hitler could be reasoned with, but nevertheless prepared for war.

Memories of the failed attempts at peace in 1938 and '39 are filled with thoughts of what might have been done to stay the onslaught of the Nazi warmongers. Perhaps things would have been different if a firm stand had been taken earlier. But with the League of Nations impotent to keep the peace, and the dogs of war baying in the Nazi kennels, it's hard to see that any actions by the democracies would have had more than a brief mitigating effect.

On the other side of the world, the Divine Emperor Hirohito had long since become a lackey of his own military establishment. The invasion of China in 1937 marked the start of Japan's move towards hegemony in the western Pacific. In China, Mao Tse-tung, temporarily allied with Chiang Kai-shek in order to fight the Japanese invader, was cautiously courting the Russian bear and planning the ultimate triumph of communism.

The Austrian *Anschluss* and the invasion of Czechoslovakia brought Europe to the brink of war. England finally informed Germany that an invasion of Poland would mean war, but the warning was ignored and German forces poured into a helpless Poland. The Nazi-Soviet pact divided Poland between the two dictatorships, but for Hitler this was only a brief interlude prior to his planned invasion of Russia. The German invasion of France soon had the Allies with their backs to the wall and it was clear to all that victory would be neither easily achieved nor soon in coming.

The Battle of Britain in 1940, and the invasion of Normandy in 1944, marked the first arrest and the beginning of the final death knell of Hitler's Reich. But the turning point of the war undoubtedly came in Russia. It was in the depths of winter before Moscow, and on the plains of western Russia, that the back of the German war machine was ultimately broken, in the titanic struggle between Teuton and Slav.

If there was one major turning point of the war, it came in the great climactic battle for Stalingrad. Both sides staked everything on the outcome of the struggle for this strategic city on the Volga. The battle raged street-by-street and house-by-house throughout the bitter winter of 1942-'43. Piles of rubble became havens for the defenders, and blocked the movement of tanks and field guns. Finally, a counter attack by the Russians succeeded in cutting off the Germans from their supply lines, and the besiegers became the besieged. Hitler ordered the beleaguered Sixth Army to resist to the last man, but Field Marshal Friedrich Paulus decided that further resistance was simply a waste of human lives. So 150,000 Germans were forced to surrender, and the battle, not only for Stalingrad, but also in fact for Russia, was lost for the Germans.[10]

Although the famous tank battle at Kursk was still to come, the tide of war definitely shifted after Stalingrad, and the Nazi invaders were steadily and inexorably pushed back to the lands from whence they came. The pursuit finally ended when the hammer and sickle was raised in triumph over the battered *Reichstag* in Berlin in 1945.[11]

In the Pacific, the Americans had the daunting task of rolling back the Japanese war machine after its attack on Pearl Harbor in December 1941. Here there were two climactic battles. The first at Midway, 1,100 miles northwest of Honolulu, where the Japanese carrier fleet was dealt a crippling blow from which it never fully recovered. The second was at Leyte Gulf in the Philippines, where the Japanese navy suffered another major defeat.

Battles for the strategic pacific islands: Tarawa, Guam, Guadalcanal, Corregidor, Saipan and Iwo-Jima among others, took a fearsome toll in human lives on both sides. Only the atomic bomb prevented further slaughter on the shores of the Japanese homeland, the final objective of the Allied armies.

In the end the combined industrial might of the United States, Great Britain and Russia proved superior to that of the Axis, and ensured ultimate victory for the Allies. But the casualties and the destruction were on a scale unimaginable in the days of Napoleon, or even Kaiser Wilhelm II. The term "total war" had taken on a new meaning. In Russia, the Herculean struggle of the two dictatorships had finally begun to sound the death-knell of the Third Reich, but not before the slaughter and destruction had reached gargantuan proportions. Never had such suffering been visited on a civilian population, and never before had the brutality and savagery of war been displayed in such naked fury. Unspeakable atrocities were committed by the Germans against the people of western Russia and the partisans fighting behind the lines. The partisans themselves were guilty of atrocities against the Germans, together with those who had collaborated with them.

AFTERMATH OF WAR

The indiscriminate bombing of cities and towns meant that civilians were involved in war as never before. The firebombing of Hamburg, Dresden and Tokyo, as well as the atomic destruction of Hiroshima and Nagasaki, to say nothing of the devastation of cities like Stalingrad and Leningrad, are only extreme examples of the general level of destruction. The city of London suffered major damage and 50,000 civilian casualties during the *blitz* of 1940-41. But Berlin was subjected to far worse, and had to endure the final assault of the Soviet armies, who vented their fury on the German capital in revenge for the atrocities committed against their homeland.

The fascist dictatorships of Germany, Italy and Japan having fallen, there remained only that of Franco, who had confined himself mostly to the oppression of his own people. In Russia, Stalin's communist dictatorship retained its iron grip on an exhausted nation, and in China, Mao Tse-tung was about to drive the Nationalists to Formosa and set up the machinery of his Communist Peoples Republic.

The world had by no means seen the end of tyranny, for oppressive regimes were also springing up in Africa, South America and elsewhere. The next forty years saw the two communist giants looking for new fields in which to plant the seeds of revolution.

Instead of being given a chance to recover from the devastation of the war, the Russian people were allowed no respite by a paranoid dictator. Stalin, whose one constructive decision had been to let his generals decide on military strategy during the crisis at Stalingrad, now claimed all credit for the victory himself. General Georgi Zhukov, the real architect of the Russian triumph, was relegated to the background, while Stalin, to divert attention from unrest at home, commenced a ruthless campaign for communist world domination.

Thus the gallant allies of the West, who had played such a decisive role in the defeat of Hitler, were changed overnight into enemies. Stalin renewed the purges of the 1930's with the same ferocity as before. The non-Russian peoples of the Soviet Union were condemned to second-class citizenship, and any signs of incipient nationalism were ruthlessly suppressed. The persecution of the Jews differed only from that carried out by Hitler in the matter of degree.[12]

The resulting cold war split the world into two opposing camps. The "war" was fought on far-flung battlegrounds in many different parts of the world. The quest to win over allies gave no thought to the welfare of ordinary citizens in the countries concerned. Harsh dictators were pandered to in spite of their ugly regimes. Arms and military training were provided so that these despots could fight "subversives," which in practice meant anyone opposed (or thought to be opposed) to the regime. The result in most cases was the harassment, abuse and death of many innocent people.

As historian Fernand Braudel points out, what happened in the cold war transferred the balance-of-power scenario, which had played itself out among the European states for the past few hundred years, onto the global scene. The global balance now adjusted itself around the two superpowers in the same way that the most powerful powers in Europe had attracted coalitions of lesser powers to balance them. But the big difference was the introduction of atomic weapons, which made the old balance-of-power game much more dangerous.[13]

The cold war bred a particularly destructive form of irrationality, not just on the Russian side. Anyone who could be bought with arms or money was accepted as an ally. Vast sums were spent on arms of all kinds. The two main adversaries developed increasingly powerful nuclear weapons, far more than were needed for any legitimate defense, and more and more powerful rockets were designed to deliver them. All this caused heavy strains on the economies of both countries.

The atmosphere of suspicion tended to poison the political climate even in those countries not directly involved.

Even after Stalin died, the cold war lost none of its sting. Nikita Khruschev, sensing weakness in the young American president John F. Kennedy, precipitated a confrontation in Berlin in 1962, followed by the Cuban missile crisis, which very nearly caused a nuclear war. After that the realization slowly set in on both sides that things had begun to get out of hand. In the end the "war" continued, not because there was any real reason for it, but because no one knew how to stop it.

One irony of the cold war was that the Russians were often supporting those who had legitimate grievances against tyrannical regimes, while the United States felt obliged to support these regimes, even while holding its nose. Those who received aid from the Russians were perceived as being communist pawns. This gave the United States an excuse for opposing the valid grievances of those who were oppressed. On the other hand, the Americans were also found supporting "revolutionaries," basically gangsters, against established governments supported by Russia, as in Angola and Nicaragua. Needless to say, the legitimate aspirations of the poor and the oppressed remained unmet.

All in all the cold war was a disaster for all concerned, but it was Stalin who had started it, and there the responsibility must lie. The idea put forward by some in the West that the United States was as responsible as Russia for the cold war is clearly a fiction. In fact, as Robert Conquest tells us in *The Dragons of Expectation,* it was Stalin alone who bore the ultimate responsibility, while many in the Soviet Union were actually in favor of detente with the West. The communist parties in the West were instructed to pursue the aim of world domination by any means possible, and anyone suspected of insufficient zeal for the cause was promptly eliminated. At the same time, all proposals by the Allies for compromise were immediately swept aside.

Although America could be said to have won the cold war, Russia came out with at least one positive result. In losing the war, the Russians managed to rid themselves of communism! Surely that was a significant bonus. Not that the situation in Russia improved right away, but at least she was finally on the right track and in a position where progress was possible. The Russians also lost their empire—for the second time in a century—and this should prove beneficial, since all the other empires have now been terminated, with no appreciable harm to the parties involved.

For all its heavy-handedness, the United States—at least domestically—came out more or less unscathed. The witch-hunts of Joe McCarthy were mild (except to their victims) compared to those of Stalin or Mao Tse-tung, whose ruthless pursuit of capitalist sympathizers made McCarthy seem like a Sunday school teacher. But the support of unsavory regimes for political motives would come back to haunt America.

The futility of the cold war was exposed immediately after it ended, when the two erstwhile bitter enemies started to cooperate as if there had never been any serious differences between them. The space program, which had been at the heart of their rivalry, instantly changed into a co-operative effort, with both countries sending astronauts to the other's space stations in a spirit of friendship and cordiality.

At the dawn of the twenty-first century, conventional wars, although still frequent, seem to be on the wane. It is doubtful that anything like the two world wars of the twentieth century will occur again, at least not in the immediate future. Even so, we are finding new ways of dividing the world into us versus them.

Guerrilla wars are the most likely kind to occur in the future. But the terrorist and the fanatic are now the main threats to the industrial powers, rather than aggression from other nations. Ways will be sought to counter these threats by increasingly sophisticated technology and all manner of electronic surveillance. This can result in a serious loss of individual rights by the average citizen.

The terrorist attacks on New York and Washington in 2001 showed just how lethal such attacks could be, when a well-financed group of fanatics carry out a strike that is carefully planned and executed. The kamikazes of World War II introduced this new kind of atrocity to the world. One shudders to think what such people could do with an atomic bomb. And it is not just the atomic bomb or the chemical weapon that we now have to fear. In addition, we have the possibility of the "cyber-terrorist," who could access control systems through some sophisticated electronic device, and cause havoc by issuing false instructions to computers that control government operations, air traffic, or vital communications networks.

Since they target civilians, terrorists are considered to be common criminals by their victims. Terrorism is not a legitimate means of making war for those who have no need to use it. But in reality, there are no legitimate or illegitimate ways to win wars. Wars have always been fought with any tactics that are available, regardless of how brutal or "illegitimate" they may be, and civilians can never expect to be spared. The notion that civilians are not targeted in war is just pious nonsense. Civilians have always been considered as part of the "enemy," and have been attacked whenever this would cause additional harm to an opponent.[14] With the coming of air power, however, the targeting of civilians has occurred on a much larger scale. The Japanese and the Germans attacked civilians on a regular basis in World War II. But the firebombing of major cities, such as Dresden, Hamburg and Tokyo, to say nothing of Hiroshima and Nagasaki, was done with full knowledge that it would result in appalling civilian losses.[15]

The motives of the current crop of Islamic terrorists are not immediately apparent. A vague "hatred of modernity" does not seem to be a convincing answer. Although some have argued that Al Qaeda's wrath has been aimed at the American military presence in the Middle East, Afghanistan and elsewhere, this too is not wholly convincing. The American invasions of Iraq and Afghanistan occurred after 9/11, so there may be other reasons involved. Obviously the terrorists have very strong motivations, for they are willing to sacrifice their lives for their "cause." The West, and especially America, would be making a great mistake in thinking that there are no legitimate reasons behind their hatred of the West. The feeling that they have been humiliated and exploited by the "white" Westerners has caused intense feelings of envy and hatred in the Moslem and developing worlds. Americans have been slow to acknowledge the existence of this hatred, since their intentions are usually good. They tend to see the problem as basically the inadequacy of the Moslems, who have failed to modernize their societies as the West has done.

Another explanation, that "the terrorists' only true cause is global Islamic dominion" is espoused by Olivier Roy, author of *Globalized Islam*. This involves a sort of global jihad, which at first sight seems utterly outlandish. But most fanatics have hopelessly impractical goals, so this explanation may in fact be close to the truth.[16]

The imagination often seeks supernatural explanations or remedies to problems that are not properly understood, and a lot of this sort of thing has been going on in the world of Islam. As Lee Harris explains in his book, *Civilization and Its Enemies*, radical Islam has become a "fantasy ideology." Harris says that 9/11 was the enactment of a fantasy.

> The terror attack of 9/11 was not designed to make us alter our policy but was crafted for its effect on the terrorists themselves and on those who share the same fantasy ideology: it was a spectacular piece of theater.... The unlooked-for collapse [of the Towers] gave to the event—in terms of Al-Qaeda's fantasy ideology—an even greater poignancy: precisely because it had not been part of

the original calculations, it was immediately interpreted as a manifestation of divine intervention. The nineteen hijackers did not bring down the towers; God did.[17]

The so-called war on terror is not a war in the conventional sense, so cannot be fought by conventional means. It's doubtful if it can actually be "won" at all. Discovery of the *exact* motives and intentions of the terrorists would surely be a positive first step in combating this scourge. People who blow themselves up on airplanes, trains and buses are not crazy in the conventional sense. It's just that their worldview has been turned upside down by some sort of extremist ideology, or by the mindless pursuit of an impossible dream.

PART II
THE BIGGER PICTURE

o o o o o o o o o o o o o o o o o o o o o o o o o o o o o o o o o
Scientific knowledge and technical mastery of nature daily win new and unprecedented victories. But in man's practical and social life the defeat of rational thought seems to be complete and irrevocable.

—*Ernst Cassirer*
The Myth of the State

PRELIMINARY THOUGHTS

Let us take a deep breath at this juncture, and consider how far we have come in our quest for insight into the character and behavior of the human animal. Most of you will agree that as far as history is concerned, the first part of this volume has been woefully inadequate. A mass of important material has been left out, and those parts that did find their way in have been excessively abbreviated.

Well, no attempt was made to write history in the conventional sense. I warned you at the beginning that what I was after was an *overall* picture of the human context, with primary emphasis on what I consider to be the four most important areas in which man differs from his fellow animals: science, culture, religion and war. I freely admit that in the realm of culture I have left a lot out. This is partly due to sheer ignorance on my part, but also to the fact that much of the vast subject of human culture is only peripheral to our quest. The development of culture—or the evolution of culture if you will—is important to the story only in so far as it has led to genuine progress towards a more civilized human society. Aspects of culture such as art and literature measure this to a certain extent. But they may vary greatly from one geographical location to another. This makes them more valuable as indications of the differences between the various cultures, rather than as an objective standard by which the progress of mankind as a whole can be evaluated. On the other hand, science and technology are much more reliable barometers of human progress, so they have been given greater emphasis than some of the other, more subjective, aspects of culture. Since they transcend national boundaries, science and technology are culturally independent. They are universally accepted as the means by which man can improve his material and intellectual condition.

At the dawn of the new millennium, advances in science, especially in the realm of biology, give us hope for a more enlightened to-morrow. But the forces of ignorance will not be easily overcome. Irrational beliefs and hatreds, those potent barriers to progress, are still threatening to destroy us as we struggle towards a better future.

When talking about religion, it is important to note that God and religion do not necessarily go together, certainly not if one considers the broader definition of religion that I prefer. But even if we stick to the more conventional meaning, we find that some religions, such as Buddhism for instance, are basically non-theistic, in that they get along quite well without any specific reference to a deity. In any case, I wish to discuss belief in a much wider sense than just conventional religious belief, which is really only one aspect of a much wider phenomenon. Thus I have introduced "secular" religions, such as nationalism, which have much in common with ordinary religious beliefs, without including any concept of God.

What has been stressed above all else is war, that most distinctively human activity, which has been man's constant companion from time immemorial. It almost seems as if mankind's principle activity has been either fighting wars or preparing for them. Advances in technology have fueled the search for better and more lethal weapons, resulting in ever more destructive wars. This process reached its climax in the truly horrendous levels of destruction that occurred in the twentieth century.

It might be argued that most of this recent violence has been caused by a handful of evil, deranged, or just ruthless and ambitious men. These include Napoleon, Bismarck, Kaiser Wilhem I and II, Lenin, Stalin, Hitler, Mao and Tojo as some of the worst offenders. They are the leaders of the various nations that engaged in excessive brutality and aggression. With the possible exception of Bismarck, none of them could have been mistaken for a statesman. (Actually, Machiavelli would have considered Bismarck to be the ideal statesman.)

One is tempted to say that without these particular leaders much bloodshed and suffering could very well have been avoided. But this idea is altogether too simplistic, because none of them would have gotten anywhere without willing accomplices. It was really their ability to transport their followers into a world of fantasy that made them so powerful. There always seems to be a steady supply of individuals of this kind. All they need is the right set of circumstances to put their particular talents to work. The horrendous levels of violence that have been produced by such individuals in more recent times merely reflect the ever-increasing power and availability of weaponry. The existence of better communications and transportation has enhanced their ability to recruit and organize large numbers of fighting men. The addition of some kind of ideology to this mix has served to further increase the scale of destruction that these people are capable of. But the type of leader that is able to ignite this sort of mayhem is no different now than in the past. If one imagines what Genghis Khan or Attila the Hun could have done with a few panzer divisions or missiles at their disposal, one realizes that it is not the leaders that have become more lethal, but the instruments at their command.

Some have attributed the rise of German militarism to the influence of Karl von Clausewitz on German leaders in the 19th and 20th centuries. His book *On War* advanced the notion that war and politics were inextricably linked, and this idea was extremely influential, not only in Germany but throughout the rest of Europe as well.

Clausewitz (1780-1831) was a Prussian general during the Napoleonic wars, and his book was not published until after his death. He advanced the idea of "total war"—that all citizens, territory and property of the enemy should be attacked in any way possible. According to military historian John Keegan:

> Clausewitz's intellectual ambitions verged on the megalomaniac. Like his near contemporary Marx, he claimed to have penetrated the inner and fundamental reality of the phenomenon that he took as his subject. He did not deal in advice; he dealt in what he insisted were inescapable truths…. *On War* was a book with a slow fuse. By the time the Prussian army came to fight its wars for hegemony in Germany, however, his ideas had penetrated it, and the victories it won in 1866 and 1870-1 ensured that they would thereafter direct the course of the new German empire as well. By an irresistible process of osmosis, they then percolated throughout the whole European military establishment; by 1914, it is true to say that its outlook was as Clausewitzian as the continent's coalition of socialist and revolutionary movements was Marxist.[1]

To shift the blame for all the horrors of the 19th and 20th centuries onto Clausewitz is obviously going too far. But there is no doubt that his influence was very potent in the thinking of both politicians and military men of that period. It's tempting to ascribe the rise of militarism to this kind of thinking. But the "citizen army," originating with the French Revolution, probably had more influence on its rise than did Clausewitz.

Without question, man can be a nasty and aggressive animal, but as previously pointed out, if he had not had such traits, he would almost certainly have been extinct by now. Our selfishness has been basic to our survival, as Richard Dawkins explains eloquently in *The Selfish Gene*. The selfishness of our genes has been our most valuable asset. According to Dawkins, it is the genes rather than the species that are "selected for" in Darwin's theory of evolution.[2] However, not only selfishness, but also altruism occurs in nature, so this concept must also be included in our view of the evolutionary process.

Altruism appears at first sight to run counter to the theory of evolution, because, rather than perpetuating one's genes, one is sacrificing them for others. But an individual's genes are shared by other people, especially by those in a tight-knit group, and even more so by one's next of kin. So the closer the kinship, the stronger should be the impulse towards altruism. And this in fact is what one sees in nature, although selfishness is by far the most dominant characteristic.

Altruism complements rather than contradicts the theory of the selfish gene. People can actually be both selfish *and* altruistic, and still not violate the dictates of evolution. The latest thinking seems to be that the theory of evolution can be applied to groups as well as to individuals. According to psychologists David and Ann Premack,

> "The problem of altruism has disappeared because evolutionary theory now accepts what it rejected earlier: evolution at the level of the group as well as at the level of the individual."[3]

This analysis puts altruism on a much firmer footing. But the present challenge lies in taming our more aggressive survival instincts, now that they have become part of the problem, rather than part of the solution, as they were previously.

The combination of strongly held beliefs and aggressive behavior seems to be one of our most serious shortcomings. The division of society into friend and foe, believer and unbeliever is now no longer an option if we are to build any kind of civilized global society. Tolerance is the only acceptable choice, but it has been in very short supply throughout human history. It is to be hoped that greater insights into the origins of war, and gratuitous violence in general, will aid in the eventual elimination of such barbaric behavior. But the taming of the beast will surely not be easy.

In what follows I will take an even broader view than in the first part, where I sought to explain the basic context in which we find ourselves. After a quick survey of some major scientific achievements, we will look at our place in the larger cosmic realm, with its vast oceans of space and myriad galaxies, stretching back all the way to its origin in the Big Bang.

The core subjects of science, technology, religion and war will continue to hold center stage. The bewildering concepts of consciousness and mind are now a legitimate part of the domain of science, so these will be examined in some detail. The laws of physics will also be looked at from several different points of view. Those wary of things mathematical or technical should not find these sections unduly challenging.

Other subjects relating to culture will also be discussed; these include politics, law, morality, work, art, philosophy and sports. In the philosophical realm, all opinions are necessarily subjective, so I do not necessarily agree with those who are quoted. For instance, Nietzsche is frequently cited in regard to things like good and evil. By giving his views I hope to bring a balance to the discussion, since he is often impatient with conventional opinions. But even his most outrageous views have verve and panache. Walter Kaufmann, his biographer and translator, has this to say about him:

> Unlike most scholars, Nietzsche sees vital things and has the power to communicate them vividly. And as he himself noted at twenty-three: The errors of great men are more fruitful than the truths of little men.[4]

The indispensable key to insight into the human condition is the theory of evolution, with its central concept of natural selection. Someone who does not accept this theory, at least in its main outlines, is missing the whole picture. Until someone thinks of something better, which seems very unlikely, Darwin's theory will remain the only satisfactory account of our origins.

Once one understands the basic mechanism of evolution, the whole process of biological development suddenly becomes comprehensible. Vast eons of time are necessary for it to do its work. The process of natural selection is incredibly slow. But given enough time it can produce wonders—the human brain for instance.

It is a shame that many people are afraid to leave the comforting harbor of old beliefs, lest they become wrecked on some new and alien shore. Modern science threatens the old certainties on every side. But the truth is that the old certainties are not capable of adapting to a changing world, and the tension between the old and the new becomes greater all the time. However, once the choice is made to look beyond the bounds of our traditional beliefs, a whole new world opens up, one that is much more exciting than the static world of established truths, which has little place for new ideas.

Those who reject evolution because it seems to contradict their deeply held religious beliefs, have fallen into the old trap of trying to mix religion with science, just as the Catholic Church did in the days of Galileo. Science and religion simply do not go together, they are basically incompatible. Religious truth and scientific truth are quite different. Religious truth is absolute and cannot be questioned; it is accepted on faith. Scientific truth is provisional and needs experimental verification; it can never be established beyond doubt. Biological evolution is a well-established and well-tested scientific theory, which has held up magnificently under innumerable attacks from those who have wished to discredit it. Its detailed mechanism is just now beginning to be revealed in all its majestic and subtle detail. Those who refuse to accept evolution will never be able to make sense of human behavior, because it is the key to the human condition. We will therefore look at its implications from several different viewpoints.

The continued proliferation of violence forces us to ask serious questions regarding the future of the human race. Are we doomed to continue this self-destructive behavior, and so risk ultimate extinction? Will it become necessary to change human nature itself? And if we acquire the means to do so, how can we be sure that any change would be for the better? These are questions that cannot be answered at the present time. Hopefully such radical solutions will not be necessary. But our addiction to war must surely be met and conquered if our life on earth is to have any kind of viable future.

9

SCIENTIFIC MILESTONES

Physical concepts are free creations of the human mind, and are
not, however it may seem, uniquely determined by the external
world.

—Albert Einstein
Evolution of Physics

FOUNDATIONS OF SCIENCE

Although our ancestors in different cultures thought seriously about physical science—in Greece Democritus discussed an atomic theory as early as 400 B.C.—it
was only the "pure" science of mathematics that got a solid start in the early days.
As opposed to physical science, which postulates a theory and then tests it by
experiment, mathematics is essentially abstract in character. It proves "theorems"
by logical deduction from a set of assumptions, or axioms.

We will see later that the abstract nature of mathematics poses questions as to
the validity of the laws that we have formulated to describe the physical universe.
Is mathematics really the language of nature, as Galileo and Newton thought, or
have we forced it into a mathematical matrix that does not accurately reflect its
essential reality? These questions will be considered at the end of this chapter, and
also in chapters 11 and 14.

The early agricultural communities of the Middle East, India and China made
observations of the moon and planets, which led to predictions of lunar eclipses,
some of which were surprisingly accurate. They were also interested in mathematics—for instance, the Babylonians apparently knew about Pythagoras' theo-

rem c.2000 B.C.[1] Nevertheless it was the Greeks who succeeded in putting mathematics on a solid foundation.

Thales of Miletus is said to have brought the knowledge of geometry from Egypt c.600 B.C. and developed it into a series of theorems.[2] His work was continued by Pythagoras, and later by Euclid. It should be pointed out that Euclid's geometry developed out of practical pursuits such as surveying. For instance, it was noticed that on a flat surface the internal angles of a triangle add up to two right angles. So even though mathematics is an abstract science, its origins lie in observations of the natural world. Incidentally, Pythagoras' theorem showed that there were *irrational* numbers. A right-angled triangle, with the two short sides of unit length, has a hypotenuse whose length is the square root of two, an irrational number. (An irrational number is one that cannot be expressed as a fraction.)

Can an irrational length like $\sqrt{2}$, which in its decimal form has an infinite number of digits that never repeat, be actually "measured" in the real world? We see from this simple example that Pythagoras' theorem is actually part of the abstract (Platonic) mathematician's world. The Pythagoreans did not consider quantities like $\sqrt{2}$ to be numbers at all, even though a geometrical "length" could be irrational. To get around this problem, they treated such lengths as geometric objects and developed an ingenious "theory of proportions" to deal with them. It wasn't until the nineteenth century that mathematicians like Dedekind and Hilbert were able to incorporate these numbers into the mathematical lexicon. This revealed the subtle connection between arithmetic and geometry.[3]

About the third century A.D.—the exact date is uncertain—Diophantus began to investigate algebraic equations. He looked for equations with positive integer solutions, and such equations are now referred to as "Diophantine." His ideas set in motion the study of numbers, which gradually expanded into the vast edifice of abstract concepts that makes up the modern world of mathematics.

The Arabs and the Indians built on the foundations that the Greeks had laid down, by giving us algebra and the decimal system respectively. The Moors—Moslems who occupied Spain until the fifteenth century—transmitted many of these ideas to the West, where they provided much of the inspiration for the birth of modern physics, which took place in the sixteenth century, when the first giants of Western science: Copernicus, Kepler and Galileo came onto the scene.

Nicolaus Copernicus, in his book *De Revolutionibus Orbium Coelestium,* or *On the Revolutions of the Celestial Spheres,* asserted that it is the sun, rather than the earth, which is at the center of our solar system. The book was published after his death in 1543, as he was afraid of the controversy that it might cause if published in his lifetime. His fears were indeed justified, because the Catholic Inquisition duly condemned the book. The Church maintained, as Plato and Ptolemy had done, that the earth was the center of the solar system. The earth therefore did not move; it was the sun that moved. It is worth noting that Aristarchus of Samos (c.310-230 B.C.) also proposed a heliocentric system, but the idea was considered to be contrary to the Greek religion. Forgotten until the sixteenth century, it was again considered heretical, this time by the Christian Church!

Tycho Brahe (1546-1601) was an eccentric Dane who made extensive observations of the planets, from which Johannes Kepler worked out his laws of planetary motion. Kepler endorsed the heliocentric theory of Copernicus, and after much painstaking work, found that the planets moved in ellipses rather than circles, as had been previously asserted. Although this explained the movements of the planets, it did not *prove* that it was the earth, rather than the sun, that moved. This had to wait until Newton's time.

With the development of the telescope, Galileo was able to confirm Kepler's laws. But unlike Copernicus, he published his work openly. This precipitated his famous trial by the Inquisition, which had already condemned the work of Copernicus. The trial ended with Galileo being forced to renounce his work in order to avoid execution. At age 74 he was confined to house arrest in Siena. Later he was allowed to live near Florence, where he continued experiments relating to the law of gravity. In spite of being nearly blind, he produced some of his finest work in his later years. Incidentally, the Church did not admit that it was wrong about Galileo until well into the twentieth century.

By the latter half of the seventeenth century, Isaac Newton had introduced his theory of gravitation, which expressed Kepler's laws in mathematical form. He then went on to propose his three famous laws of motion, which were later codified into the conservation laws of Energy, Momentum and Angular Momentum. These have remained the cornerstones of physics up to the present day.

Newton's astonishing achievements were all the more remarkable since he was the son of an illiterate farmer. But he was not very attractive on a personal level. Although he became president of England's prestigious Royal Society of scientists, he treated his fellow members with considerable disdain. When Gottfried Leibniz invented the calculus independently, Newton refused to correspond with him. He spent the last years of his life dabbling in the occult, trying to make contact with the spirits of the dead.

By the time of Newton's death in 1727, man's awareness of his place in the universe had changed forever—from an earth-centered world to a heliocentric solar system, with the "fixed" stars and constellations located on some kind of huge sphere beyond. Man's basic image of nature had also changed—to a mechanical universe, where the earth moved according to physical laws based on mathematics, and where the movement of all objects could be predicted from these laws.[4] Instead of random motion, there was order. Everything seemed to operate like clockwork. God had made the clock, and then just wound it up and left it to run by itself.

With the help of Gutenberg's printing press, which was invented in the fifteenth century, these ideas began to spread gradually from the educated few to the general populace. Meanwhile the Industrial Revolution was well under way, and other branches of science were also making progress. This was true of medicine, which up until the seventeenth century was based mainly on the writings of the second century Greek physician Galen. But anatomical studies in the late Middle Ages showed much of Galen's teaching to be erroneous, and corrections were gradually made. The first real breakthrough came when William Harvey (1578-1657) demonstrated the circulation of the blood.

Further progress was made in the eighteenth century with the introduction of a smallpox vaccine, and by the nineteenth century modern medicine had begun to take shape. But genuine knowledge of the inner workings of the body, including the structure of the cell and the process of cell division, would have to wait until the twentieth century.

NINETEENTH CENTURY HIGHLIGHTS

The development of mathematics was rapid from the seventeenth century onwards, with such greats as Fermat, Euler, Lagrange and Gauss contributing to advances in number theory, which had been initiated by Diophantus. In the nineteenth century, the development of complex numbers by Gauss; of number fields by Galois (who died tragically in a duel at the age of 21); and group theory by Cauchy, Lie and others, ushered in the era of modern mathematics. Bernhard Riemann made important advances in geometry, and pioneered the mathematical treatment of curved surfaces and multi-dimensional spaces.

Among the many outstanding physical scientists of the nineteenth century, two stand out in particular: Michael Faraday and James Clark Maxwell. These two were responsible for the introduction of the theory of electromagnetism, which lies at the heart of modern physics. Faraday introduced the idea of an electric field and Maxwell formulated the basic equations of electromagnetism.

Chemistry also made significant progress with the discovery of the periodic table by Dmitri Mendeleev. This was a major step towards unraveling the mystery of how matter is composed, and paved the way for major breakthroughs in the twentieth century.

Up till now we have only considered those branches of science that are based on mathematics. But of course there are many others that do not have a mathematical basis. Sciences such as geology, archaeology, biology and anthropology are all essential to the study of the human condition, and these began to make significant progress during the nineteenth century. But it was the English naturalist Charles Darwin who made the greatest intellectual breakthrough with his book *Origin of Species,* which was published in 1859, and was followed by *The Descent of Man* in 1871. From that time onwards, the self-image of the human animal would never be the same.

The first jolt had come when Copernicus had pushed mankind away from the center of the universe. But this was much more serious. The theory of evolution pictured him as descended from other animals, specifically apes, and not specially created by God, as he had previously assumed. It was a big blow to man's ego, and the reaction was swift, especially from the Church. The first natural response was to brand the whole thing as false, and even in the twenty-first century there are still those that refuse to accept evolution. Ironically Darwin, who was a believer, did not intend his theory to deny that God had created life. In fact, as Daniel Dennett points out in *Darwin's Dangerous Idea,* the title of Darwin's first book, *Origin of Species,* was unfortunate, since it did not really deal with the origin of life, only with the way new species develop from those that already exist—through the process of natural selection.[5]

Like Copernicus before him, Darwin was anxious not to upset the powers that be, but it was all to no avail, the cat was now out of the bag. Of course he had many defenders, who thought his theory was magnificent (as indeed it was), but, as he himself had feared, his work was met with less than universal acclaim.

Mendel's laws regarding heredity, although published in Darwin's lifetime, were unknown to him. But when these laws became widely known at the end of the nineteenth century, they cleared up a problem that Darwin himself had wrestled with. It was commonly held that sexual reproduction led to a blending of traits or characteristics in the offspring of species. This blending tended to wipe out *variation,* which was necessary for Darwin's theory of natural selection to operate effectively. However, Mendel showed that the characteristics were not blended, but appeared unchanged in subsequent generations, even though they would sometimes skip a generation. If Darwin had known about this all would have been well. Ironically, a copy of Mendel's work was found in Darwin's library after his death—but it was apparently unopened.

Although Darwin thought that acquired characteristics could be inherited, which turned out not to be correct, this was not part of his theory of natural selection. One of the first proponents of evolution, J-B Lamarck, had advocated this idea, and so Darwin, who respected Lamark's thinking, simply went along with it. The fact that he did so does not detract from the overall significance of his work.

The final synthesis of Darwin's theory with the work of Mendel, now known as neo-Darwinism, was not achieved until the 1940's. As Gerald Edelman writes:

> This "modern synthesis" accounted (as Darwin could not) for the origin of genetic variation as mutations in deoxyribonucleic acid (or DNA) as well as for the rearrangement of genetic structures in a process called recombination.[6]

The general body of Darwin's work has stood up magnificently to incessant attacks from all sides. The discovery of the structure of the DNA molecule by James Watson and Francis Crick in 1953, which will be discussed later, further demonstrated the validity of Darwin's theory.[7] Evolution is now acknowledged by the scientific community as the only legitimate account of the development of living species.

The prevailing assumption in Darwin's time was that species had been created independently, in the locations where they were found at the time. The supposition that the earth was only a few thousand years old seemed to support this. But it was beginning to become apparent, by looking at the geological record, that the earth was in fact much older, and Darwin showed that independent creation was a completely erroneous reading of the evidence. He asserted that *all* life had a common origin, and that all species, belonging to all genera, families, orders and classes, were ultimately descended from the earliest and simplest forms of life.

Sir Charles Lyell (1797-1875) had done much pioneering work in geology, a relatively new science in the nineteenth century, and Darwin was able to use both the fossil evidence and the newly acquired knowledge of the various geological epochs, to support his ideas. From these geological discoveries, and from observations made during his worldwide travels on the research ship *Beagle* (1831-36), Darwin was led to the conclusion that the present distribution of species could best be explained by their having been transported from one geographical location to another. The means by which this was accomplished is explained at length in *The Origin*. Some of his best insights come from taking into account the most recent glacial period, or ice age, and by showing how this affected the way that the various species have become distributed throughout the world's continents. Here are some of his thoughts about the basic unity of all life.

> If the difficulties be not insuperable in admitting that in the long course of time the individuals of the same species, and likewise of allied species, have proceeded from some one source; then I think all the grand leading facts of geographical distribution are explicable on the theory of migration (generally of the more dominant forms of life), together with subsequent modification and the multiplication of new forms.... We can thus understand the localization of sub-genera, genera, and families; and how it is that under different latitudes, for instance in South America, the inhabitants of plains and mountains, of the forests, marshes, and deserts, are in so mysterious a manner linked together by affinity, and are likewise linked to the extinct beings which formally inhabited the same continent.[8]

The multitude of genera and species, and also the many varieties that do not qualify as separate species, were all carefully documented and analyzed by Darwin, especially with respect to their location and distribution. The vast number of existing species, and the even greater number of those that have become extinct and can only be found in the fossil record, made the whole enterprise a monumental task. But even though the record was incomplete—and Darwin himself was very much aware of this—he showed that the only satisfactory explanation that fitted the facts was his theory of natural selection. This is basically the survival of the fittest, meaning that slight variations in the offspring of organisms (we now know that these are caused by mutations in the genes), if they happen to be beneficial in the struggle for survival, will cause these organisms to eventually displace the ones that are not so well adapted to their environment. And indeed as time has gone by, and more evidence has accumulated, this explanation has remained the only one that adequately fits the facts.

Even though the general public was loath to accept Darwin's ideas, his professional colleagues gradually came around to supporting him, especially the younger ones. One of his stoutest defenders was the anatomist Thomas Huxley, who had a famous debate about evolution with the Bishop of Oxford, Samuel Wilberforce, in 1860.

The good bishop was not particularly interested in how other species had arisen. It was the origin of man that concerned him most, and he insisted that mankind had been specially created by God and was not the mere product of natural selection.

But Darwin provided convincing evidence that this was in fact so. Here is some of what he has to say about man:

> His body is constructed on the same homological plan as that of other mammals. He passes through the same phases of embryological development. He retains many rudimentary and useless structures, which no doubt were once serviceable. Characters occasionally make their re-appearance in him, which we have reason to believe were possessed by his early progenitors. If the origin of man had been wholly different from that of all other animals, these various appearances would be mere empty deceptions; but such an admission is incredible. These appearances, on the other hand, are intelligible, at least to a large extent, if man is the co-descendant with other mammals of some unknown and lower form.[9]

Evolutionary theory has been applied not only to living species but also to society and culture among other things, and this will be discussed later. So let's leave Darwin and his theory for the moment and return to science based on mathematics.

In the nineteenth century, mathematics began to break up into specialized areas: the theory of functions, differential equations, groups, matrices, tensor analysis, as well as the old staples of number theory, calculus and geometry. In many instances these studies were undertaken purely as exercises in abstract thought, without any practical applications in sight. But in fact quite a few of them eventually did find applications in physical science. One example is tensor analysis, which was used by Einstein to present his general theory of relativity. Another is quantum mechanics, which relies heavily on the theory of complex numbers, and also Lie groups. Lie groups and Lie algebras became very important tools in particle physics during the twentieth century. Their inventor, Sophus Lie (1842-1899) was a pioneer of "continuous" groups, which were also used in other areas such as differential equations.[10] More about Sophus Lie in chapter 14.

THE TWENTIETH CENTURY

Now let us look for a moment at man's understanding of his environment at the beginning of the twentieth century. A question that had been asked since biblical times concerned the age of the earth. One of the first attempts at an answer was given by St Augustine in the fourth century. By using biblical genealogies, he estimated the age of the earth (and the universe) to be about 6,000 years. Various estimates at later dates—some giving the actual day of creation—did not differ much from this until the nineteenth century. Darwin guessed the earth's age at roughly 400 million years, but it was not until the advent of methods using the decay of radioactive elements in rocks, that the true age of the earth became apparent. By 1956, using such methods, the age of the solar system was estimated at about 3 billion years, and the present figure is around 4.6 billion. The age of the universe is now estimated to be about 15 billion years.[11]

Investigations into the size of the universe have also produced a completely different picture, even from the days of Isaac Newton. A major contributor to our knowledge in this field was Edwin Hubble (1889-1953), who discovered huge star systems, or galaxies, beyond the Milky Way, and was able to show that the universe is in fact expanding. Einstein later supplied an explanation for this. Now, with the Hubble telescope, we are able to see vast distances—over thirteen billion light years—enabling us to see stars and galaxies from a time when the universe was much younger than it is now.

Not only the extent of the universe, but also the nature of space and time began to be examined in greater detail in the twentieth century. Einstein has been mentioned only in passing, but of course he has been tremendously influential in shaping our views of the physical universe. Newton envisaged absolute space and time, meaning that the yardsticks with which they are measured do not change in different frames of reference. Einstein destroyed this Newtonian world and substituted space-time, where measurement depends on relative motion. The key postulate in Einstein's special theory of relativity—dealing with reference frames in linear motion at constant speed—is the constancy of the velocity of light. Light is always found to have the same velocity regardless of the motion of its source, or that of an observer. This led to a completely new conception of space and time.

The *general* theory of relativity deals with frames of reference that are *accelerated* with respect to one another. Einstein's major insight, that gravity and acceleration are essentially equivalent—the equality of gravitational and inertial mass—led to his theory of gravitation.

[Say you are standing in a closed box, which—as far as you are concerned—could be anywhere. Without looking outside the box, you cannot tell whether you are in a gravitational field, which is pulling you down towards the floor of the box, or the box is being accelerated upwards, causing the floor to push upwards on your feet. The two possibilities are interchangeable.]

Einstein postulated that gravity is due to the curving of space-time, the curvature being caused by material objects within the space. The curvature, or warping of space, causes objects to accelerate towards one another *as if* a gravitational force is acting upon them. In Einstein's general theory it is the *curvature* of space-time, rather than the *force* of gravity, which causes bodies to move towards one another. This was a radical departure from Newton's conception of gravity, and showed the breadth and originality of Einstein's ideas.

In both his theories of relativity, rather than trying to fit a new theory into the existing framework of space and time, Einstein abolished the old framework and created a completely new one. This brilliant conceptual breakthrough helped usher in major advances in physics in the twentieth century.

There is no question that Einstein's two theories of relativity are among the most brilliant achievements of the human mind.

Now we move on to the big topics of the twentieth century. Having briefly discussed relativity, the next big item is quantum mechanics, or QM. This is a difficult subject for almost everybody, and not even its creators fully understood it. This is what string theorist Brian Greene has to say about QM:

> Unlike relativity, few if any people ever grasp quantum mechanics on a "soulful" level. What are we to make of this? Does it mean that on a microscopic level the universe operates in ways so obscure and unfamiliar that the human mind, evolved over eons to cope with phenomena on familiar everyday scales, is unable to grasp "what really goes on"? Or, might it be that through historical accident physicists have constructed an extremely awkward formulation of quantum mechanics that, although quantitatively successful, obfuscates the true nature of reality? No one knows.[12]

Because of its abstruse nature, quantum mechanics has acquired an almost mystic stature, somewhat like a religion. But it is actually a rarefied branch of mathematical physics. Max Planck probably has the best claim to the title of founder of QM, since he was the first to solve the "black body" problem.[13] Niels

Bohr, Werner Heisenberg, P.A.M. Dirac and Erwin Schröedinger were among the "disciples."

Einstein was never comfortable with quantum mechanics, because of its statistical nature—dealing with probabilities rather than definite quantities. However, it was he who confirmed Planck's original idea concerning the black body, when he discovered the photoelectric effect. This established that the energy of electromagnetic waves comes in little packets, or photons.

Readers who know something about QM are probably familiar with some of its strange aspects. Its essence is revealed in the famous double-slit experiment. Here a light shines towards a barrier with two narrow slits in it. Behind the barrier is a photographic plate that records the pattern of light passing through the slits. The results show that strange things happen. The light acts like a wave, with interference between the two beams issuing from the slits. But when the intensity of the light is significantly reduced, *single* photons of light appear to pass through *both* slits, and interfere with *themselves*!

These phenomena are described by means of wave functions—otherwise known as state functions—which represent the exact "state" of an object or system.

Another fairly well known feature of QM, apart from the fact that energy comes in little lumps, is Heisenberg's uncertainty principle. This states that the exact location and momentum of an object cannot both be known simultaneously. If the location is known exactly, the momentum will be indeterminate, and vice versa. Such is the peculiar nature of the quantum world. But it turns out that this subtle little quirk of the quantum process permits many important reactions to occur that would not otherwise be possible. "Virtual particles," which appear to violate the law of conservation of energy, and which mediate many reactions between particles, can get away with such violations only because of the uncertainty principle. So, far from being just an interesting detail, it is a vital part of quantum mechanics.

The wave function formulation gives rise to the idea of "superposition of states," whereby an object can be in two or more states simultaneously. But when an observation is made, the wave function "collapses" into a single state. A famous example of this involves Schröedinger's cat, where the poor animal is kept inside a closed box, and its wave function consists of the superposition of two states: "cat is alive" and "cat is dead." Only by opening the box can one ascertain which state the cat is actually in, and if the box remains closed, the cat continues to be both alive *and* dead.

Finally there is the many-worlds interpretation of quantum mechanics. This says that when a measurement is made, the wave function does not collapse into a *single* state; *all* possible states are in fact realized—but in different universes! In other words, the states that were previously super-imposed, now exist in parallel universes. In the case of Schrodinger's cat, a dead cat would exist in one universe and a live cat in another!

In spite of its weird characteristics, quantum mechanics can be considered as one of the most important advances of the twentieth century. Its principles are used in many of the electronic devices that lie at the heart of modern technology. Such things as transistors, lasers, and computer chips are all based on quantum mechanical principles.

Quantum mechanics deals with the micro-world, and strange things seem to go on there. However, very powerful tools have been developed by the physicists to describe the behavior of matter in this micro-world. When Einstein was working out his relativity theories, there were only two known forces in nature: gravity and the electromagnetic force. But by the 1950's the physics community had become aware of two more: the strong and weak nuclear forces.

The electromagnetic force was incorporated into quantum mechanics by Richard Feynman, who developed a "field theory" called QED—Quantum Electrodynamics. This succeeded in reconciling Einstein's special relativity theory with quantum mechanics.[14]

When the two nuclear forces were discovered, attempts were made to expand QED to include these as well. In the 1960's Sheldon Glashow, Abdus Salam and Steven Weinberg worked out a field theory incorporating the electromagnetic and weak forces, for which they ultimately received the Nobel Prize. In 1974, Howard Georgi and Glashow proposed an extension of this "electroweak" theory to include the strong force. All this was eventually developed into what became known as the Standard Model, which incorporated all of the non-gravitational forces.[15]

This was a great achievement, but the celebrations were somewhat muted because of the fact that gravity was not yet included in the theory. The elusive Holy Grail of the TOE, or Theory of Everything, had not yet been attained. To make matters worse, there seemed little immediate prospect of achieving this, because the gravitational force is so much weaker than the other three.

Einstein's general theory of relativity deals with large objects and large distances, whereas quantum mechanics deals with very small objects and microscopic distances. And besides, the gravitational force is some hundred million billion billion billion (10^{35}) times smaller than the weak force, the smallest of the other three, and so it can effectively be ignored in most quantum mechanical calculations.

Gravity and quantum mechanics seem to be fundamentally incompatible. Nevertheless, the physics community will not be satisfied until the two have been united into one grand theory. It seems that man is never satisfied until he can explain things in a neat and simple way, which is aesthetically satisfying and which brings out the underlying beauty and rationality of what he is trying to explain. This is probably why crossword puzzles are so popular. Everything fits together exactly, and when one is finished, the solution is revealed as being not only correct, but uniquely so.

So the search goes on. Every attempt to enlarge the Standard Model by including gravity has so far met with insurmountable problems, so it seems that a whole new approach is required. And this brings us to the final episode in this part of the story.

The holy grail has still not been reached (at the time of writing), but more and more physicists are coming around to the view that string theory, or its more comprehensive cousin, superstring theory, has the potential to become the long-sought final theory.

String theory, in one form or another, has been around for more than 30 years, but interest in it by the pros has waxed and waned during this time, as various developments have either looked promising or seemed to lead nowhere. The basic idea of string theory is that matter consists, not of particles that essentially have no dimension and are described mathematically as points, but of tiny one-dimensional strings, whose length is approximately 10^{-33} cm (the Plank length), and which vibrate like a violin string at different frequencies. The different frequencies represent different fundamental particles and force carriers: electrons, quarks, photons, etc. The latest version of string theory, the so-called M-theory, which is really a unification of previous theories, requires the strings to exist in an eleven-dimensional space, with one time dimension and ten space dimensions. Seven of the space dimensions are tightly curled up, so as to be essentially invisible to even the most powerful instruments available for probing microscopic distances. Thus our four-dimensional world of space-time may have these seven extra space dimensions tucked away so tightly that no one except a string theorist is really sure of their existence.

There are many other aspects of string theory that are too involved to be discussed in this survey, but these are explained for the general reader by Brian

Greene in *The Elegant Universe,* which I recommend to all those who are interested.

Having brought the discussion of particle physics up to the present, we can quickly survey the other major scientific developments of the twentieth century. One such development that has not received the attention it deserves is plate tectonics, which has revolutionized our thinking about the nature of planet Earth.

The German meteorologist Alfred Wegener first proposed the idea of continental drift in 1912. He noticed how the shape of the continents seemed to resemble a giant jigsaw puzzle and surmised that they were once actually in contact, but had subsequently drifted apart. He studied the rocks on either side of the Atlantic Ocean, where the coastlines of the two continents seemed to correspond, and found the formations to be almost identical. Wegener then postulated that a huge super continent, which he named Pangaea, existed about 225 million years ago, and that it later broke up into two smaller super continents, Laurasia to the north, and Gondwanaland to the south. These in turn broke up into smaller pieces during the Mesozoic era, and eventually coalesced into the continents that we know today.

Like many a radical new theory, this was at first pooh-poohed by the scientific community. But subsequent discoveries only tended to confirm Wegener's brilliant conjecture. It was found that the earth's crust, or lithosphere, is divided into approximately seven enormous plates. When the plates meet along a coastline, the ocean plate, which is thinner, gets pushed down under the continental plate, and the continental coastline gets pushed upwards, forming a mountain range. This process is called subduction. The North and South American Pacific coastal formations are good examples of this process.

Incidentally, when the distribution of species and the fossil record was correlated with the way that the continents had shifted over time, Darwin's ideas about the distribution and development of species were further confirmed.

We now come to what is perhaps the crown jewel of twentieth century scientific discoveries. This one occurred in the field of molecular biology. I am referring of course to the discovery of the structure of the DNA molecule—the double helix—by James Watson and Francis Crick in 1953.

The significance of this discovery can hardly be exaggerated. In one giant leap, the machinery of life itself was revealed. Prior to this, scientists had been groping for answers as to how living things grow and develop, and although they had a rough picture of the process, the actual details of the mechanism remained hidden. Now this mechanism, right down to the molecular level, was revealed in all its subtle details. Not only did this spectacularly confirm Darwin's theory of evolution, it opened the way for the mammoth strides in biology that were made in the second half of the twentieth century, and set the stage for what is likely to be even greater progress in the century to come.

What this discovery reveals is the essential unity of all living things. All life, including plant life, carries the same DNA code. The "alphabet" consists of four letters: A, G, T and C, which stand for the bases: adenine, guanine, thymine and cytosine. These letters make up "words" of three letters each, and these in turn make up the genes.

The double helix consists of two helical sugar-phosphate chains, or backbones, situated on the outside, running in opposite directions, with pairs of bases strung between them. "Seen in this way, the structure resembles a spiral staircase, with the base pairs forming the steps."[16] The bases are always paired in the same way: A with T, and G with C. As Watson himself tells it, in the *Double Helix:*

> I became aware that an adenine-thymine pair held together by two hydrogen bonds was identical in shape to a guanine-cytosine pair held together by at least two hydrogen bonds.... Always pairing adenine with thymine and guanine with cytosine meant that the base sequences of the two intertwined chains were complementary to each other. Given the base sequence of one chain, that of its partner was automatically determined. Conceptually, it was thus very easy to visualize how a single chain could be the template for the synthesis of a chain with the complementary sequence.[17]

Thus the DNA molecule contains two copies of the entire sequence of genes. The number of genes varies from approximately 10,000 for the less complex life forms, to about 30,000 for a human being. It was thought until quite recently that humans might have as many as 100,000 genes, because of their greater complexity as organisms. But it turns out that the number of genes is less important than the way that they are "wired up" in the intracellular network.[18] Each gene can consist of anything from just a few three-letter words, to several thousand. The whole "book" is divided into chapters, or chromosomes, of different length. The number of chromosomes increases with the complexity of the organism—the lowly bacteria have only one chromosome. Human genes are located on twenty-three chromosomes. Chimpanzees have twenty-two, but their genes differ only very slightly from ours. In all, the human genome contains over a billion words.

A human being has more than 100 trillion cells, each of which contains two copies of the complete genome. Whenever a cell divides and becomes two cells, the DNA molecule duplicates itself. It is so configured that the two chains of the helix can be "unzipped." This is accomplished by breaking the hydrogen bonds between the paired bases. Each helix is copied, and then everything is zipped up again to form two replicas of the original molecule. This copying procedure is performed through the actions of various proteins, or enzymes.

It's one thing to discover how the book is put together and quite another to actually read it, let alone *understand* it. But good progress has been made in both of these endeavors. Each word specifies one amino acid, so the relationship between the word and the acid constitutes a code. This basic code is common to all life, and all forms of life can be traced back to the earliest one-celled organisms. The idea that human beings were somehow created separately will not hold water. The likelihood of there being two separately evolved life forms with the same DNA code is extremely small. Although the structure of the code is not the result of pure chance—if it was the odds against it being duplicated would be astronomical—nonetheless the chances of the same code arising independently are very small indeed.[19] Separate *creation* with the same code is also extremely unlikely, because, as Darwin himself explained in *The Origin of Species*, there is compelling evidence that it is variations in species which lead to the creation of new species. So there is an unbroken causal chain connecting all living things, starting from the earliest forms of life. There is no need for any outside intervention in a process that, once started, continues indefinitely.[20]

The picture of the world that has now begun to take shape for us at the beginning of the twenty-first century is one of vast size and complexity. Just as we can barely imagine the extent of the enormous oceans of space that surround us, so also we are only dimly aware of the worlds within worlds that are contained in each one of us.

The mechanism of life can be found inside every living cell—each one being a world unto itself. It operates continuously and without our conscious knowledge. Inside the cell is a nucleus, containing the DNA—the formula, or recipe for life itself. It has taken hundreds of scientists, working with the most powerful computers, many years to unlock the secrets of this tiny masterpiece. But the human genome project is now just about complete, and the ability to understand and cure the most deadly diseases is almost within our grasp. There is a huge mine of information sitting literally inside each one of us, but on a scale so minute that it takes long and tedious research, using the most modern techniques now available, to pry loose just a few of the secrets that lie so close to our grasp, yet remain so stubbornly elusive. Slowly and laboriously the inner sanctum of life itself is being revealed in all its wondrous power and subtlety.

Science is even beginning to probe the hidden secrets of the mind. To discover just how we perform all the miracles of speech, reasoning and cognition that we take so much for granted, and which operate mostly outside of our immediate consciousness. Will we eventually be able to create artificial minds, even more powerful than our own?

ASPECTS OF MATHEMATICS

Finally I would like to discuss some features of the "queen of the sciences." Since so many branches of science need mathematics for their exposition, one could say that it is the one indispensable ingredient in our search for answers regarding the nature of our world. This being the case, the nature of mathematics itself becomes something that should be looked at a little more closely.

At the turn of the twentieth century, Bertrand Russell and Alfred North Whitehead published their voluminous *Principia Mathematica,* which laid down the axioms of set theory and the rules of inference that could be used to prove theorems within the theory. This seemed to set mathematics on an unshakable foundation. However, the foundation remained unshakable only until 1931, when Kurt Gödel published his famous Incompleteness Theorem.[21] This demonstrated that any system of axioms is incomplete, in so far as there are sentences, or theorems, that are in fact true, but are not provable from the axioms. This was a big blow to the mathematical community, but nothing could be done, the limitations of any logical system had been exposed.

A scientist often likes to quantify a problem, and to do this he usually sets up some kind of mathematical model. This reduces the problem to a form that is more amenable to numerical analysis. For instance, a river can be studied by assuming a certain profile (width and depth), a rate of flow and a gradient, or slope. Many minor deviations from these assumptions are ignored, and depending on how accurately the river matches the model, such things as the volume of water passing a given point in a certain time can be calculated more or less reliably.

This idea of a model extends to many branches of science (and non-science). But making a model is more of an art than a science, because models cannot always be trusted to give accurate, or even useful answers. An example where this approach is fraught with danger is economics. This is a large field, and there are many economic models in circulation, with many parameters involved, such as rates of inflation, unemployment, average income, interest rates, consumer demand, etc. All these parameters are put into some kind of mathematical formula, which hopefully will supply answers to many of the questions that an economist might ask. But serious pitfalls await the unwary economist along the way. Most of the correlations between the various parameters are ignored, and so the answer is often meaningless. Another serious problem occurs when parameters that can in fact make a great difference are left out altogether. A well-known example concerns the supposed relationship between unemployment and inflation. In America it was assumed for years that a rate of unemployment below 6% would cause inflation.[22] So when the rate went to 5¾%, many economists predicted that inflation was about to occur. Well, to cut a long story short, it did *not* occur, and the unemployment rate went all the way down to 4%, and there was *still* no inflation. Obviously something had been left out of the original model that connected unemployment with inflation. More parameters were needed, but which ones, and how should they be correlated?

On top of all this there is the problem of the accuracy of the data that is fed into the model. Often this involves assumptions that are little more than educated guesses—and perhaps some *un*educated ones as well. Much of the data and statistics are later revised, at times quite radically. And nobody has the faintest idea how accurate the revisions are!

This shows the shaky foundations on which much of economics is based. Many of the parameters that are used are actually correlated in ways that are quite unpredictable, and what's more, these correlations are often continuously changing. Why is this so? Basically because they are based on the behavior of human beings, and we all know how unpredictable *they* can be. The famous economist Maynard Keynes was fully aware of this, and warned that an economic system could not be accurately modeled with the mathematical tools that are currently used to do the job. As an example of how naïve the economists can be, it has been something of an axiom that people will naturally make rational choices as to what is in their own best interest. Well, anyone who knows the first thing about human nature knows that this is the *last* thing that most people will do. Actually, I believe that some economists are finally beginning to realize this.

So is economics a science or not? Since it possesses some of the attributes of a science, let's be charitable and call it a science in the making.[23] Recent economic models based on networks show some promise, but the human factor is always lurking in the background, waiting to upset the calculations.[24] All the same, you have to admire the tenacity of the economists. Come what may, they are determined to turn economics into a science. They are confident that an incredibly complex system like an economy can somehow be completely understood, if only they can come up with the correct mathematical model.

Economics, being poorly understood by almost everyone—including the economists—is an ideal vehicle for the flimflam of politicians. Phony explanations for recent economic trends are used to justify policies that are favored by one party, while the other party uses the same data to explain how ruinous such policies are.

The nature of mathematics itself can also be a problem. As mentioned before, mathematics is essentially an abstraction. How well it functions when used to describe the physical world is unclear. It is obviously well able to add up a grocery bill in the supermarket. But there are more important things than grocery bills.

A *mathematical* line is made up of points, which have no size and therefore occupy no space—and there are an infinite number of them, *however short* the line is! In the real world, a point with no size makes no sense—because it isn't there. Neither is a line with no width or a plane without thickness. In our world, even a very thin string has a cross-section with a definite area, so one cannot say that it is one-dimensional, it actually has *three* dimensions. Similarly, a flat plate has a finite thickness, so it too is three-dimensional. In the mathematical world there are one-dimensional lines, and two-dimensional planes, and three-dimensional solids, each of which are made up of zero-dimensional points!

[Things have gotten even trickier lately. We now have *fractional* dimensions. These came about with the introduction of fractals—those strange things that look the same at different scales, like coastlines and snowflakes. Anyway, if you take a flat piece of paper, which is approximately two-dimensional, and crinkle it up, it becomes something that looks like a cauliflower or a sponge, which is not really two-dimensional any more. If you go on scrunching it up into a tightly compressed little ball, it becomes *three*-dimensional! So the stage when it looked like a cauliflower was sort of half way between two-dimensional and three-dimensional—let's call it two-and-a-half-dimensional. This sort of thing is now done with a straight face, and one can get any fraction of a dimension that one desires, by simply creating what can be considered an intermediate stage between two integral dimensions. Personally I consider this sleight of hand—or perhaps sleight of dimension. As far as I can see, there are still only three-dimensional objects in this world of ours, because the original piece of paper was actually three-dimensional, if you consider it as a real piece of paper, not just a mathematical abstraction.]

Mathematicians love to talk about infinity, as if an infinite number is nothing very special. However, an infinite number of material things, *however* small each one of them may be, would not fit in any space that was not itself infinite in size. That is why the mathematician's point must not occupy *any* space at all.

In the real world there are only *three-dimensional* objects. There are also no infinities—except in a mathematician's head—unless the universe itself is infinite, which is not known at the present time. A finite piece of matter has only a *finite* number of atoms in it, whereas a mathematical line of finite length (however short) contains an *infinite* number of points! Matter cannot be divided up indefinitely, so a mathematical point does not exist in the real world.[25]

The "continuum" of the mathematician is also an abstraction. It turns out that neither space nor *time* can be divided up indefinitely.[26] Although we perceive such things as lines and planes to be continuous, this is because we can only see the general outline, rather than the real object in all its microscopic detail. This is also why there is no exact dividing line between one object or material and another, there is only a fuzzy transition zone where one cannot say where one thing ends and another starts. At the atomic level, there are no precise dividing lines.

Calculus and other branches of mathematics that use variables whose magnitude can tend to zero are abstractions from reality, they are idealizations that allow us to measure and quantify the physical world. The word "infinitesimal" is used a lot by mathematicians. It serves as a sort of bridge between the real world and the abstract world of mathematics. An infinitesimal object is smaller than any conceivable object—*however small*—and yet it has a definite size! There is a whiff of paradox here.

[Actually, the calculus can be formulated without the use of infinitesimals, as Karl Weierstrass showed in the nineteenth century, but mathematicians and physicists accept infinitesimals because they are easy to use and make everything nice and neat.]

Of course there are no negative quantities in the real world either—have you ever seen *minus* three cows in a field? (But you *have* seen zero cows!) And what about complex numbers? These other kinds of number came to be considered when mathematicians began to solve different kinds of equations. Gerolano Cardano (1501-1576) was one of the first to introduce them in connection with the solution of cubic equations. But it wasn't until the nineteenth century that complex numbers were generally accepted.

In the days of Diophantus, only positive real numbers were considered to be valid solutions to an algebraic equation, so some equations did not appear to have any solutions at all. But negative numbers were eventually included, and finally, with great reluctance, the mathematical community swallowed the idea of complex numbers. These are numbers of the form A + iB, where A and B are real numbers, and i is $\sqrt{-1}$. Complex numbers occur naturally when one is looking for *all* the solutions to a given algebraic equation, not just the simple positive or negative solutions.

If A + iB is a complex number, then its *complex conjugate* is A - iB. When these two are multiplied together we get $A^2 + B^2$, which is the square of the modulus, or magnitude, of the complex number, and it is always a *real* number. To get the magnitude one takes the positive square root of $A^2 + B^2$. This is an extremely important relationship, which is used frequently in many branches of mathematics, especially in quantum mechanics. Complex numbers can be represented on a two-dimensional plane, where they can be added and subtracted like vectors. But the important thing about complex numbers is that the common operations of multiplication, subtraction, division, etc., can all be carried out in the same way as with real numbers.

[The complex numbers that we have been considering are some of the simplest. The simplest of all are called Gaussian integers, where the numbers A and B are just ordinary integers (whole numbers). Instead of using $\sqrt{-1}$, we can form other "integers" A $\pm$ B$\sqrt{-p}$ where p is a prime number. Complex numbers of the form A $\pm$ B$\sqrt{-5}$ can be used to factor certain primes. For example $29 = (3+2\sqrt{-5})(3-2\sqrt{-5})$. Or they can provide alternate factors for non-prime numbers, e.g. $6 = 2\times3 = (1+\sqrt{-5})(1-\sqrt{-5})$. This is all part of the fascinating subject of number theory.[27] The complex numbers using $\sqrt{-1}$ are the most useful, because they have other interesting properties, for example the exponential formula. This is the famous function $e^{i\theta}$, where "e" is the base of natural logarithms and i is $\sqrt{-1}$. It can be written as a complex number $\cos\theta + i\sin\theta$, which is equal to +1 or -1 according as θ is an even or an odd multiple of π.]

Once mathematicians began to include complex numbers in their solutions, many other avenues of research were opened up. So the introduction of first negative, and then complex numbers was a significant development, which had far-reaching implications for many sciences, especially mechanics, engineering and physics. This is why I have covered this subject in a little more detail.

The probabilities that we use in quantum mechanics are all real numbers, because they are the moduli of complex numbers, as explained above. But in order to arrive at these real probabilities, we have had to use mathematics involving complex numbers (the "state functions" are complex functions). So you may well ask: If I can get solutions to real problems using complex numbers, does this mean that, in its essence, nature "understands" complex numbers and is somehow intimately bound up with them?

Is mathematics really the language of nature, as Newton thought? Or is it just an artifice concocted by the human brain? Actually, the modern view is that it is basically the latter. Nevertheless it does seem to provide useful (and accurate) descriptions of certain aspects of nature.

Clearly mathematics *is* the language of music, with its notes and harmonies, each note having its own precise mathematical frequency. But one has to bear in mind that music is a creation of man, whereas nature is not. So it seems appropriate that mathematics should define music, whereas with nature one is not so sure.

Although mathematics can be used to describe certain aspects of nature very accurately, it's clear that many things in nature cannot be so described. Mathematics only deals with an *idealized* version of nature—an idealization created by man. According to Newton's law of gravity, a feather and a stone will fall at the same rate. But this is only true in a vacuum. In the real world they do not fall together because of air resistance. The only reason that Newton's equations of planetary motion work so well is because we are dealing with only two bodies, the sun and a planet in this instance, which are moving in what is essentially a vacuum. We also assume that the mass is concentrated at the center of gravity. But as soon as we introduce other bodies, like a second planet, we encounter the "three body problem," and it becomes impossible to get exact answers. So even Newton's laws are not as widely applicable as is generally assumed.

Further discussion regarding the relation of mathematics to the natural world will be taken up in chapter 14.

10

THE PHYSICAL CONTEXT

Oh, write of me, not "Died in bitter pains,"
But "Emigrated to another star!"

—Helen Hunt Jackson
Emigravit

THE BIG BANG

Let us now turn to the most important theory of modern cosmology: how everything got started in the first place. This entails going back literally to the beginning of time—to the Creation. The Big Bang theory is relatively recent, but is now accepted by nearly all scientists. The evidence is still fairly sketchy, but it's beginning to add up to something quite persuasive. You might ask how we can be sure about something that happened 15 billion years ago. Of course we can never be *sure* of something like that, but let's see what we have to go on.

In the 1920's Edwin Hubble discovered that the universe is expanding, everything is moving away from everything else at an ever-increasing speed. So if things get farther apart as time goes on, in the past they must have been closer together. And if you could go back far enough into the past, they would be very close together indeed. This is one of the main arguments for the Big Bang, but there are others.

If the universe really did start with a big fireball, then this would have left some telltale evidence behind in the form of microwave radiation. Well, the microwave radiation was in fact discovered in 1965, and so the Big Bang theory started to look a lot better. In addition to this, further explanations by the physicists as to how things developed in the first few fractions of a second have begun to flesh out the whole picture in a much more convincing manner.[1]

Einstein's general theory of relativity postulates the existence of "singularities," where gravitational forces can become incredibly large. These are the black holes, and their existence has been confirmed with a high degree of reliability. The Big Bang has the appearance of a black hole in reverse—everything going out instead of coming in. But why shouldn't the universe actually be oscillating back and forth, expanding to a great size, and then contracting back into a black hole, only to explode forth into another period of expansion? In the contraction phase maybe time runs backwards! Perhaps we are just in one of the outgoing phases. This depends to a large degree on the rate of expansion. If it is slow enough to allow gravity to eventually stop it altogether and commence a contraction, then we are headed for a "big crunch," a black hole from which another Big Bang may produce another expansion. Or, if the rate of expansion is too great, the universe will just keep on expanding indefinitely.

To complicate things, there is the question of the "dark matter." This must exist to account for the behavior of stars in the outer regions of spiral galaxies. As Wallace and Karen Tucker explain in *The Dark Matter:*

> The force of gravity should be strongest near the center of a galaxy, where the matter appears to be concentrated. As the matter thins out along the spiral arms, the gravity should decrease. It follows then that the speed of rotation of the stars and gas clouds should decline from the inner to the to the outer regions.
> This is *not* what is observed.... An analysis of these measurements has shown that the stars are not slowing down; they are moving at the same speed as the ones closer in.
> The observations imply that a substantial part of the mass of spiral galaxies is not concentrated toward the center of the galaxy, as the distribution of light would suggest. Rather, it must be in some dark, unseen cloud of matter that pervades the galaxy and extends far beyond it.[2]

Whatever this dark matter is, there is a lot of it; its total mass must be greater than all the matter that is visible. So far all efforts at discovering it have been in vain. This is one of the secrets of our weird and wonderful universe that is particularly elusive. All sorts of theories have been proposed to account for the dark matter, but it remains stubbornly—and literally—out of sight.

In addition to the dark matter, there is also what might be termed "dark energy," or vacuum energy. It turns out that there is no such thing as a real vacuum, with nothing in it at all. There always exist quantum fluctuations—a sort of froth of particles slipping into and out of existence, even when there is no other matter around.[3] As a result of this, inter-galactic space possesses a special kind of energy, and this causes a repulsive force, which tends to counteract the gravitational forces between the galaxies. And indeed it has recently been discovered, through the study of supernovae, that the universe is expanding at a much faster rate than was previously thought.

So when we talk about the expansion of the universe, and the gravitational forces which are tending to slow it down, we have to take into account not only the mass of the dark matter, but the vacuum energy as well.

The theory of the Big Bang has done wonders to revive the practice of cosmology, the science of the universe as a whole. Now almost every physicist has become a cosmologist. The Big Bang has even brought the idea of God into the discussion. The physicists have been forced to think about how the whole process got started. In other words, the Creation has now reached the realm of scientific inquiry.

[I know I said that science and religion don't mix. Well, they still don't. This situation just makes it *seem* as if they do.]

This is not necessarily all good news for the believers, because it means that any intervention that God could have had during the history of the physical universe must have occurred right at the very beginning, at the time of the Big Bang. Because after the Big Bang, everything just unfolds (evolves) automatically. Ten billion years later life appears on Earth (it may have appeared in other places as well), without the necessity for any intervention by God. Biological evolution then takes over, and *voilà*, another four billion years or so and you have the human animal—who eventually manages to figure out what has been happening for the past 15 billion years!

But *before* the Big Bang, who knows? And what about *time*? Surely it must have had a *beginning*. And how did the laws of Nature come about? As astronomer John Barrow writes:

> The ultimate cosmological conundrum appears to be the question of how and when the laws of Nature came into being, if the Universe of space and time is imagined to arise spontaneously out of nothing.[4]

Maybe there really is a God who is not just a figment of the human imagination. But if his purpose was to create human beings, he chose an incredibly elaborate way of doing it, the whole process taking 15 billion years (give or take a few billion).

The God that we are now talking about is quite different from any of the conventional Gods. "It" is a God that we cannot even think about, except in the most indirect way. It is *unimaginable*, because we have no concept of what kind of being it really is. The conventional Gods: Allah, Yahweh, Ahura Mazda, Vishnu, etc., are all projections of human beings and have many human characteristics (a sex, a shape, emotions, thoughts and the like). But a *real* God could not have any of these things.

Now I am well aware that many of those who belong to the various religions, and who are of a more progressive turn of mind, already *do* think of a deity as being something that is basically unimaginable. It has already been noted that the Hindus have always thought of God in this way. So maybe the gap between the believers and the unbelievers (with the possible exception of the atheists) is beginning to close somewhat. We should not get too excited over this, however, because there is still a considerable disparity between the worldview of those who adhere to some kind of religious belief and those who do not, and I'm talking here about the more liberal believers.

Of course if the universe is actually in one phase of a periodic expansion and contraction, maybe there is no need for a creator. The system would be in a state of perpetual motion, without the necessity for a precise beginning. On the other hand, if what has been said above about the speed of the expansion is correct, the universe will probably just go on expanding forever. Instead of the "big crunch," when the universe contracts back into a black hole, we would have the "big chill," where everything would get further and further apart. All the stars would eventually die; everything would get colder and colder, until it finally reached absolute zero.

JOURNEY TO THE STARS

Imagine yourself way out in space, a light year from earth, en route to the center of our Milky Way galaxy. (Light travels at 300,000 kilometers per second, so in a year it travels about ten thousand billion kilometers, or 10^{16} meters. This is the distance we call a light year).

When you look back towards the earth, it's not there, and even if you had brought along an extremely powerful telescope, our sun is the only part of the solar system that you would be able to see from that distance. The earth would be gone, swallowed up in the black void of space. But you are only *one* light year from earth, and the center of the galaxy is still 26,000 light years away!

Our galaxy is one of the smaller ones, containing about a hundred billion stars. The shape of the galaxy is roughly that of a disc, 100,000 light years in diameter. Its average thickness is about 10,000 light years, increasing to about 30,000 at the center. If you had continued on to the center of the galaxy you would almost certainly have fallen into a black hole, for it's now thought that nearly all galaxies have black holes at the center.

The Andromeda galaxy, our nearest galactic neighbor, is actually moving towards us, and may crash into us in about five billion years. This may result in one galaxy "swallowing" the other, or else with the two galaxies circling one another in a perpetual embrace. Beyond Andromeda there are millions of other galaxies that are visible with the most powerful telescopes. The total number of galaxies in the universe is estimated at over a hundred billion. Most exist in clusters, separated by vast regions of intergalactic space. This space is constantly increasing in size, due to the expansion of the universe.

The stars in our Milky Way galaxy are separated by several light years on average. To get an idea of the scale of things, imagine our own sun, whose radius is 696,000 km (109 times that of the earth), shrunk down to the size of a tennis ball. At this scale, the nearest star, Alpha Centauri, which is 4.3 light years away, would be more than 6,000 kilometers from the sun!

Even a single light year is a distance whose magnitude is hard for the human mind to comprehend. A thousand light years becomes even more difficult. And when we start talking about millions, or even billions of light years, we feel as if we have passed beyond the reaches of the human imagination. These kinds of distances, together with the number of stars that are contained in this seemingly infinite ocean of space, do not initially register their magnitude in the human mind.

For thousands of years man had no inkling of the true reality of which he is a part. Something like the sun was simply there in the sky, its distance not really considered, except by a few who sought answers to difficult questions. The stars were just "up there," part of the "roof of the world." This was the realm of the gods, and did not really concern human beings.

It was not until the late Middle Ages that this picture began to change dramatically, when the Copernican Revolution started man on a quest for answers as to the true nature of the world that he inhabits. The range of man's thinking began to dramatically expand, and much of what was previously considered beyond the scope of human knowledge was reexamined in the light of these new discoveries. A totally different kind of universe started to emerge.

The old ways of looking at things were discarded by those who were aware of the new discoveries. But the old conceptions died hard, because they were based on tradition and faith, not observation and reason. There was a tension in the society, between those who wished to stay with the old established truths, and those who looked for a more solid basis on which to construct their worldview.

In the nineteenth century, Darwin's theory of evolution further shook the world of established ideas. And when at the turn of the twentieth century Edwin Hubble discovered that the universe is actually expanding, and that the faint blotches of light just visible in the most powerful telescopes of the day were in fact other galaxies far beyond our own, the old ways of thinking had gone forever. It was found that the universe was in fact thousands, even millions, of times larger than anyone had previously imagined. Science, germinating in the human mind for centuries, had come alive with a vengeance and started to replace mythical beliefs with a more accurate picture of reality. For thousands of years, these beliefs had gone unchallenged. There was no objective standard by which the validity of a belief or theory could be judged. But now the light of reason began to shine into the dark recesses of ignorance, and what it revealed was unsettling to the human psyche. We still live with such tension, and it will probably increase, at least for a while, as science continues to uncover nature's secrets.

All the same, many people, especially the young, are adapting to the new truths and expanding their capacity for learning. Having established his mastery over much of the natural world, man now seeks to *understand* nature, in all its fantastic subtlety and depth. The heavens, once the mysterious homeland of the gods, are turning out to be immeasurably greater, and vastly more complex than was ever previously imagined. The mind of man expands to meet the challenge of the new, and the frontiers of knowledge reach into areas never before thought accessible to human understanding.

But can we ever really explore this vast New World other than through a telescope? We have certainly made a good start in our own solar system. But this is like exploring one drop of water in an ocean. Even traveling *at the speed of light,* a journey to the nearest star would take over four years. And what would we do if we got there? We could of course orbit the star. But that is about all we could do at Alpha Centauri, because it has no planets in orbit around it. If we want to find a planet to land on we will have to go much further out into space.

Although several stars with accompanying planets have been found, it is not clear just how hospitable they would be to human life. And in any case, the logistics of such an enterprise, assuming that we could build a rocket ship capable of making the journey, would be formidable indeed.[5]

For the time being space travel outside of our solar system is beyond our capabilities. So these more ambitious journeys will have to wait. However, there are still many exciting things that can be done closer to home. Establishing an outpost on Mars is already in the planning stage, and building a base on one of the moons of Jupiter should be well within our capabilities within the next fifty years or so.

There are some wild speculations about how we might overcome the light-speed barrier. The use of "wormholes" is one that is bandied about a lot, another is the possibility of creating a tear in the fabric of space-time, whereby one might jump to another place and time almost instantaneously. But such notions really belong in the realm of science fiction—at least for the present.

ARE WE ALONE?

Then there is the possibility of life on other worlds, which is a popular topic of science fiction. Everyone is familiar with UFO stories of one kind or another. My own opinion, for what it's worth, is that UFO's can, in almost all cases, be explained as natural phenomena such as stars, or the lights from a plane, or some other everyday object, which has been misinterpreted as a UFO. Even if they do not have such an easy explanation they could still be the result of some other, as yet unexplained phenomenon. The least likely explanation is that they are space ships from other worlds. In other words, I'm a skeptic, since there seems to be no *convincing* evidence that would make me into a believer. UFO's make wonderful subjects for movies and science fiction, but that's about all. It would seem that even if there *were* more advanced civilizations out there somewhere, they would nonetheless encounter many of the same difficulties that we ourselves face in regard to space travel. This is because it is reasonable to presume that the laws of physics, as we know them, apply uniformly to at least the visible universe from which these visitors would presumably have come. In the same way, stories about space ships having landed in South America and elsewhere in the distant past do not hold much water for me. But everyone is entitled to his or her opinion and—heaven forbid—I could be wrong!

The question as to whether there is life elsewhere in the universe is one that we can more easily get our teeth into. While not being able to take really big bites, we can at least nibble at it a little.

Speculation about life on other worlds is older than science itself, but nothing more than wild conjecture on the subject has been possible until quite recently. The question still cannot be answered definitively, but there are now some new tools at our disposal, which were not available in the past. Once it is known exactly how life started here on earth, we will be in a much better position to assess the possibility that it has also started elsewhere in the universe. But even now we can at least make a start, because there is already considerable information available regarding the origin of life, even though it is not yet complete. So a few general observations can be made.

The basic chemistry of life is now known in considerable detail. Elements such as carbon, nitrogen, sulfur and phosphorus, when combined with oxygen and hydrogen, make up the proteins, amino acids, sugars, etc., which are the basic constituents of the huge organic molecules which give rise to the living cell, with its self-replicating systems of DNA and RNA. These basic elements came together in the warm seas some 4.6 billion years ago to form the primitive organisms that were the ancestors of all life on earth. This, or something close to it, is the scenario for life's first appearance on earth.[6]

But a lot more questions remain to be answered before we can draw any final conclusions. Did life suddenly appear spontaneously? And if so, how probable is such a spontaneous occurrence? If in fact the probability is quite high, then we should not be surprised to find that it has happened more than once, and in several different locations. Thus we might imagine that each form of life that we see had its own individual (spontaneous) beginning. But the evidence now available to us shows that this cannot be the case. It is clear from the study of DNA and its unique code that all life arose from a *single* source. This discovery has several implications. If life did occur spontaneously, this was probably a rare occurrence, otherwise we would expect to see more than one code exhibited in organic DNA.

The rarity of the initial occurrence of life helps to explain the difficulty that scientists have had in producing life artificially. From a religious point of view, if God did have anything to do with creating human beings, this puts his hypothetical creative act much further into the distant past. Because after the initial beginning of life, the process of evolution would unfold automatically, and eventually produce—or maybe not produce—a human being, without any outside assistance. As paleontologist Richard Fortey explains:

> That vital spark from inanimate matter to animate life happened once and only once, and all living existence depends on that moment. We are one tribe

with bacteria that live in hot springs, parasitic barnacles, vampire bats and cauliflowers. We all share a common ancestor.

This astonishing fact carries an obvious corollary. The genesis of life was not easy; rather, it must have been an exquisite gamble in the face of thermodynamic odds, which work against self-replicating systems—those which *acquire,* rather than lose, energy. If it were not so difficult, there should be evidence that some creatures were not born of the same clay as others. The primeval fingerprints of creation should still be ingrained in the molecules of every tissue of their bodies, and they should be different fingerprints from those identifying the rest of life. But this is not so.[7]

As mentioned in chapter 1, the idea that a certain level of "complexity" among aggregations of certain molecules could spontaneously give rise to self-replicating systems was popular among biologists and those in related fields for some time.[8] This seemed to imply that there may exist a "law of self-organization," which could be responsible for the appearance of life. If this were indeed the case, then it might not be so difficult to produce life from inanimate matter. However, the fact that life seems to have originated only once on Earth strongly implies that the process is one that occurs only under very special circumstances.

The suggestion that life in our solar system actually originated on Mars rather than here on Earth has lately been given serious consideration. Strongly doubted at first, but now taken much more seriously, this theory states that life was transmitted to Earth from Mars via meteorites. These may have contained bacteria, or other life forms, which had been dislodged from the Martian surface by the impact of asteroids or other space-traveling bodies. This seems at first glance to be utterly fantastic, but it may not actually be so far fetched. Apparently the time period when the environment was most suitable for the propagation of life was actually longer on Mars than it was on Earth. In any case, we will have to wait and see if this theory can stand up to further scrutiny.

The question of *where* life originated in our solar system is not nearly so important as *how* it originated, and how rare such an occurrence is likely to be. The answer as to whether there is life elsewhere in the cosmos depends heavily on the relative rarity of its possible occurrence. And we are at some disadvantage in answering this question. If we had discovered even *one* other instance of life outside our solar system, we would be in a much better position to decide the probability of its occurrence elsewhere. But we have not as yet found evidence of life beyond Earth itself. This has not been for want of trying. We have scanned the heavens on every radio frequency, to see if there are signals that might give evidence of intelligent life somewhere "out there," but to date nothing has turned up. Of course, differentiating any meaningful signals from the background noise is an extremely difficult task, but quite a lot of progress has been made in this regard.

What our scan of the heavens has been seeking is *intelligent* life, and it is this kind of life that we are most interested in. The existence of life on a planet may be inferred from the study of its atmosphere, but this does not tell us anything about intelligent life. If the probability of finding *any* kind of life in the universe is small, not only because of the complexity and uniqueness of the process itself, but also because of the relative rarity of planetary systems with suitable environments, then the probability of finding *intelligent* life is surely a great deal smaller. Just because life has arisen in a particular planetary system, does not mean that *intelligent* life will necessarily follow, given the requisite time. It may or it may not, but there is no guarantee that intelligent life will inevitably result from the process of evolution, however long it is allowed to continue. The appearance of our big brain may well have been a fluke, since it does not seem to serve any vital survival need. But if it *did* develop as part of our need for survival, then the chances of intelligent life evolving somewhere else would seem to be much greater.

From what has been said, we can conclude that the occurrence of any kind of life is extremely rare, and that of intelligent life is much rarer still. So it is *possible* that we are indeed unique, and that no other life, let alone intelligent life, exists anywhere else in the universe. This is possible, but it's *extremely* unlikely. The reason for this is because of the *vast size* of the universe. The number of star systems where planets can exist is quite small relative to the total number of stars. The probability of such a system occurring is probably less than ten per cent. But even if it were only a hundredth of this percentage, there would still be hundreds of billions of star systems with planets that were potentially hospitable to life. And even if only a tiny percentage of these actually produced life, we would still have hundreds of thousands of them dotted about the universe. So what we should really ask is, How much *intelligent* life are we likely to find elsewhere in the cosmos?

It is possible that there are myriad instances of life, but no other intelligent life—possible, but again very unlikely. We have to conclude that there is a substantial probability of other intelligent beings inhabiting other parts of the universe, and it's also likely that some of these can be found within our own galaxy. But we cannot know for certain until some of the little (or big) fellows actually emerge from one of their space ships and say "hello" in some kind of language that we may—or may not—be able to understand. Or alternatively, until we are able to travel to *their* homeland and communicate with them, and tell them how happy we are to see them. We could then ask if they would be nice enough to put us up for a week or so, after which we would have to depart on our thousand-year-plus journey back to Earth.

The possibilities of life elsewhere that I have just outlined are roughly those put forward by Carl Sagan and Frank Drake in the 1970's. Sagan estimated that there might be a million other civilizations in our own Milky Way galaxy. But even though this came to be thought of as an exaggeration, the general projections of Sagan and Drake have been pretty much accepted for some time. However, Peter Ward and Donald Brownlee, in a recent book *Rare Earth,* have questioned the assumption that "complex" life is common in the universe. They think that *primitive* life, which does not include either animal or advanced plant life, may be extremely common. However, more complex forms of life may be very rare indeed. They point to many unique features of the Earth and of our solar system. The fact that the Earth has a core of molten iron is something that is probably vital to the occurrence of complex life, but such a core may be extremely rare. They also point to the fact that for 3 billion years after life first occurred on earth, only primitive organisms existed. Then suddenly there was a marked increase of quite different, and much more complex species. This is known as the Cambrian explosion, about 550 million years ago. Only then did complex life forms begin to proliferate. Ward and Brownlee think that something like the Cambrian explosion required such a confluence of special circumstances as to make it an extremely rare, and possibly unique, occurrence. All in all they make a fairly persuasive argument, but they nonetheless admit that there is not enough data to reach any firm conclusions.

I think that we tend to look at our own case as being more or less the only way life could occur. This point of view involves the so-called Anthropic Principle.[9] However, even if the Cambrian explosion *is* unique, I'm not convinced that it was *necessary* for the development of complex life. I don't see why there should not be many other evolutionary paths that could be taken in order to arrive at complex life forms. Given the vast size of the cosmos, there could be regions where life formed in other ways, with different elements and in other types of environment.

In any case, the opinion of the experts is divided. In *Vital Dust,* the Nobel Prize winning biologist Christian de Duve says that a cosmic cloud of organic, carbon-based molecules pervades the universe, and that life is almost certain to be abundant throughout the cosmos.

> If I am right, there are as many living planets in the universe as there are planets capable of generating and sustaining life...Trillions of biospheres coast through space on trillions of planets, channeling matter and energy into the creative fluxes of evolution.... The Earth is not a freak speck around a freak star in a freak galaxy, lost in an immense "unfeeling" whirlpool of stars and galaxies hurtling in time and space ever since the Big Bang. The Earth is part, together with trillions of other Earth-like bodies, of a cosmic cloud of "vital dust" that exists because the universe is what it is.[10]

De Duve imagines islands of life and culture sprinkled throughout the universe. But the distances between them are such that the laws of physics, specifically the light-speed limit, would preclude them from interacting with one another. It may eventually be possible to communicate with such islands of culture, should they exist, within a distance of about thirty light-years. But we will probably never be able to extend our reach very much further than that. De Duve continues:

> We could, by enlisting future generations, extend this range to a few hundred light-years, but surely not much further. Compare this distance with the diameter of our galaxy (about 100,000 light-years) and you can see that our access is perforce limited to only a small number of star systems in our own galaxy, a miniscule fraction of the universe...[11]

Of course, we do not know what is really out there. But as I have said, a visit from some strange beings in funny looking machines would put us well on the way towards clearing up some of these thorny questions.

ASPECTS OF EVOLUTION

From the preceding discussion, it is clear that the question of intelligent life, how it arose and how frequently it has occurred, is a key topic in our study of the overall context of human existence. All I can do here is point out some of the aspects of this inquiry, because there are still large gaps in our knowledge, which prevent us from making any definitive judgments in the matter.

So what are some of the facts that *do* bear on the subject of intelligent life? First of all, we must have at least a rough idea of what we mean by "intelligent."

(As with "life," a precise definition may ultimately elude us.) Every animal (or even plant) can be said to have a certain measure of intelligence. In fact many creatures, for example those that inhabit the ocean depths, can be described as highly intelligent in their ability to understand and exploit their environment. So how do we differentiate man from all the rest? As noted in Part I, it is the fact that man has language, culture, and above all, imagination that makes him different from his fellow animals. The other aspects that we talked about, namely art, science, technology, religion and war are basically cultural phenomena. Many other animals, especially our nearest relatives, the chimpanzees, exhibit some of these same traits, but only to a very limited degree. While many have rudimentary language, and presumably also some aspects of imagination, none have the slightest acquaintance with art, religion, science or war. These seem to be the distinguishing characteristics of "intelligent life."

Does the intelligent life that we have postulated to exist elsewhere in the universe exhibit the same characteristics as humans do? We would certainly expect them to have art, technology and science, but what about religion and war? If they have the latter two, might it not be better for us to avoid making contact with them at all! It's quite possible that they would treat us as an enemy, rather than greet us as friends, and in that case we would probably reciprocate with hostile actions of our own. Maybe the congenial meeting envisaged in the previous section is not the most likely to occur. Even if we ourselves have been able to curb our more aggressive instincts by the time we are able to make such a journey, we have no reason to assume that our aliens will have done the same.

But we must not be too quick to jump to conclusions. The direction of our own evolution has been very much dependent on geographical and climatic conditions here on Earth. These would obviously differ greatly in other planetary systems. So even if life arose in a similar manner, from the same, or nearly the same, combination of elements, there is little likelihood that evolution would have taken a similar path over a period of three or four billion years. In fact there is a high probability that it would have been radically different.

Given these different evolutionary paths, would intelligent life be more, or less likely to emerge? It's impossible to say. In our science fiction we tend to depict aliens as similar to us in many ways—just as in our religions we depict God as having human characteristics. But the aliens are likely to be a big surprise to us. As already stated, we also have to consider the possibility that self-replicating systems may have arisen from different combinations of molecules in radically different environments. This cannot be ruled out, given our sparse knowledge of what most of the rest of the universe is like.

Obviously the greater the number of different ways life *can* occur, the greater the likelihood that it *has* occurred—or *will* occur. But different circumstances may alter the actual process of evolution, and could make it less likely, or perhaps more likely that intelligent beings would ultimately appear.

At the present time man is the only "intelligent" animal on earth, among hundreds of thousands of different species, and most of the species that have come into existence are now extinct. The way evolution works, every species, however successful, eventually becomes extinct, and presumably mankind is no exception. Our intelligence might help to prevent this of course, but so far there is little evidence that it will.

Perhaps there is only room for one intelligent species of animal on any given planet. You will remember that the Neanderthals, another intelligent species, became extinct some 35,000 years ago, and modern Homo sapiens may well have destroyed them.[12] Two separate species, each with cultures, religions and the proclivity towards war, may not be able to exist side by side on the same planet. It's hard enough for different cultures created by the *same* species to co-exist.

Our warlike tendencies are obviously more self-destructive than the phenomenon of religion, but these two do seem to go together to a considerable degree. Is it possible that intelligent beings on other worlds might not have our addiction to war? It is certainly possible. But in our case, since carnivores tend to have bigger brains than herbivores, our higher intelligence seems to be correlated with this fact, which in turn can be linked to the origins of warlike activity. So war may be a pathology that's linked to intelligent life.

The elusive concept of higher intelligence continues to baffle the neuroscientists, the anthropologists and many others in related fields. How has evolution, in its hit-or-miss way of operating, managed to produce something like the human brain? Once this question is seriously addressed, another one arises. Was the human brain an accident?

As Robert Ornstein writes in the *Evolution of Consciousness:*

> Since early humans did not need a great brain to deal with the hunter lifestyle, it is unlikely that any cultural adaptation was responsible for this new anatomical complexity. Why build a bigger brain than you need to survive? The question is, what kind of an adaptation might have increased the brain in size, and what does it tell us about our mind now?
>
> We have a brain that is four times as large as our nearest "neighbors" and capacities beyond their farthest horizon. It is natural to regard ourselves as something special....

Obviously, all the suggestions—bipedalism, language, and other hypotheses—contributed to the change. But all these events, though clearly important, don't justify the major leap between the great apes and us....

A group of papers published in 1989 and 1990 makes the surprising suggestion that a spur for the brain's enlargement came from engineering and "packaging" considerations. Then the increase in size combined with other events to produce further changes. While, again, this is certainly speculative, the great increase in the cortex, I believe, must have been fueled by factors other than social because the brain grew explosively *in advance* of the characteristics we associate with being human.[13] (author's italics)

The fields of biology, anthropology and genetics are very active these days, and lots of interesting ideas are being bandied about. Another way to explain human intelligence is cited by Matt Ridley, in his book *Genome*. He says that we may have developed our greater intelligence through intra-species competition. In other words it became necessary to out-smart our fellow humans.

The notion that our brains grew big to help us make tools or start fires on the savannah has long since lost favor. Instead, most evolutionists believe in the Machiavellian theory—that bigger brains were needed in an arms race between manipulation and resistance to manipulation.[14]

Whatever the reason for our acquisition of higher intelligence, it should not materially affect the probability of big brains occurring elsewhere. Once a brain such as ours has come into existence, for whatever reason, it stands as evidence of what evolution is ultimately capable of. In other words, we ourselves are evidence that higher intelligence is possible. So if it can happen here, surely it could happen in other places as well—the Anthropic Principle notwithstanding.

Before we leave the subject of higher intelligence, one other intriguing question comes to mind. Since the DNA of a human being and that of a chimpanzee differ by only a miniscule amount—less than two percent—what accounts for the vast difference in mental capacity, learning ability and imaginative breadth? A clue to this disparity may lie in the different amount of time that each takes to reach maturity. Obviously the brain must develop differently after birth, since the basic hardware is just about the same.

Most other animals are able to walk and take care of themselves far sooner than a human being, which is helpless at birth, and needs to be constantly looked after for many years. The learning period for a human being is extremely long when compared to that of other animals. Actually, the extended human childhood may very well be the key to the difference in mental capacity, for it gives extra time for the complex neuronal networks—the wiring of the brain—to establish the right connections before everything gets set in place and flexibility becomes limited.[15] This allows us to build a much more powerful thinking machine. So our lack of early maturity may actually be the vital ingredient in our success.

This idea is not new, it goes back at least to Darwin's time. He does not find much difference in the length of childhood from man's nearest relatives.

> It has been urged by some writers, as an important distinction, that with man the young arrive at maturity at a much later age than with any other animal: but if we look to the races of mankind which inhabit tropical countries the difference is not great, for the orang is believed not to be adult till the age of from ten to fifteen years.[16]

But Darwin was trying to show how little difference there is between man and the other mammals. The question of greater intelligence is not discussed. The orang is one of our closest relatives, and has a brain very similar to ours, even though it is somewhat smaller. But brain size is not the only criterion for intelligence. Elephants have larger brains than humans, but they need it to control their larger body, so this does not say anything about their intelligence. How the brain is wired up is the significant factor.

Extended childhood may not be the *only* thing that gives us our superior intelligence, but it is surely an important contributing factor. The fact that we have a larger brain than the orang, as well as having an even *more* extended childhood, may go a long way in explaining our superior intelligence.

There is a big difference in brain size between the chimpanzee and the human—500 cc. vs 1300 cc. So in spite of the close similarity of the DNA, the brains of the two species are quite different. Psychologists David & Ann Premack point out that this could be accounted for by what are called regulatory genes. The similarity of gene structure between species is not the only factor to be considered. Which genes are *expressed* is actually more important. Gene expression in the human brain is apparently quite different to that in the brain of the chimpanzee, resulting in a far greater capacity for learning on the part of the human.[17]

Darwin does make some observations about our higher intelligence. But much of his thought is clouded by the fact that he was both a racist and a male chauvinist—as were the majority of British males in the nineteenth century! However, the development of advanced language and higher intelligence surely go together.

As the voice was used more and more, the vocal organs would have been strengthened and perfected through the inherited effects of use; and this would have reacted on the power of speech. But the relation between the continued use of language and the development of the brain, has no doubt been far more important. The mental powers in some early progenitor of man must have been more highly developed than in any existing ape, before even the most imperfect form of speech could have come into use; but we may confidently believe that the continued use and advancement of this power would have reacted on the mind itself, by enabling and encouraging it to carry on long trains of thought.[18]

Darwin thought that our superior intelligence could be accounted for by natural selection. "The difference in mind between man and the higher animals, great as it is, certainly is one of degree and not of kind."[19] Given time, chimpanzees and other close relatives of ours, could develop a similar aptitude for complex mental processes. He found the idea that we are somehow "specially endowed" with superior intelligence wholly unacceptable.

The key difference, as Darwin saw, lies in the ability to construct complex language. This helps the brain consider more and more abstract concepts, and expands the imagination into ever more sophisticated realms of thought and reasoning. The linguist Noam Chomsky showed that we possess a special innate ability for language, which other mammals lack.[20] A human child is able, not only to learn a language, but also to master its grammar with surprising ease. This makes possible the expansion of knowledge at a far greater rate, and in a much more comprehensive manner, than would otherwise be possible. This ability must surely have been correlated to the increasing size of the brain.

CONSCIOUS AND UNCONSCIOUS MINDS

Intimately related to the subject of higher intelligence is that of consciousness, another elusive concept that is only now being seriously investigated in scientific circles.

Today, the brain is slowly and reluctantly starting to give up its secrets. But consciousness is something that is hard to put one's finger on. One can argue that the world we see around us is actually an illusion, and that we are merely part of this illusion. (But if life is a dream, then who is the dreamer?) Descartes' famous declaration "I think therefore I am" seemed at first to have settled the question of whether we really exist. But this was not enough to satisfy the curious for very long.

Speculations regarding consciousness gave birth to the idea that there is some kind of center in the brain, where the input from the senses is analyzed and decisions are made as to what the appropriate responses to the various stimuli should be. Some thought that there was a little "homunculus," or engineer, sitting inside the brain, watching something like a movie screen and controlling the body's reactions in an appropriate way. But the trouble with this idea is that the brain has no focal point that could act as a control center—and anyway, there would have to be another, even smaller, homunculus inside our homunculus's head, and so on and so on. As Daniel Dennett says:

> No part of the brain is the thinker that does the thinking or the feeler that does the feeling, and the whole brain seems to be no better a candidate for that very special role. This is a slippery topic. Do brains think? Do eyes see? Or do people see with their eyes and think with their brains? Is there a difference? [21]

This brings up the subject of dualism. The idea behind dualism is that the mind and the body are separate entities. If the brain doesn't do the thinking, then the *mind* has to do the job. In *Consciousness Explained,* Dennett asserts that the mind is not made of the same material as the brain, it is made of what he calls "mind stuff."

A lot of our body's actions, in fact most of them, are automatic reflexes of one sort or another. But there are times when decisions have to be made and the question arises, Who makes these decisions? Who is in charge? Isn't it the *mind* that is in charge? But here we run into the same problem that we ran into when discussing the soul in chapter 2. According to dualism, the mind, like the soul, is nonmaterial and thus incapable of affecting the physical substance of the brain. Dennett continues:

> A fundamental principle of physics is that any change in the trajectory of any physical entity is an acceleration requiring the expenditure of energy, and where is this energy to come from? It is this principle of the conservation of energy that accounts for the physical impossibility of "perpetual motion machines," and the same principle is apparently violated by dualism.[22]

This is essentially the same argument that I made in chapter 2 regarding the soul. So what about the opposite point of view: that the brain actually *is* the mind? This is called materialism and Dennett doesn't like this either. He says that if we think of a purple cow, then this idea, or thought, has to exist somewhere. So he goes out on a limb and postulates the existence of "mind stuff."

This leads us round in a circle. The mind cannot be immaterial because of the laws of physics. But, according to Dennett, we can't do without some kind of mind stuff. He says that consciousness is still a mystery, but that we will eventually figure it out.

So how can we begin to make some sense out of this? We should remember that consciousness can be *altered* though the ingestion of certain chemicals contained in plants such as marijuana, opium, etc. These, together with other chemicals, such as alcohol, are often referred to as "mind-altering" substances, and this implies strongly that the mind is not made of "mind stuff" but, like consciousness itself, is actually just a *chemical process*. (It is interesting that certain cultures have banned the use of some of these substances, while others have cultivated their use.)

I disagree with Dennett about "mind stuff," I think it is pure fantasy. You can't have it both ways, either you have dualism or you don't. Just like the soul, mind stuff is a figment of the imagination, and the imagination itself is a *function* of the brain. It is the *brain* that produces thought, and also controls it. The individual self consists of the physical body and its *functions*, and nothing more.

Erwin Schrödinger (he of Schrödinger's cat) has some interesting things to say about mind and matter. He notes that not all neural networks are "conscious," apparently only those in the brain, although many have the capacity to *learn*. The fact that many of the physical movements that we make are essentially unconscious does not mean that they always were. Many unconscious actions were once conscious. They have just become routine and slipped into the unconscious. Only when the routine is broken by something unusual or unexpected is the conscious mind made aware of what is going on.

Schrödinger asserts that consciousness is needed for us to learn. Once something is learned, it becomes automatic, and so consciousness is no longer needed. This is how he puts it: "Consciousness is associated with the *learning* of the living substance; its *knowing how* (*Können*) is unconscious."[23]

In my view this applies not just to physical movements, but to thought processes as well, which come about by learning how to navigate in the physical world. Pure thought results, indirectly, from the process of learning through the senses. Like the imagination, it's a function of the brain. The fact that animals can also learn implies that they too have consciousness.

The brain/mind connection can be very confusing. But if thought about logically it is not that difficult. The word *mind* describes, or represents, an *abstraction*. Rather surprisingly, almost everyone understands what you are talking about when you use the word "mind," even though the *concept* of mind is somewhat nebulous.

Consciousness and mind are similar, but consciousness describes a *phenomenon,* rather than an abstraction. The mind and the brain come in one neat package. But the mind cannot exist without the brain, whereas the brain—in a slightly less developed form—could exist without the mind. In other words, there are aspects of the brain that have nothing to do with the mind (or consciousness), but not vice versa. One cannot consider the mind as a separate entity from the brain, they are inseparable, and the mind is just one part of the brain's *function.* It's not necessary to postulate something like mind stuff, this just confuses the issue. The so-called mind-altering substances, referred to above, are of course *brain-altering* substances, because they affect the chemistry of the neural networks in the brain. They are "mind-altering" in the sense that they alter the *function* of the brain, i.e. the mind.

Short-term and long-term memories are the stuff of thought, and they are also the stuff of dreams. And what *are* dreams anyway? According to Levi-Strauss they are *bricolage*—like the content of myths. They are an assortment of memories, both old and recent, real and imagined, which appear as a kind of kaleidoscope in our subconscious mind while we are asleep (in computer parlance, they are the contents of the recycle bin). I like this idea much better than Freud's theory of dreams, which tries to explain in logical terms something that is basically illogical. Since many other animals also appear to dream, it is surely just a natural phenomenon, which has little to do with culture.

Logic comes from the sequencing of neuronal structures. Their actions are driven by electronic pulses, regulated by networks built up over billions of years of evolution. Our brain is the creation, not of a single stroke of luck, but of a *process,* started when the first forms of life arose from inorganic matter.[24]

Experiments have shown that awareness (consciousness) of a physical movement comes only *after* neuronal activity connected with the movement has already been initiated in the brain.[25] Thus, if there were a conscious "decision" to make the movement it would be ex post facto—the decision would have already been made *subconsciously!* This ties in with what Schrödinger says about the learning process.

But there is an additional subtlety here, as microbiologist JohnJoe McFadden points out in *Quantum Evolution.* Even though there is neuronal activity prior to any conscious awareness, the movement itself does not actually take place until this awareness has occurred. There is a time lapse of about four hundred milliseconds until the action actually commences. But *conscious awareness* of the decision occurs two hundred milliseconds later—leaving enough time to stop the movement. So the conscious "will" is able to veto the action before it is carried out—if it so desires.[26] Of course the action can only be vetoed if it becomes conscious, i.e. it has not already been learned, or some unusual circumstance occurs! It looks as if free will may just survive—under certain conditions—since although the decision has already been made subconsciously, it can be cancelled by a conscious act. Thus we do not actually *make* decisions we just decide (within two hundred milliseconds) whether or not to carry them out! Free will seems to be still there—just—but it's not *completely* free.

Whether there really is such a thing as free will is debatable. Newton's assertion that any outcome is the end result of a chain of causation is basically correct, quantum mechanics notwithstanding.[27] Actually, nothing is *really* random. Even a coin toss could be predicted if one had enough information, though in practice this is not possible. So how we act in any given circumstance is foreordained in a sense, because it is the end result of a causal chain. It just *seems* as if we made a decision. However, there is another element to consider, and that is the imagination. Our imagination allows us to reflect on different courses of action, and then choose one of them. *How* we will choose may be foreordained, but we make a choice nonetheless! There certainly could not be any free will without the imagination—nor consciousness for that matter.

[Actually there is a growing realization in the field of molecular biology that decision-making is intimately connected with quantum mechanics! After all, quantum mechanics operates at the molecular level, and this is precisely where the living cell also functions. McFadden thinks, "Quantum measurement may be behind the phenomenon of conscious choice."[28] So the action of the *will* may involve quantum de-coherence, or the collapse of the wave function!]

And what about the imagination? We seem able to change the topic of our thoughts voluntarily, so who is in charge here? The answer is that nobody is in charge. No special guidance center is needed. The whole system is in charge of itself—it is self-controlled. Decisions are part of a seamless progression of action and reaction in the brain, which presents our conscious self with a "picture" of what is going on, and the imagination is part of this picture, or rather an extension of it. However, by far the greatest part of this process of action and reaction takes place subconsciously.

The primary difference between humans and other animals is that the former have the conscious part of their mental functions more highly developed, and this in turn is a reflection of their greater learning ability. The more sophisticated imaginative part of the mental process must be kept on the conscious level. The interplay of the conscious mind and the imagination creates a thinking machine of incredible subtlety and power, which far outdistances the mental capacities of our fellow creatures. The picture in the imagination takes its structure from our experience of the world—from our memories. Without experience there is no imagination.

THE COMPUTER AND THE BRAIN

The picture that we construct of the world around us is created by electromagnetic waves. The true nature of the *real* world is beyond our comprehension. What we "see" through our eyes is merely a "construct" in the brain, which *represents* the world that we inhabit. There are also backup systems of hearing, touch, taste and smell. These also help us to "see" the world, and they complement the picture created by the sense of sight.

All this equipment allows us to find food and avoid danger. It also informs us of the existence of other people just like us. The ability to communicate with them through speech is one of the vital characteristics of being human—other animals having speech only to a very limited degree. Evolution is the mechanism that has created all of this, because all these things, except perhaps for more advanced speech, are essential to survival. Our big brain, plus our imagination, has given us the ability to dominate the world. It has also given us the ability to destroy it.

The primary reason for the development of the brain was to procure food. As Tom Siegfried says in *The Bit and the Pendulum:*

> Plants have no brain because their ancestors made their own food. Of course, making your own food is not all that easy—photosynthesis is pretty sophisticated chemistry. But it doesn't require a brain. Eating food is the more complicated task. It requires a sophisticated system to control the muscular motions enabling an organism to see and catch edible life forms. The nervous systems used by primitive life for eating were probably the first step on the evolutionary path to a brain. In other words, we eat, therefore we think.
>
> Computers, on the other hand, don't eat, but they do think—sort of. So the comparison of computer thinking to human thinking is not entirely parallel.... Both computers and the brain process information by manipulating symbols. In computers, the symbols are electronic patterns. In brains, the symbols are molecules.[29]

The brain is a complex processor of information. While it has some of the aspects of a computer, it has many characteristics that a computer lacks. Some have likened the difference between the brain and the mind to that of hardware and software in a computer. But the analogy is inexact, because both the computer and its software are designed by an outside agency, namely man. Neither the brain, nor the mind is *designed* at all.

The mind is a *function* of the brain, and arises directly from it.[30] Mind and consciousness are intimately related, but are not the same thing, because there is both a conscious and an unconscious mind. You might say that consciousness is the spectator of what the mind is doing. But one should remember that consciousness, like the brain itself, is the result of natural selection.[31]

One can say that the human brain has been "designed" by natural selection. But this unique—and very lengthy—process is quite different from anything that human beings are capable of. That may help explain why AI (artificial intelligence) has been so difficult to accomplish. The brain just doesn't function like an ordinary computer. It has multiple (parallel) connections, whereas a conventional computer has much simpler (serial) connections. As Steve Grand says, "Intelligence is the result of billions of unintelligent processes operating concurrently."[32] But computers that function more like the neural networks in the brain may soon be a reality, although progress along these lines has been slow and intermittent.[33] (Of course it is their own brains that the scientists are using to discover exactly how the brain works—the brain's own incredible subtlety makes this introspection possible! The brain is helping us to expose its own secrets!)

We have our way of designing things and Nature has hers. We tend to design things from the top down, whereas Nature does it from the bottom up. So in order to do the things that Nature does, we will have to start doing things her way. Top-down control means that there is a *controller,* who knows about everything that goes on in the system, and constantly regulates its operation. This is possible in a relatively simple system, with only a moderate number of parts. But it is clearly impossible in complex systems, like those that occur in Nature, with literally billions of sub-systems, each with sub-systems of their own. The only way that such a system can work is from the ground up. Each part neither knows nor cares what any of the other parts are doing. If one thinks about it, one realizes that not even super-human intelligence could exert top-down control of all the complex structures and organisms in Nature. Only by having *no one* in overall control can such things function at all, although at first sight this seems to be impossible. The concept of bottom-up control is fundamental to any proper understanding of how Nature operates—and evolution as well.

[Although we may think we are in complete control of our bodies, this is not really so. Only a very limited amount of top-down control is possible. By far the greatest part of the controlling mechanism is bottom-up. It occurs automatically—and subconsciously.]

Another big difference between the brain and a computer is that the brain is alive—or at least it's in a body that's alive. One must surely assume that there is a fundamental difference between two things: one made of living organic material, and the other of some *inorganic* substance, even if they both function in a similar way. Then again, maybe there wouldn't be so much of a difference. We are, after all, made up of ordinary chemical elements. Jeffrey Satinover asks, "Will we be able to tell the difference between a trillion-neuron silicon-based brain and our own 20-billion neuron, carbon-based one?"[34]

A computer serves as an extension of the human brain, since it can process data in far greater quantities and at much higher speeds than the brain can. Since man created the computer, it is fitting that it should be his servant and helper. But if the computer does start to act like a sentient being, as some of its advocates predict that it will, then we may be in for some rude surprises.[35] We would have a "being" with a thinking mechanism similar to the human brain, that did not need food! Since the human brain evolved for the primary purpose of obtaining food, this seems a bit peculiar. We would have created something that was "alive" in some sense, but that did not require food (apart from a little electrical "juice").

I don't consider a robot as being alive because it can't think for itself. The fun will start if and when robots or computers *do* start thinking for themselves.[36] Will our new digital friends develop emotions like ours? And will they have consciousness? [37]

But we may not be so happy with our new creations. As the Nobel Prize-winning chemist Roald Hoffmann says, "The psychology of human beings is not well suited to admitting that we can be replaced by a computer program, only that others can be."[38]

Not only do we have artificial intelligence, but also artificial life (a-life). In his book *Creation,* Steve Grand claims to be able to create life. But it is actually *virtual* life, which exists in cyberspace. Nonetheless he claims that it really is life. The trick is to simulate a basic entity, like an atom, or a neuron, by means of a computer program, and then, by further computer operations, induce such a simulation to create a more complex object such as a molecule, and ultimately some kind of automaton. This process is called *emergence* in computer parlance.[39]

A simulation of a living thing is not alive, and a simulation of intelligence is not intelligent. On the other hand, intelligent, living things can be made out of simulations.... If we simulate nerve cells using computer code, then they are not really nerve cells. But if we use these simulated nerve cells to build a brain and the brain thinks, it is not the brain's fault that its constituent neurones are a sham; it will still be a brain and its thoughts will be real thoughts. If it then goes on to proclaim itself to be conscious, who are we to deny it? On the other hand, if we simply try to write a computer program that behaves as if it is conscious, then I think it is wrong to say that the result really is conscious.[40]

Steve Grand's book is fascinating, in that it dares to go beyond conventional ways of thinking about life and intelligence. Here is another quote:

Life is not the stuff of which it is made—it is an emergent property of the aggregate arrangement of that stuff. Even the stuff itself is no more than an emergent property of a still smaller whirlpool of interactions. Living beings are high-order persistent phenomena, which endure through intelligent interaction with their environment. This intelligence is a product of multiple layers of feedback. An organism is therefore a localized network of feedback loops that ensures its own continuation.[41]

Even though a-life is not "life" as we know it, this fact is not important to those in the field. They feel that there can be other manifestations of life besides the one that is familiar to us in the biological realm. The computer is the key to discovering the principles on which any kind of life must depend. Just as the telescope and the microscope were the instruments that led to the opening up of a more comprehensive understanding of the physical world, so the computer is helping us to unravel the mysteries of life itself. This is what the Danish biologist Claus Emmeche has to say about artificial life in *The Garden in the Machine:*

Today it is the computer that permits us to see the deepest structures, that has taken the microscope's place as the *speculum mundi* or mirror of the world. It is, of course, a world based on mathematical formalism, formalisms that nonetheless contain such dynamic forms of movement that they hold the promise of being able to describe both the quivering of earthly life and the complex mechanics of heavenly bodies.... Is what we see simply a human construction, or do the computer-generated pictures describe an independent reality?.... The pictures that computers construct are the world of the biology of the possible, a synthetic world of artificial life that, despite its artificiality, must conform to the universal laws of self organization and evolution.[42]

This idea of computer-generated worlds can lead to all sorts of fantastic scenarios. The possibility that our universe is just a small part of some vast multiverse is the subject of debate by cosmologists. But how can we know that we are not part of someone else's computer-generated world? Paul Davies looks at the possibilities:

> Eventually, entire virtual worlds will be created inside computers, their conscious inhabitants unaware that they are simulated products of somebody else's technology. For every original world, there will be a stupendous number of available virtual worlds—some of which would even include machines simulating virtual worlds of their own, and so on ad infinitum.
>
> Taking the multiverse theory at face value, therefore, means accepting that virtual worlds are more numerous than "real" ones. There is no reason to expect our world—the one in which you and I are reading this right now—to be real as opposed to a simulation. And the simulated inhabitants of a virtual world stand in the same relationship to the simulating system as human beings stand in relation to the traditional Creator.[43]

Interesting though these speculations are, we must return to the more familiar surroundings of our everyday world (regardless of whether it is real or simulated). We will now look at some of the institutions that man has created, starting with the various rules and laws that have been found necessary for the proper functioning of human society. We will also look at the laws that Nature herself appears to obey.

11

LAWS OF MAN AND NATURE

○ ○
The duping of the many will always be a condition of the rule by
the few

—Lee Harris
Civilization and Its Enemies

LAW AND ORDER

Laws or rules have been a part of the social scene since the earliest days of human
settlements. As culture developed, the necessity for rules became more apparent,
for man in his natural state is not adapted to the unnatural conditions of life
within any kind of structured society. As time went on, more rules were created,
and it ultimately became clear that almost any kind of human activity needed to
have its laws, whereas the only kind of law that had existed hitherto was the law
of the jungle.

In Mesopotamia, the advent of writing soon brought forth the first examples
of law codes. The most famous of these early codes is that of Hammurabi of
Babylon (1792-1750 B.C.). It was by no means the first of its kind, as archaeolo-
gist Jack Finegan tells us:

> As for Hammurabi's well-known code of laws, with its nearly three hundred
> paragraphs of provisions touching commercial, social, and domestic life, and
> the relations of the *awilum* or noble, the *mushkenum* or commoner, and the
> *wardum* or slave, it is evident that it draws upon a legal heritage already
> reflected in the Sumerian code of Ur-Nammu, the Akkadian laws of Esh-
> nunna, and the Sumerian code of Lipit-Ishtar, even as it is also related at not a
> few points to the later laws of Israel.[1]

Assyrian and Hittite law codes soon followed. It was thus generally apparent that in order to strengthen the fabric of society, rules of conduct and operation were essential. But as with any human enterprise, there were difficulties that had to be overcome.

Once you have introduced the idea of law, there are several considerations that become evident. First of all, who or what is to be the lawgiver? Secondly, who is to interpret the law? And third, who is to enforce it? All these can, and have, caused major problems through the centuries.

Laws or rules have to be promulgated by some individual or group, and it must be agreed upon as to who has the authority to create laws. But theory and practice seldom coincide in this regard. If an individual or group of individuals has sufficient power and ambition, they may be able both create the laws and also to enforce them, without having to obtain agreement or permission from anyone else.

As for interpreting the laws, this can also be done by those who make them, or their representatives. In fact the first law codes were seldom, if ever, accepted by general agreement. They were created directly by decree of the ruler or king. But an interesting feature of this process began to arise in many communities that were widely separated geographically. The ruler began to acquire divine status; in many cases he actually became a god. Once this occurred, the legitimacy of the laws that were promulgated was no longer in question. If a god created the laws, they would have to be obeyed, with no questions asked. For example, in such an out-of-the-way place as Polynesia, we find that this has been going on for centuries. As Robert Wright explains:

> The generic Polynesian chief had plenty of sacred clout. He was an earthly representative of the gods, the conduit through which divine power or *mana*, flowed into society. Indeed he possessed *tapu*—such sanctity that commoners were not to come into direct contact with him. (Hence the modern word *taboo*.) Some chiefs were carried around on litters and had spokesmen, "talking chiefs," who handled the dirty business of communication. The Polynesian chief, observed one western scholar, "stands to the people as a god."[2]

This tendency towards deification of the ruler has been widespread, and it has also served well to quell thoughts of rebellion among the common people. From Hammurabi to the Roman Caesars, and even to the crowned heads of Europe, who created the *divine right of kings*, rulers everywhere sensed that they were safer on the throne as a god, or the representative of a god, than simply as an ordinary mortal. And that laws could be made, and obeyed, without nearly so much fuss if the ruler remained on an altogether higher plain than those who were required to do his bidding. From our longer perspective, we might imagine that talk of divinity could have aroused suspicions of tyranny, but the idea of having a god as ruler seems to have suited people remarkably well. All that was necessary was some kind of myth, to explain the process of deification.

The Athenians, those pioneers of logical thought and democratic government, although their myths and legends were full of stories about gods and mortals performing heroic deeds, attempted during their classic age to put both government and laws on a sounder basis. In the *Republic,* Plato envisages a group of "guardians" (philosophers), who would promulgate laws and administer them with justice and equity. The assumption was that a group of people should be assembled from within the community, who could be relied upon to govern without bias or favor.[3] This idea, or something close to it, was actually put into practice in some of the city-states, although it fell somewhat short of Plato's ideal, since there was still a king who was the nominal ruler. But the king was really a "first among equals," a sort of chairman of the board. However, the "board" consisted of the heads of the community's leading families. The notion that they would consider the welfare of the whole community as more important than their own interests was somewhat naïve, to say the least.

Plato's idea seems anti-democratic. One worries that the elders or guardians will abuse their power. After all, power corrupts does it not? But Plato's idea may save us from the "tyranny of the majority," which can become a problem in democracies.

As time has gone by, more enlightened governments have in fact arisen, and the idea of democracy, originated by the Greeks, is increasingly accepted worldwide. But the road has been a long and rocky one, and the struggle against tyranny has by no means been won. Many of the European nations, in spite of their warlike tendencies, have pioneered the creation of more enlightened leadership, introducing the idea of parliamentary government, which has gradually wrested power away from the entrenched elites. But progress has been uneven and the forces of reaction are always lying in wait.

More recent attempts to grant power to the people by abolishing the elites have been dismal failures, from the French Revolution to the present. In the twentieth century, "people's representatives" sometimes replaced the elites. They maintained their positions of power by means of secret police organizations, which were used to intimidate and coerce the very people they were supposed to serve and protect. At least the old elites knew how to live, as evidenced by their beautiful homes and estates. At least they had education and good taste. The comrades of the people shared with the elites only a lust for power.

The idea of God-given law, as opposed to that promulgated by a god-king, had its initial impetus after the Jewish people adopted monotheism and introduced the Ten Commandments, reputedly given by God to Moses on mount Sinai. These formed the basis of moral teaching for both the Jews and the Christians. Other religions, especially the major ones of both East and West, also introduced the concept of *moral* law. This was over and above the civil law, and although the areas covered by both types of law overlapped, the moral law was more concerned with individual or personal behavior.

Different cultures can in fact have different moral laws, and this can cause considerable difficulty when they come into contact. The situation with civil law is even more complicated. There are national laws, state laws, county laws, municipal laws and local laws of all kinds and description.

As with many other human activities, once the process of lawmaking starts, it is almost impossible to stop it. This is especially true with civil laws. In most countries, they have governing bodies—such as parliaments, senates and houses of representatives—that do little else but make laws. This in spite of the fact that there are already far too many laws! Old laws are hardly ever abolished, even though many of them no longer serve any practical purpose. The lawmakers must go on creating new laws, whether or not they are needed, just to justify their status as law-makers. This situation illustrates how lawmaking, like many other activities, can easily get out of hand.

RULES OF THE GAME

There are a host of human activities that have their own laws or rules. Sports and games, for instance, form a broad category where rules are needed. In addition to rules and laws, there are also customs, which differ in subtle ways from conventional types of regulation. The penalty for breach of a custom is not well defined, and can range from something quite severe to nothing at all. But breach of a custom can seriously damage one's standing in the community, as much, if not more than breach of a law.

Sports and games play a very important role in human society. They are rituals of competition, which have far more significance than meets the eye. Individual games can be likened to duels, and have much in common with mating rituals in the animal world. The knightly jousts of the Middle Ages had obvious parallels in this regard. Today, boxing and fencing are contests that are reminiscent of duels. But practically all games have something of this element in them. Competition is a very basic part of all societies. A society has a tendency to divide itself into winners and losers, and games and sports are a means whereby this distinction can be made. (Could this possibly be because the ladies are more attracted to a winner than a loser?)

Both sports and games involve the strange human phenomenon of transference, or identification—only vaguely connected to the term used in psychoanalysis. Just as the members of a community identified with their heroes in the days of single combat, so the people of today identify with their sports heroes and with their national and local sports teams. Without this psychological attachment, which in essence entails *virtual* war, these activities would lose much of their meaning and significance. Blood sports, such as bullfighting, reminiscent of the ritualized war of the gladiators, are variations on a similar theme, where the audience enters vicariously into the action of the spectacle or sport. Other sports, such as horseracing or cockfighting are betting games, although the latter could also be considered as a blood sport. Of course there's more to horse racing than betting—there's also snobbery. Like fox hunting, horse racing got its start as the sport of kings. The purest form of sport is athletics, which probably originated with the ancient Greeks. Although adulterated by professionalism and drugs, the modern Olympic games are actually less corrupted than the ancient ones. Cheating and brutality were widespread in the original games. The Roman Emperor Nero managed to have himself declared the winner of a chariot race, even though he did not finish.

While individual games are substitutes for the duel, team games can be considered as a substitute for war. Football is a prime example. But this is much more than just an analogy. The Duke of Wellington's remark that the battle of Waterloo was won on the playing fields of Eton was very close to the truth. The concept of the *team*, which Lee Harris traces back to Sparta, has been central to the superiority of Western armies.[4] The French Revolution produced the *citizen army*, which proved far superior to professional armies. The emphasis on team games in the English public schools is intended to inculcate much more than fair play in the participants, it is meant to encourage individual initiative, which was vital to the success of the British imperial armies. (Some other, less savory, "teams" appeared in the twentieth century, to wit: the Fascist, Nazi and Communist parties. These could better be described as gangs.)

[The recent phenomenon of "soccer hooligans," especially those of the British variety, illustrates another connection to war. People like this were the cannon fodder in the great battles that marked Britain's rise to greatness. They were the first over the ramparts, and the first to meet the charge of the onrushing enemy. In war they were (unsung) heroes, but in peacetime many of them were criminals. They were on the bottom rung of the social ladder, and so were given little credit for doing the hard fighting that led to victory. Just as manual laborers do the really important work, but are nonetheless looked down upon socially, so these "outcasts" were shunned, even though they were essential to the success of any military campaign. However, in this day and age, such people may not have the skills to become members of a modern army. So they have to create their own war, in which they can fight for their country, with the "enemy" as the opposing team's supporters. They are not satisfied with the *virtual* war of the more conventional soccer fan. As a result, they squander their talents in gratuitous violence. Far from being hailed as heroes, they are lucky if they escape being sent to jail. In a real war one is applauded for acting in this way—perhaps even given a medal. But in the ersatz war of the hooligans, no one recognizes them as the warriors of yesteryear.]

The best players are said to have the "killer instinct"—echoes of the primordial beast. This surely tells us how important competition is in any society. In fact a case could be made that the more competitive societies are the most successful, in the material sense anyway. Intense competition seems to be a vital ingredient to success in many fields. This ensures that the cream comes to the top—just the way evolution intended.

Other games are more individual in nature. Golf, for instance, is like life, in that it reflects the individual's struggle with his own inner self. The shifts of fortune, which are often due to luck rather than skill, or the lack thereof, are paralleled by life's changing fortunes, and must be dealt with through self-control and patience, just as in real life. The true test of the golfer comes when things are going badly, when luck seems to have deserted him and his game is threatening to unravel. In some ways the contest is not with his opponent but with himself.

Although most sports or games of the "active" variety are played by the younger folk, this is not at all true of golf. In fact one of the great achievements of a golfer is to play eighteen holes in fewer strokes than his age. This cannot be done until the golfer is at least in his late 60's, and then only by those with exceptional health and ability. So these *real* golfers are very few in number.

Another interesting thing about golf is how badly most people play it. Although they try valiantly to improve their games, spending hour upon hour in search of a better golf swing, and avidly reading the latest instructional literature, only a very few are successful in actually making progress. In fact, for the majority, the more they practice, the worse they get. But however badly they play, they hardly ever consider giving up the game. The secret of a better swing may suddenly be revealed in a flash of inspiration.

There is actually a scientific explanation for the golfer's unhappy state. The reason most golfers play badly is because the human brain cannot work out exact solutions to problems such as hitting a golf ball so that it will travel 300 yards and land within a few feet of a given target. As Frank Vertosick explains in *The Genius Within,* a serial computer can work out an exact solution to that kind of physical problem, whereas the human brain, with its network of neurons, is more suited to finding fairly good approximate solutions, rather than exact ones.

> Exact solutions come at too high a price and are almost never necessary in the real world. The average person is a lousy golfer because the human brain didn't evolve to execute movements *perfectly each time.* Perfect execution is the province of serial computers, not living machines.[5]

While we are on the subject of golf, the elaborate rules of the game, which are known in their entirety by only a very few, seem to parallel the situation in society itself, where the intricacies of the laws of the land are known only to judges and lawyers. And like the civil laws, the rules of golf are constantly being changed and extended.

This obsession with rules is not confined to golf. Many other sports have rules that are not well known in their entirety by either spectators or participants. Who, other than a tiny minority of players or fans, really knows all the rules of such games as baseball, hockey or football—in any of its varieties—or even tennis? The list could go on and on. A small army of officials is required for practically every professional sport, to see that the rules are not infringed, and to interpret them when necessary.

Why is it necessary to have such elaborate rules for every kind of human activity? Cannot those involved be trusted to act, or compete, in a fair and sportsmanlike manner, without being subject to the rulebook at every twist and turn? Isn't golf supposed to be played by gentlemen, who would never think of cheating? Alas, in a world where cheating is considered sinful, the cheat has a tremendous advantage, and so he cheats whenever he thinks he can get away with it.

Games such as chess and bridge are on a more intellectual level. And the rules are not nearly so elaborate. Nevertheless, cheating, or unsportsmanlike conduct, is apt to occur from time to time. One can hardly describe such activities as sports or games in the conventional sense—"intellectual pursuits" seems to be a more apt description. The simple rules of such games as chess and checkers allow them to be modeled by computer programs. But even though the rules are simple, the number of possible positions, or states, of the board is enormous, and the result of a given move on the overall course of the game is very hard to foresee. This is what makes these games interesting.[6]

With almost all laws, there is a distinction between the *letter* and the *spirit* of the law, and therein lies the rub. Human nature being what it is, most people will try and find ways to evade laws or to discover loopholes in them. But this violates the spirit of the law. A truly civil society will be achieved only when the spirit, not just the letter of the law is observed. But this is asking too much of human nature in its present state.

INTERPRETING THE LAW

Now we come to the second important question, Who is to interpret the law? As far as civil law is concerned, there is an elaborate machinery of judges and lawyers who are ready, willing—and sometimes even able—to interpret the law. As far as the moral law is concerned, things get murkier. The question of *authority* is paramount in this case. When we are dealing with religion, it is usually God that is the ultimate authority. But who is to say what is the law of God? And who is to interpret it?

The law of God is usually "revealed" to a holy man or prophet, and then written down in a "sacred book." But who is to interpret the law so written? This generally falls to an officially sanctioned body of "wise men" (hardly ever women!), whose job it is to make sure that the laws are known and understood by all the faithful.

The fact that civil law is not universal is not an impediment to its operation, since it is expected, and accepted, that such laws will vary from place to place and country to country. But the moral laws are often thought of as universal. And since such laws can in fact vary from society to society and religion to religion, considerable problems may arise. In the days when the human family was split up into widely separated communities, which seldom came into contact with one another, this problem seldom arose. But if contact *was* made between different cultures, the stark contrast between both moral laws and customs became readily apparent. Today, with contact between cultures an everyday occurrence, these contrasts have become somewhat blurred, but they are still very real, and show that moral laws and customs can vary considerably from culture to culture.

Would it be possible to agree on universal moral laws? After all, many of these laws *are* in fact the same in many different societies. But in truth, this task would be all but impossible. Not only do people of different religious persuasions within the same society disagree as to what is morally right and what is not, even those of the *same* religion often fail to agree among themselves regarding the moral laws.

So we have to come to the conclusion, in spite of all the talk about moral law being God-given and universal, that it is in fact a relative thing. In the final analysis, it is the *individual* who has to decide what is moral and what is not.

But wait a minute. Surely this is just permissiveness gone wild. If everyone can make up their own moral code, then there will be no valid standards and chaos will reign. There are several reasons why such fears are unfounded. To begin with, in nearly all societies, the moral code and the civil code overlap in many instances. In addition, as noted above, the moral traditions and customs of the various societies and cultures also tend to overlap in the case of serious transgressions such as murder and theft—and also regarding many lesser offences. In other words, for the most part there is a consensus among intelligent and reasonable people, as to what constitutes proper behavior. (The Golden Rule: "do unto others as you would have them do to you," goes a long way towards establishing a basic standard for interpersonal behavior of all kinds.) The fact that individuals can differ on certain matters does not alter this. For although morality is not something that is absolute, reasonable people should be able to come fairly close to agreement on the basics of proper conduct. The Ten Commandments have lasted exceptionally well because they have in fact stressed standards of behavior that most societies adhere to anyway, and the civil laws reflect these same standards. It is in private matters that the differences become more apparent.

[The fact that morality varies between different cultures and countries is not sufficient reason to account for the lack of moral behavior in international relations, or its complete abandonment in war. This tells us that there are times when morality has to take second place to more import things, such as the pursuit of power. Even within a community or nation the quest for power pushes aside any compulsion to abide by the civil or moral laws. But in this case, when the laws are broken, care must be taken to avoid penalties if possible. With actions *between* nations no such care is necessary, because normally no penalties will be imposed. In fact, in the case of international relations and war, the abandonment of morality is (unofficially) sanctioned by the state!]

On a personal level, reasonable people can differ on questions of moral behavior, just as they can on many other things. In fact, no amount of teaching, indoctrination, or exhortation can impose uniformity. Any attempt to legislate personal or private morality by the self-appointed guardians of public virtue is almost always counterproductive.

All the same, we do not lack for "authorities" that insist on explaining to us just what is moral and what is not. Part of the function of religion is to expound the laws of God. So there are professional interpreters whose function is to explain the moral law, just as there are lawyers who are expert in the interpretation of civil law. These are priests, rabbis, clergymen, swamis, and other holy men (again, not usually women), who are essentially middlemen between God and the common people, and whose special function is to explain and interpret his teachings. None of these professionals would be anxious to allow the transfer of their authority in moral matters to the individual, as this would be usurping their prerogative. Indeed, in the Christian Church, the heretics (or reformers)—Gnostics, Manichaeans, Arians, Cathars (Albigensians) and various kinds of Protestants—all strove to make the spiritual life a more *personal* thing, whereas the Roman Church insisted on keeping the keys to the kingdom of heaven to itself. Sometimes, for example in the case of the Cathars, the Church was willing to use torture and execution to retain control over the teaching of morality. Incidentally, heresy seems to be mostly a Western phenomenon. The Eastern cultures are more tolerant. And another interesting fact, many of the Western "heresies" were Eastern in origin.

Darwin says that morality, rather than being God-given, arises from the social instincts: love, sympathy for one's fellow man, etc.

> The moral sense follows, firstly, from the enduring and ever-present nature of the social instincts; secondly, from man's appreciation of the approbation and disapprobation of his fellows; and thirdly, from the high activity of his mental faculties, with past impressions extremely vivid; and in these latter respects he differs from the lower animals.... After some temporary desire or passion has mastered his social instincts, he reflects and compares the now weakened impression of such past impulses with the ever-present social instincts; and he then feels that sense of dissatisfaction which all unsatisfied instincts leave behind them, he therefore resolves to act differently for the future,—and this is conscience.[7]

But many other animals have social instincts, which strongly suggests that they also have a sense of morality. Some psychologists, and others in related fields, maintain that animals do not have a sense of self, and so cannot be said to have a personality like that of a human being. But one only has to look around to see that many, if not most, animals do indeed have personalities, so how can these scientists say that they have no sense of self, or of morality? This smacks of hubris to me. And many animals obviously have a well-developed sense of aesthetics. What would be the point of the beautiful display of the peacock, if the peahen could not appreciate it? I'm happy to report that some recent studies have shown that my opinion may indeed be correct.[8]

LAWS OF NATURE

Another system of laws relates to the natural environment, namely the laws of physics. At first sight, these appear to be another set of "God's laws." But while the moral laws can be broken, if the physical laws are broken, it means that they are not the correct ones! So they are quite different from the other laws that we have looked at.

We cannot be sure that the laws of physics would have existed in the way that we have formulated them—or even whether they would have existed at all—had man not come along and discovered (or created) them. This is so whether or not they really *are* God's laws. Because if they *are* Gods laws, it's well nigh certain that he would not have framed them in the same way that we have. And if they are *not* God's laws, then whose are they, Mother Nature's? (Whether or not they *are* God's laws is discussed further in chapter 14, *Does God Know about Lie groups?*)

Since Einstein's laws have now superseded those of Newton, one cannot truthfully say that Newton's laws are the laws of physics, although they are obviously a good approximation. But even Einstein's laws are surely just a *better* approximation.[9]

Certainly we want to find the *exact* laws, not just approximations to them. But this may not be possible. For the laws of physics, as formulated by man, which have been either created or discovered, are essentially *man's* laws, and are at best approximations to the *real* laws, whatever they may happen to be, and whatever their ultimate origin.

Consider, for example, the famous equation $E = mc^2$. This is a simple and very powerful equation, which lies at the heart of our understanding of the physical universe. But each term in this equation has been *defined* by a human being; namely Einstein. It is a relativistic equation, and the terms have been carefully formulated so that they will fit precisely into it. The "m" stands for the "relativistic mass," and E is a component of the "4-vector of momentum and energy" (does God know about 4-vectors?), while "c" is the velocity of light in vacuo.[10] Surely, if the laws of physics *are* God's laws, he could have come up with another equation, involving other terms, or could perhaps have framed the same, or a similar law, without using *any* kind of equation at all. Some scientists would say that this equation represents a kind of logical imperative—it *has* to be true, and we have merely discovered it. But since man (specifically Einstein) has "invented" all the terms that go into the equation, I don't see that this is necessarily true.

One soon realizes how difficult these things can get when one reaches the philosophical level. This is why the physicists tend to leave such questions alone. Personally, I can't resist taking a crack at them. You just never know what you may discover.

Whether or not they are God's laws, our physical laws are nonetheless very powerful, and they are vital to our understanding of the universe. So even if the laws that we use are not the *real* ones, they are nevertheless essential to our scientific endeavors.

CRIME, PUNISHMENT AND JUSTICE

This brings us to the other important question regarding our civil and moral laws, Who is to enforce them, and what should the penalties be? It turns out that it is much easier to create laws than to administer justice when laws are broken. And justice itself can be very elusive. Plato tried to define what he meant by justice in the *Republic*, but he shed very little light on the matter. In any case, his idea of justice was different to ours. One must not forget that justice is a human invention, but nonetheless an important one, for it is a vital part of any human society. It does not exist in nature.

As in the interpretation of the law, so in the matter of punishment, fairness and justice are essential. But throughout history they have both been in very short supply indeed. It is not a pleasant story, and reflects badly on all concerned, except perhaps the poor devils that have been caught in the web of injustice. Stories of dungeons and torture are familiar to all those who have studied history. Indeed, little effort was made to improve the lot of prisoners until the nineteenth century, and then only in the more "enlightened" countries. That punishment was only rarely appropriate to the crime was not of any particular concern to those who administered the law. Sadistic physical punishments and gruesome methods of execution were common. The English reserved special treatment for those considered guilty of treason. Being hung, drawn and quartered was their fate, well into the nineteenth century. To spare the sensitivities of the reader I shall refrain from describing this sadistic form of execution.

The methods of torture that have been used throughout the ages have been refined and improved, as if the process of inflicting pain were a science. Far from being discontinued, this grisly research still goes on today in many countries—even in the more "enlightened" ones.

The question of deterrence has been central to any discussion of crime. It has been maintained that sufficiently severe punishment is bound to act as a deterrent against further transgressions of the law. This theory has very little actual evidence to support it. Nobody who commits a crime does it in the expectation that he will be caught. On the contrary, he expects *not* to be caught. The thought of punishment, for the type of people who are likely to commit crimes, is usually vague at best. Those who are very *unlikely* to commit crimes may indeed be deterred, but this kind of deterrence is not likely to reduce the prison population very much.

In medieval England, pickpockets were often executed for their crimes. But they found that one of the best opportunities to ply their trade was at public executions! While the crowd was intent on watching the grisly spectacle, the pickpockets could easily relieve them of their money and valuables. These miscreants obviously thought (correctly) that the chance of their being caught was extremely slim.

Public executions could, however, serve as a deterrent, as indeed they were intended to. But this was by no means always the case. Rebellion against an unjust authority could bring swift and severe punishment, usually in the form of public execution. But many of these unfortunates were considered martyrs to their cause, and so were honored as heroes rather than reviled. This in turn inspired others to follow their example. For instance, the early Christians were severely persecuted by the Romans because they were considered to be subversive. Many of them were crucified on crosses set up along the highways for all to see. But this did not serve as much of a deterrent, because they were considered martyrs for Christ, and as such, assured of heaven. Indeed, the only effective way the Romans found to deal with the Christians was to join them.

The conditions in modern penal systems, even in Western democracies, are not much improved from those of past centuries. Crime and punishment are something that the average citizen would prefer not to think about, except in so far as it affects him personally. In other words, he is mainly interested in not becoming a victim of crime. He is in favor of harsh punishment for the criminal, the harsher the better. The politicians try to convince the public just how tough they intend to be on crime, and so a rational approach to the problem is well nigh impossible. By seeking to deter crime one can easily lose sight of any commitment to justice.

Once a prisoner is incarcerated, the chance of him or her ever again becoming a productive member of society is small. In the United States, two million people are in prison, at vast expense to the state. Many of these are mentally ill when they are incarcerated, and many others will suffer sufficient psychological damage to render them incapable of returning to a normal life after they are released. A large percentage of these prisoners are there for some minor violation of the drug laws, for which they have received mandatory sentences. This is hardly an enlightened approach to crime. It can basically be described as medieval.

In many countries the solution to the problem of crime has been largely confined to the building of more prisons. The human cost of this approach is not of much interest to the general public, and even the economic cost is considered to be worth it. The problem is left to those who run the prisons and the judicial system. It is ignored by just about everyone else. But it should be obvious that we cannot have a more civilized society by simply sweeping such problems under the rug.

Harsh sentences in fact do little to *prevent* crime. The best opportunity for preventing a crime comes *before* the crime is committed. This should be obvious, but few societies consider putting it into practice. And punishing the criminal obviously does little to help the victim.

Until we start studying the nature of criminality from a more rational point of view, and acknowledge that most criminal behavior is the result of many factors, most of which are beyond the control of the individual criminal, we will never come close to solving the problem of crime. Rather than just locking criminals away in prisons, surely it would be better to study them, and hopefully discover the reasons for their antisocial behavior.

New research into the workings of the human mind brings into question many of our assumptions concerning personal responsibility. If we are simply a mass of little particles that obey the laws of physics, how much responsibility for our actions do we really have? Since anger, love and sexual attraction consist mainly of chemical reactions—which are largely beyond our control—where does genuine responsibility lie? Surely we will have to revise a lot of our thinking in this area.

Once we have realized that the old ideas of free will and responsibility have to be modified, we can start putting together a more realistic description of what a genuine value system should look like. But it's not going to be easy, and there will be a lot of weeping and gnashing of teeth by the traditionalists. However, if we are ever going to create a truly just society, we have no choice in the matter. Drastic reform of our criminal justice systems is vital if we are to make any real progress towards this goal.

Today, in most democratic countries, they deal out something that could only very roughly be described as justice. But in the case of authoritarian regimes, justice is still almost non-existent. With such regimes, political crimes are treated as harshly as real crimes, if not more so. The search for suspects is undertaken by some kind of secret police, beholden only to their masters in the seat of power. Although such organizations are nothing new—the Inquisition and the Committee of Public Safety are early examples that come readily to mind—they proliferated markedly during the twentieth century, when the fascist and communist dictatorships held sway. The Gestapo, the Stasi and the NKVD were just three of many such groups of "enforcers," who terrorized and intimidated the populace in the name of the law. The only difference between these people and ordinary criminals was that they were sanctioned by the state. It is indeed depressing how easily these thugs were recruited, and how little encouragement they needed to carry out their sadistic tasks.

So justice is mostly a stranger in the halls of power. Crime can be anything that those in authority decree it to be, and if they themselves commit crimes, where is the court that will try them?

But in spite of everything, justice is still around, and all efforts by tyrants to remove her from the scene have been unsuccessful. Even though she is largely ignored, she refuses to go away. Justice is a concept that man ultimately cannot live without. The atrocities committed by the villains of the past are seen to be just that—atrocities. Hitler, Stalin and countless others have been exposed in the court of world opinion, and will forever live in infamy.

Unfortunately the dictators that remain are not much interested in what the world thinks of them. There are still many corners of the world—in Africa, the Middle East, South and Central America and Asia—where appalling atrocities, on a par with Hitler's, are still being committed, with little complaint from the international community. So the brutalities of the human race are by no means a thing of the past. Injustice is still the rule, rather than the exception.

History records that the just have been revered and extolled above the merely powerful. The appeal of Christ was his commitment to justice, and the injustice of his death stands as a rebuke to those who wished to silence him. His offence was to point out the cruelty and injustice of the mighty Roman State. This was considered treason, and the only punishment was death. But long after his death, his plea for justice has not been forgotten. His followers have had difficulty living up to his lofty ideals, but those that did not abandon them stand out like beacons in the darkness.

Mahatma Gandhi, like Christ, fought the injustice of the British by peaceful means. But this was possible only because the British were more civilized than the Romans. One can imagine how Gandhi would have fared if he had tried similar methods on the Nazis.

12

POLITICS AND POWER

o o o o o o o o o o o o o o o o o o o o o o o o o o o o o o o o o o o o o
Politics ruins the character.

—Otto von Bismarck

POLITICS IN EUROPE

Under the feudal system, which existed in Europe during the Middle Ages, the king was the owner of all the land. The barons, or other royal appointees, were nominally his vassals. But in practice the king's power over the barons was limited to a considerable degree. This was demonstrated when the English king John was forced by the barons to sign the Magna Carta in 1215. However, by the end of the fifteenth century a much stronger monarchy arose, claiming a divine right to rule from God himself. Such kings as Henry VII and Henry VIII of England, Louis XIV of France and Philip II of Spain, exercised almost supreme power as absolute monarchs. But the rise of the bourgeoisie helped to gradually undermine the authority of the king and, as related in Part I, this eventually resulted in the establishment of a constitutional monarchy in England and a Republic in France, although in the French case the transition was considerably more traumatic. The other monarchies of Europe, notably that of Prussia, found themselves in danger of having their authority eroded by reform-minded members of the middle class, who were not impressed by the idea of the divine right of kings. The resistance that the Prussian and Russian monarchies exerted against the forces of reform had far-reaching consequences for Europe. Most of the other monarchies, while opposed to any liberalization of their regimes, did not put up much active opposition, and so there was a gradual erosion of their traditional power.

The nineteenth century saw various reform movements in Europe, and even some in the United States. There were many debates over reform by the two main political parties in the English Parliament. The labels of Whig and Tory had been in use since the seventeenth century, but in the course of the nineteenth century the Tories became the Conservatives and the Whigs became known as the Liberals. However, these labels of Liberal and Conservative bear little relation to the same names that are used today to describe political parties. Both the Liberal and Conservative parties were what we would now call conservative, the main difference being that the Liberals were in favor of free trade and religious liberty, and the Conservatives were opposed to both. Later the gap between the two parties widened as the Liberals became disenchanted with colonialism.

Dating from about the middle of the eighteenth century, there had been a general weakening of the idea that the traditional elites were the only ones fit to govern. In the early Chinese culture it was considered legitimate to remove a ruler who failed to carry out the Mandate of Heaven and abused his power. In Europe also, the ideas of the seventeenth century political philosopher John Locke proclaimed a contract between government and people, stipulating certain natural and inalienable rights for all citizens. Such ideas greatly influenced the writing of the new American Constitution.

With these notions of rights for the people came the extension of the suffrage, or the right of the people to choose their own leaders. But anything like genuine universal suffrage was not contemplated in the nineteenth century. For instance, in England neither women nor Roman Catholics were allowed to vote. And for the most part, neither were those who did not own property.

The famous democracy of the Greeks also restricted the suffrage to those who owned property, so technically the Greeks had a *timocracy*, where property is a qualification for full citizenship, rather than a true democracy. Political rights were extended to those who participated in the military forces, mainly the hoplites, who manned the famous Greek phalanx, and who consisted mostly of small farmers. Later the oarsmen who manned the galleys were also granted citizenship even if they did not own property. These were not slaves but free men.

The Greeks had one very interesting feature in their democratic system. Officials were selected by lot, and all qualified citizens were eligible to hold office. On the minus side, the Athenians had their own version of the Inquisition, or "thought police." Anyone suspected of subversive activities, or of not paying due respect to the gods, was put on trail and could be punished with death or banishment. Socrates was a victim of the thought police.

During the nineteenth century in Europe, a tug-of-war developed between those who wished to see the traditional elites retain their power, and those who wanted to let some fresh air into the system. There were those, like Jose Ortega y Gasset, who thought, "A society without an aristocracy, without an elite minority, is not a society."[1] But there were others who considered that the rights of the people were more important than the privileges of the few.

An example of what could happen if the old power structure was overthrown had already occurred in France, and this gave the old monarchies an excuse for dragging their feet when it came to reform.

In our discussion of the social development of England, France and Germany in chapter 7, we saw that England took the peaceful road to the resolution of this conflict. The struggle was played out in Parliament, much of the time between the powerful personalities of two prime ministers: Benjamin Disraeli the Conservative, and William Gladstone the Liberal. But contrary to what one might think, they both supported Reform Bills, although Disraeli showed a little less enthusiasm for them than did Gladstone.

POLITICAL CURRENTS IN AMERICA

Soon after the new government of the United States was established, there arose a split in the administration of president George Washington, between the followers of Thomas Jefferson on the one hand, and those of Alexander Hamilton on the other. The partisans of Jefferson, known as Jeffersonian Democrats, sought to nurture a nation of small farmers, whose rugged individualism made them suspicious of a strong centralized government. The Hamiltonians, or Federalists, wanted firm fiscal control by the central government, and favored policies that supported the urban commercial interests.

As the young country developed, and sectional rivalry between the North and the South became more pronounced. The Federalists gradually lost support and a split opened up within the Democratic Party, or Democratic Republicans as they liked to call themselves. This division gave rise to the creation of the Northern and Southern Democrats. Meanwhile the Whig party was formed in 1824, mainly in opposition to Andrew Jackson, a military hero who advocated increased popular participation in government. The Whigs gained strength after Jackson became president. But they soon split into competing factions, till by 1852 they were no longer able to exert any meaningful political influence. Most of their members joined either the Democratic Party or the new Republican anti-slavery party.

By 1850 slavery became the main issue dividing the nation and this further emphasized the split in the Democratic Party. The anti-slavery Republican Party, which arose in Michigan in 1854, soon became well established in the North. But the Democrats remained the party with the widest following. The Southern Democrats were pro-slavery, while the Northern Democrats were further split between the anti-slavery wing and those who supported what was termed "popular sovereignty," which allowed the individual territories to make their own decisions regarding slavery.

In 1860, the Northern and Southern Democrats each nominated their own candidate for the presidential election. As a result of this split, Abraham Lincoln, who was nominated by the new Republican Party, was able to win the election.

The Civil War between North and South left the South defeated and resentful, and failed to resolve the underlying question of racial inequality. So the politics of the United States, especially in the South, continued to be affected by the results of the Civil War well into the twentieth century and beyond.

Abraham Lincoln's Emancipation Proclamation had freed the slaves, but any attempt to give them their rights as citizens was met with fierce resistance in the South. The impeachment of president Andrew Johnson, Lincoln's vice president, was directly related to this conflict. A Southerner himself, Johnson refused to enforce the new laws giving equal rights to the freed slaves in the South.

During the era of Reconstruction after the war the Republicans lost ground in the South, while the more conservative Northern Democrats, who had supported "popular sovereignty," became increasingly powerful.

As time went by, the Republican Party gradually transmuted itself, so that it became more the party of business than an advocate of civil rights. The Democrats, on the other hand, began to espouse the lot of those less fortunate, a move that tended to make them less popular in the South, where the Republicans began to make inroads among the whites. This process continued as the Republicans appealed more and more to the economic interests of traditional Southern whites, while the legacy of Lincoln and his opposition to slavery began to fade. By the turn of the twentieth century the transformation of the Republicans into the party of "traditional Southern values," and as a strong supporter of business and the military was complete. While many southerners remained nominal Democrats, their allegiance to the party continued to decline.

Unfettered laissez-faire capitalism eventually led to a boom in stock prices during the 1920's, followed by the crash of 1929 and the subsequent depression. The Republicans, as the party of business, fell out of favor with the American people, and it was up to the Democrats to try and put the nation back together again. By the mid 1930's the Democrats, under Franklin Roosevelt, had taken the lead in establishing a national system of social security, whereby workers were protected against temporary unemployment and provided with retirement benefits. This series of laws was called the New Deal.

The Republicans regarded the New Deal as excessive government intervention in a free enterprise system. And the War on Poverty, sponsored by Lyndon Johnson in the 1960's, got them talking about wasteful government programs that were akin to socialism, the latter being anathema to the party of business and laissez-faire capitalism. But in fact socialism was shunned by both major parties, and the New Deal and the War on Poverty had little to do with it. The main feature of socialism, public ownership of the means of production, was never seriously contemplated in America. The Republicans, in deprecating these social programs, started to use the word "liberal" to describe them, while the implication was that they were really tending towards socialism. By the 1970's, they had succeeded in making "liberal" into a pejorative term, which was more or less synonymous with wasteful government spending, and both parties tended to avoid the term. Ironically, the word itself accurately describes the true nature of these programs, which embodied the noble idea of trying to protect the more vulnerable members of the society from the ups and downs of the capitalist economy. It was in fact an example of America at her best and most generous, whereas it was being made to look like a costly mistake. And so in America, the word liberal came to mean something close to socialism, almost the exact opposite to its meaning in England.

After the assassination of president John Kennedy in 1963, the civil rights laws that he had proposed before his death were duly enacted by Lyndon Johnson, but over fierce opposition from the South. As Johnson himself had predicted, the passage of the civil rights laws marked the beginning of the Democratic Party's decline and the resurgence of the Republicans in the South. This in turn resulted in the gradual weakening of the Democrats' overall hold on political power. By the turn of the twenty-first century, the dominance of the Republicans in the South had resulted in the virtual eclipse of the Democrats in that region, with the consequence that congress and the presidency were both firmly in the hands of the Republicans. This provided an opportunity for the neo-conservatives in the

Republican Party to try and repeal many of the provisions of Franklin Roosevelt's New Deal.

[I have tried to give a broad outline of how politics has developed in the United States, in contrast to what was happening in Europe. Obviously many of the details of this complex subject have had to be omitted. For this I beg your indulgence.]

COMMUNISM, CAPITALISM & SOCIALISM

Contrary to what was happening in the United States, socialist parties came to power in several European countries. In Britain, the working classes, especially those belonging to the trade unions, became disenchanted with their traditional allies in the Liberal party and started their own Labour party, which by the 1930's had just about eclipsed the Liberals.

After the Second World War, there arose a widespread debate among economists, businessmen and intellectuals generally as to whether socialism, capitalism, or perhaps a mixture of the two, was the best political and economic system. In other words, should the marketplace be left to operate without government intervention, or should the government guide and direct the economy, making sure that it not only serves the national interest, but also promotes the general welfare of the population.

The United States was the most dedicated to pure capitalism. However, in Britain the Labour party, which came to power after the war, decided to nationalize some of Britain's industries, notably the coal mines and the steel industry. Other countries also experimented with socialism, and the debate over the merits of the different systems spread to countries outside Europe as well.

The ensuing struggle between government and the market place is too involved to discuss in detail, but it is well described by Daniel Yergin and Joseph Stanislaw in *The Commanding Heights*. This book gives a broad view of the world situation during the postwar period, and explains the interplay between the different economic systems.

After the fall of communism in Russia and Eastern Europe, it was generally acknowledged that the market place had proved triumphant in the aforementioned struggle, although some pockets of socialism still remained. Scandinavia stood aloof from the battle and continued with its socialist system, and China still clung to communism, although its grip grew weaker as market forces started to exert themselves within the Chinese economic sphere. A few other relics from the communist era, such as Cuba, became basically irrelevant in a capitalist-dominated world.

The economic policies of communism included the concept of central planning, which turned out to be a major misstep. But it took the Russians seventy years to remedy their mistake, and to introduce the Western concept of free markets, which are inherently decentralized. The Chinese have been quietly adopting many features of the capitalist system, without admitting that their own communist system has been a failure. Just by letting farmers lease the property that they work on, not actually giving them outright ownership, has caused yields to increase significantly.[2] Collective farms and communes, once important features of the communist system, have long since been abandoned.

Human nature is not well adapted to working for the common good. Some kind of profit motive is essential to keep the wheels of progress turning. An individual must also be assured that he can keep a good portion of the profit from his labor, and not have it expropriated at the whim of the government.

But this does not mean that socialism is a failure, far from it. Socialism is much more flexible than communism, and in fact they have little in common except the idea that government can provide some kind of overall guidance for the system. This need not entail central planning on anything but the most modest scale. And socialism can only work properly in a democracy, whereas communism is by nature anti-democratic.

In fact, a judicious blend of socialism and capitalism is probably the ideal makeup for a human society. Many features of the welfare state—much derided by laissez-faire capitalists—can in fact ameliorate some of the harsher effects of capitalism, without in any way upsetting the operation of a market economy. Accordingly, many countries have deemed it appropriate to incorporate certain aspects of socialism into their economic systems. The amount of socialism can be varied according to taste, from very little in the case of the United States, to quite a lot in the case of the Scandinavian countries.[3]

Although the overall economy works better if it is not centralized, some parts of it function more effectively when run by the government. Health care, for instance, is much better if it is kept out of the private sector. Introducing the profit motive into medicine inevitably results in inferior health services for the general public. Doctors and hospitals tend to forget that their primary duty is to care for people, not to make money.

As far as both health care and public education are concerned, the communists, for all their faults, did a much better job than many democratic countries, including America.

The great strength of socialism is that it is inclusive. It tries to insure that no member of the society is left behind. And it seeks to ameliorate some of the rough edges of capitalism, which tends to leave the losers behind. The Scandinavian countries illustrate this well. Their citizens feel that they belong to a larger community, which will aid them in times of need. The Americans, by contrast, are more individualistic, and if competition winnows out some of the weaker players, then it's just too bad, they've had their chance, like everyone else. Although there is a "safety net" in America, which insures that those at the bottom of the social ladder are not left destitute, the needy are not embraced by the community as they are in countries that put more emphasis on community. For those at the bottom, the American dream becomes a mirage.

Communism was a wonderful idea in theory, much more idealistic than dog-eat-dog capitalism, with its survival of the fittest. Everyone is on the same level, helping each other and sharing Nature's gifts. Christ was a communist—at least he had strong communist tendencies! Communism should have brought out the best in people. Instead, it brought out the worst, not only in its adherents, but also in its opponents.

This really should not have been a surprise. The human race is not ready for brotherly love—and may never be. A realistic look at the human animal shows that in spite of his trappings of civilization, he is much more suited to the law of the jungle—the capitalists are certainly more realistic as far as their assessment of human nature is concerned. Genuinely trying to "civilize" man is indeed a frustrating endeavor. Of course I am talking here in general terms. On the individual level, there are many fine people who can most certainly be described as civilized. Unfortunately there are not nearly enough of them, and one finds very few in positions of authority. Perhaps they are not tough enough to wield power effectively.

On a personal level, most people are helpful and pleasant. If one treats others in a reasonable manner one usually gets reasonable behavior in return. It is human nature *en masse* that is so scary. Many of those nice reasonable people can become part of a howling mob at the drop a hat. As Nietzsche aptly puts it, "In individuals, insanity is rare, but in groups, parties, nations, and epochs it is the rule."[4]

Communism will only work if we change human nature. But maybe any kind of *really* civilized society is impossible without such a change. Could this be where our new knowledge of biotechnology might come in useful?

And what about capitalism? Did the triumph of the market place over government control mean that capitalism was the only way to go? Since all capitalist countries, including the United States, have *some* government control over the private sector, *pure* capitalism does not in fact exist. But in any case, there are serious problems with capitalism, which make regulation of some kind essential. Just as communism is too idealistic as far as human nature is concerned, so also is capitalism, although admittedly to a lesser degree. Private companies fiercely resist almost any kind of regulation. But protection of workers, consumers and the environment requires constant oversight.

Unbridled capitalism can lead to an increasing gulf between the rich and those less fortunate, to say nothing about the corruption of the political process by private interest groups. Here we encounter the heart of the problem of private enterprise. All institutions and communal activities conducted by human beings are subject to corruption. So both the government and the private sector can fall victim to this scourge. When the government steps out of its regulatory capacity and becomes involved with the private sector, corruption becomes even more prevalent. Tax loopholes, rigged contracts, sweetheart deals of every type and description become the normal order of the day. As Herbert Hoover succinctly observed, "You know, the only problem with capitalism is capitalists. They're too damn greedy." [5]

As the communists found out to their sorrow, economies work best when they are decentralized. The capitalists are right that too much government regulation can kill the free market—but they are seldom willing to admit that too little regulation can also be a problem. A market works like a biological system, from the bottom up. But capitalism can come off the rails, given the imperfections of human nature. Although markets work with simple rules, the extra element of human involvement makes them unpredictable to a large degree. Nevertheless, even though markets operate on the principle of trial and error, and are sometimes manipulated by dishonest individuals, they are remarkably robust. They keep operating in a reasonably efficient manner, even under difficult conditions. But there is a limit to how much disruption the market can stand. If corruption becomes too widespread, the system will ultimately break down.

ASPECTS OF GLOBALIZATION

The fact that too much pure capitalism can be bad for one's political and economic health has recently been demonstrated by the actions of the International Monetary Fund (IMF) and the World Bank, in trying to promote economic development in poor countries. These two institutions were created at the end of World War II, to help the post-war recovery in Europe and Japan, and in this they were remarkably successful. However, as related by Nobel prize-winning economist Joseph Stiglitz in *Globalization and Its Discontents,* ideological rigidity has hindered their more recent efforts in this field. As Stiglitz says:

> Over the years since its inception, the IMF has changed markedly. Founded on the belief that markets often worked badly, it now champions market supremacy with ideological fervor. Founded on the belief that there is a need for international pressure on countries to have more expansionary economic policies—such as increasing expenditures, reducing taxes, or lowering interest rates to stimulate the economy—today the IMF typically provides funds only if countries engage in policies like cutting deficits, raising taxes, or raising interest rates that lead to a contraction of the economy.
>
> The most dramatic change in these institutions occurred in the 1980's, the era when Ronald Reagan and Margaret Thatcher preached free market ideology in the United States and the United Kingdom. The IMF and the World Bank became the new missionary institutions, through which these ideas were pushed on the reluctant poor countries that often badly needed their loans and grants.[6]

The great economist John Maynard Keynes advocated government spending and the lowering of interest rates during economic slow-downs, in order to "prime the pump" and encourage an economic recovery. But any kind of government intervention with the free market was anathema to the laissez-faire capitalists of the Reagan-Thatcher years. Inflation was considered more serious than unemployment, and so Keynesian economics was relegated to the trash pile. But a funny thing happened on the way to the twenty-first century; Keynesian economics was resurrected in the halls of the high and mighty—but for domestic consumption only, and without the despised name of Keynes ever having been spoken aloud. The United States and the other leading industrial nations advocated belt-tightening and high interest rates for the countries seeking help from the IMF and the World Bank, whereas they themselves employed good old Keynesian pump-priming policies for their own economies if they started to slow down! In other words, Keynes was fine for the rich and powerful, but not for the have-nots of the Third World. Painful medicine should be given to these people, so that through suffering they may be brought back to health.

So globalization has hit a few snags. These include both rigid ideology and an ample helping of hubris from the major powers, especially the United States.

Stiglitz cites the different approaches to the conversion from communism to the free market that have been undertaken by the two erstwhile communist giants: Russia and China. Russia fell prey to the prescriptions of the United States, the World Bank and the IMF—these included "shock therapy" and other painful remedies. On the other hand, China took a more gradual route and proceeded at her own pace. The results are clear for all to see. China has been making solid progress, and Russia has mostly been going backwards, with the economy little better than it was under the communists. Although nominally democratic, Russia has become what Fareed Zakaria calls an "illiberal democracy." China is still a dictatorship, and its leaders hope to modernize its economy without making any political changes. But the introduction of capitalism has required reform of the legal and administrative systems as well. Zakaria says that this process will inevitably lead to democracy, either peacefully or by the violent overthrow of the communist regime.

To be fair, one must remember that the powerful industrial nations, headed by the United States, are not *trying* to wreck the economies of the countries with whom they have been dealing—they are trying to *help* them. The World Bank was founded in order to try and eliminate poverty. So why are the results of their labors so unsatisfactory? As noted above, inflexible ideology is partly to blame, but lack of consultation with the countries concerned is also the cause of many problems. Put bluntly, the big guys are trying to play God with the little guys. They have only made a cursory effort to understand the problems of these countries, and much of what they have done has in fact been counterproductive. Author and activist Arunthati Roy has some harsh things to say about the "globalizers."

> Today corporate globalization needs an international confederation of loyal, corrupt, preferably authoritarian governments in poorer countries, to push through unpopular reforms, and quell the mutinies. It's called "Creating a Good Investment Climate." [7]

Let's look a bit further into the globalization process.

For the capitalists, the apparent victory of their system over communism brought a sense that the only true and viable system had prevailed over one that was not only wrong, but also palpably evil. The shortcomings of capitalism were conveniently forgotten in the flush of victory, and a conscious effort was made by the United States to spread both democracy and free-market capitalism throughout the developing world. This, in combination with the developing process of globalization would surely result in a better world for all. Such a rosy scenario has already encountered some major obstacles. In fact, it is now clear that it is fundamentally flawed.

We have already seen that the free market needs to be properly regulated if it is to function properly, and many in the capitalist world strongly resist any kind of regulation. But this is by no means the only problem. A recent book, *World on Fire: How Exporting Free Market Democracy Breeds Ethnic Hatred and Global Instability,* by Amy Chua, an American of Chinese descent, points out that the problem of "market-dominant minorities," although it is not a new phenomenon, is a serious impediment to progress in many third world countries. Globalization, with its push for democracy and free markets, has only exacerbated the problem.

The dominant minorities, which are described by Ms. Chua, involve outsiders, usually of a different ethnic group, that hold the reins of power over major portions of a nation's economy. Examples are: the Chinese in much of Southeast Asia, including Indonesia and the Philippines; the Tutsi in Rwanda; Eritreans in Ethiopia; and Indians in Uganda. Whites constituted dominant minorities in many colonial countries, and Americans now comprise such minorities in several developing nations.

In South America, the great landed estates, or *latifundias,* whose owners are descendents of the original Spanish and Portuguese colonists, constitute tiny minorities that control large amounts of the wealth in many of these countries, the indigenous populations having long since been reduced to poverty. Countries such as Brazil, Uruguay and Chile also have acquired imported business elites. These include especially Jews, Lebanese and Germans. In all these cases, resentment by the indigenous majorities is inevitable.

Democracy tends to *empower* these oppressed majorities, and this frequently leads to the election of demagogues. Violence can result when the pent-up grievances of the majority come to the surface. An example is Zimbabwe, where the white settlers, who owned the choicest land, are now being expelled from their property by radical elements encouraged by President Robert Mugabe, who was "democratically" elected.

As in South America, the legacy of white colonialism has left its mark on Africa. But in this case there are some *indigenous* dominant minorities, such as the Kikuyu in Kenya and the Ibo in Nigeria.

The Arab-Israeli conflict in the Middle East has many complex causes, but one that is stressed by Ms. Chua is the position of Israel vis á vis the surrounding Arab states. She identifies Israel itself as a market-dominant minority situated amid a group of poor and oppressed nations, ruled by indigenous demagogues who stir up hatred for Israel to camouflage the failings of their own regimes. As Ms. Chua points out, bringing democracy to these Arab states would, at least in the short term, exacerbate the situation, because the people are even more vitriolic in their hatred of Israel than are their leaders.

Finally, America itself is seen as a market-dominant minority in relation to the rest of the world.

> Just 4 per cent of the world's population, America dominates every aspect—financial, cultural, technological—of the global free markets we have come to symbolize. From the Islamic world to China, from our NATO allies to the southern hemisphere, America is seen (not incorrectly) as the engine and principal beneficiary of global marketization. For this—for our extraordinary market dominance, our seeming global invincibility—we have earned the envy, fear, and resentment of much of the rest of the world. Of course, not everyone who envies and resents us wants to destroy. But there are those who do.[8]

Although America is a global dominant minority when considered as a whole, the benefits of her global dominance are very unevenly distributed at home. In fact, as America has become economically and politically more powerful, the gap between rich and poor among her own people has widened. But those less well off do not resent those at the top—at least not yet—because the latter do not represent an ethnically separate minority of outsiders, like the Chinese do in the Philippines. The American dream imbues all Americans with the same belief in the possibility of fame and fortune.

Ms. Chua has some suggestions for ameliorating the problems related to market-dominant minorities. In spite of the fact that they are resented, envied and despised, they still perform functions that are vital to the economies of the countries in which they operate. So eliminating them is not the answer. They have to improve their image by behaving more responsibly towards the ethnic majorities over whom they exert power. By exercising more sensitivity and contributing to the welfare of the community they can counter their reputation as greedy exploiters. This approach has been successful in Malaysia:

> Along with foreign investors, Malaysia's entrepreneurial Chinese minority controlled all of the country's most lucrative, large-scale commercial enterprises, both agricultural and nonagricultural.
>
> To redress these extreme ethnic wealth imbalances, the Malaysian government adopted sweeping ethnic quotas on corporate equity ownership, university admissions, government licensing, and commercial employment. It also initiated large-scale purchases of corporate assets on behalf of the Malay majority.[9]

The results so far have been very encouraging. An indigenous Malay economic elite has been created alongside the existing Chinese minority and this has brought native Malay participation in areas of the economy that were previously the exclusive preserve of foreign investors or Chinese and Indian Malaysians.

So the solution would seem to be the reform of the minorities themselves. They should seek to improve their image by increasing the participation of the indigenous majority in the power structure.

13

PURPOSEFUL PURSUITS

o o o o o o o o o o o o o o o o o o o o o o o o o o o o o o o o
Let not ambition mock their useful toil, Their homely joys, and
destiny obscure; Nor grandeur hear with a disdainful smile, The
short and simple annals of the poor.

—Thomas Gray
Elegy in a Country Churchyard

MEN AT WORK

What is it that drives man to work so hard at many things that do not seem to be
really essential to his survival? Compared to most other animals, who prefer eating, sleeping and mating to most other activities, man is a veritable dynamo. But
it is interesting to compare modern man with his more primitive ancestors in the
very early stages of culture. The latter were mostly content to take care of the
basics, without indulging in large building projects and constantly seeking to
advance their material comfort. But as culture has developed, all sorts of new
occupations and enterprises have opened up. Why all this frantic activity? Culture must have done something to man to make him behave in this way. It seems
to have made him a lot more ambitious. It has made him want to better himself
and to climb the social ladder, whereas in ancient times he was hardly aware that
such a ladder even existed. But now that he has reached his present level of culture, it is almost impossible for him to opt out and return to a more primitive but
less stressful existence. He either becomes part of the rat race, or is left behind and
ends up as a cultural dropout. It's true that there are a few eccentrics who manage
to achieve a less stressful existence without partaking too strenuously in the rat
race. They seem to be able to strike a nice balance between enjoying many of the

benefits of modern life, while still leaving time to smell the flowers. But these are people who are satisfied with less than what is usually aspired to by today's man or woman. They tend to agree with philosopher Jean-Jacques Rousseau, who thought that man is corrupted by culture, rather than improved by it.

Just as biological organisms have become more complex since the early days of life on earth, so human society has also become more complex as it has developed, and this has caused stresses and strains that were absent in more primitive cultures.

In order to see how this situation came about, we have to go back a few thousand years to the dawn of culture. It's likely that the advent of agriculture gave impetus to the idea of work, or at least working for someone else. According to psychologists Ann and David Premack, ownership, or control of *land* is the key:

> Agriculture changed ownership. Farmers claimed land as individuals. Yet even personal claims to land did not constitute a true economic factor until increased population had made land scarce and introduced one of the principal novelties on which economics rests, permanent scarcity. The scarcity of land and the ever-increasing population led people to claim not only the land, but its resources—water, salt, timber.
>
> Agriculture divided the world into rich and poor, a condition unknown among hunter-gatherers. The rich owned the land, and increasingly, the resources of the land, thus setting the stage for the single most powerful economic factor—work.[1]

To cut a long story short, the non-owners had to work for the owners if they were to obtain the goods (or money) that they desired. And who were the owners? Those who could not only take land, but hold onto it as well. From then on, if you were not an owner, you had to work for your living. This caused society to become much more stratified than it was in the days of the hunter-gatherers. A case can be made that private property constitutes one of the major shortcomings of human society. However, attempts at getting rid of it have not been successful. So apparently it's a necessary evil.

Ambition occurs only in a rudimentary way in the animal world. Most animals' main occupation is finding food, sleeping and doing a little mating on the side. If the search for food is not too strenuous, life can be very relaxing. Take the giant panda for instance; eating and sleeping are his main activities; he only eats bamboo and he mates only occasionally. It's a great life, so long as the supply of bamboo holds out. However, his lack of enthusiasm for mating has left him on the verge of extinction. But not to worry! He's so cute to look at that humanity has fallen in love with him en masse. He is taken care of like royalty, and his bamboo supply is guarded like a treasure!

Ambition implies working towards a specific goal, which is visualized in advance. It's surprising how much effort some people are willing to expend in order to attain what others might consider to be only a marginal amount of satisfaction. There are countless examples of this, for instance a skater who spends thousands of hours preparing for a competition that lasts only a few minutes. Almost any kind of professional career, and many that are non-professional, requires years of study and large outlays of money and effort, in order to acquire the necessary level of proficiency. Such things entail an extended period of learning; something the human animal seems to be very good at if he puts his mind to it. And he can indeed put his mind to it if he so desires. He can set goals that may take years to attain, and when they *are* attained, satisfaction is only temporary, and so further goals are set. Life for the human being is working towards an unending series of goals.

Although some animals are able to complete tasks that are superficially similar to the sort of tasks that humans do, these tasks are not learned, they are simply carried out instinctively. A beaver is not taught by his parents how build a dam. He does not *learn* how to build one. He instinctively *knows* how to do it. Similarly, a spider does not learn how to create a web, and a bird does not learn how to fly, or build a nest. All these skills are directly related to survival. The ability of even "intelligent" animals, such as ravens, parrots, dogs, horses, or chimpanzees to learn new skills is very limited. A human being has a capacity for learning that is on an altogether different scale. And what he learns is generally not directly related to survival, but is the result of his ambition to improve himself either intellectually or socially.

Self-image is all-important. Perhaps it's a lack of a self-image that allows the rest of the animal world to forgo the human being's constant struggle for improvement. But I doubt if this is true, for many animals appear to have well-developed self-images—the peacock for example. No, the human being is motivated by something much more powerful than just his self-image, and in the next chapter we will take a guess at what that something is.

One thing that many animals *do* seem to learn with alacrity is how to manipulate humans! The domestic cat or dog enjoys a thoroughly relaxed life, which consists mostly of eating and sleeping, while his master is rushing around, busying himself with endless tasks, which include buying and preparing meals for his pet. Although the human may be considered the smarter one according to some man-made standard of intelligence, it turns out that domestication is actually a two-way process. Animals, and even plants, are able to use human beings and other animals in order to enhance their survival in an evolutionary sense. In *The Botany of Desire,* Michael Pollan explains how dogs and cats alter their behavior so that human beings will be attracted to them and look after them. This may be one of the reasons why there are more dogs than tigers in the world! Pollan's highly original and informative book is mainly about the interplay between plants and humans, especially four particular plants: the apple, tulip, cannabis and potato. It is full of interesting insights related to evolution.

The domestication of certain animals is a very old custom that cuts across all cultural boundaries. With the larger and more powerful animals, this necessitated killing off the more aggressive ones, so that only the more docile animals were permitted to breed. But it's worth noting that the vast majority of animals will not allow themselves to be domesticated. They have more pride than to accept food and lodging in return for giving up their freedom. The unnatural conditions of their life in captivity prevent most species from breeding, and when they do breed, their young are often sickly.

Nevertheless man has been able to domesticate many species of animals, some of which have been raised for food, as well as such things as wool, fur or milk. Others have been used for entertainment, as in circuses, or for medical research. Even birds have been put to work for man, like the trusty carrier pigeon. The ones that have really done hard work are the so-called beasts of burden: the ox, the elephant, the horse, the mule, the llama and the camel. The horse has worked for man more than any other animal. For transportation, for war and for sport, the horse has had a long inning, which is only now coming to a close. The racetrack and the polo field are now its principle habitat, since the royal sport of hunting is rapidly fading away, and the horse and buggy is gone forever.

The horse has a strange personality, which humans have been able to exploit in many ways. Some people have a fear of horses, since their very size can be intimidating. But the horse is really quite docile, and most of them can be bent to man's will with only a modicum of effort. However, this docile animal has carried man into the thick of battle and proved its courage again and again.

The zoo is an institution that is supposed to tell us something about animals. But it tells us a lot more about human beings. The animal in the zoo is really there to exhibit man's superiority over the animal world. Rather than respecting his fellow creatures, man removes them from their natural habit and exhibits them before groups of gawking kids and adults, who enjoy feeding them junk food and otherwise abusing them. The sheer hubris of this exercise seems altogether lost on the public.

I remember once going to the Central Park zoo in New York City, where they had a particularly handsome polar bear. It was the middle of summer, and the temperature was in the nineties. The poor animal, in his great fur coat, now a sooty gray from the perpetual smog, was just lying there in a pool of warm water, looking forlorn and miserable, which he undoubtedly was. The arrogance and lack of respect that is shown towards the marvelous natural world of which we are a part was forcefully brought home to me. From that moment on, I have hated zoos with a passion.

I thoroughly enjoyed the film *Planet of the Apes*, in which the roles were reversed and the apes put the humans into cages. Too bad it was only a movie. The idea that animals are "improved" by being tamed is obviously just a fiction. Nietzsche has some scathing things to say about the "improvement" of both animals and humans:

> To call the taming of an animal its "improvement" sounds almost like a joke to our ears. They are weakened, they are made less harmful, and through the depressive effect of fear, through pain, through wounds, and through hunger they become sickly beasts. It is no different with the tamed man whom the priest has "improved."[2]

The idea of a "work ethic" is something that has had considerable circulation in the West. The *virtue* of work is also a notion that has crept into the Christian ethos. The Calvinists are probably responsible for its origin, since they considered the accumulation of wealth to be a sign of virtue—God having rewarded the virtuous man with riches. Of course the obverse of this coin implies that the poor lack virtue—a convenient way of rationalizing a love of money and riches.

The Americans seem particularly fond of the concept of the work ethic. Perhaps this has something to do with their Puritan roots.[3] Anyway, the idea that work is somehow ennobling, whereas idleness is close to sin (the devil makes work for idle hands) is fairly widespread, and not only in the West. The principle involved here is that one should *work* for one's living—there should be no free lunch. So the work ethic, or the culture, has contrived to make us feel guilty if we sit around doing nothing. Other animals don't seem to feel this way at all—they certainly don't *appear* to worry about doing nothing, and it seems to have no ill effect on their health.

But there are all sorts of different kinds of work, and only a small proportion of these activities could be called essential to the operation of society. The production of such things as food and housing are obviously essential, but if one starts to look carefully at how human beings occupy themselves, it's surprising how many jobs one notices that are only marginally important at best. Interestingly enough, most of the work that is considered menial, and perhaps even slightly degrading, is in fact vital to the life of the community, whereas many of the more highly paid jobs are essentially superfluous. In fact the prestige of a job is often inversely proportional to its basic value or importance. For instance, it is the anonymous bureaucrats that actually keep a country running, rather than the leaders who get the publicity and the high salaries. The leaders like everyone to think that they are the only ones capable of running things, but this is basically a mirage.

It seems to me that many of the menial jobs deserve more recognition. Consider the garbage man for example. Surely his work is vitally important. Without him everything would be chaos. Yet he gets scant reward and almost no prestige for the vital work that he does. I know that people like firemen and doctors are important too, but I've got a soft spot for the garbage man, because few people recognize how important he is—and there are a lot of others like him that get very little recognition for the essential jobs that they do. I know that we have to have some Einsteins and Newtons if we are ever going to make any *real* progress, but geniuses are rare and very special. The rest of us are not that important, even though we may have high opinions of ourselves.

Although there are exceptions to this overall assessment, as a general rule one might say that the more prestigious the job, the less likely it is to entail a genuinely honest and useful day's work—and we should emphasize the word "honest."

But, you may say, this is a highly subjective point of view—and you may be right. We'll try and look at things a little more objectively. There are basically two groups of people: the leaders and the workers. The workers carry out the plans or orders of the leaders. Each group needs the other in order for anything constructive to be done. Without the leaders, the workers would have nothing to do. Without the workers, the leaders would just sit around, talking about schemes that would never be implemented (we can be almost certain that they will never go out and do the hard work themselves).

The unfair part, it seems to me, is that one of these groups is given more credit than the other, in spite of the fact that they are both essential to the success of any enterprise.

The way different jobs are evaluated has a lot to do with the concept of status. This is an important factor, which distinguishes the various layers of society. In fact, status is an all-important defining characteristic of human societies. The type of work that one does reflects one's *status*, regardless of its basic utility.

In the early societies, slaves did most of the menial work, so this type of labor tended to be regarded as somehow inferior. Even nowadays, menial work tends to be done by those at the bottom of the social ladder. So the importance of the work is not necessarily related to the status that is connected with it in the public mind. The general consensus is that *manual* labor has a lower status than that involving the intellect, in spite of the fact that it is, in general, just as important as mental work.

Actually, the idea that ordinary manual labor is somehow inferior is an old one. Confucius looked down on manual labor and exalted the intellect, as did the Greeks. But just the fact of using one's hands is not sufficient to imply lower status, since a pianist uses his hands. The difference of course is that the pianist is an artist, and an artist works primarily with his *mind*. Aristotle says there is a difference between just doing things by rote and having knowledge and understanding of what one is doing. Experience is essential for both artist and laborer, but the artist has knowledge of *causes*. This is how Aristotle explains it:

> Men who have experience know that a thing is so, but not why it is so; those who know why a thing is so also know its cause. This is why we regard the master craftsman in any field as more deserving of respect, more knowledgeable, and wiser than manual workers. Thus it is not on the grounds of their greater success in doing things that we judge some people to be wiser than others, but because of their grasp of principles and knowledge of causes.[4]

One must realize, however, that the method of according status to a particular job is highly subjective. It depends on who is doing the classifying. Remember, Aristotle was a philosopher, so he was definitely biased as to the status of those who work with their minds. The manual laborer may think that the artist is actually a good-for-nothing lay-about, but few people are interested in his opinion. The artists and philosophers are more articulate, so they are the natural arbiters of status. (It is sometimes possible to *buy* status, although this sort of thing tends to be sneered at by the traditionalists.)

The concept of status is reflected in the *class* divisions that were so strong in the past, and still retain their influence today. Only certain jobs were considered proper for the upper classes, and these were naturally accorded a higher status. Nonetheless, there is a subtle difference between class and status. Status can sometimes override class, and vice versa. But the exact way that these things work is complex and subtle, and there are no hard and fast rules to guide the uninitiated.

Even though the work ethic seems a bit artificial, experience tells us that we *do* feel better for doing a good day's work. However, there is a tendency to assume that one only gets real satisfaction from *good* work, and the better the work, the more satisfaction one gets. But is this really true? For the average person, whether the work is useful or worthwhile is of little consequence, it's the money he makes that is the all-important factor. And this is a good thing, because most jobs are neither particularly interesting nor useful. After all, someone like a stockbroker does little or nothing for his clients—most of the time he helps them lose their money—let alone for the larger society, and the stock *analyst* makes the stockbroker look all-important. But both are extremely well paid in most cases. All the same, the stock market is an important part of the economy, and stockbrokers do have their legitimate place. It just seems that, like lawyers, there are too many of them, and some of them are basically parasites. The stock market seems to have acquired a lot of people that are not strictly essential to its proper functioning—they are just dead wood. (Since the stock market is the very lifeblood of the capitalist system, maybe it needs some reserves of manpower in case of an emergency!)

Please do not think that I am singling out the financial community for special criticism, because the same thing applies to myriads of jobs in practically all walks of life—look at the military if you want to see an example of pointless jobs and bloated bureaucracy. (If your country is attacked, you definitely need the military. The rest of the time, they waste money and tend to get you into wars that you are better off staying out of!) And look at the "media," which has expanded to produce "news and entertainment" on a gargantuan scale, most of which neither informs nor entertains anyone with even a modicum of intelligence or education. The sole motivation of the producers of this trash is to make money at the expense of an ignorant public, rather than trying to inform said public.

Then there are professional sports. Huge salaries are paid to athletes for doing nothing except play games that they happen to be good at. The money that they earn is not related in any meaningful way to the importance of what they do.

Modern economies have created vast numbers of jobs, which have come into existence, not because they are vital to the proper functioning of society, but simply because modern-day economic systems have become more and more complex. It is the complexity of the system, rather than its utility or efficiency, which is the driving force behind the expansion of the job market.

So it seems that we have become fairly good at manufacturing, or inventing jobs, which pay people a living wage—and in some cases an exorbitant one—regardless of whether they are really useful or not. We have created whole industries apparently for the sole purpose of giving people something to do. Of course we must then persuade the public to buy their products, which is done by advertising. The unfortunate consumer, like the goose that creates the foie gras, is being force-fed all kinds of merchandise that it doesn't really need, just to keep the wheels of industry turning.

So far we have been talking mostly about *men* at work. But *women* are more than half the population. Until quite recently women were actively discouraged from entering the workforce on most levels, since motherhood was considered to be their proper station in life. Only certain occupations, like nursing, teaching or clerical work, were considered to be "woman's work." But this has changed radically in the past hundred years or so. All the same, most women do not seem to seek status through work in the same way that men do (some do of course). And it's hard to challenge the accepted notion that the chief purpose in life for a woman is motherhood. But although a job can get in the way of this, it's surprising how many women are able to have both a job and a family at the same time. Now that women are free (in many countries) to take more or less any job they wish, many of them have in fact done so. A job can provide security if a woman doesn't marry, or is divorced.

There are still those who say that the place of a woman is in the home. But it's evident that the society is healthier if women can chose to do what they want. Having equality between the sexes is not only right and just, it makes for a more stable and prosperous society. One only has to look at the countries where women do *not* have equal status with men, to see how important it is.

So equality for women is a fine thing, except that there are only a limited number of jobs to go around, and if the women take half of them, many more men will be unemployed! In the future, will the number of available jobs be sufficient to accommodate anyone who desires to find work?

In the past, as society became more complex, more jobs were created. But there is a limit to this process, and we are fast approaching the time when things may go into reverse. This will happen when more and more jobs are taken over by machines or robots, and the population grows so large that we simply cannot go on manufacturing enough jobs to go around. This will really play havoc with the work ethic, because instead of four or five percent unemployment, we may have fifty percent or more. And unless we can discover some other kind of useful work for these people, they will either be permanently unemployed or take turns working at the jobs that still remain. One can envision all sorts of scenarios. Vacations could expand to six months or more—this would at least create more jobs in the tourist industry. Make-work projects would proliferate, or people could actually be paid a living wage for doing nothing. Perhaps literally millions of people would become artists or entertainers of one kind or another. (Of course this sort of thing requires talent, which most people lack.)

The prospect of a lot of idle people with nothing to do except make mischief is somewhat frightening. But this problem will almost certainly have to be faced in our brave new world of the future. Most work as we now know it may simply fade away. Even the garbage man, God bless him, may be replaced by a robot! But think of the opportunities that this could bring. Remember that Bertrand Russell said we have to have leisure time in order to get a *real* education? Well, now everyone would be able to acquire a first class education!

Not every one agrees with me about the future of the job market. Stuart Kauffman, in *Investigations,* has constructed an algorithmic model of an economic system. He represents people as automata; and with certain simple rules of interaction, he creates a model of the economy, which goes on creating jobs ad infinitum.

> Consider the economy as forever becoming, burgeoning with new ways of making a living, new ways of creating value and advantages of trade, while old ways go extinct. The economy, like the biosphere, is about persistent creativity in ways of making a living.
>
> Think then of the role of laws and contracts, whose constraints enable the linked flow of economic activities down particular corridors. The web of economic activities flows down channels whose constraints are largely legal in nature. The coming into existence of enabling constraints of law is as central to economic development and growth as any other aspect of the bubbling activity.[5]

There is an obvious parallel to biological evolution here, as Kauffman points out. I have previously stated my opinion that the study of biological evolution and social and economic evolution are basically different. Of course there are parallels between the two, but one has to be careful about taking the analogy too far.

Kauffman likes to think big. Having got the idea of autonomous units on an increasing scale of complexity—molecules, cells, organisms, societies—he proceeds to build an all-encompassing model, in which he can insert different kinds of autonomous objects. The model is mathematical in nature, so the old question of how accurately such as model can represent reality again rears its head. If he's right in projecting his model onto a real economic system, we need not worry about the pool of jobs drying up some time in the future. But I still have a strong suspicion that we can't go on creating new jobs indefinitely. The jobs of the "people," who Kauffman considers as automatons in his model, will surely be taken over by *man-made* automatons, or robots! So the number of jobs available to humans will in fact be limited.

What actually will happen depends on the rate of increase in the population, which no one has ever been able to forecast accurately. (The present estimate is that there will be zero population growth by 2050-70.) Another consideration is the retarding of the ageing process, which could soon begin to cause a significant increase in the population, even with a constant birthrate. Some of these older people could stay in the work force, but many will need others to look after them.

WESTERN ADVENTURERS

What is it about Western society that makes it so pushy? It was Westerners that crossed the oceans in search of riches and treasure. They were not stay-at-homes like the Chinese, who did not much care about what went on elsewhere. The West had a wanderlust, which propelled them to foreign shores in search of who-knows-what. No challenge was too great for them. The oceans had to be navigated, the highest mountains climbed, the hottest desert crossed, the densest jungle searched for lost cities with streets paved with gold. Curiosity is a characteristic of the human species, but it's particularly strong in Western man.

Maybe it was because they just happened to develop the kind of technology that would allow them to do all this. Or maybe they developed the technology precisely so they *could* do these things. It was probably a combination of the two.

One has to have ocean-going ships and instruments for navigation in order to travel the high seas. The Chinese had both, and they made several voyages to foreign parts, but they never followed them up. The spirit of adventure just wasn't there.

The inhabitants of Oceania *did* have the spirit of adventure. They set sail on a vast ocean in tiny boats, not knowing who or what they might encounter. But although they eventually occupied hundreds of Pacific islands, they did not change the world in the same way that the Western adventurers did.

The ocean-going ships that the Europeans built were intended to open up trade between the Mediterranean and northern Europe. But this was not enough for them. They expanded their horizons across the unknown oceans. For this they needed sophisticated instruments of navigation, some of which they borrowed from the Chinese, and others they invented themselves.

As we saw in part I, the motivation was primarily the attainment of riches. But there were other motives as well. In chapter 4 we saw how the Greek colonies came about partly because of a lack of social mobility in the city-states. Young enterprising Greeks found that the best avenue for advancement was often to establish an outpost of their city in a foreign land, where they would not be restricted by the established elites in the home city. The same motivation drove many of the European colonists and adventurers. Many were the younger sons of noblemen or merchants, whose paths up the social ladder were impeded by those in more favorable positions. Darwin had some interesting thoughts on the subject:

> The restless who will not follow any steady occupation—and this relic of barbarism is a great check to civilization—emigrate to newly-settled countries, where they prove useful pioneers.[6]

In any case, the structure of European society was probably a factor. But it was the confluence of many factors that caused the Western expansion. Just the spirit of adventure was not enough. The means and the opportunity had to be there as well. The advances in science and technology, as well as the development of commerce and industry, all combined to create a more dynamic society, which could not be contained within its geographical boundaries, and consequently spread itself out across the globe. Religion's part in all this was to provide a justification for the exploitation of foreign peoples. Since they were not considered part of God's family, they had to be converted. It was a variation of the old idea of war being permitted against the heathen.

There is no question that the primary reason for the success of the West was its superior military force. As Samuel Huntington puts it in *The Clash of Civilizations*:

> The West won the world not by the superiority of its ideas or values or religion (to which few members of other civilizations were converted) but rather by its superiority in applying organized violence. Westerners often forget this fact: non-Westerners never do.[7]

The story of this expansion and its interplay with the history of other cultures is elegantly told in William McNeill's classic, *The Rise of the West*. It was this book that first sparked my interest in world history, and started my quest for a better understanding of man's place in the universe. I can recommend no better starting place for such a quest.

There is nothing innately different about Western man. There have been lots of theories about the white race being superior to those that it has exploited, but these are idle tales, and usually put forward in order to justify the cruelty and other excesses of the Western adventurers. There are, in fact, many reasons why it was the West that gained prominence over the rest of the world. But there are also many other reasons, having to do with climate, geographical location, natural resources, and the prevalence of certain diseases, as to why other cultures and peoples did *not* come into prominence in a similar manner. In *Guns, Germs, and Steel,* Jared Diamond traces some of these reasons, and thus helps to paint a more balanced picture of the overall scene.

Once the juggernaut of Western industry had been started, it was impossible to turn it off. The rise of the cities meant that the bucolic country life was mostly a thing of the past. The belching smokestacks of the industrial towns created a new landscape that removed man from his rural past.

All this did not happen over night. But once started, its progress was inexorable. First of all the railroads, then the car, and finally the airplane, meant that people could travel great distances, even if they had no overriding reason to do so. This created a new type of creature altogether—the tourist. Previously confined almost exclusively to the rich, tourism is now a pursuit of the masses. To some extent this has led to better understanding between cultures, but it's nonetheless surprising how little the average tourist learns when visiting foreign shores.

RENEWAL AND REBIRTH

It might have been expected that the horrendous devastation of World War II would have destroyed much of the structure of the modern world. But, partly due to the fact that the heartland of the United States, the most powerful of the industrial nations, was not damaged during the war, Europe and Japan made a remarkably rapid recovery with the help of American aid. Even the cold war, with its waste of resources and poisoning of the international climate, did little to dampen the pace of recovery. One of the exceptions was Russia, the prime insti-gator of the cold war.

The great international cities, embodying the rise of culture through the cen-turies—monuments to man's striving for dignity and knowledge—have been built and rebuilt bit by bit, and altered many times in order to accommodate new ideas and changing aspirations. The comparison to organisms seems somehow apt, since the wounds of the war have now healed and the life of the great cities goes on. Even a city such as Berlin, devastated by allied bombs and Russian armor, has risen phoenix-like from the ashes, although in this case it has taken more than fifty years. London, Tokyo, Dresden, Hamburg and Leningrad (St Petersburg)—even Stalingrad—have mostly recovered from their frightful wounds. Only Hiroshima and Nagasaki remain as reminders of the ultimate weapon of destruction. Even there, life still goes on, but it's doubtful if the wounds will ever completely heal.

In looking at the great cities of the world, one often appreciates the depth of their character only when this is changed in a radical way. There was a phase after World War II when the planning of cities became the plaything of architects and city planners. "Urban renewal" was thought to be the way the run-down parts of existing cities could be improved, and even the planning of new cities from scratch was attempted. The results were horrible. Urban renewal created soulless neighborhoods, bereft of character. Jane Jacobs' classic book, *The Death and Life of Great American Cities,* argued strongly against this approach and helped to stem the tide of mediocrity.

The character and charm of almost all great cities lies in the fact that they are *unplanned.* The ingredients for a successful neighborhood involve the interplay between residential neighborhoods and the commercial life of the city, in a way that is almost impossible to plan for in advance. But there are some general prin-ciples that should be followed with respect to the general layout. Jacobs was the first to draw attention to some of these basic concepts, and many of them were in conflict with the prevailing ideas regarding urban renewal.[8]

One can *renew* a neighborhood while preserving its basic structure, but this takes much more effort than simply leveling it and replacing it with something that lacks the subtle interplay of functions that characterizes a successful urban neighborhood. Such a neighborhood cannot be created over night; it takes time to form the intricate fabric of relationships that is its essence. The early urban planners failed to appreciate this, and the results were dismal. Some totally new cities that were actually built, like Brasília (in Brazil) and Chandigarh (India), proved just as unsuccessful. In Brasília, the temporary housing built for the construction workers became the most popular place to visit!

It's not impossible to design a city from scratch. St Petersburg, built by Peter the Great of Russia, is an example of a great city that rose from a designer's mind. Another example is Christopher Wren's plan for rebuilding the city of London after the Great Fire of 1666. But it takes talent and resources to carry out such large-scale projects, and only a very few have been successful.

The fact that the greatest cities are unplanned reflects an essential characteristic of the natural world. The whole thing works so well precisely because there is no overall design, and hence no designer. In particular, biological evolution is an *unplanned* process. In the same way, human institutions "evolve" without any overall design.

Urban planning imposes an overall plan on a process that works best if it is unplanned. Individual buildings can be planned, and even groups of buildings, but if one goes much further than this one usually gets into trouble. Of course if a city has been very badly bombed, say like Dresden, one has to start more or less from scratch, in which case it is difficult, if not impossible, to recapture the true character of the original.

Most cities have grown up over the years without any overall plan, but some have had their growth directed right from the beginning. The grid plan, for instance, has been used not only in modern cities, but in ancient ones as well. In early Chinese culture and in the Indus valley, many of the cities were laid out on a grid. This kind of layout was also used in Mesopotamia, and later in Greece and the Roman Empire. Of course such a plan had obvious practical advantages. But since it can only be used successfully in flat locations, the flatness of the terrain, together with the grid pattern, made for a lack of interest and character, which may explain why it was not used more often.

A grid system can be called "minimal planning," and so long as the city is otherwise left to develop on its own, the result is usually quite satisfactory. But a city with a lot of variation from neighborhood to neighborhood seems to suit the human psyche better than one that has more of an overall uniformity.

Cities are not the only things that are better left unplanned. Utopian schemes, such as collectivization in Russia and the Great Leap Forward in China—as well as communism itself—have all proved unsuccessful.[9] The same thing with parliaments. "Messy and unsupervised" seems to work better than "tidy and strictly controlled." The free input of different ideas produces the best results. It seems that many things work better *without* any kind of centralized planning. Although there are instances when one has to have a master plan, say when one has to design a major road system, in general it's better to avoid overall plans whenever possible.

The evolution of man and society are both unplanned. There is no master plan or designer, and none is necessary. In both cases it is the process itself that drives it. No guidance is required; any attempt to guide or direct it will almost certainly be counterproductive.

But man can affect the process of biological evolution, as Darwin himself pointed out. This involves the difference between natural and artificial selection. Artificial selection occurs when man attempts to alter the natural process of reproduction by encouraging the development of desirable traits in plants or animals by means of interbreeding or cross-fertilization. Not only has man interfered with the natural evolution of plants and animals, but as a direct result of his acquisition of culture, he has also introduced artificial elements into the process of his own evolution.

An example of this is given by Richard Dawkins in *The Selfish Gene*. He explains that in nature those animals that have too many children tend to be eliminated from a population. This is because there is usually an insufficient food supply for all of their young to survive, and many of them starve. Thus the genes for producing a lot of children tend not to be passed on to future generations. However, man with his modern welfare state, takes care of any excess children and does not allow them to starve.

> Individuals who have too many children are penalized, not because the whole population goes extinct, but simply because fewer of their children survive. Genes for having too many children are just not passed on to the next generation in large numbers, because few of the children bearing these genes reach adulthood. What has happened in modern civilized man is that family sizes are no longer limited by the finite resources that the individual parents can provide. If a husband and wife have more children than they can feed, the state, which means the rest of the population, simply steps in and keeps the surplus children alive and healthy...But the welfare state is a very unnatural thing. In nature, parents who have more children than they can support do not have many grandchildren, and their genes are not passed on to future generations. Contraception is sometimes attacked as 'unnatural'. So it is, very unnatural. The trouble is, so is the welfare state.[10]

Let's take a quick look at the way this very important natural function fits into the cultural context, because culture changes how it operates in important ways.

THE MATING GAME AND THE GAME OF LIFE

We have not yet talked about the most important of all human activities—reproduction. But it's difficult to do justice to this fascinating and important subject. One approach is to discuss it scientifically in relation to the theory of evolution. But this is sort of dry and technical, so we'll just have to settle for a somewhat superficial treatment rather than an in-depth study. The following is a sort of *potpourri* of observations, which I hope will shine a little light on the subject. However, you *could* just skip this section altogether without any serious loss.

It is curious that many activities connected to the process of procreation are carefully camouflaged, so they are not readily apparent to the casual observer. We are all familiar with the elaborate courtship rituals that take place in the natural world, so one might expect similar rituals to occur in human societies. However, one might also expect that culture would have changed these rituals. And indeed, although there is a lot of similarity, man does many strange things that seem, at first glance, to have nothing whatever to do with reproduction—until one realizes what is really going on.

It's easy to get the impression that things are being made a lot more complicated than they need to be. Unlike other animals, which have few inhibitions where sex is concerned, man has developed a certain diffidence with regard to the natural function of procreation, which compels him to keep it hidden for the most part. Some parents find it easier to tell their children that babies are delivered by storks, rather than to simply tell them the truth. This can result in the child getting all sorts of distorted views with regard to the reproductive process.

Different cultures have different ways of ritualizing the process of courtship. Many have developed customs and modes of behavior that betray a desire to hide the basic functions of the flesh behind an elaborate facade. In many Christian and Moslem countries they seem almost ashamed of the reproductive process, as if it were somehow unnatural (what, in fact, could possibly be *more* natural). It's as if it would be nice to do without it. But of course we can't do without it. So, like it or not, we have to go through with it. This leads to a sort of game of hide and seek, where as much as possible of the process is covered up. The Moslems take this to the extreme, by covering up their women from head to foot in what's called a *burka*. This tends to put a damper on the mating game. Nonetheless, the more enterprising of the young people find ways of getting around this and other obstacles. Alas, the *burka* not only hampers the mating game, but also helps to keep women in an inferior status.

Although other cultures indulge in this kind of charade to a certain extent, the Christians and the Moslems have a tendency to overdo it, probably because they both have a propensity to look upon the flesh as basically corrupt. Fortunately nature's evolutionary imperative provides enough "primitive urge" to overcome these inhibitions, otherwise these cultures might have become under-populated in comparison to the others. Actually, such cultural inhibitions hardly dampen the fun of the mating game, which is endlessly fascinating to participants and observers alike. And besides, these cultures are by no means monolithic in their attitudes. Compared to the more puritanical behavior of the British and Americans, the French get endless fun out of the mating game, and have few inhibitions about it. Actually, the attitudes of the older folk are dictated as much by custom as by religion.

But behind the ritualistic facade the serious game of life is playing itself out. Of course there are many human activities that have nothing whatever to do with reproduction, but there are also many that *are* related to it, even though at first glance it seems that they are not. If society is not actually one big mating ritual, it is not nearly as far removed from it as one might think.

The general rule is: the more desirable the mate, the more elaborate the mating ritual. So the higher up the social ladder one goes, the more serious the mating game becomes. At first glance, the elaborate balls and other get-togethers of the rich and powerful appear as mere competitions to show how much money and effort can be wasted on frivolous things. But the object of the exercise is by no means frivolous. For those giving and attending the balls are telling those who care to listen that the avenue to success in the game of life is open only to those in the exclusive set of invitees.

In the days of kings and queens, the monarch would not allow his offspring much choice in the matter of mates. The royal children had marriages arranged for them with other crowned heads, and this ensured that the exuberance of youth, or even Cupid's dart, would not interfere with dynastic ambitions. Nonetheless, Cupid's dart could not be completely avoided, and the will of the monarch was sometimes thwarted.

Almost every kind of fashion, whether in clothes, jewelry, art, and even sport, is essentially part of the mating game. The type of job one has, where one lives, what kind of car one drives, where one goes to school, or on vacation, and especially the type of friends one has, are all related to the mating game. They are related to it because both parents and children (especially the former) are striving to climb the social ladder—or at least trying to make sure that they don't slip down it. Some version of this struggle takes place in almost every society, although it obviously takes different forms in different cultures, and, as I said before, it becomes more frantic, and more expensive, the higher up the social ladder one goes.

In modern Western society, with its lack of class divisions and greater freedom of opportunity, there is more scope for the mating game. But the rest of the world follows a similar, if less frantic, pattern. Similar kinds of behavior were common among the Greeks and the Romans, the Aztecs and the Incas. And the things they competed for were also quite similar. Even so-called primitive people compete with regard to clothes, body paint, houses, hunting grounds, etc. The only type of society where the mating game is seriously compromised is one where matches are made by the parents, and the young people have little choice of whom they can marry. This is the same procedure that was employed by the crowned heads of yesteryear. But when it's extended to the general populace it has a stifling effect on the whole society. All the same, it seldom functions as intended, because in many cases a prospective bride will refuse to marry someone she doesn't like—let alone love—and there is not much that the parents can do about it.

The idea that parents are more competent at finding mates for their children than the children themselves is definitely spurious. But that doesn't stop parents from trying to influence these matters as much as they can. They forget that they themselves were once children, and usually did precisely the opposite of what their parents wanted.

It's probable that clothes were originally used for ornament rather than for warmth, especially in hot climates. The use of ornament has been almost universal among all races and cultures since the earliest times. But there are radically different ideas of what constitutes beauty among the various races and cultures of the world. The white race has an inflated idea of its own superiority and attractiveness. But the other races have similar notions. This of course makes the world much more interesting, but frustrating as well.

In addition to the different fashions in all types of clothing, the use of tattoos and body ornament is widespread in many societies. In primitive tribes this includes such things as removing the front teeth or enlarging the ears, lips, or noses in ways that would seem grotesque to outsiders. Various types of mutilation, especially of the face and head, are often practiced in these societies. All this is done for beautification, and to enhance one's attractiveness to the opposite sex.

The color of the skin is of great importance as a criterion of good looks for the various races of mankind. The reason for the different skin colors is not known with certainty. In any case, the separation between the races is of fairly recent origin—within the last 30,000 years or so.[11] Most of those not belonging to the white race consider white skin to be unattractive. Of course many white people have a similar aversion to darker skin. So the idea of what constitutes beauty varies, not only among individuals, but even more markedly between cultures and races as well. The remarkable thing is not that the criterion of beauty varies—this one would expect to some degree—but the striking thing is how *much* it varies. And just as the idea of beauty is relative, so sexual mores and morals can differ considerably between the various cultures.

Darwin says that the "most vigorous and best adapted" males are the ones most likely to be successful in the mating game. But this does not necessarily mean that the best interests of the society are served.

> The very poor and reckless, who are often degraded by vice, almost invariably marry early, whilst the careful and frugal, who are generally otherwise virtuous, marry late in life, so that they may be able to support their children in comfort.... Thus the reckless, degraded, and often vicious members of society, tend to increase at a quicker rate than the provident and generally more virtuous members.
>
> There are, however, some checks to this downward tendency. We have seen that the intemperate suffer from a high rate of mortality, and the extremely profligate leave few offspring.[12]

So civilization has upset the process of natural selection to some degree, but not entirely. It has not done away with the idea that the main purpose in life is procreation. And to emphasize its importance the institution of marriage has been created. But marriage is something that is a relatively late phenomenon in human society. Either polygamy or semi-monogamous relationships were the norm in early communities, and this is still the case today in some societies. It roughly reflects what goes on with our closest relatives in the animal world. Monkeys and apes practice monogamy some of the time, but polygamy is the general rule. It is perhaps surprising that promiscuity is not more widespread among both animals and humans. But the probable reason is because jealousy is such a pervasive natural emotion, and unless there are established rules of behavior in this area, chaos will result.

The established rule in modern societies is of course marriage, which seems to work fairly well. It's obviously sensible to allow for divorce, otherwise marriages can become too burdensome and cease to serve any practical purpose. Another important function of marriage is to ensure that the offspring continue to be looked after during the extended time that a human being needs to reach maturity.

An interesting footnote on the subject of marriage relates to the best man in the wedding. The role of the best man was originally to help his good friend obtain a wife from a neighboring tribe. "In our own marriages the best man seems originally to have been the chief abettor of the bridegroom in the act of capture."[13] His present role is purely ceremonial, so we can think of him as rather like the appendix in the body—something that once had a practical purpose, but is now a possible source of irritation.

Not only the mating game, but the whole game of life is played quite differently in far-off places like Polynesia, where the influence of Western society has not yet made itself felt to any great degree. The frantic "pursuit of happiness," which defines the Western, and especially the American way of life is almost entirely absent in this type of society. As Ivar Lissner tells us:

> We must always be on our guard against the temptation to apply the restless, progressive standards of the West to civilizations which should be assessed by quite different criteria. Our Western standards are not by any means applicable to every race on earth. Neither dynamism nor progress, in the Western sense, necessarily make for human happiness. The slumbering, dreamy existence of the Pacific races, for instance, with its careless tranquillity and unconsciousness of sin, its elemental rhythms of joy and sorrow, is probably much closer to the secret of living.[14]

But this idyllic way of life cannot long survive the relentless advance of global civilization. "Progress" is its implacable enemy. As with Stone Age man, its days are surely numbered. Even though we probably exaggerate its innocence when compared to our frantic world, it might be nice to give it a try before it goes the way of the dinosaur.

SURVIVAL OF THE FITTEST

Things like the pursuit of science and the search for knowledge are only peripherally related to either survival or the mating game. So the human animal has created other interests and occupations for himself besides the basic ones of survival and reproduction. Although these activities are not directly connected to the imperatives of biological evolution, many of them are essential to the preservation and advancement of culture. Medicine is clearly a constructive activity, and it has now become a major source of benefit to the human race. Other types of science increase man's understanding of himself and the physical world, and ultimately hold the key to any meaningful progress towards a more civilized society. The production of art can be considered as an important, perhaps even essential, part of the progress of mankind on the intellectual level. But these kinds of activity are anti-evolutionary in a certain sense, in that they allow man to bypass the process of evolution. It's as if we have changed the course of our own evolution. Perhaps the most obvious example of this is that *everyone* may now have a chance to survive, not just the fittest.

War can hardly be said to accord with the evolutionary idea of survival. It is not necessarily the fittest that survive in war, but usually those with the most destructive weapons. This distorts the natural concept of who constitutes the fittest. So this kind of activity is something foreign to the evolutionary process. Nevertheless war can be considered to have its roots in the struggle for survival, from the days when one-on-one combat was the norm. It's the addition of ever more lethal weapons and the organization of armies that sets it apart from any kind of natural process. In an analogous manner, it was teamwork and tools that allowed mankind to rise to the top of the animal world and begin the development of culture. But once the need for teamwork became less vital, there was a subtle change from co-operation to competition.

Success on the ladder of evolution has in fact radically altered the nature of human development. But although man has changed the process of his own evolution, he has not yet become master of it. Prior to his ascent to the top of the food chain, all his energies went into physical survival. There was fierce competition for food and other necessities. But after mankind's emergence as king of the beasts, the fight for survival was essentially over, and so a lot of the energy that had gone into this struggle was no longer needed for the same purpose. (It's true that the battle against things like microbial predators has continued to this day, but this battle is internalized within each individual member of the species.)

The cultures that man has created were possible because the battle for supremacy in the animal world had already been won. The competition for food became much less arduous, since there were no large predators that could not be defeated. So there existed a lot of surplus energy, which had to go somewhere. Part of it went into hunting, but as we have seen, this resulted in the extinction of many other species that had previously been able to hold their own in the competition for food. Humans started to use their excess energy in hunting not only animals, but also one another.

The transition must have taken many centuries, because isolated human settlements that seldom came into contact with each other could probably have lived in peace, with only minimal internal strife. But as the total population increased and the distribution of settlements grew denser, both internal and external conflict must have become more common. The fact that man is a territorial animal encouraged competition between groups. Much of the excess energy was thus aimed at other human communities, which now took the place of the ancient predators that had been defeated. The drive for survival had become self-destructive. Other groups became the enemy, the foreigner, the stranger, rather than being partners in the struggle for survival. Any slight difference in physical appearance or social custom was taken as a sign that they were outsiders, and essentially different.

Some of the excess energy went into the more constructive aspects of culture, such as the improvement of agriculture and the erection of elaborate buildings. New tools and better methods of construction; more efficient organization of the community and the introduction of law codes; more sophisticated forms of art; and more elaborate forms of ritual, both religious and secular.

The competitive energies that had helped man to win the primal battle for survival could not all be channeled into constructive paths. Competition between communities, and within the same community, became a constant feature of human societies. The struggle with the rest of the animal kingdom had already been won, but the struggle within the human family was to grow ever more violent with the passage of time. Warfare became an inseparable part of human culture.

POWER AND PRIVILEGE

The Darwinian theory stresses selection for those variations (in the genes) that are best able to ensure survival and produce offspring, thus providing for the perpetuation of the species. But human society works in quite a different manner, in that the competition is artificially limited. Those at the top want to make sure that they and their offspring remain in a position of privilege. You might ask what is wrong with that; isn't it just the survival of the fittest? Actually it's not, because the whole system is now stacked against those who are not at the top. The playing field is no longer level. This does not necessarily lead to the survival of the fittest, but could very well lead to the demise of the fittest, and the survival of the unfit.

But surely the survival of the fittest still holds, because monarchies can be overthrown and elites can be replaced? This is only partially true, because dynasties and their supporting elites are (or were), to a large extent, self-perpetuating. This is why it usually took a revolution to get rid of them, or a foreign conqueror. There was often a struggle for power among the offspring after a monarch died, and each one would raise an army to support his cause. But when all was said and done and the winner emerged, the dynasty lived on. Even if a clear winner failed to emerge and there was a partition of the country between the claimants, the dynasty could still be considered to have survived, albeit in a weakened state. In the case of the Ottoman and Mughal Empires, there was always a fight to the death among the claimants, which insured that the strongest ultimately won—a brutal but effective means of weeding out the less qualified claimants. No sibling of the winning party was allowed to survive. Although monarchies that had an established method of succession were more stable, fights among the kin of a deceased monarch were nonetheless frequent.

As far as privilege and power are concerned, surely the elites are the most qualified to lead their fellow men? Well, experience has shown that if the elites are in fact excluded from power, as they were under communism, things can go rapidly down hill. So those "born and educated to lead" cannot be idly tossed out without considerable injury to the body politic. Plato may have been right that not everyone is fit to govern (notice how Plato keeps coming back into the discussion). The ghastly examples of Pol Pot in Cambodia and Mao in China, who brutally murdered all those considered to be intellectuals, should remind us that a culture is dependent on its talented and educated citizens in order to preserve its structure and integrity. Darwin noted the importance of those who are better educated in a society:

> The presence of a body of well-instructed men, who have not to labor for their daily bread, is important to a degree which cannot be overestimated; as all high intellectual work is carried on by them, and on such work, material progress of all kinds mainly depends, not to mention other and higher advantages. No doubt wealth when very great tends to convert men into useless drones, but their number is never large; and some degree of elimination here occurs, for we daily see rich men, who happen to be fools or profligate, squandering away their wealth.[15]

But talent is not confined to those in the upper echelons of a society. And there is no guarantee that the offspring of those in power will have the necessary abilities to carry on after their elders have passed away. In fact the sons and daughters of the rich and powerful are often a source of disappointment to their parents. Being born to privilege provides little incentive for self-improvement. A fresh infusion of talent from outside of the governing class is constantly needed in order to maintain the requisite standard of competence. (This is what the biologists call the expansion of the gene pool.) So in order to maintain a standard of excellence, it is necessary to open up the exclusive club to newcomers from beyond the inner circle of the elite.

Until the coming of democracy, human society has seldom allowed this to happen. Almost all the older societies quickly became stratified. The layers were rigid, and although one could go down, one could seldom if ever go up. The slave class was at the bottom; then there was usually a rudimentary merchant class; the other categories generally comprised the military and ruling classes, together with a priestly class.

After the introduction of agriculture, some kind of class system has been the norm in practically all societies. And class systems are still in place today in many countries, although the divisions may be based upon different criteria. The breakup of the old type of system, or at least a significant change in it, came about with the expansion of the merchant class. This has been discussed already in connection with the rise of capitalism and the resulting shift in the power structure in many European countries.

The class structure certainly helped to keep a society together, providing it with a certain measure of stability. But such things as the expansion of trade and advances in technology put a strain on such a rigid social fabric. Those at the top could not stop these developments, but they were reluctant to allow the rising middle class a share in the privileges of power. Carefully developed institutions and customs might become compromised by an influx of ruder citizens from below. These upstarts simply did not possess the carefully cultivated tastes in the finer things of life, which were the hallmark of those who held the reins of power. The inner circles of the elite could only be attained through special breeding (the gene pool was intentionally restricted). Their claim to power rested on heredity, on bloodlines and on property. This was an exclusive club, and outsiders were not encouraged to apply for membership.

But the merchant class, or bourgeoisie, kept on getting more powerful, at least economically. In China they were looked down upon as engaging in sordid moneymaking, and in Europe there was something of the same attitude. But from the Renaissance on, their power and influence steadily increased.

Those at the bottom of the class structure were not initially helped by the rise of the middle class. But there were a lot of them, and if they really got together, they could make their influence felt. This could only be done, however, with competent leadership. Lack of leadership among the masses has been a constant problem, and this has allowed them to be continually exploited by those standing higher on the social ladder. But as the middle class rose, so the working class became more aware of the fact that maybe their lowly status was not necessarily permanent after all. If the merchants could start moving up, why shouldn't they? The French Revolution is the classic example of what can happen when this kind of movement starts to occur in a rigid class structure. The failure of the elites to adapt to change ended up causing the whole edifice to collapse.

But any attempt to change the class structure overnight is fraught with danger, as attested by the French, Russian and Chinese Revolutions. Evolution rather than revolution is much the safest course. The American Revolution made an effort to produce a more egalitarian society, by introducing democracy and abolishing titles. The English colonies had sought to reproduce the same class distinctions as those that pertained at home, so the American Revolution made a definite break in this regard.[16] This has permitted those with the requisite talent and ambition to rise in the society. There is no doubt that the flood of immigrants seeking equal opportunity has contributed mightily to America's strength and economic growth.

AMERICAN SLAVERY AND CLASS STRUGGLE

In spite of her achievements, a dark cloud has hung over the American success story. First of all it was the treatment of the Native Americans. This was a continuation of the policies of the British, who, when the indigenous population refused to kowtow to them, proceeded to try and exterminate them. Then there was the question of slavery, which was also a holdover from the colonial era. The blacks were considered a separate class of people, born into an inferior status, like the *sudras* in India. This was a fiction of course, since most of them had been obtained through the raiding of their African homelands by rival tribes, who then sold them to European or Moslem slave traders. Being captured or defeated in war meant relegation to the slave class, regardless of one's previous status. The slave trade simply relegated these unfortunate people to the level of ordinary merchandise.

So after having been consigned to a lower class, from there it was only a short step to imply their inferiority as human beings. This supposedly justified their harsh and inhuman treatment. The fact that the pigmentation of their skin was different from that of the slave-masters helped to bolster the proposition that they were "not like us." That all this was totally un-Christian hardly seemed to matter, although there were a few who did draw attention to this fact.

Having rationalized to themselves their treatment of the blacks, the Americans fiercely resisted any change in their status. The whole structure of the South was built up around the "peculiar institution" of slavery. So when the American Revolution proclaimed that all men were created equal, the blacks were conveniently forgotten. The class system was firmly in place, and change was almost unthinkable.

On top of the normal rigidity of the class structure was the fact that the South, and to a lesser extent the North also, was economically dependent on slavery. The American South was part of the vast slave-based plantation system of sugar, coffee, cotton and tobacco, stretching all the way from Brazil, through the Caribbean, to Maryland on the Chesapeake Bay. This system was so profitable for the plantation owners that they were able to import luxuries from Europe, while the slaves got nothing for their labor.

The fact that the leaders of the Revolution were mostly rich slave-owning Virginians was somewhat embarrassing, but human beings have a marvelous capacity for rationalizing away unpleasant truths. Although the slave trade was officially abolished in 1807, this was widely disregarded. The status quo was not interfered with, and life for the slave-owner went on as before.

But this could not go on indefinitely and the problem of slavery finally erupted in the Civil War. There were other causes for the Civil War, but above all else was this dark cloud that refused to go away. The people of the South fought bravely for the right to choose their own way of life. The essence of their struggle was the defense of white supremacy. Southerners were determined to preserve their part of America as "white man's country." The abolition of slavery threatened to destroy their world.

In retrospect we can see that the South was unlucky with the timing of the Civil War. For millennia slavery had been not only legal, but also morally and socially acceptable. However, after the 1820's, slave trading was largely abolished, and slavery gradually changed its status from a moral to an immoral institution. As J. R. & William McNeill write in *The Human Web:*

> Just as the world's systems of forced labor attained their maximum historical size, something strange happened: the systems were dismantled. Slavery, which had existed for at least 5,000 years, and had seemed part of the natural order of human affairs, in many societies came to be seen as immoral. Simulta-

neously its economic logic began to weaken, its political support waned, and its opponents organized.[17]

The effect of the Industrial Revolution and the rise of liberal democracy had changed the way the European powers, especially Britain, looked upon slavery. It was seen as incompatible with the new ideas concerning the rights of man, and it would not be very long before the rest of the world came to look at slavery in the same way.

But the Civil War did not settle the matter of the treatment of the ex-slaves. The Southern whites, fiercely resisting any change in their privileged status vis à vis the blacks, refused to accept the freed slaves as equal citizens. In many ways the treatment of the blacks was worse after the Civil War than before it. Lynching and other abominations were widespread, and went on well into the twentieth century. In fact, the ex-slaves did not begin to enjoy their legitimate rights of citizenship until the 1960's, a hundred years after the Civil War, when the civil rights movement at last began to redress the wrongs of slavery.

The Anglo-Saxons did not invent slavery. In fact they came to it by accident rather than design. The enslavement of those who had been defeated in battle was common practice among the early cultures that we have considered, except in the case of the Chinese, where it was a rare occurrence. The slaves were usually the lucky ones, because it was customary to kill a defeated enemy, and often many of their women and children as well. The Aztecs sacrificed their defeated enemies to their gods. In fact it seems that the principle object of warfare for the Aztecs was to obtain captives that could be ritually sacrificed. According to their system of belief, the gods needed a constant supply of human blood in order to replenish the fertility of the soil and to maintain the welfare of the community. The more captives that were sacrificed, the better things would be. This manner of behavior, which can only be described as barbaric, did not prevent the Aztecs from producing extraordinary works of art and architecture, and otherwise exhibiting many aspects of an advanced society.

The actual treatment of slaves varied considerably. Those who were made to work on public monuments had a miserable existence, while domestic slaves were very much better off. In Greece, many of the domestic slaves became almost part of the family, and were sometimes even granted their freedom. This was also true in the United States, though freedom was seldom granted. But to make any kind of sense out of the phenomenon of slavery we have to consider it in the larger context of class and privilege. More modern instances of slavery, such as occurred in Germany under the Nazis and continues today in parts of Africa, are more the result of a breakdown of civilized society, rather than being part of a traditional institution.

The cruelty associated with slavery is certainly shocking from a more modern standpoint. But excessive cruelty has been a characteristic of the struggle for power from very ancient times. In fact one can list extreme cruelty as another distinguishing feature of the human race. The struggle for dominance is fierce and unrelenting, and the end usually justifies any means that are available.

Communism keeps cropping up along the way in various contexts, and another way of looking at communism is as class warfare. This is exactly what Marx intended it to be, but he was probably unaware of the underlying forces that he was dealing with. He thought a quick and victorious war against the capitalist exploiters would lead to justice for all in a workers' paradise. This was a utopian scheme that was hopelessly unrealistic. But a look at the methods of communism can be instructive. In all the communist revolutions: in Russia, China, Cambodia, Cuba, and even Vietnam, there was a vicious campaign against "intellectuals." The intellectual posed a threat to the power of the communists, and they had to be eliminated one way or another. In the case of Cambodia this meant literally extermination. In China, during the Cultural Revolution, not only university professors and anyone with a university degree or other kind of special training, but also artists and musicians, were treated like outcasts. Many died of ill treatment, and others barely survived. This was an example of class warfare. The leaders of the masses ignored the fact that these intellectuals were needed to keep the society functioning. They were not so much interested in the welfare of the masses as in the maintenance of their own power, and the intellectuals represented a direct challenge to that power. The irony is that Marx himself was an intellectual.

As far as class warfare is concerned, the power struggle between the middle and upper classes has been of a basically different character. While the middle class has been known to take up arms against the power elites, and the elites themselves have jealously guarded their privileged status, on many occasions it has been to their mutual advantage to cooperate. After all, the bourgeoisie produced many of the goods and services that the elites needed to retain their power. This resulted in the steady rise in power and influence of the middle classes. Rather than trying to forcefully remove the elites, they were generally content to gradually replace them as the effective instruments of power. In most countries, this process has now resulted in the virtual elimination of the old aristocratic class from the power structure. Where they still exist, they have mostly been relegated to a ceremonial status. The process of industrialization has forced them either to adapt to the world of business or lose their privileged status. The mere ownership of land no longer guarantees them a position of power in the community.

In America there is no mention of an upper class—or lower class for that matter. One only talks about the middle class and the lower middle class. The upper middle class is occasionally mentioned, but no one seems to be quite sure who actually belongs to it.

The strange nature of the American class structure reminds me a bit of the British railway system, which used to have three classes: first, second and third. After World War II they decided to eliminate one of the classes in order to save money. This was done in a quintessentially British way. They eliminated not the third class, or the first class, but the *second* class. So now there was no in-between, you were either at the top of the heap or at the bottom—on the railway that is. In America they did the opposite; they got rid of the top and the bottom, and left the middle! It just shows what can happen if you move from one side of the Atlantic to the other! But in fact the British still have the remnant of an upper class, which considers itself a bit above the ordinary folk. So the choice they made with the railway classes was appropriate in a roundabout sort of way.

14

PHILOSOPHICAL VIEWPOINTS

o o o o o o o o o o o o o o o o o o o o o o o o o o o o o o o o
Mathematics takes us still further from what is human, into the region of absolute necessity, to which not only the actual world, but every possible world, must conform.

—*Bertrand Russell*
The Study of Mathematics

QUARKS AND OTHER STRANGE OBJECTS

I hope that those readers who may have skipped some of the more technical parts of what has gone before will not abandon this section too readily, since it should be easily comprehensible by those with only a modest scientific background, and it is an important part of the story. So please do not head for the exits before the play has even begun.

Ever since the days of Copernicus in the sixteenth century, the twin sciences of mathematics and physics, with the help of some key technological advances, have steadily changed our perception of the universe. By the turn of the twentieth century, many great minds had built an imposing edifice of abstract theory, which helped to explain many of the natural phenomena that were being studied by increasingly sophisticated scientific instruments.

It was mathematics that led the way. Pure logic applied to many disparate concepts revealed patterns within patterns that suggested an underlying structure to the abstract world of numbers, which had by then been enlarged to include a more comprehensive picture of the concept of number, considered on an increasingly abstract level. Complex numbers of many different kinds—some of which have already been mentioned in chapter 9—opened the possibilities of even larger logical structures underlying those already uncovered. The theory of groups was the key idea that allowed the development of these lines of inquiry. It is group theory that underlies much of the mathematical formulation that is used in modern physics, and much of this was already in place by the second half of the nineteenth century.

In scientific circles, it was fairly well accepted that only a strictly mathematical approach could provide an accurate description of nature. After all, Newton's laws, which were formulated mathematically, had so far stood the test of time. So it looked as if nature operated according to strict rules, which could be expressed in terms of mathematics. Even after Einstein's theory of relativity had superseded Newton's gravitational laws—in theory but not actually in practice—the concept that physical laws, expressed in mathematical terms, were a valid description of nature was not seriously questioned by the scientific community. Indeed, how else could we describe nature except by laws expressed mathematically? Since these laws agreed exceedingly well with observation, there was no reason to doubt their validity. Surely it is philosophers rather than physicists that worry about such things.

Group theory was one of the key ideas that emerged in the nineteenth century. The notion of a group is one of the most important unifying ideas in mathematics. It draws together a wide variety of mathematical objects, which include not only numbers and geometric objects, but also "functions" of many different types. The group concept can be applied to such things as reflections, rotations, permutations, etc.

There are many different types of group, but the ones that the physicists are most interested in are *non-commutative* groups. These groups have typical elements A and B, where the "product" of A and B, written AB, is not necessarily equal to BA, which means that the elements cannot be ordinary numbers, they have to be *matrices*, and the product of A and B involves *matrix* multiplication rather than ordinary multiplication.

Lie groups, mentioned in chapter 9 in relation to particle physics, are actually groups of *matrices*. These groups occur frequently when one is studying things like rotations, and they can tell us a great deal about the symmetries of physical systems. They are the meat and drink of the particle physicist, who looks for symmetries wherever he can find them.

The advent of quantum mechanics put the study of the micro-world onto an altogether different plane from the world of Isaac Newton. With Newton, the laws of the physical universe made intuitive sense; the forces and orbits seemed to be in accord with the world that we observe on a daily basis. For instance, they account logically for what happens when a ball is thrown into the air. But the mechanisms of the micro-world do not make intuitive sense; in fact they are *counter-intuitive*, as was shown in chapter 9 with the double-slit experiment. What happens is something one would *not* expect to happen. But it *does* happen, and only quantum mechanics can describe mathematically the phenomena that occur at this level. It is the only language that can be used to describe the micro-world accurately. And it turns out that theory and observation correspond to an astonishing degree—all one has to do is throw one's intuition out the window. So until something better comes along to describe the world of the very small, quantum mechanics is our only reliable tool.

In the latter part of the twentieth century, all sorts of new particles were discovered by the physicists, in addition to things like the proton, the neutron and the electron, which had been known for some time. Smashing high-energy beams of particles into one another in "accelerators" is the means by which these new particles are created and observed. Most appear as "resonances," which exist only for a fraction of a second and then decay into some other particle or particles. By studying the behavior of these short-lived objects, it is possible to find out things like their mass, electrical charge and spin.[1]

In order to account for the behavior of the new particles, the physicists turned to mathematics. The most appropriate tool for this was the theory of groups, and in particular Lie groups, whose "representations" provide a wonderful basis on which to study the symmetries of these strange and wondrous inhabitants of the micro-world.[2]

And this is where the quarks come in. In the 1960's, Murray Gell-Mann, a top physicist who was also conversant with Lie groups, came up with an ingenious scheme whereby the behavior of most of these particles could be explained by thinking of them as *representations of various Lie groups*. In order that everything should fit together neatly, like the pieces of a jigsaw puzzle, it was necessary for Gell-Mann to postulate the existence of "fundamental" particles called quarks. According to him, the quarks were the *constituents* of known particles like the proton and neutron (but not the electron), which had previously been thought to be indivisible.[3]

What I have been describing, in very rough outline, is part of the basic formulation of what the physicists call the Standard Model, which we came across in chapter 9. As an abstract theory—a pure construct of the human mind—it is very impressive. But the quarks, those ultimate building blocks of the physical world—that actually come in different *colors* and *flavors*—cannot be observed directly, even with the most powerful of modern instruments. Any attempt to separate the proton or any other particle into its constituent quarks is doomed to failure. They are tucked in so tightly that it is impossible to break them apart. Only through painstaking analysis of sophisticated accelerator experiments could their existence be verified.

For a while it was thought that maybe the quarks were just a mathematical construct, which was needed in order to provide an explanation for the observed behavior of the proton and the neutron. But more recent evidence from collision experiments has confirmed their existence with reasonable certainty.

According to the theory, there are six flavors of quark: up, down, strange, charmed, top and bottom! And they all come in three different colors! The top and bottom quarks proved to be the most elusive, but persistent research was eventually rewarded. The bottom quark's existence was confirmed in 1977, at the Fermi National Accelerator Laboratory, near Chicago. The top quark was also found there, but not until 1995.[4] It turned out that Gell-Mann's ingenious hypothesis was not just a flight of fancy after all.

There are quite a few important features of the theory that I have left out, such as the elusive Higgs boson, which is necessary to account for the fact that the symmetries of the Standard Model do not quite match the experimental data. But I have tried to explain the theory without going into too much detail, and I hope that the gist of it has become reasonably clear. The point I am trying to make is that there is a kind of chicken-and-egg quality to creating mathematical models of the physical world. Is the physics creating the mathematics, or is the mathematics creating the physics? Sometimes one gets the impression that the physical world is being pushed into a mathematical mold, but loose ends keep on popping out, and a frantic effort has to be made to stuff everything back in again. However, one has to say in defense of the physicists that many of the phenomena that they have predicted, purely on the basis of mathematical models, have later been found to actually occur. So there is no denying that this group-theoretical approach is a very powerful tool, and a very successful one.

All the same, in addition to the question of the Higgs boson, there is also the problem of reconciling gravity with quantum mechanics, and this brings such concepts as string theory (also introduced in chapter 9) into the picture. The latter theory postulates the existence of still more exotic particles, which could not be detected with the energies now available in the most powerful accelerators.

Without this kind of verification, string theory remains just an idea in the minds of the physicists. But since the quarks turned out to be real, it would be unwise to dismiss string theory too lightly. In its essence, string theory is not incompatible with the Standard Model.

So there is more work to be done before everything finally falls into place. But there are a lot of very smart people working on these things and it seems certain that all the outstanding questions will eventually either be answered, or found to be unanswerable. How long this will take one cannot predict with any certainty. Meanwhile perhaps we should ask:

DOES GOD KNOW ABOUT LIE GROUPS?

One can be fairly certain that the physicists are not particularly interested in this question. But it's an intriguing one nevertheless. If there *was* a Creator in the very beginning, surely "he" must have known what he was creating and what its potentialities were. If there *are* such things as fundamental physical laws, surely he would know about them, even if he did not actually *create* them. However, upon reflection we see that this does not necessarily follow. Isn't it possible to postulate some kind of motivating force—an alternative definition of God, which could start the whole thing off (with a bang) and not know what was going to happen afterwards? The laws of physics could have been unknown to him (it), and only discovered after 15 billion years by an intelligent creature that just happened to evolve on a planet in an obscure corner of the universe! But if we assume that the laws of physics are pretty much what we have postulated them to be, then they must have existed from day one, from the time of the Big Bang, without God knowing anything about them!

I admit that this scenario is a bit strange. But the assumption that God *did* know about the laws of physics can lead us to even stranger conclusions. If we assume that God knew all about the laws of physics; that in fact he really *created* them in order to make his original handiwork function in the way that he wanted it to; and if we assume further that we are at least on the right track in our search for the ultimate physical laws, then surely God must have known all about Lie groups 15 billion years before Sophus Lie was born! [5]

There is another possibility, and this seems at first to be a bit more reasonable. It is that Bertrand Russell was correct in his surmise that there is an underlying logical structure to the material world which is unchangeable and expressible in mathematical terms. And what's more, any conceivable reality cannot exist without it. In other words, the laws of physics are part of a logical imperative; they could not be any other way, even if God wanted to change them. This infers that the abstract structure of mathematics (or at least part of it) is not just a construct of the human mind, but reflects the very essence and fabric of reality itself.[6] (See my discussion about the *Laws of Nature* in Chapter 11.)

Although at first sight this looks like a way out of the dilemmas caused by the first two scenarios, it too has its drawbacks. The vast edifice that is modern mathematics is a totally abstract structure, which apparently has no direct connection to physical reality at all, even though some of it may have been motivated by observations of the physical world. This remains true even though many natural phenomena can be fairly accurately described in mathematical terms.

At the end of chapter 9 we concluded that mathematics is solely a creation of the human mind. But Russell contends that the physical universe is compelled to obey certain abstract principles, which can *only* be expressed mathematically, and that its very existence is somehow contingent upon these principles being obeyed. In other words, mathematics exists *independently* of the human mind. This contradicts our conclusion that mathematics is purely a human invention. The only way out of the dilemma is to say that if indeed the universe is compelled to obey certain abstract principles, they do not necessarily have to be expressed mathematically.

All this does not mean that the universe, or at least parts of it, cannot be *described* by physical laws like the one's that we have formulated. It only means that these laws are probably not the essence of reality that Russell supposed them to be.

As noted in chapter 9, mathematics cannot really be described as the *language* of nature, as Newton and others have asserted, even though many natural phenomena can be described using mathematics. There are actually only a few areas of mathematics that have any demonstrable relation to the real world. And even though some other parts of the vast mathematical realm may be found to have practical applications, it's safe to say that this will not happen very often.

So we have this vast theoretical structure—and it's getting bigger all the time—with some special parts that may be able to capture certain aspects of reality. But the main bulk of it consists of wonderfully ingenious exercises in abstract thought, having little or no connection to reality at all. What is it, we may ask, that makes the part that is useful so special? In particular, what is it about Lie groups that make *them* so special?

Actually, we can answer this last question fairly well. It's because in many cases Lie Groups are related to rotations, which in turn are related to symmetries, and *symmetry* is the key concept that lies at the heart of modern physics.[7] At the core of both Newton's and Einstein's physics is the idea of symmetry. The Standard Model, with all its different kinds of quarks and other particles is, *au fond,* all about symmetry. Lie groups are in essence symmetry groups.

There is a basic symmetry that lies at the heart of our conscious awareness of the physical world, which allows us to relate our experiences of the world with those of others. Without this symmetry, communication would be difficult if not impossible. So if there is a principle that governs our knowledge of the physical world, it is the concept of symmetry. But this does not mean that there is something magical about the mathematics of symmetry that makes it the "essence of reality." As mentioned in chapter 9, mathematics describes an ideal (Platonic) world, rather than the real one.

In any case, the concept of symmetry alone is not nearly enough to describe the physical world. If everything were symmetrical it would be a very dull world, and that is not the way things really are. It's only in a perfect world that everything would work out like it is supposed to in the Standard Model, and evidently the world is not perfect. (This is where the Higgs boson comes in; it provides a little *asymmetry.*)

It's worth noting that although the physical laws of conservation are based on symmetry, and material things like crystals have a symmetrical structure, life itself is based on asymmetry in a very real sense. It is the *asymmetry* of the chemicals in the egg that leads to the birth and development of a living organism. Like the human body, the exterior of the egg itself is quite symmetrical—they both have an axis of symmetry—but what's inside is not at all symmetrical. Chemical reactions come from asymmetrical relations between atoms and molecules.

The superficial symmetry of the double helix hides the basic asymmetry of the chemistry of life. Many molecules come in both left-handed and right-handed versions, and this asymmetry affects how they react with other molecules. In the same way, some elements are more symmetrical than others. The electrons that surround the nucleus are arranged in "shells." If one or more electrons are missing from a shell, the atom is less stable and will react with other elements more readily. Lack of symmetry encourages more complex chemical reactions.

What the physicists have created is a *model* of the material world, just like any other mathematical model. How closely this corresponds to the real thing is anybody's guess. But surely there must be a strong correlation between the model and reality, otherwise it would not be possible to predict what goes on "out there" with the kind of accuracy that the physicists are capable of, or to test the accuracy and consistency of our theories by experiment.

Some philosophers have maintained that the world that we perceive is just a construct of the human mind, and of course that is literally true. But this does not mean that there is no reality behind such a construct. The picture that is painted in the brain does not have to be an illusion, as some have thought (it may be difficult, however, to *prove* that it's not an illusion).

Does the world actually exist if there is nobody, or no creature, to perceive it? This is the same idea as that of a tree falling in the forest with nobody around to hear it. Does it make any noise? The answer seems to be both yes *and* no. So we'll leave that one to the philosophers. But it's interesting to note that there was nothing around to *perceive* the universe for at least 10 billion years! It was there all by itself, with nobody to admire it but God. However, God obviously would not *see* things the way we do, he does not have a body like ours—neither would he think like us. So in a very real sense, the world that we now experience did *not* exist during all that time. It only began to come into focus with the advent of living creatures.[8]

All this is in the realm of philosophy rather than science, and the philosophers have been arguing about such things for centuries. But many of these concepts are germane to our quest for enlightenment regarding the human condition. Of course there are often more questions than there are answers. But the application of logic can sometimes yield some degree of illumination.

The question as to whether God knows about mathematics may actually be irrelevant. Any being that was truly omnipotent would already know all the things that mathematics is able to demonstrate, so what would he (it) need mathematics for?

It's doubtful that a *real* God would know or care much about the sort of laws that we have formulated to describe natural phenomena. And anyway, our laws deal with the physical world only in a piecemeal fashion. This is because these laws are formulated at different scales. Quantum mechanics deals with the micro-scale; Einstein's relativity deals with astronomical scales; and Newton's laws deal with ordinary everyday scales. Since solid bodies are made up of atoms, the behavior of the body and the individual atoms cannot be studied together. You either study the whole or the individual parts (this is at least partly why we are having such difficulty in reconciling quantum mechanics and gravity). In a gas the atoms or molecules fly all over the place, but the gas as a whole can be studied statistically, as regards its temperature, pressure, etc. So we seem to be finding different laws for different scales. We can have chaos at one scale, and order at another. As astronomer John Barrow says, in *The World Within the World:*

> Often, chaos leads spontaneously to order. The atoms around us move haphazardly, each in its own way, yet there is comparative order over a large scale.... There is no 'law' of evolution which directs the course of biological development over aeons of time: only the statistics of the independent results of adaption and survival. Yet the flora and fauna of our planet exhibit what we would have to admit as 'order'. This impressive state of affairs makes it reasonable to ask if it is not possible that there is no 'unseen hand' at work in the Universe at large. Could it be that there are no laws of Nature at all? Perhaps all the order we see is a manifestation of that particular type of lawlessness and independence that leads to predictability? [9]

In the foregoing, we have assumed the existence of some kind of Supreme Being or "motivating force," otherwise there would have been no point in posing our basic question, Does God know about Lie groups? But even if no such Being exists, our conclusions regarding the laws of physics should still be valid. These laws, being a product of the human mind, cannot be expected to represent the true nature of our physical world, even though they may be able to capture certain elements of reality.

CULTURAL PERSPECTIVES

History is a fascinating subject for those who are interested in the past. And indeed the study of history is essential for anyone who wants to have a balanced view of the world. But it is also frustrating, because is it very difficult to obtain any kind of objective view of history. For instance, in the case of a battle, the story of what actually *happened* in the battle differs with every single participant—providing he survived to tell the tale. The side that won the battle is going to have a totally different version of it than the side that lost, and even those on the same side will have very different stories. Thus the "history" of the battle will depend to a large extent on the source of your information. Sometimes the different accounts do not seem to be describing the same event at all. It's up to the historian to try and distill the essence of the story from these conflicting sources. Hopefully there are some "hard facts" that can provide a framework on which the historian can build, and the various stories can be compared, in order to decide which ones are the more credible, and which are clearly exaggerations or distortions.

A good historian is often able to produce a reasonably objective account. As historian John Gaddis explains in his excellent little book *The Landscape of History*, it's neither possible nor desirable to capture every detail of history. He makes clear how important a knowledge of history is, and how it can be written effectively. History is not just a catalog of facts; it is a *representation* of the past, something like a landscape painting, which represents far more than is actually contained in the picture itself. History should represent the historical "landscape," and indicate how each aspect of the story fits into the larger context of its physical and cultural background. Historians need not agree on their *interpretations* of the truth, in fact competing views are healthy. Gaddis says of the historical method:

> Nor does it demand agreement, among its practitioners, as to precisely what the "lessons" of history are: a consensus can incorporate contradictions. It's part of growing up to learn that there are competing versions of truth, and that you yourself must chose which to embrace. It's part of the historical consciousness to learn the same thing: that there is no "correct" interpretation of the past, but that the act of interpreting is itself a vicarious enlargement of experience from which you can benefit.[10]

But to get a really comprehensive view of our world, we need more than history, because written history only goes back about five thousand years. Before that we have oral history, which most certainly influenced the first written history. But we need sciences like archaeology, anthropology, paleontology, geology, evolutionary biology, and finally astronomy and physics, to take us all the way back—eventually to the Big Bang. All these sciences, including history, have advanced tremendously in the last few decades. But they still have a long way to go. What they give us is still rather rough and ready, and has huge gaps in it as well. But at least we have made a start at finding out what our world is really like. Not that we can ever expect to know *everything* about it.

But even though these sciences tend to present a fairly uniform view of the world to those who study them, different people can still interpret the facts in different ways. Consequently there is no completely objective view, which we can confidently say is the correct one—even the scientists and the historians have their little biases. There are only a multitude of different views—as many as there are people.

One has to get literally outside of oneself in order to get any kind of truly objective view. You may think that you are looking at *the* world, but you are actually looking at *your* world, and in many ways it is quite different from *my* world. Of course my world is undoubtedly closer to your world than, say, a *chimpanzee's* world, but it still differs in a multitude of ways. The fact that people's views differ radically about politics, art, religion, morality, the opposite sex, entertainment, etc., reflects their diverse personalities, which in turn reflect different levels of education and differences of culture and life-style, to say nothing of the structure of their genes, as well as many other environmental influences. So in spite of the fact that there *is* only one world, the worlds that we individually inhabit are very different. (This is really what makes things interesting, for if everyone looked at the world in the same way, things would surely be a lot duller than they are—but probably a lot more peaceful.)

[When I am talking about an individual's view of the world, I mean that part of his consciousness that deals with the society and culture in which he lives. The picture of the *physical* world that is constructed by the senses will be discussed below.]

In *The Decline of the West,* Oswald Spengler claimed that each culture tends to promote its own worldview, or weltanschauung, which is unique to that particular culture. Recent studies have gone even further and found that people in separate cultures actually *think* differently.[11] So it's no wonder that people tend to search out those who share a similar worldview. Nevertheless, trying to understand how other people see the world can be extremely rewarding, if one refuses to be put off by what seem to be unbridgeable cultural differences.[12]

When human beings were finally able to spread out over the entire earth (except for the poles), widely separated groups developed different languages, and this has emphasized the separation even more. The fact that this dispersion took place over a span of more than 100,000 years should remind us how far apart we have drifted in the course of our journey into the world of different cultures that we see today.

Each individual is a little world unto himself. I know they say that no man is an island, but to a large extent we are indeed islands. Our big brain allows us to create a more complex world, which is expanded with the aid of our imagination into something much more significant than anything that exists in the rest of the animal kingdom. This makes us not only more aware of the extent of the earth itself, but also gives us a sense of our place in the wider universe. It also reveals the differences that exist between man and his fellow creatures.

Self-awareness, or consciousness, is a direct result of the increase in capacity and complexity of the human brain. This in turn has led to the rise of culture. So now the natural instincts of man must be re-channeled, from the necessity for survival in the wild, to the ability to live productively in the culture that man himself has created. Consciousness continues to evolve, but in a different milieu.[13]

Like all primates, man lives in groups, but the struggle for survival within the group has intensified with the rise of culture, as has the tension between the old survival instincts and the new rules and customs that the individual cultures have created. The problem now is how to acclimatize ourselves to a radically new world, because the world we originally adapted to is long since gone.[14] Myth and religion were one means to ease this transition, but they are now inadequate for the job. The culture itself is changing so fast that our adaptive capabilities are having a difficult time keeping abreast of the latest developments.

During the journey to where we now find ourselves, we have grown apart as a species. In spite of modern travel, much of the world's population lives in ignorance of how the rest of the world lives and thinks. We will have to reverse the process of alienation that has brought us to this state, because our world is becoming interconnected as never before, and the instincts that helped to preserve us for millions of years are ill-suited to the cultural environment in which we now find ourselves. Paradoxically, these instincts now threaten to destroy the very civilization that they once helped to create.

THE WORLD OF THE SENSES

Whereas there are major differences of character, temperament, opinion and worldview between individuals, there is one aspect of consciousness that does not vary nearly so much from person to person. This is the actual perception of physical reality that we construct through our senses. It varies little between individuals, simply because it is essentially an involuntary process, and the mechanism by which it operates is very similar—although not identical—in different individuals. (The neural circuitry is connected differently, even in identical twins, but the basic mechanism is the same.[15])

But the image created in the brain, *and the reality behind the image,* are two entirely different things, which have only a very tenuous connection. It is strange but true that we will never have more than the tiniest inkling of what lies beyond our world of the senses. What we create in our minds is a *construct* that allows us to navigate within our immediate surroundings in a satisfactory manner. This construct is created through various chemical processes; in the case of sight it is generated by electromagnetic waves emitted from the objects in our field of view. These waves consist of untold billions of little blobs of energy called photons, whose different frequencies determine the colors that we "see." The waves are absorbed by the retina in the eye; then transmitted into the brain through the optic nerve. This is the process we call sight.

Just how the image that we "see" is formed in the brain, or its exact nature, is not well understood; nor can we know for certain that what *you* see and what *I* see is really the same thing. But the fact that we can communicate our impressions of the world to one another, and to coordinate our activities and relationships in a satisfactory manner, implies strongly that our individual "images" are essentially the same. But these images do not give us an accurate picture of *reality* at all. The solid objects that we see around us are, in fact, composed almost entirely of empty space. Remember that any atom, of any element, consists of very little except empty space. Without the aid of our senses we would have no idea of what is really "out there," and the "sensual" picture that we paint for ourselves bears only a tenuous relationship to the real thing.

When you look into the sky on a starlit night, you see stars that existed in the distant past, and perhaps do not still exist. But even if you look around your room you actually see the past. As physicist Lee Smolin puts it:

> We are very used to imagining that we see a three-dimensional world when we look around ourselves. But is this really true? If we keep in mind that what we see is the result of photons impinging on our eyes, it is possible to imagine our view of the world in a quite different way. Look around and imagine that you see each object as a consequence of photons having just traveled from it to you. Each object you see is the result of a process by which information traveled to you in the shape of a collection of photons. The farther away the object is, the longer it took the photons to travel to you. So when you look around you do not see space—instead, you are looking back through the history of the universe. What you are seeing is a slice through the history of the world. Everything you see is a small part of that history.[16]

Although the world that you and I perceive with our senses is not the *real* world, which exists above and beyond our sensual experience, it is the only one that we will ever know. The "real" world is forever hidden from us; it can never be part of our reality, as far as we are concerned it does not exist at all. So

Nietzsche is essentially correct when he says that the world of the senses is the *only* world.

THE GARDEN OF GOOD AND EVIL

As far as the various intellectual disciplines are concerned, philosophy is in a category by itself. Although it is definitely not a science, it has made important contributions to mankind's intellectual development, and has remained a vital part of all major cultures from very early times, right up to the present.

Bertrand Russell says that philosophy has two major divisions:

> Philosophy, throughout its history, has consisted of two parts inharmoniously blended: on the one hand a theory as to the nature of the world, on the other an ethical or political doctrine as to the best way of living. The failure to separate these two with sufficient clarity has been a source of much confused thinking.[17]

Given the nature of philosophy—essentially the accumulated opinions (wisdom) of a variety of individuals—its content is highly subjective. It ranges all the way from amazing insights into abstruse questions relating to every aspect of human experience, to what amounts to just about pure nonsense. These extremes can often be found in the same individual!

Before we leave these philosophical meditations, a few words seem appropriate on the subject of good and evil. Here we will be dealing mostly with the moral connotations of these terms, since if we try to extend the discussion into too broad a field we are liable to get lost in endless thickets of logical complexities. The terms good and bad can be applied to just about anything, but good and evil has much more of a moral connotation, and morality is concerned with people, so this is what I would like to discuss.

The nature of good and evil has been much debated by philosophers, but generally more shadow than light has been cast upon the subject. Friedrich Nietzsche's ideas about them are interesting, not because I necessarily agree with them, but because he presents an unconventional point of view. Radical as it is, *Beyond Good and Evil* is must reading for the serious student of morality.

Nietzsche thinks we should not think of good and evil as opposites:

How could anything originate out of its opposite? For example, truth out of error? or the Will to Truth out of the will to deception? or the generous deed out of selfishness? or the pure sun-bright vision of the wise man out of covetousness? Such genesis is impossible; whoever dreams of it is a fool, nay, worse than a fool; things of the highest value must have a different origin, an origin of *their own*—in this transitory, seductive, illusory, paltry world, in this turmoil of delusion and cupidity, they cannot have their source. Rather in the lap of Being, in the intransitory, in the concealed God, in the 'Thing-in-itself—*there* must be their source, and nowhere else! [18]

In spite of what Nietzsche has to say on the subject, it is commonly accepted that many things come in pairs, and are essentially defined by their opposites. However, Nietzsche is right in saying that it can be misleading to define things in terms of their opposites, because although they may be thought of as opposites, when considered more carefully, they turn out to be radically different rather than opposite. And besides, what *exactly* do we mean by opposite? Black and white, love and hate, day and night, etc., are more accurately described as "complementary terms," rather than opposites. The *exact* opposite of some quality or qualitative term is an elusive concept.

Plato held that all things that are opposites are generated from their opposites. This really means that one can't have one without the other. But simply saying that evil is the absence of good, or vice versa, is not really good enough, because rather than demonstrating that they are opposites, one is simply defining them to be so. One must admit, however, that good and evil *do* seem to go together, because if evil did not exist, then good would lose its meaning, and *vice versa*. Looked at in this way, good and evil cannot exist separately.

Nietzsche's premise regarding evil is that it has to be judged against man's primeval instincts. Here he is right on target. *Man behaves the way he does because he is the product of evolution.* Those who do not accept evolution are missing the most important part of the picture. Consequently, their ideas on morality are hopelessly distorted.

Nietzsche says that self-preservation is *not* man's primary instinct.

A living thing seeks above all to *discharge* its strength—life itself is *Will to Power;* self-preservation is only one of the indirect and most frequent *results* thereof.[19] (Nietzsche's italics.)

I tend to agree that many things that are considered evil can be seen as consequences of the Will to Power, so perhaps it's a mistake to call them evil.

Nietzsche concludes that the Christian idea of good and evil is hopelessly distorted. Bertrand Russell, in *The History of Western Philosophy*, looks at some of Nietzsche's ideas on the subject:

> Christianity is to be condemned for denying the value of "pride, pathos of distance, great responsibility, exuberant spirits, splendid animalism, the instincts of war and conquest, the deification of passion, revenge, anger, voluptuousness, adventure, knowledge." All these things are good, and all are said by Christianity to be bad—so Nietzsche contends.
>
> Christianity, he argues, aims at taming the heart in man, but this is a mistake. A wild beast has a certain splendour, which it loses when it is tamed. "What is it that we combat in Christianity? That it aims at destroying the strong, at breaking their spirit, at exploiting their moments of weariness and debility, at converting their proud assurance into anxiety and conscience-trouble; that it knows how to poison the noblest instincts and to infect them with disease, until their strength, their will to power, turns inwards, against themselves—until the strong perish through their excessive self-contempt and self-immolation: that gruesome way of perishing, of which Pascal is the most famous example."[20]

Nietzsche is right that the adjectives good and bad, when applied to people, have basically arisen by dividing the world into the good (us) and the bad or evil (them). To Nietzsche, all men are most definitely *not* created equal. The word "noble" gives this away. Although we have now just about got rid of the nobles (aristocrats), we still retain the connotation of "noble." From very early times, the aristocrats (according to the aristocrats) have been true and good, whereas most of the common people have been worthless wretches—Rousseau's "noble savage" notwithstanding. Unfortunately this classification has been very hard to erase. The rich are generally considered to be better than the poor. This is easily extended to other categories: the powerful and the weak, winners and losers, etc.[21]

This brings us back to the Will to Power. Could man's propensity for war have its origin in the Will to Power? Could some of his other unpleasant characteristics have their roots in the same source? Nietzsche contends that we have created the idea of good and evil to try and make sense out of human behavior. But this has only succeeded in making the whole thing more difficult to understand. He proposes that we move beyond the concept of good and evil. Maybe man treats his fellow humans so abysmally, not because he is basically evil, but because of the Will to Power, which, being a natural instinct, can hardly be considered evil. In fact Nietzsche considers it to be good.

This is a seminal idea, and although it is widely discussed in philosophical circles, it has not been given the attention it deserves by the educated public. Walter Kaufman, in *Nietzsche: Philosopher Psychologist Antichrist,* freely acknowledges the inaccuracy of many of Nietzsche's statements. But Kaufman feels his (Nietzsche's) analysis of mankind is more accurate than his critics are willing to admit. In his preface to the above work Kaufman writes:

> First, there is the scholar's interest in correcting what he takes to be misapprehensions. Then certain aspects of Nietzsche's critique of modern man may deserve serious consideration: ever more people seem to realize that their pleasures do not add up to happiness and that their ends do not give their lives any lasting meaning. Properly understood, Nietzsche's conception of power may represent one of the few great philosophic ideas of all time.[22]

I'm not sure how the Will to Power can be reconciled with Darwinism, which Nietzsche did not entirely agree with. However, it does seem to exist in the animal world as well, albeit to a lesser extent.

Nietzsche enjoyed shocking people because he was impatient with conventional ideas. But in fact his view of mankind is similar to that of Heraclitus, one of the early Greek philosophers, and also to Hobbes and Hegel among others.

But even if Nietzsche was right in saying that it is not accurate to label many of these human characteristics as evil, this does not get us very far. If they are not evil, they are certainly undesirable traits to have in a modern society. And this reinforces what I said in the last section about having to adapt anew to a changing environment.

Actually a lot has already been accomplished in this direction. Since the aristocratic classes no longer hold power, Nietzsche's splendid aristocratic beast has essentially been de-fanged. Nor is this beast likely to be much of a bother in the future. The fact that we now have a more democratic society—which seems dull and unromantic compared to the old aristocratic type—should not bother us the way it would have bothered Nietzsche. *Noblesse oblige* was about all that the lower classes could hope for in the old days, and most of the time it was very thin gruel. One has to add, however, that democracy has not cooled off the urge to produce ever-more lethal weapons of war. If anything, it has increased the amount of money spent on armaments. The military-industrial complex continues to race ahead at full throttle with no sign of let-up.

Although Nietzsche worked hard to get rid of evil—mostly by calling it something else—there still seems to be plenty of it around. I don't agree with his romanticized view of war. Men have constantly deluded themselves about its nobility and glory, only to find that the reality is a monstrous nightmare. The last two world wars should have made this clear. And if something like the Holocaust was not evil, then indeed there *is* no evil.

This brings up the idea of a just war, a war against injustice and tyranny. Seldom is the issue clear-cut, but in the case of World War II it would certainly seem to have been justified. However, one is left with the nagging doubt as to whether the end really *did* justify the means, and whether all the destruction and suffering might somehow have been avoided, or at least mitigated.

St. Augustine raised doubts about the justice of war in *The City of God.* As historian John Lynn writes:

> For St. Augustine, a just war could only be fought by a legitimate ruler, and then it should only be directed towards righting an injustice. He also insisted that the suffering caused by war be less than that caused by the wrong that one is combating.[23]

Although morality is often thought of as something intrinsic or God-given, it is in fact a human invention. Conventional notions of good and evil do not usually recognize this fact. An exception is Michael Shermer's book, *The Science of Good and Evil,* which looks at religion and moral behavior from an evolutionary standpoint, in a similar manner to David Wilson's analysis of religion, discussed in chapter 2. Here is what he has to say about our "evolved moral sense."

> By a moral sense, I mean a moral feeling or emotion generated by actions. For example, positive emotions such as righteousness and pride are experienced as the psychological feeling of doing "good." These moral emotions likely evolved out of behaviors that were reinforced as being good either for the individual or for the group. Negative emotions such as guilt and shame are experienced as the psychological feeling of doing "bad.".... This is the psychology of morality—the feeling of being moral or immoral.[24]

We should remember that most moral sanctions run counter to the imperatives of natural selection. Although certain animals may experience good and bad "feelings," morality, as we know it, only came onto the scene with the rise of culture. Before that, morality would have been a definite hindrance. In fact, if man had been "moral" in the days before his intelligence was able to give him a leg up on all other creatures, he would not have survived as a species. But now man must somehow become *more* moral, in order to avoid destroying himself—as well as the rest of the planet!

15

THE PATHOLOGY OF WAR

As long as war is regarded as wicked, it will always have its fascination. When it is looked upon as vulgar, it will cease to be popular.

—Oscar Wilde

THE LURE OF BATTLE

During the last four or five millennia, there has been a steady increase in war's destructive capabilities, due to the increasingly lethal nature of the weapons involved. But the actual propensity towards war has not changed much over the years. The variables have been the size and organization of armies, as well as the weapons employed, and these have kept increasing the level of violence, until it finally reached a crescendo in the twentieth century.

Ancient myths are filled with stories of heroes in mortal combat, so one might infer that this form of combat was the preferred method of settling disputes, the theory being that this was a ritualized form of warfare, which avoided the unnecessary shedding of blood. But recent studies have concluded that individual combat was not widely used, and that warfare between groups was the norm.[1]

By the time that the first cultures arose in Mesopotamia and Egypt, the concept of war on a much larger scale was well established. But the "armies" involved were in fact little more than an armed rabble. It took some time before anything like an army in the modern sense came into being.

The Greek phalanx represented a notable step in the organization and discipline of armies. The use of horses and chariots meant that armies became more specialized as to their weapons and manpower. But it was not until the coming of the Roman legions that an army in the modern sense came into existence. Here

311

we see order and discipline imposed on a hierarchical structure, and a command system capable of directing large numbers of men in a reasonably efficient manner. As a result of this, the barbarian hordes, and even the Greek armies, were no match for the fighting prowess of the Roman military machine. The barbarians learnt quickly, however, and it was not long before they began to give the Romans serious trouble. A major turning point was reached at the battle of Adrianople, where the Emperor Valens was defeated by the Visigoths in 378, and it was not long before the barbarians were at the gates of Rome.

The Roman army was a brutal instrument of destruction that showed no mercy to its defeated enemies, just as the heroes of old had shown no mercy to their fallen foes. The vanquished could expect slavery or death as their fate. It was only later that any idea of ethical conduct with respect to war was introduced. Even though Christianity abandoned the concept of pacifism, it did eventually exert some civilizing influences on warfare, as did Islam with regard to its holy wars.

The Christian knight and the Islamic holy warrior were supposed to conduct their violence in a more seemly manner than the vulgar hordes of heathens, but these so-called ethical standards were honored mainly in the breach. Chivalry only extended to the knightly class. Defeated knights were held for ransom if they were considered important enough. The ordinary foot soldier was lucky if he escaped with his life. As related in Part I, when it comes to war, morality is a very scarce commodity indeed.

Military historian John Keegan points out that in more modern times there has been a distinction made "between the lawful bearer of arms and the rebel, the freebooter and the brigand."[2] The professional bearer of arms is supposed to do his fighting according to the rules of war, while the rougher types are not so fastidious about their conduct. However, the "irregulars" have often been used by the regular armies for special missions, and have frequently been accepted as on a par with the regular troops.

Many of those that would be considered criminals in times of peace can become heroes in war. Medals are given for unspeakable acts of butchery! And even those considered exemplary citizens in peacetime can commit the most horrendous acts during war. The reality of war compels the realization that abiding by the rules—any rules—places one at a distinct disadvantage, and so the distinction between the behavior of the freebooter and the professional soldier soon evaporates. It is no use pretending that war can be anything other than the brutal activity that it has always been. Trying to "civilize" war is basically a futile endeavor. The fact that the ancient Greeks had elaborate "rules" of war does not mean that their wars were somehow more civilized. It just underlines the fact that they were addicted to war. One of their "rules" was that hostilities should be suspended during the Olympic games. But war went on as usual after the games.

The legal bearers of arms were the ones that Clausewitz had in mind when he said that war was the continuation of politics by other means. However, Keegan is of the opinion that the way war is *conducted* has more to do with culture than politics. Clausewitz's idea of the decisive battle, which probably originated with the Greeks, certainly affected the way military men in the West thought about war. That war can be conducted on a more or less continuous basis, without any kind of a decisive battle, was quite foreign to Clausewitz's way of thinking. But in fact many warrior societies, such as the nomads of the steppe, conducted their wars in this manner. The set battle, although it has occurred throughout history in many parts of the world, represents, according to Keegan, the "Western way of war." The West, as inheritor of the Greek cultural legacy, has persisted in this more dangerous way of making war, at least until very recently.

The case of the Tokugawa shogunate nicely illustrates Keegan's view that the methods of warfare are largely dictated by culture rather than politics. The cult of the sword dictated how battles should be fought.

> The Tokugawa shogunate was more than a political institution. It was a cultural instrument.... In ensuring that warriors had a monopoly of swords, the Tokugawa were guaranteeing the samurai's place at the pinnacle of Japanese society.[3]

Of course this kind of thing was utterly impractical, and could only be maintained while Japan was essentially cut off from the rest of the world. But it does illustrate how culture can influence the methods of warfare. Other historians, notably John Lynn, in *Battle*, also stress the cultural, rather than the political nature of warfare. Lynn says there is really no "Western Way of War," which was an idea put forward by Victor Hanson in his book of that name. Lynn says the thesis that Western warfare originated with the decisive battles fought with the Greek phalanx does not hold up to historical scrutiny.[4]

The idea that gentlemen conduct war in a more civilized manner than the coarser folk was never more than a myth. It's true that most modern armies treat their fallen foes better that the Romans did—the Geneva Convention has now improved the treatment of prisoners of war. But in the main, war is pretty much the beastly business that it has always been. In fact, up until very recently, the level of violence, as well as the involvement of civilians, has been on an ever-increasing scale. The improvement in medical assistance to the wounded is one of the few plusses in an otherwise dismal story.

It is indeed ironic that war has progressed, in a few thousand years, all the way from individual hand-to-hand combat, to push-button warfare, conducted from a distance of hundreds, or even thousands, of miles. Any individual glory or prestige that might be gained from victory in physical combat has been removed completely from the scene. So it might appear that one of the main motivations for war has been removed.

Nonetheless the production of arms goes on unabated. The machinery of war continues to grind out its lethal wares. It is as though the virus of war has adapted itself to a different environment. Now it attacks the economic fiber of its victims. Money that could be used for essential services is instead wasted on armaments that would almost certainly be useless in any future war.

AMERICAN POWER

In America the virus of the military-industrial complex has taken hold in a particularly virulent form. It has become politically impossible to dismantle the mechanisms of war, for they have become embedded into the life of the nation. No congressman or senator dares to vote against an increase in the national defense budget for fear of being branded as unpatriotic, even though no potential enemies exist that could possibly justify such an increase. The industry of war has taken root in so many places that any attempt to reduce this bloated structure is met with overwhelming opposition. Even President Eisenhower, a soldier himself, warned of the growing power of the military machine. Here is his famous quote from a farewell speech:

> This conjunction of an immense military establishment and a large arms industry is new in the American experience.... We recognize the imperative need for this development. Yet we must not fail to comprehend its grave implications.... In the councils of government, we must guard against the acquisition of unwarranted influence, whether sought or unsought, by the military-industrial complex. The potential from the disastrous rise of misplaced power exists and will persist.[5]

This was back in 1961, and the president's timely warning has gone unheeded. The peculiar phenomenon of American patriotism has been called upon to insure that nothing shall upset the smooth running of this fearsome machine. And patriotism in America is a powerful force indeed. The term origi-nated at the time of the American Revolution, when patriots were those who opposed British "tyranny," and loyalists were those who opposed these "traitors" to the English crown. But after the revolution was won, the term patriot, far from being forgotten, took on a kind of mythology of its own. Barbara Ehrenreich describes this phenomenon:

> In the American vernacular, there is no such thing as American nationalism. Nationalism is a suspect category, an ism, like communism, and confined to other people—Serbs, Russians, Palestinians, Tamils. Americans who love their country and profess a willingness to die for it are not nationalists but some-thing nobler and more native to their land. They are "patriots."
>
> In some ways this is a justifiable distinction. If all nations are "imagined communities," America is more imaginary than most. It has no *Volk,* only a conglomeration of ethnically and racially diverse peoples, and it has no feudal warrior tradition to serve as a model for an imaginary lineage the average citi-zen might imagine himself or herself a part of. But at the same time, there can be no better measure of America's overweening nationalist pride than the fact that we need a special "American" name for it. Nationalism, in the contempo-rary usage, is un-American and prone to irrational and bloody excess, while patriotism, which is quintessentially American, is clearheaded and virtuous. By convincing ourselves that our nationalism is unique among nationalisms, we do not have to acknowledge its primitive and bloody side.[6]

America's fascination with guns has helped to consolidate the arms industry's hold on the public purse. "The right to bear arms" is the rallying cry of the gun lobby, otherwise known as the National Rifle Association. This stems from the Constitution's Second Amendment, which supposedly sanctions an individual's right to carry a gun. The Amendment itself is ambiguous, and was probably only intended to permit arms to be used by state militias. But at the time that it was written the only guns available to private citizens were pistols and muskets, which were highly inaccurate and somewhat dangerous to operate. It's well nigh certain that the writers of the Amendment would never have permitted the carrying of weapons such as the modern handgun or automatic pistol, let alone any kind of automatic rifle. But the cult of the gun is now so etched into the American con-sciousness that the gun itself has become something sacred, which, like the sword of the *samurai,* every patriot has a right, even a duty, to own. As a result, the per-centage of guns owned by the general public is far greater than in any other coun-try on earth, and the number of crimes committed with firearms is proportionately much higher.

Of course, legitimate defense is perfectly valid in a dangerous world, but excessive spending on arms can create problems of its own. Deterrence is in the eye of the beholder. One man's deterrence is another man's aggressive build-up.

To a large extent, the Unites States is a prisoner of its own history. As has been the case for many millennia, the only really effective kind of power on the international level is military power. Any country that wishes to play a role in world affairs must have a sizable military establishment. When one looks at America's history one sees a country that acquired military power reluctantly. The founding fathers of the United States tried to avoid "entangling alliances," and sought to remain largely isolated from the global stage. But this soon became impractical, and she was drawn into wars with Mexico and Spain, as well as with her old colonial ruler, Great Britain. The Civil War involved the manufacture of weaponry as never before, and the twentieth century saw America involved in two world wars. After that, as the greatest economic power, she was thrust into competition with the Soviet Union in the cold war. This necessitated maintaining a large military establishment. Her earlier reluctance to acquire such power was quickly forgotten, and weapons systems were piled one upon another until she had accumulated a vast arsenal of armaments, far greater than was necessary for any legitimate purpose. The result of all this has been that other nations have sought to expand their own military establishments lest they fall too far behind in the global power game.

So America finds that she has acquired, almost unintentionally, a military establishment that has taken on a life of its own, and which is never satisfied unless it has obtained the latest and deadliest weapons of destruction to add to its already massive arsenal. This huge supply of weapons has now become more of a liability than an asset. The idea that one can buy safety by possessing a monopoly of the most modern and destructive weapons is a dangerous illusion. Far from making America safer, it has undermined her economy and encouraged terrorists to attack her wherever they see an opportunity. While seeking to limit the spread of nuclear weapons to countries that she considers threatening, America not only retains 8,000 of her own, but is also creating additional warheads that would be more effective in a possible nuclear conflict!

With her vast supply of technologically sophisticated weaponry, America is able to destroy any forces ranged against it, by targeting them with pinpoint accuracy from enormous distances. She is thus seen more as the destroyer than the builder of nations, an image precisely opposite to the one she seeks to convey, that of a peacemaker and a promoter of democracy.

America's image among the peoples of the world has become distorted in ways that her leaders often seem unaware of. Her intentions are usually good, but she somehow fails to convince the world of her basic benevolence.

Until quite recently, few people feared that the huge American arsenal of arms would become a cause for apprehension in the world community. But with talk of pre-emptive action, many of the world's leaders have become deeply suspicious of American intentions. The attempt to spread free markets and democracy at the point of a gun has caused alarm around the world. America's reputation as a force for peace and a promoter of human rights has been seriously eroded. Let's hope this is only a temporary aberration.

BULLIES AND VICTIMS

Every state or nation will try to act in its own best interest, just as each individual will attempt to do the same. But sometimes what is in one's best interest is not readily apparent. A classic case in point arose during the Peloponnesian war between Athens and Sparta, an account of which was written by the Greek historian Thucydides. It involved what has been called the Melian Dialogue.

In 416 B.C. Athens approached Melos, an Aegean island that had traditionally been a colony of Sparta, with a view to securing it as an ally. Melos would have preferred to remain neutral, but Athens was not satisfied with that, and sent a delegation whose purpose was to bend the will of the Melians to the Athenian point of view. Thucydides gives an account of the meeting between the Melians and the Athenians, and John Keegan nicely summarizes this in his book, *War: Great Military Writings*.

> The Athenians put self-interest first. They tell the Melians that Athens must take possession of Melos if the other islands they have conquered, and which they need for their security, are to remain under their control. The Melians first ask why they cannot merely remain friendly neutrals. When told that such neutrality does not satisfy the Athenian's needs, they advance the argument that it would be dishonourable to break with Sparta, which they trust to come to their help if threatened. The Athenians reply that force, not trust, is what counts in war, and that honour is a costly position unless it can be defended with arms.
>
> The Melians nevertheless refused to surrender their freedom. War broke out and, as the Athenians had warned, ended in the Melians' utter defeat.[7]

Here we encounter the doctrine of "might makes right." The British cited this incident between Melos and Athens when attempting to justify their pursuit of empire. Keegan continues:

> Thomas Hobbes, the seventeenth-century English philosopher of state power, translated Thucydides and used the Melian Dialogue in particular to illustrate the *debt the weak owe to the strong*. Thucydides' history became, in the nineteenth century, a key text in the education of the British ruling class, at a time when their country's naval power was its principal instrument in the creation of a world empire.[8] (my italics)

The Melian Dialogue can be looked at in different ways. In hindsight one can say that the Melians were foolhardy. But they undoubtedly thought that defeat was not necessarily inevitable. Who knows? A lucky break, or the timely arrival of the Spartans, might have saved them. And then they would have been genuine heroes, instead of heroic losers. The British themselves turned their own argument on its head during the Battle of Britain, when they fought on against all odds against Hitler and came out victorious. But before the battle there were those who counseled negotiations with the Germans, and in fact these were seriously considered.[9]

Throughout history there have been many such incidents. Fighting on against all odds has not always led to defeat. And sometimes an honorable defeat is better than a dishonorable surrender. The real warrior will almost never accept defeat. But this notion has to be part of a tradition, which the society inculcates into its citizens.

The British, themselves a warrior nation, were not able to defeat the Native Americans, because the latter would rather die than accept British rule. As a consequence, the British felt no compunction in killing them. The Japanese, another warrior nation, were indoctrinated with the cult of their God-Emperor. Suicide rather than surrender was the only acceptable conduct.

But there is more to war than the actual fighting. Intimidation is very much part of the exercise. Sometimes it's possible to get what you want without doing any fighting. But you have to be able to make a credible threat or your bluff may be called. One of the oldest and most successful strategies is to play one party off against another. The enemy of your enemy can be your ally, but he must be watched carefully and not given a chance to change sides. Above all, one must forget all about morality. Otherwise the enemy will have you at a distinct disadvantage.

FAMILY TENSIONS

The potential for conflict lurks at the heart of all human societies. The complex interactions of the "civilized" world make for tensions that are unique to man, and serve to exacerbate many natural tendencies towards conflict. Such tensions, when relieved in one area, tend to come to the surface in another. This is illustrated nicely when a country goes to war. The stresses in the society are forgotten as the nation unites against a common enemy, only to reappear once the war is over.

The family itself, as a microcosm of society, acts in somewhat the same way. A nasty neighbor or an unwelcome suitor will unite the family against him. But without such diversions, the tensions within the family will naturally come to the surface.

Family friction is illustrated in the case of dynasties. The founder of the dynasty is usually a strong individual, confident of his abilities, who is able to unite his nation in the establishment of a strong and viable state. But all sorts of problems arise when the founder dies. Not only the family, but also the whole community is liable to fly apart into competing factions. The result is often civil war, resulting in the division of the country into separate kingdoms, or the defeat of all but one of the pretenders. In the latter case the lucky winner then establishes himself on his father's throne. But his seat is often insecure, because the tensions and enmities created in the dynastic struggle are still simmering below the surface. Dynasties thus become weaker as the generations pass.

There are many variations on this theme, which reflect the different personalities involved and the changing landscape of the world outside of the dynastic realm. The Holy Roman Empire of Charlemagne is a good example of the unpredictibility of dynastic structures. The multitude of internal and external influences that came to bear on this huge aggregation of diverse peoples and geographical regions played itself out over a thousand years of history. But a prime shaper of this history was the internal friction of the various parts, which caused them to interact in ways that tended to relieve the tension. Every now and then these internal stresses would result in an adjustment in the configuration of the parts—some might break off altogether, while others would acquire new territory. This relieved things for a while, but it was not long before tensions started to heat up again. The Thirty Years War can be regarded as one particularly violent instance of this phenomenon, involving nations outside of the Empire as well.

Another example of family tensions, similar, but not identical to the external war syndrome, comes in the aftermath of a revolution or the expulsion of an invader. When the revolution is over, the victorious revolutionaries invariably start fighting among themselves, because the tensions between them were suppressed during the revolution. Civil war often comes on the heels of a revolution. The Americans, having expelled the British, took only half a century to commence their own Civil War. The Russian revolution of 1917 was followed by a brutal war between the Reds and the Whites. Numerous other examples come to mind. The Greeks, after they had defeated the Persians and secured their homeland against the threat of foreign invasion, proceeded to tear themselves apart in the Peloponnesian war between Athens and Sparta. In India, after the withdrawal of the British, the Hindus and Moslems fought each other to such an extent that the country had to be partitioned. Many African countries, having rid themselves of the colonial powers, have gone on rampages of civil war. The Chinese, after finally expelling the Japanese invaders in 1945, proceeded to fight a brutal civil war between the Nationalists and the Communists. The Incas, after they had consolidated their Empire in Peru and Ecuador, began almost immediately to fight among themselves. This contributed to their downfall at the hands of the Spanish conquistadors. But as soon as the Spanish had defeated the Incas, they too commenced their own civil wars!

The French Revolution had a slightly different twist to it—the French always enjoy being a bit different from everyone else. The original revolution was submerged in a second revolution, which attacked the instigators of the first one. But a civil war was averted only when Napoleon, ever the opportunist, managed to channel all these internal tensions into an external war of conquest. But for Napoleon, this war had to continue, since he was not capable of keeping his empire together in peace.

Now we might ask whether the phenomenon of war is becoming outdated. Is the virus finally losing its deadly hold on human society? Could it be viewed as perhaps having been beneficial in the long run? Maybe it helped to build more viable communities, in spite of all the suffering and devastation that it caused.

Aggressive wars permitted larger states to be created. Was not the building of empires a constructive development, which allowed the transition from tribal societies to larger and more culturally advanced polities? And did not the maritime empires at least promote world trade, even though they exploited the people whom they colonized? War, like pestilence, is supposed by some to have a beneficial effect, by getting rid of the excess population. This last is questionable, since the "best and the brightest" are often the victims, rather than the survivors of war.

But since war goes far beyond the natural struggle for supremacy that takes place in the animal world, it cannot be considered as part of biological evolution, only an indirect result of it. Any seemingly beneficial effects of war would appear to have come at an unacceptable price. One can only conclude that war is a perversion of the evolutionary process, and represents a failure of culture and the concept of civilized behavior. Indeed, while we still practice war we do not really have the right to call ourselves civilized.

THE NATURE OF THE BEAST

So what about the primordial beast? Is he likely to be tamed any time soon? Actually, he does seem to be losing some of his hold on the collective imagination of nation states. This is partially a consequence of globalization and the ensuing increase in general knowledge through the Internet and global television. But the vastly more destructive weapons that are now available will not allow the beast to die. And the military-industrial complex is also helping to keep him alive. He can be made just as fierce as he ever was with the help of modern weaponry, in the same way that the older folks are getting a new lease on life with the help of modern medicine. Senior golfers are hitting the ball as far as they ever did with the help of new equipment. So too the beast of war is showing some of his old vigor with the help of more and more lethal and sophisticated weapons. As we have seen, the advent of terrorism has led to the democratization of lethal violence.

War seems the epitome of evil. "War is hell," said William Tecumseh Sherman, and surely he knew what he was talking about.[10] The romanticizing of war is a recurring theme throughout literature and myth, and there have been many attempts to bring a religious aspect to war. The religions of Islam and Christianity have been caught in a paradox regarding war. They know it is wrong, but they rationalize their way out of the dilemma by declaring the conditions under which it is justified, and proposing rules for its conduct. They cannot bring themselves to denounce it altogether. In fact it was war that basically destroyed these religions as a moral force. We have seen how this came about with Christianity, when it became the religion of the Roman Empire. In the case of Islam, aggressive war against the infidel was practiced almost from the beginning, and rationalizations for this have never carried any moral conviction.

War was too powerful for religion to fight in the West, because it has always been the quintessential Western activity. War, trade and technology, allied with science, have been the foundation stones of Western supremacy. Religion has been the glue that helped to keep everything together. So it could not oppose one of the chief building blocks of the culture. If religion wanted to be part of the power structure, it was impossible to remain unsullied by the beast of war.

Buddhism has by and large succeeded in separating itself from the power structures of the Eastern countries where it has maintained its influence. As a result, it has been able to retain its moral authority to a much greater degree. Ironically, this may be due in part to the fact that it was expelled from India after the Islamic invasions in the eleventh century, which caused it to spread into Tibet and China. Although it did become part of the power structure in Tibet, Buddhism was still able to retain much of its moral authority, due to the more pacific nature and relatively isolated position of the Tibetan culture. In China it has remained largely outside of the power structure and this has been beneficial to its ethical and moral standing in the community. The communists tried to wipe out all conventional religions, but Buddhism has managed to survive nonetheless. It has been easier for Buddhism to remain above the fray because the Eastern cultural mystique is much less aggressive than that of the West.

Hinduism, the most ancient of all the major religions, with its roots stretching back to the Aryan hunter-gatherers, has not been seriously compromised by the beast of war, because war has always been accepted by it as part of the human scene. Not having a founder, Hinduism is based on the teachings of the Vedas. "Abiding peace and blessedness" are attained by the ideal of freedom, but this freedom comes only after a spiritual discipline has been attained. However, this does not exclude the enjoyment of esthetic and sensual pleasures. But the fact that one of the castes of Hinduism is that of the warrior, or military class, suggests that the concept of war has been basic to the society since early times. "The *kshatriyas* were the kings and military protectors."[11] Armies and warfare were part and parcel of the culture, long before the invasion of Alexander the Great. Any kind of prohibition against war was never overtly a part of Hindu teaching. In spite of this, one can say that Hinduism has been much more tolerant than the Western religions; nothing like a holy war or a crusade has been called against the heathen. On the whole, the Hindus have been more realistic about human nature, and so have not gotten themselves into so many embarrassing and contradictory moral dilemmas as the Christians and the Moslems.

Just as the caste system of the Hindus is finally dying, so the warrior tradition of the Junker, the Zulu, the *Samurai* and the Plains Indian is finally yielding to a more rational outlook on the world. And none of them will be missed. But the American marine still rises at 4 a.m. to make sure that the world is safe for capitalism, and Moslem fundamentalists of various kinds are still plotting dreadful deeds in the name of Allah. The Palestinian and the Israeli are unable to bridge the chasm of a religious, cultural and territorial divide, and the Serb still dreams of revenge for past betrayals. Africa is still consumed in an orgy of tribal violence, and rogue states dream unspeakable dreams of mass destruction. So peace and tranquility is hardly likely to break out any time soon.

But we may nonetheless be inching towards a world where the divisions of the past will be seen in a different light, and the necessity of overcoming them should become more and more apparent as time goes on. A hopeful sign is that the armies of the democracies are beginning to be involved in peacekeeping, rather than in their traditional pursuit of war. Nowadays, with the Internet intruding into every dictator's backyard, life is not so secure for the bad guys. Their ability to prevent outside news from seeping into their domains is rapidly eroding. More and more emperors will be revealed as having no clothes. And perhaps most significant of all, some of the perpetrators of atrocities are at last being brought to justice.

The final elimination of the primordial beast will surely require a sustained effort by the world community, an effort that has been woefully lacking up to the present time.

ART AND WAR

The fact that war has been a recurring theme in the world of art is an indication of its centrality in the cultural life of man. War, rape and massacre have been depicted over and over by the great artists of the past. Sculptural friezes on palaces and temples from Egypt, Assyria, Persia, Greece, Rome and Central America all depict the violence and cruelty of war in a fairly realistic manner. These scenes are not hidden from the people but exhibited for all to see. The aim is clear: to impress upon the people the ability of rulers and gods to bring their enemies into submission. The implication is that war is part of the function of a great state, that it strengthens the sinews of the society and confirms both gods and rulers in their respective realms. Thus art is employed in the service of the state, to exhibit its power and to glorify the concept of victory in war.

The artists of the Renaissance also depicted scenes of violence, war and mayhem. The connoisseurs and patrons of art were not shocked to have such subjects displayed in their elegant palazzos. In any case, practically all these gory images were scenes from Greek or Roman history and myth; the subjects were far enough removed in time that they were able to take on a certain surreal quality. The paintings were also quite stylized, and so did not render the images in an overly realistic manner. But the gruesome nature of the scenes was nonetheless apparent.

As we move towards the modern era, we find pictures of warfare to be just as popular as ever. It seems that violence never loses its appeal. But of course it is sanitized violence—violence without the blood and horror of the real thing. Apparently what fascinates us is *vicarious* violence, not so much actual violence, which would repel us. Pictures of the gladiators in Rome's Colosseum do not evoke much more than a vague revulsion, but few modern citizens of Rome, or anywhere else, would have the stomach to watch the real thing. The same is true of war. It is glamorized in books and pictures, which insulate us from the horror. Knowing this to be so, we can let our imagination bring us ever closer to the reality, but the image can be turned off if it gets too disturbing.

Art frequently depicts cruelty of one type or another. The greatest epic of the Western world, Homer's Iliad, is filled with violence and slaughter, while its basic theme is that of lust and deceit. Can we really claim that these forerunners of Western culture were civilized? Are we really proud that they have bequeathed to us their accounts of brutal and senseless behavior, which we like to call heroic?

Opera, that quintessential expression of culture, has provided a meeting place for the members of high society to show off their fancy clothes and fine jewelry, while indulging their exquisite taste in music. Only the work of the finest composers is good enough to be performed before such august gatherings. Night after night, the rich and the influential have flocked to the magnificent baroque cathedrals of operatic splendor, to listen to gory tales of incest, rape and murder. All this set to the most sublime music and performed with the aid of elaborate and costly scenery. Villains are constantly lurking in the wings. Perfidy, betrayal and revenge are presented for the entertainment of the distinguished audience. Even in the citadels of culture, the thirst for stories of violence and mayhem cannot be denied.

The coming of motion pictures has revolutionized the depiction of warfare and violence. All the talent of the motion picture industry has been harnessed to give us the vicarious pleasure of watching our fellow human beings get slaughtered en masse. It is given to us just the way we want it—lots of violence, but not *too* realistic. This kind of thing hardly ever fails at the box office. And nobody actually dies—or is even wounded—unless there is some terrible accident on the set.

The murder mystery is the most popular form of light reading, besides being a staple for television audiences. Another favorite is the serial killer, whose gruesome and sadistic compulsions never fail to fascinate. Such killers, like other notorious criminals, often become so famous that they are memorialized in art and literature.

The theater has always been popular because human beings love make-believe. But motion pictures and television have catered to this trait on a much larger scale. The popularity of themes of horror and violence never seems to wane. Adventure, romance and romantic comedies are the only other topics that come close to having a comparable appeal. But violence and mayhem win practically every time. Not even sex—at least in the manner that it is permitted to be presented to the general public—can compete with violence. Anything of a serious or educational nature is overwhelmed by the sensational and the violent.

LEADERS AND FOLLOWERS

In the last two hundred years individuals have arisen who occupied positions of immense power, and who were able to cause, directly or indirectly, enormous suffering and devastation. Napoleon, Lenin, Stalin, Hitler, and Mao Tse-tung are prime examples.

With all of these leaders, what one might call the Will to Power and Prestige—a more extreme form of Nietzsche's Will to Power—was combined with some sort of ideology. But in every case there were two essential ingredients in their rise to prominence: the means and the opportunity. Both of these involve chance to a high degree. But it is one thing to be given the opportunity by fate, and another to take it. None of these leaders were of a kind that was likely to let a good opportunity go begging. They recognized it for what it was—the opportunity of a lifetime.

The means that was ready at hand for these leaders was the availability of huge numbers of potential followers. But the combination of circumstances did not end there. They instinctively realized that their following could be expanded exponentially through the appeal of an existing and potentially explosive ideology, or ideologies, which they found ready-made at their fingertips. Most importantly, these ideologies could be used as the basis of some kind of mythology.

Once the myths began to take hold, they spread like wildfire, and galvanized large numbers of people into an unstoppable force. The power of these myths enabled the mythologizers themselves to ascend to the pinnacle of power. As you have no doubt guessed, these ideologies included: nationalism, populism, communism, fascism, racism and militarism—in various combinations.

Lee Harris, in his book *Civilization and Its Enemies,* calls these "fantasy ideologies." In order to attain their goals these leaders had to implant in their followers the spirit of ruthlessness.

> To see these movements as driven by their ideology is a tremendous error. Rather, they were driven by men who had been transformed by the fantasy contained in the ideology: the whole purpose of the fantasy ideology was to permit the true believer to overcome the middle-class and bourgeois inhibitions on violence that had been built into the character structure of the nineteenth-century European personality. It was a way of psyching themselves up to commit acts that they knew to be violations of the civilized norm, in order to achieve the degree of ruthlessness necessary to intimidate their opponents into acceding to their demands.[12]

It was an accidental circumstance that these leaders happened to be at the confluence of several converging historical movements, and it was this that made their influence so potent and their power over the ideological forces that they were able to manipulate so compelling. Hitler's rise to power illustrates how a fortuitous set of circumstances can thrust an individual to the fore—someone who would almost certainly never have gained prominence under normal circumstances.

In most cases, these leaders genuinely believed in the ideologies that they championed. Their own sense of mission served as an inspiration to their followers. The fact that they were willing to sacrifice millions of lives in pursuit of their fantasies belies any contention that they were actually seeking some worthwhile end. Nietzsche's Will to Power, together with the desire for prestige, was the main motivating force.

Here again is the power of belief. We saw the galvanizing effect of religion in the jihad and the crusades. Here we see the secular religions having an even stronger effect. The combination of belief and the Will to Power is an incredibly explosive mixture. Followers of this type of leader can commit almost any kind of atrocity once they are caught up in the leader's spell. Moral inhibitions are quickly forgotten, as the believers are overwhelmed by the righteousness of their cause.

DESCENT INTO HELL

When he is very young, the human animal is cute and cuddly like most other animals. Although he can grow up to be warm and caring in his relations with his fellow man, too often the selfishness that is his legacy from the evolutionary past comes to dominate his behavior when he grows older. Sad to say, he *can* grow up to be a fiend! In truth, while the human animal can rise to incredible heights of intellectual achievement, artistic creativity, selflessness and valor, he can nonetheless descend into the deepest abyss of evil. And when he does descend into this dark abyss, the horrors that he is capable of inflicting on his fellow man are almost beyond belief in their monstrous enormity.

Since nothing comparable happens in the rest of the animal kingdom, this potential for extreme cruelty must be a part of being human. Since the dawn of prehistory this propensity for cruelty, over and above that inflicted in the normal course of war, has dogged the human race, until in the twentieth century it reached its apogee in the Nazi Holocaust. But even such a ghastly example has not prevented the recurrence of similar episodes. In the Balkans, in Africa, in Indonesia, in Cambodia, in China and elsewhere we have seen similar behavior to that exhibited by the Nazis, albeit on a smaller scale. And there has been little international outcry over these horrors. Is our species incapable of learning from its mistakes?

In the last section we saw how strong leaders could use the magnetism of a cause to lure their followers into the wild pursuit of conquest. But in this instance we are talking about sadistic cruelty inflicted mostly upon civilians, rather than those actively engaged in war. The Nazi atrocities were frequently committed against unarmed civilians, both before and during World War II, and it was special units, rather than the regular forces, that were mostly to blame. It seems that they were created for the express purpose of committing the most sadistic crimes. And they were quite prepared to do such things, even though they would have been put in jail for doing them under normal peacetime circumstances. Similar paramilitary units, often designated as death squads, have committed most of the atrocities that have occurred since the Nazi era. Ruthless leaders have recruited these people to do their dirty work, and the regular soldiers, while not much liking what they see, in most cases have done nothing to prevent it.

Actually such horrors are not really new, it just seems that they are now better organized. Rape, pillage and massacre have always been part of war. In days gone by the violence against civilians was carried out by practically all the fighting men, although it was usually after, rather than during a battle. Even the concept of "ethnic cleansing" is not really new. The difference now is that these atrocities are frequently committed outside of the normal confines of war. No mitigating circumstance of the heat of battle can be claimed. This is just cold-blooded cruelty for its own sake. Now, in our supposedly more civilized times, the rougher types are specially recruited to lead the way down the path to hell, where the more squeamish are hesitant to go. Instead of random atrocities, carried out on the spur of the moment, we have *organized* atrocities, planned and carried out with ruthless efficiency, either in the name of some half-baked cause or ideology, or just to keep a ruthless dictator in power.

War correspondent Chris Hedges describes the contemporary scene this way:

> The ethnic conflicts and insurgencies of our time, whether between Serbs and Muslims or Hutus and Tutsis, are not religious wars. They are not clashes between cultures or civilizations, nor are they the result of ethnic hatreds. They are manufactured wars, born out of the collapse of civil societies, perpetuated by fear, greed, and paranoia, and they are run by gangsters, who rise up from the bottom of their own societies and terrorize all, including those they purport to protect.[13]

The Roman Emperors had their Praetorian Guard; Napoleon had his Imperial Guard; the Ottoman sultans their Janissaries. These were "elite units," whose object was to protect the state's leader from his enemies, not to indulge in wanton atrocities. Today's dictators possess elite units that are little more than gangs of paramilitary thugs, whose express purpose is the murder and mutilation of their fellow citizens.

There has to be an atmosphere within a nation that will permit the formation of these units of sadistic henchmen. Once Hitler's spell was cast upon the German nation, many people who appeared to have been exemplary citizens became capable of the most abominable crimes. Although there were a good number who resisted this horror, there were far too many who not only went along with it, but actively aided and abetted it as well. Here we have supposedly upright citizens doing the devil's work!

The dehumanizing of the German nation as a result of this Nazi poison has not yet been fully acknowledged, although significant progress has been made towards an acceptance of some kind of accountability. As usual, there are the deniers, who maintain that the Holocaust never happened. But the evidence is irrefutable, so the denier's case is indefensible.[14]

The enormity of the Nazi Holocaust is hard to appreciate at first. It is only when the unspeakable horror of what actually took place begins to sink into one's consciousness that one becomes aware of the true depths of evil to which human beings can sink. It's a nasty shock, from which one never fully recovers.

We have read so many times about war and massacre, and even genocide, that to a certain extent we have become anaesthetized to the shock of such things. That human beings are capable of these kinds of barbaric behavior is accepted as an unpleasant truth. Nevertheless the scale and brutality of what the Nazis did was beyond anything that had occurred before. The fact that it was planned and carried out so meticulously; that it continued over such a long period of time; that special facilities were planned and built for the sole purpose of destroying innocent human beings; that it was rationalized as something that would benefit the German people; and the callous way that many of the practitioners of this monstrous evil went about their work. All these things together put the Nazi atrocities on a slightly different plane from even the worst of what had gone before. This was truly a descent into the lowest depths of hell, and it cast a dark shadow not only over the Germans, but also over the whole human race.

Could this happen in any nation? One can never be sure, because in fact many nations had their Nazi sympathizers, who came out of the woodwork to sing the führer's praises. But it needs a combination of circumstances to bring these abominations up from the depths.

As for the sadistic killers themselves, the question arises, Is anyone capable of such behavior, or are there special types of individual that are susceptible to such a demonic spell? Maybe a certain genetic makeup is responsible for this ugly flaw. The plain fact is that there are killers and gangster types in every nation, and once they become part of the power structure almost any kind of atrocity is possible. The ordinary citizen sometimes gets swept along in the heat of the moment, but most of the time he is an unwilling participant in the worst acts of barbarism.

Could the capability for extreme cruelty be a genetic defect? Here we have to be careful not to draw any hasty conclusions. For just as the ordinary citizen can be caught up in the fever of war, so he can sometimes commit crimes in the heat of the moment that he would normally never think of doing. This "heat of the moment" can be artificially created, in circumstances that we have already considered. So there may be a bit of the primordial beast in all of us.[15]

JUST AND UNJUST CAUSES

We have already seen that morality is a very scarce commodity when it comes to war. But many of those who go to war do not see it that way at all. Far from it!

Invariably, they see themselves as fighting for a righteous cause, and all sorts of moral justifications lie ready at hand. The mythology of war creates a frightful picture of the enemy as inhuman beasts, ready to destroy everything that is good and pure and worthy of the blood of heroes. The enemy sees the same picture, or rather its mirror image.

War correspondent Chris Hedges describes how a "cause" can be transformed into something sacred, which affects the thinking of the whole nation.

> The cause, sanctified by the dead, cannot be questioned without dishonoring those who gave up their lives. We become enmeshed in the imposed language. When any contradiction is raised or there is a sense that the cause is not just, the doubts are attacked as apostasy.[16]

To the hard core of professional soldiers the cause is of no great moment. War is war, and what they have been trained to do is to kill the enemy and destroy his property. So causes or justifications are of no particular interest to the professional, who is expected to carry out orders and to accept whatever justification his leaders may choose to proclaim. In the case of Clausewitz, he was more interested in the morale of his soldiers than in the moral side of war. He thought of war as an extension of politics, and morality, if he considered it at all, was relegated to a minor status.

> "War is not merely a political act, but also a real political instrument, a continuation of political commerce, a carrying out of the same by other means."[17]

We must remember, however, that when Clausewitz talked about politics it was not really the same thing as the politics that we are familiar with today. His politics was more akin to what we would now call statecraft.

Like the great Chinese master Sun Tzu, who wrote *The Art of War*, Clausewitz considered war to be more of an art than a science. As with economics, it has too many variables that are subject to human whim, and so it is impossible to construct a comprehensive theory of war. Once war starts, all the best-laid plans go out the window.

For Clausewitz, war is fought for the most part by professional soldiers, not by riff-raff, and he likes to play down its brutality. But his ideas are by no means simplistic, and are still applicable to the modern world. *On War* is must reading for anyone who is seriously interested in the history and nature of warfare. His account of how war has changed through the centuries, reflecting how the various political systems and cultures have evolved, gives an insightful picture of how warfare and human culture have developed together over the centuries.[18]

In the vast majority of cases both sides proclaim what they consider to be valid reasons for going to war. They are both fighting with the firm conviction that their cause is just, or at least they have managed to convince themselves of this. And what's more, they invariably believe, not only that their cause is just, but also that *God* is on their side as well. Indeed, how could God *not* be on their side if their cause is just?

Here we have another example of what hubris can do to the human mind. But one can appreciate how nations might want some moral justification for going to war. So it becomes necessary to convert the enterprise into some sort of *moral* crusade.

It's true that there are cases when one side appears to be the clear aggressor. This does not prevent the aggressor from claiming that he is fighting for a just cause. But it nonetheless puts the victim of aggression on a much firmer moral basis, and occupying the moral high ground is definitely good for morale! Indeed, defense against an aggressor does seem to be justified, providing of course that the "aggression" was not actually provoked by the victim. The aggressor often claims that he is merely defending himself against his enemy's hostile actions. (Incidentally, Clausewitz thinks this is a good tactic!)

It's usually clear to an outside observer whether genuine aggression is involved. Germany and Japan in World War II are good examples of aggression against apparently innocent parties. How could supposedly civilized nations embark on an orgy of savagery and destruction and nonetheless proclaim that their actions were entirely justifiable? In both these cases the aggressor nation was highly motivated and considered its cause to be just. Elaborate justifications were fabricated and duly swallowed by the populace, almost without exception. Among other things, Japan claimed that the United States was preventing her from obtaining vital resources, especially oil. Actually, some of the complaints of the Japanese were not without foundation, but her brutal treatment of the Chinese and other foreigners, and finally the unprovoked attack on Pearl Harbor, put Japan firmly in the role of the aggressor. Hitler claimed that Germany had been unfairly treated by the Allies at Versailles, but this was hardly justification for starting another war. He said the Germans needed *liebenstraum*, or breathing space, where her population could live freely and without overcrowding. Those who pointed out that this meant taking other people's land were told that Germany's destiny was to rule the Slavic nations. All this nonsense was accepted by a majority of the German people.

In the 1930's the Japanese had invaded China and Manchuria, where they committed numerous atrocities. The most brutal example was the "Rape of Nanking," in 1937, where Japanese soldiers went on an orgy of brutality. The citizens of Nanking, especially the women, were attacked, killed and mutilated without mercy. Japanese soldiers, asked after the war why they had behaved in such a way, replied that at the time they did not consider the Chinese to be human beings! There were similar "explanations" for Nazi crimes against the Jews and other minorities. As members of a master race, the Germans and the Japanese were persuaded that these people were simply inferior to them. They were not worthy to be treated as human beings, and should be exterminated. It is almost unbelievable that such specious arguments could be used to justify these campaigns of unspeakable brutality. But alas they were.

Surely civilized people would not even treat animals in the way that the Germans and the Japanese (and the Russians) treated their enemies. So the excuse of not considering them to be really human is altogether lame.[19] We can only conclude that the Germans and the Japanese had literally been brainwashed into believing that, as superior beings, they had a duty to exterminate these unfortunate people. To an outside observer this seems utterly incredible, but to those who had fallen under the spell of the mythologizers it all made perfect sense.

When we look at the broader picture, it becomes somewhat less surprising that a whole nation can fall under such an evil spell. At least part of the answer seems to lie in *education,* because, unhappily, education can easily be used for subversive purposes. Education can become an outlet for propaganda, and its effects can be lethal.

Hitler realized that if he took people young enough, and exposed them to his ideas about the master race, he could create a whole mass of obedient followers. He was already aware that the German people were predisposed to blame many of their misfortunes on the Jews, and so he played on this theme for all it was worth. The Hitler Youth was created in order to produce willing followers who would carry out the Führer's policies without question. And, as they say, the rest is history.

In the case of the Japanese, the education of the citizens took a subtler turn. One could even say that the end result was an unintended consequence of a genuine attempt to modernize Japanese society. We saw in chapter 3 that the Meiji Restoration of 1868 resulted in a frantic attempt to catch up with the rest of the world, and that one priority was the introduction of an effective system of education. The emphasis on subservience to the Emperor and the furtherance of Japanese interests seemed quite innocent at the outset. But by the 1920's, when the militarists had taken control, this system of education became perverted into what amounted to a form of indoctrination, by which the Japanese people were persuaded that they were a superior race, and were therefore justified in expanding Japanese control over the territory of their neighbors. Ian Buruma, in his book *Inventing Japan,* has this to say about the siege and massacre of Nanking:

> It was not enough to kill; the victims had to be humiliated and dehumanized first. This makes the killing easier, for it strips the victims of their humanity. But it is also the result of vicious indoctrination. For years, Japanese had been told the Chinese were inferior and the Japanese a divine race. Government propaganda, parroted by the jingoistic Japanese press, told soldiers they were fighting a holy war. Anything they did in the name of the emperor, no matter how savage, was sanctioned by the holiness of their cause.[20]

The militarists were well aware of the xenophobic tendencies of the Japanese, which had often been in evidence throughout their history. Like Hitler, they exploited the existing characteristics and traditional biases in the social fabric of the nation.

The communists were also adept at the art of indoctrination. They "educated" their followers to believe that a war against the capitalist exploiters would lead inevitably to a worker's paradise. This communist propaganda was very effective. But we have to remember that this kind of indoctrination, which was actually not very sophisticated, worked best on those without much of a basic education, and the younger they were the better. In other words, as with the Taliban and the Hitler Youth, there has to be a certain degree of ignorance in the potential believers before they will swallow the party line that is fed to them. This is why Marx's ideas fell on fertile ground only in countries that were relatively backward in regard to the general level of education. The intellectuals were feared and persecuted by the communists because they were difficult to indoctrinate.

In the above examples, the well of knowledge was intentionally poisoned. But there is always the danger of any educational system being perverted by those who are afraid of genuine knowledge, and who wish to perpetuate their own version of the truth. This is why educational establishments must always maintain strict independence. Education is the key to a better life, but there are always lots of busybodies around, trying to subvert it.

The examples of Germany and Japan illustrate unambiguous cases of aggression. But in other cases the aggressor is not so easily identified. The causes that are espoused often seem hollow to the outside observer. The people of the countries involved have simply been brought up to *think* in a certain way. At first sight this appears harmless. You may say, Of course they are brought up to think in a certain way, isn't everybody? Well, some habits of thought are more harmful than others. If one is brought up to believe that certain people—Frenchmen, Jews, Arabs, Indians—are inferior in some way, this can radically alter one's whole worldview.

So fighting bravely for a cause that seems to an objective observer to lack any kind of reasonable justification is by no means unusual. However, even though the population may be predisposed to think in a certain way, systematic psychological persuasion is usually necessary for a particular cause to be embraced with the requisite fervor. To turn a naked act of aggression into a moral crusade still requires skillful application of the propagandist's art. But it should not surprise us how often this has been successfully accomplished, given the gullibility of a human being, especially one that is young or poorly educated—or both.

REALISTS AND UNIVERSALISTS

Niccolò Machiavelli (1469-1527) was one of the most influential thinkers in the realm of political philosophy. The average person will probably know something about him, even if such names as Hobbes, Locke, Kant or Ibn Khaldun may be unfamiliar. This indicates that his ideas have been of lasting influence, even though much of what he had to say about human nature was decidedly unflattering.

One of the recurring themes that we have encountered is that morality seems to disappear when it comes to relations with other states. We have also seen that war itself tends to brutalize the combatants, and that the ruthlessness of certain leaders is *intended* to remove any moral scruples from those who carry out their orders. So although we consider morality to be extremely important, little progress has been made in applying it *between* nations. In fact, the only kind of morality that seems to make any real sense is *individual* morality. When it comes to the morality of governments, or states, or empires, the rules immediately start to break down. This is strange, because all these entities are made up of people, and so one might expect that there would be some kind of communal morality, analogous to the individual kind.

When it comes to interstate relationships, leaders soon discover that if they base their actions on ordinary standards of personal morality or ethical conduct, they can put their country at a considerable disadvantage in any negotiations that they may wish to enter into. Although the members of a government are people, the *state* is impersonal. So when dealing with another state, personal morality no longer applies.

There is an interesting book by Jonathan Haslam called *No Virtue Like Necessity: Realist Thought in International Relations Since Machiavelli*. This sets out the case for the realist point of view, by presenting the opinions of some influential philosophers, including Machiavelli, who have advocated it. But it also chronicles the ideas of those who have rejected the thinking of Machiavelli, those who have denied that morality must necessarily stop at the water's edge—the Christian Church for example. It is a well-researched book and is not amenable to easy summation, so I recommend it to anyone seriously interested in this subject. Haslam discusses four aspects of the political scene: Reasons of State, balance of power, balance of trade, and geopolitics. In doing so he gives us a picture of how political thought has evolved during the past 500 years.

The trouble with those who have challenged the realist point of view is that their ideas have tended to be impractical, bordering on the utopian. But there is a serious vein of thought that challenges the realist point of view, and this is what Haslam describes as "universalist." It envisions the eventual creation of a universal (global) state as a substitute for the present individual states. Obviously this would be very difficult to accomplish, given the history of international bodies up to this time. But we *are* gradually—and haltingly—moving towards such a thing.

Haslam describes the way in which a state functions in the phrase "Reasons of State." This emphasizes what we said above about the state being essentially a separate entity. Here is some of what he says:

> Realist thought depends on a premiss which universalists refuse to accept: namely, the primacy of the state. At the core of the realist tradition also lies the insistence that considerations of morality which would normally apply to the individual within the society should not apply to society acting in relation to other societies. Rules of prudence take precedence over rules of morality, since the dominant community—the state or society—has transcendent needs and commands prior loyalty. It is this that most clearly marks the realist from the universalist.[21]

The fact that the state has primacy over the individual is the crucial assumption of the realist. This puts the statesman at the service of the state, and nullifies any moral scruples that he may have as an individual.

The realist will argue that this must be the case, because any moral inhibitions that the state might be subject to would surely put it at a fatal disadvantage in relation to another state that wished to attack or dominate it. However, this is not always what happens in practice. There are often *personal* relationships between kings and monarchs, prime ministers and presidents, and these can build up trust and confidence in relations between nations. And besides, it's not that a state *never* does something simply because it's the "right thing to do."

In truth, the Machiavellian picture seems to be rather extreme, for without *any* kind of trust between states, we would surely have chaos—or perpetual war. And what about international law? In addition to treaties, there have been many attempts to frame international laws, and this shows the existence of a general desire to improve relations between states and to avoid conflict as far as possible.[22] But we obviously still have a long way to go.

The key to the problem between nations is the question of national sovereignty. It is the fear of losing national sovereignty that keeps nations from cooperating with one another on a more meaningful basis. But behind this looms the concept of the state itself.

What exactly *is* the state? It certainly is not an organism, as some have argued. The state comprises the citizens under its jurisdiction, together with the territory that they inhabit. But each citizen thinks of it in his own particular way, as something above and beyond the land and the people. In this sense it's an *abstraction*. Like its twin brother nationalism, it doesn't really exist at all, except in the minds of its citizens, and especially in the minds of their leaders. Some heads of state, like Louis XIV of France, have thought of themselves as actually *being* the state—*l'état c'est moi*.

Although Machiavelli's ideas are well known, they most certainly have not been universally accepted. In fact the merits and demerits of his writings continue to be debated to this day. Even though one can object to his "realistic" approach, there is nonetheless a solid basis of truth in what he has to say. As Robert Kaplan writes:

> The core of Machiavelli's wisdom is that primitive necessity and self-interest drive politics, and that this can be good in itself, because competing self-inter-

ests are the basis for compromise, while stiff moral arguments lead to war and civil conflict, rarely the better options.[23]

But the universalists have not been silenced. Universalism may seem unrealistic, but if we want to have a peaceful world, it is surely the only viable alternative. We just have to get over the stumbling block of national sovereignty, which is intimately connected to our old friend nationalism. The "idealists" who think along these lines are mostly the intellectuals in the universities or the professions. The bureaucrats and the leaders who have to make the hard political decisions usually end up in the realist camp, although they may have originally thought that they could apply their own ethical principles to the field of international relations.

In addition to Machiavelli, Haslam examines philosophers such as Plato, Spinoza, Hobbes, Locke, Kant, Rousseau and Burke for their thoughts about how states interact with one another. The core of each philosophy is its assessment of human nature. Is man naturally bad, as Kant thought? Or is he naturally good, but corrupted by society, as Rousseau believed? Is he ruled by his passions, or can these be kept in check by reason? Is war and conflict the natural state of man, as Hobbes and Hegel thought, or is peace attainable by enlightened diplomacy, or something like the balance of power? These thinkers agree that relationships between states cannot be considered in the same way as relationships between individuals. But they also agree that a state, like an individual, will pursue its own interests above all, and will defend itself if attacked. Practical considerations are likely to outweigh moral principles in most circumstances.

Machiavelli was certainly not the rogue that some have made him out to be. In fact he was honest and forthright in his own personal conduct. He had experience in diplomatic affairs, and was an avid student of history. His concern was with statecraft, and how to govern effectively. He thought that peace could be preserved if all sides maintained a realistic view of human affairs, unsullied by moralistic thinking or sentimentality. The fact that those little Italian city-states spent most of their time attacking one another—just like the Greeks before them—undoubtedly influenced his thinking. But he was also concerned with the wider world, especially with the interference of France and Spain in Italian affairs.

Machiavelli maintained that a state's success depended largely on an accurate assessment of how others would react if it undertook to increase its power or influence at the expense of its neighbors. Being honest or straightforward in the field of diplomacy can easily result in being outmaneuvered by one's competitors, so a little deceit is perfectly acceptable from time to time. As Machiavelli himself puts it:

> Everyone realizes how praiseworthy it is for a prince to honour his word and to be straightforward rather than crafty in his dealings; none the less contemporary experience shows that princes who have achieved great things have been those who have given their word lightly, who have known how to trick men with their cunning, and who, in the end, have overcome those abiding by honest principles.[24]

The basis of Machiavelli's philosophy is what he calls virtue, or more properly *virtù*. As Robert Kaplan explains in *Warrior Politics*, this is not Christian virtue, but *pagan* virtue. "Machiavelli's pagan virtue is public virtue, whereas Judeo-Christian virtue is private virtue."[25] Deceit and trickery are often necessary for the public good.

> "Virtue," or *virtù*, in Machiavelli's Italian, derives from *vir*, Latin for "man." For Machiavelli, virtue variously means "valor," "ability," "ingenuity," "determination," "energy," and "prowess": manly vigor, that is, but usually in the pursuit of the general good. Virtue presupposes ambition, but not only for the sake of personal advancement.[26]

So now at last we know why our morality cannot be used in international relations. It's the wrong *kind* of morality! It's *private* morality, quite a different thing from public morality, or "pagan virtue."

"Realists" like Machiavelli believe that war is simply a part of the human condition, and so there is not much that we can do as far as getting rid of it. But if one accepts this point of view then there is little room for optimism, given the increasingly lethal nature of the weapons employed in war. Sooner or later we will blow ourselves off the face of the earth.

The realist point of view assumes that states will always seek to expand at the expense of their neighbors, and will constantly strive to increase their power so that they can respond to any perceived threats. Nonetheless we can find states that are not nearly so aggressive or paranoid. Some are quite happy to live in peace with their neighbors. Take the Scandinavians for instance; their mildly socialistic society seeks to enhance the welfare of *all* its citizens, and does not attempt to project power beyond its borders. Or the Swiss, in their alpine paradise, making elegant watches and playing host to tourists.

The Scandinavians weren't always so pacific. For a long time they were the scourge of Europe, looting, pillaging and raping mainly for the fun of it. But they gradually transformed themselves from brigands into traders, and ultimately into responsible citizens. Their present peace-loving condition shows that a history of dark deeds does not preclude the eventual embrace of more civilized behavior.

The case of the Scandinavians is an interesting one, and tends to confirm some of the ideas of the English philosopher Thomas Hobbes. Hobbes, born in 1588, the year of the Spanish Armada, was a philosophical soul mate of Machiavelli, and like the Italian sage, he refuses to just fade into the background of history. His experience of the English civil war undoubtedly influenced his thinking to a considerable degree, but his ideas remain stubbornly pertinent to this day.

An advocate of authoritarianism, Hobbes believed that a government had first of all to create order, since man in his natural state will set upon his neighbor and there will be chaos. Accordingly, the first function of government is to save man from himself. After order is created, a more civil society can evolve, based on law and respect for individual rights. But democracy is pointless without law and order first being firmly established.

Even if human nature is not quite as brutal as Hobbes pictured it, his philosophy seems to be borne out in quite a few instances. This is certainly the case if we look at some modern experiments in creating democracy. As with the Scandinavians, a peaceful and orderly society must first be established, before anything like democracy can be attempted. A period of authoritarian rule is almost always necessary. A benevolent despot is better than a dysfunctional democracy—but he must be benevolent.

Democracy in ancient Greece was quite primitive, and was constantly in danger of reverting to oligarchy or tyranny. Even though it had features that were superior to ours, their legal and governmental institutions were not strong enough to prevent strong leaders from corrupting the system.

The danger in Hobbes' authoritarian scenario, of which he himself was aware, is that the government *itself* must be prevented from malfeasance, since it consists of the same rapacious human beings as the nation at large. Here he puts his finger on the primary weakness of all human institutions, namely corruption. Who is to govern the governors? At first glance, this is also the problem with Plato's government of "wise men," who are somehow above the fray, and are required to govern with wisdom and justice. In the Hobbsian view, such wise men are subject to the same failings as everyone else. His book, *Leviathan,* describes an *impersonal* bureaucratic state, largely insulated from manipulation by corrupt individuals, which would maintain order, but at the same time protect its citizens.

This does not mean that Plato's idea has no merit. The un-elected "guardians" could exist side by side with a democratically elected parliament or assembly, rather like the British House of Lords. They could be called upon to make policy in areas where the welfare of the nation as a whole was at stake, such as the direction of fiscal policy. The aristocratic elites in Europe and the scholar bureaucrats in China were generally able to work for the public good, because they were secure in their positions of privilege. Politicians, however, must constantly be worrying about their re-election, and dare not propose unpopular policies. Even though a few of the aristocrats may have abused their positions of trust, there was a tradition of community service for those born to privilege, and this helped to keep such abuse to a minimum. A sense of civic duty is largely lacking among today's titans of industry, although some of them do make contributions to the public welfare. This is the old idea of noblesse oblige, which has its limitations. Nevertheless it worked reasonably well in the past.[27]

The Scandinavians have achieved their enviable system of government because they have worked hard at creating a civilized society. It took a long time to convert them from a band of looters into a community of responsible citizens. But it has certainly been worth it. Actually, their socialistic state bears some resemblance to Hobbes' Leviathan.

16

CULTURAL VISTAS

o o o o o o o o o o o o o o o o o o o o o o o o o o o o o o o o o o
Every boy and every gal,
That's born into this world alive,
Is either a little Liberal,
Or else a little Conservative.

—*William S. Gilbert*
Iolanthe

LIBERALS AND CONSERVATIVES

I hope that this section will give a reasonably accurate idea of how political views seem to divide approximately into two camps. My definitions of liberal and conservative my not be universally accepted, but please give me a little leeway with this tricky subject.

The labels liberal and conservative actually cover a wide spectrum. We've seen that some European conservatives would probably be labeled as liberals in the United States, and vice versa. In Europe "liberal" is often used to describe the Liberal Democratic party, a descendent of the old Liberal party, which was not liberal in the sense that the word is used in America.

As related in chapter 12, the difference between English Liberals (Whigs) and Conservatives (Tories) was primarily concerned with trade and freedom of religion. In 1900, a third party arose, called the Labour party, which was intended to represent the working class, and which eventually displaced the Liberals as the primary opposition to the Conservatives. The Labour party had definite socialist tendencies, since it soon started to advocate government ownership of some segments of industry.

In America, the party labels of Democrat and Republican came to mean almost the opposite of what the parties originally stood for. This was primarily, but not exclusively, due to the issues of slavery and civil rights during the period of the Civil War and beyond. However, as in England in the nineteenth century, both parties were what we would now call conservative; it was only later that the Democratic Party came to be viewed as the more liberal of the two.

The word liberal literally means "generous," and although the politicians have frequently misused it, "liberal" is employed more or less in its conventional sense in America, whereas in England the word liberal has had little to do with generosity. In fact English Liberals were similar to American moderate conservatives, who could be found in both the Republican and the Democratic parties. Part of this confusion stemmed from the fact that in Europe liberalism was connected with *non*-intervention by the government in the economy. As Daniel Yergin writes:

> For Americans, the global battle between the state and the market can be puzzling, for it appears to pit "liberalism" against "liberalism." In the United States, *liberalism* means the embrace of an activist, interventionist government, expanding its involvement and responsibility in the economy. In the rest of the world, liberalism means almost exactly the opposite—what an American liberal would, in fact, describe as *conservatism*. This kind of liberalism supports a reduced role for the state.... It has its intellectual roots in such thinkers as John Locke, Adam Smith, and John Stuart Mill.[1]

In order to avoid confusion we will reserve Liberal to describe the British Liberal party, and liberal for the more commonly accepted dictionary definition, bearing in mind that this differs somewhat from the term used in current American politics.

In spite of differences in interpretation, the terms liberal and conservative do have a general connotation, which is by and large understood by politicians and public alike. The word liberal is generally understood as "progressive," while conservative has several shades of meaning, which will be explained below. By and large one might say that liberals are more interested in a government concerning itself with the people's welfare, especially those on the bottom rungs of the social ladder, while conservatives are keen to preserve what they consider to be the traditional values of the society, and to avoid unnecessary government interference in the economy or matters relating to such things as "social justice."

The terms left and right, which date from the time of the French Revolution, are often substituted for liberal and conservative. Rightists were equated with monarchists, and leftists with democrats. But like many political terms, their definitions have tended to alter over time. "Left" now has more of a connotation of socialism, while "right" takes on a hint of the reactionary.

According to conservatives, liberals are soft, woolly thinkers, whose misplaced sentimentality leads them to spend government money on those who contribute little to society. To a *religious* conservative, liberalism is equated to permissiveness in the matter of morality. On the other hand conservatives (again according to the conservatives) are realistic thinkers, who wish to preserve the basic values of the society and are not afraid to inflict stern measures on those who disobey the law. They like to support those who they consider as the most important members of the society. In their opinion these consist mainly of the rich, the business community and the military. The implication is that liberals are soft on crime and are not sufficiently concerned with preserving the society's basic values. Conservatives are resentful of government interference in their lives, unless of course the government can do something for them, like subsidize their business or offer them some form of tax relief—then they are all for it. In other words, they are not averse to government spending, provided that they are the sole beneficiaries.

From the liberal point of view conservatives are hard, greedy and self-satisfied, interested only in enriching themselves at the expense of those less fortunate. Their assumption that they hold a monopoly on virtue reveals both the emptiness of their values and their meanness of spirit.

According to my way of thinking, there are actually three distinct kinds of conservative, not just in Britain and America, but almost anywhere. Conservatism means vaguely "conserving both the traditions and institutions of society." But this is far too loose a definition, and covers a very broad spectrum of opinion, including liberal opinion. So I like to be more precise, and divide conservatives into three camps. First, there are what I call the "fuddy-duddy" conservatives, who like society just the way it is, and don't want to change anything. Then there are the "progressive" conservatives, who want to keep what is good and valuable, while at the same time trying to improve things that need to be improved, without doing anything to upset the basic traditions of the society. Finally, there are the radical conservatives, who want to make society over to their way of thinking, even if it means replacing some things that are good and valuable with other things that they consider to be more important. These are the extreme right-wingers, the *hard* right, who usually clothe their opinions in some sort of ideology, which helps to differentiate them from the first two categories. To a more moderate conservative, these extremists are not really conservatives at all. Of course to the extremists, the moderate conservatives are really liberals—which is probably not too far from the truth.

There are also extremists on the left, who wish to promote a more egalitarian society by curtailing the privileges of the rich and powerful, and "distributing the wealth" to a certain degree. To their conservative counterparts they are considered as either socialists or communists.

To a liberal, conservative thinking is *bad.* Even though he may not go so far as to say that conservatives are bad people, the wrong-headedness of a conservative's views tends to reduce his moral stature in the eyes of a liberal. Naturally the same is true when the roles are reversed. This does not preclude liberals and conservatives from being friends, for it is intriguing to see if one can disabuse one's acquaintance of his erroneous political views, and thus raise his intellectual and moral status. Usually no such thing takes place. But if it *should* happen, the satisfaction evoked is similar to having made a religious conversion.

In a two party system, or at least in a system where there are two major parties, both parties have to embrace quite a wide spectrum of political opinion, and so there are what could be termed liberals and conservatives in both parties. How then can the parties be differentiated?

In modern democratic countries the political spectrum tends to run from the extreme right to the extreme left, and many of the politically active citizens can be found on these two wings. Those in the middle do not have very strong feelings about who they vote for, and can be persuaded to cast their vote for a politician or party that happens to appeal to them at any given time. If no candidate attracts them, they may not even bother to vote at all. So the political spectrum is not static, and tends to lean sometimes towards an overall liberal bias and at other times towards the conservative end of the spectrum.

Since there is little love lost between the two ends of the spectrum, it is as inevitable as night follows day that they should end up in different parties. In a two-party system, they become the base support of the two major parties, and will almost never consider voting for the opposition, except under extreme circumstances. Once in a while a few activists on one of the extreme wings lose faith in the party of their choice. Rather than support the other party, they may jump ship and start a third party. In this case chaos will reign for a while, but usually the two-party system reasserts itself, with the disgruntled extremists reluctantly returning to the fold. Third parties can wreak havoc in a basically two-party system, by throwing an election to one side or another. However, it may happen that a third party gets strong enough to actually displace one of the major parties. The displaced party then rapidly loses its influence.

One should not get the idea that the two-party system is the most desirable. Although two-party systems are more stable than multi-party systems, they are much less democratic, and this is the fatal flaw of the two-party system; it forces the citizenry to vote for one of two alternatives, neither of which appeals to a majority. The choice then becomes: to vote for the lesser of two evils, or not to vote at all. This accounts for the miserably low turnout in most countries where there is a two-party system. Multi-party democracy, far from disregarding the basic make-up of the political spectrum, expresses it much more accurately. Multi-party systems may appear more chaotic and less efficient than two-party systems, but they are much more democratic, and tend to produce a less divided and more satisfied citizenry, feeling that its views are at least being considered in the electoral process. A much larger percentage of the people will take part in the political process in a multi-party system.

The corrosive effect of money and special interests tend to undermine all political systems, but a two-party system is particularly vulnerable in this regard.

The quotation by W. S. Gilbert at the beginning of this chapter is misleading on two counts. In Gilbert's day both liberals and conservatives were what we would now call conservatives. But the idea that one is born with a political affiliation and keeps it throughout one's life is definitely erroneous. The object of the politician is to make sure that any change of opinion will be towards his own way of thinking and that of his party. Only those on the extreme left or right wings are likely to remain firmly fixed in their beliefs. The others are liable to shift their opinions as their circumstances or their lifestyles dictate. The aging process alone can easily alter political opinions.

It is possible to find stereotypes whose political views can be fairly well predicted. But there are always exceptions to these rules. The rich, the business community, the military and most bureaucrats tend towards the conservative end of the political spectrum. On college campuses, and in the professions, you will find the intellectuals, who are likely to have more of a liberal bias. In the financial community, you will find mostly conservatives. Actually, many of the college liberals end up in business, where their political views may become more conservative. Youthful idealism can give way to the sober realities of family and responsibility. In reality, the opinions of both liberals and conservatives are quite fickle for the most part. Only those who hold deep-seated convictions of what a society's character and values should be will remain steadfast in their support of any particular political party, and then only if the party remains faithful to its professed ideals.

A true conservative thinks the world would be fine if it wasn't for the woolly-headed liberals. On the other hand, liberals feel that conservatives are indifferent to the injustice and suffering that exists in human society, and that they have no thought for anyone but themselves.

Most people have a little of the liberal and a little of the conservative in them. So it is easy to see how they can change parties. And in truth the association with a party is often of a negative character. They actually disagree with all the parties. It's just that they disagree with one of them a little less than the others.

The harmful aspect of politics is polarization. Differences of opinion are inevitable—and healthy—in a society, but there should be a better way of discussing them without demonizing the other side. Politics tends to accentuate differences, whereas the aim should be to narrow or eliminate them. The old human tendency to divide into groups of "us and them" leads to a needless increase in hostility between the parties. Happily this type of antagonism is usually confined to the extreme ends of the political spectrum, but political campaigns tend to bring out the worst in everyone, and bad feeling can easily spill over into the middle of the spectrum as well. People should be able to discuss their differences in a civilized manner. But politics makes this almost impossible.

The split between liberals and conservatives is an interesting aspect of the broader phenomenon of human interaction, which involves differences of opinion and beliefs in general. Both liberals and conservatives are looking at the *same* world, but they interpret it quite differently. They see the world—and human nature—through different colored spectacles, reflecting their own particular personal feelings and biases. Although the color of the spectacles can change, the tendency is for the distortion to grow greater, rather than less. The conservative reads conservative newspapers and magazines, and talks mostly to his conservative friends. The same is true for the liberal. In consequence, their views of reality tend to get more distorted over time, since they seldom consider an alternative viewpoint. This is true of almost all beliefs and opinions, so a really objective view of almost anything is extremely rare.

NEW DEVELOPMENTS IN THE ARTS

Since any discussion of art is necessarily subjective, I apologize in advance if what I have to say goes against any of your deeply held opinions.

It can be asserted, I think with some validity, that the increase in the spread of democracy that has occurred over the past two centuries has brought with it a decrease in the quality of art in general. It's hard to put one's finger on the exact reasons for this. One might speculate that the high quality of art in the older cultures reflects a more highly developed imagination as compared to the modern world with its greater emphasis on reason. But there are no valid criteria whereby the art of one culture can be compared to that of another.[2]

In Western architecture there was a series of "revivals" in the 18th and 19th centuries. These were usually either Greek or Gothic revivals, which was natural enough, since the two "pure" sources of Western culture were the Greek and the Gothic. But the existence of a revival of any kind signals a dearth of fresh ideas and inspiration, and indicates a turning towards the past rather than the future.

In fact, there was no new culture to inspire any great artistic expression, and the new religion of nationalism failed to tap the wellsprings of creativity in the same way that the theistic religions had done. The soaring Gothic cathedrals stand in mute testimony to the time when Western man lifted his eyes to heaven and labored mightily to build a house worthy of his God. Anyone who walks into these magnificent buildings can experience the transcendent nature of the religious sentiments that inspired them. They are truly monuments to man's desire to raise himself above his animal nature. The same striving for transcendence can be felt in all great religious structures.

But nationalism does not seem to inspire the imagination in a comparable manner. This lack of inspiration also carries over to the other arts, and this includes music as well. Even philosophy, which the ancient Greeks considered to be an art, seems to have run out of interesting ideas. Something like logical positivism is too abstract and academic for the average citizen, even if he is interested in intellectual matters. Ludwig Wittgenstein perhaps represents the extreme in this direction. Most of his work concerns the analysis of language and its meaning. He applied the same kind of analysis that Bertrand Russell had used when applying symbolic logic to mathematics (specifically set theory). But this did not impress Russell very much, because he thought that mathematics and language could not be analyzed in the same way.

Existentialism in its various different forms, as enunciated by Heidegger, Sartre and Jaspers among others, also showed a trend towards the esoteric and the abstract.[3] Although these philosophers did appeal to a limited segment of the general public, their ideas were too abstruse to generate a wide following.

Interestingly enough, a trend towards abstraction also appeared in *science* at about the same time. As Frank Vertosick explains:

> The early twentieth century brought parallel revolutions in art, science, and psychiatry—all three began detaching themselves from the world of the tangible at the same time. Art went from realistic to abstract, physics from Newtonian to quantum, and psychiatry from the conscious to the unconscious. Abstract art, quantum mechanics, and Freudian psychiatry share the common bead of the unseen.[4]

Could this trend towards abstraction be an expression of a mature Western culture, founded on the more abstract concepts of science? Be that as it may, this tendency towards abstraction was at the heart of the modern movement in both art and architecture. Its practitioners proclaimed a new and fresh approach to the conception of art, an attempt to rise above the sterile imitation of the past, and to express man's increasing freedom from outmoded ways of thought. And a fairly promising start was made in this endeavor.

The French impressionists produced mildly abstract art of superb quality, although it was a while before it was fully accepted by the traditionalists. After that, modern art began to get a bit too abstract for its own good. The main offenders in this regard were the cubists, who, having freed themselves from any cultural inhibitions, proceeded to produce new forms of art, which may have been intellectually interesting, but were aesthetically obscure.

Although the modern movement did produce much that was of high quality, there was a tendency to cater more to the cognoscenti of the world of art, rather than to the general public, and this became even more pronounced as time went on.

Most of this new art could only be properly appreciated by the connoisseurs of the avant-garde. As a result, some very strange objects and images started to turn up in art galleries and museums. Piles of bricks and random splotches of paint were exhibited in the hallowed halls where once the works of such as Rembrandt and Michelangelo had found a home. Most observers did not dare criticize such works, for fear of being labeled as mere philistines, who simply did not understand what art is all about. Sometimes it seemed as if shock value was the main criterion for a successful work of art—if it made one feel positively ill, it was accepted as the genuine article.

Of course one could argue that it's worth putting up with a fair amount of mediocrity, so long as a few works of outstanding quality are actually produced. And one has to admit that even in the days of the Old Masters a good deal of second-rate art was produced as well. But only the best works have come down to us, the rest have been filtered out along the way.

The emergence of modern Architecture had a considerable effect on the Western cultural scene, and not only in the world of art. Several strong minded and forceful architects rose to prominence in the first half of the twentieth century. These included: Frank Lloyd Wright, Miës van der Rohe, Walter Gropius and Le Corbusier. All of these were talented men who had their own ideas of what constituted good architecture, and none of them, with the possible exception of Gropius, were particularly interested in the opinions of their fellow architects. Gropius started the Bauhaus movement in Germany, which showed promise of a fresh start in architectural design, but Hitler's regime caused its adherents to seek shelter in other countries. All the same, it remained influential for some time.

The other three were prima donnas, and each had a major influence on the direction of architectural development in the twentieth century. They had their favorite materials and their favorite forms. Architectural students everywhere were encouraged to study the works of these masters, and so their influence became widespread throughout the world of architecture.

There were two catch phrases of the modern movement: "form follows function" and "less is more"—the latter slogan being attributed to Miës van der Rohe. It was Miës that started the idea of the glass box. The famous Farnsworth house in Illinois was the prototype of this architectural genre. If one liked living in a glass box this was fine, but things like privacy and practicality took second place to the overall aesthetic effect. But it was a beautiful little jewel of a house, in spite of the fact that it was hopelessly impractical in many ways—and very expensive.[5] The cognoscenti of the architectural world loved it, and the architectural students swooned all over it. The result was that Miës was emboldened to try the idea of the glass box on a much larger scale. He obtained a commission to build the corporate headquarters for the Seagram Company in New York City in 1954, and so the little glass box of the Farnsworth house transmuted itself into the glass skyscraper of the Seagram building. As before, aesthetics rather than practicality became the principal guiding factor.

From here one thing easily lead to another, and the glass skyscraper soon caught on like wildfire. Before long it was springing up everywhere, not just in America. The International Style had been born.

In the ancient cities of Europe, with their magnificent Renaissance, Greek revival and Gothic buildings, cheap imitations of Miës' New York skyscraper started springing up like weeds. To say that Miës van der Rohe was responsible for the destruction of hundreds of cities around the world is perhaps an exaggeration, but he was influential in creating a lot of buildings that fitted poorly, if at all, into the urban landscape.

Now, at the beginning of the twenty-first century, just as in the world of art, we have architecture for the architects, but not really for the people. Strange and weird structures, more like sculpture than architecture—which in itself is not necessarily a bad thing—push their way skyward like exotic growths in the urban landscape. Some of these structures have intentionally tried to imitate cubist paintings! Many of the larger commissions seem to be museums, which should tell us something about the current state of our culture, as well as that of architecture itself, namely that the general public is getting much more interested in culture and art.

Rich people not only donate art, they lend it to be hung in museums, and this tends to raise its price, regardless of its aesthetic merit. The effect of all this is to further separate the aesthetic value of the art from its monetary value. "A work is not art until someone rich comes along and buys it" may contain more than a grain of truth.

Can we conclude that the overall decline in artistic quality represents a weakening of our cultural values? Actually, the creation of great art is not necessarily a sign of a superior culture. At the time when the great Gothic cathedrals were built, the Inquisition was burning people at the stake! So it's possible that a decline in the quality of art may in fact signal the rise of a more civilized social order.

A more realistic view of the cultural scene in our modern democratic age is that the number of people who can be considered as cultured has in fact increased considerably. In the early days of Western culture, and of the other world cultures as well, only a very thin layer at the top—the upper crust—were sensitive to the world of culture. The rest were comparatively uneducated, their lives consisting mostly of drudgery. Only their religious faith gave them hope of a better life in the world to come.

This situation of having a small group at the top continued up until quite recently. But now the number of cultured citizens has expanded a great deal, not only in the West, but also worldwide. The result of this is that the cream at the top has become diluted. It is no longer cream, but ordinary milk. So maybe we should not be so surprised at the decline in the quality of art. Nevertheless we should rejoice that more people are now able to partake of the world of culture. The proliferation of museums has further encouraged this trend. The death of the old class system is letting some light into the lower echelons of society, where previously hard work, poverty and superstition held sway. So it's not so surprising that the world of art has also changed, not just with the coming of a more democratic society, but also with man's changing image of himself.

The production of art is not a rational process, just as the creation of myth and religion is basically irrational. So in a more rational world, governed more by technology and science than by pure products of the imagination, we may not have a right to expect outstanding quality in our art. But who knows? Our brave new world may yet inspire the imagination to new heights of artistic greatness.

THE DECLINE OF BELIEF

In Chapter 2 we examined how the fertility of the human imagination gives rise to many kinds of strange and exotic beliefs. But belief in myth and religion has tended to fade as the various cultures have approached the modern era. These beliefs no longer hold the imagination as they once did. Hell and damnation no longer strike fear into people's hearts.

One might be tempted to think that the recent emphasis on religion in many Moslem countries means that a religious revival is in progress in those parts of the world. But just as Christianity is not now the religion of Christ, so Islam is no longer the religion of the Prophet. As noted above, it has become politicized, and no longer represents the same cultural phenomenon that it once did. The current scourge of Islamic extremism can be seen, at least partly, as reflecting this loss of innocence.[6]

Samuel P. Huntington, in *The Clash of Civilizations,* asserts that there is a general revival of religion going on at the present time, especially in non-Western countries. This is primarily as a reaction to "modernization" and the spread of Western secular culture. He cites statistics to prove this trend. But such a revival reflects the desire to find meaning in a world that is fast changing. And this is what religion has always done, so the phenomenon is not really new. Actually, the rise of religious intolerance is more in evidence than a revival of genuine religion.

Many religions minister to the temporal as well as the spiritual needs of their adherents, so much of the "revival" can be attributed to the material benefits that religion can bring. But a religious revival is basically different from, and lacks the inspiration of the original. It is analogous to a stylistic revival in art. And besides, most of these so-called revivals entail fundamentalism or extremism of some sort, and so, rather than providing any genuine solutions to the problems of social upheaval, they simply accentuate the old bugbear of "us against them." Religion in its old form is no longer capable of easing man's adjustment to the world of culture. The process of globalization has opened up a new world of knowledge, which the traditional beliefs can no longer compete with.

All the same, the decline of genuine religious beliefs can be considered as a loss to society. Religion was the glue that kept things together, providing an anchor for humankind in its struggle to adjust to the artificial environment of human culture. With the fading of these beliefs, humanity needs new and sturdier supports, and these can only come from a more rational view of the world. It's like the process of growing up. When we are children we believe in fairy tales. But as we grow up, we begin to have a more realistic view of the world. A young culture is somewhat the same, believing in the gods and myths as if they were part of reality. But as the culture matures, they are no longer so widely accepted.

Nevertheless, the maturing of the culture does not necessarily involve the discarding of all irrational beliefs. Just as there are different stages in the life of an individual, there are various stages in the process of cultural development. As belief in the original religions started to fade, so the belief in the new religion of nationalism started to increase. And this proved to be a much more dangerous form of belief than conventional religion. The rise of nationalism, at least in Europe, coincided with the decline of religious belief and the lessening of faith in the traditional institutions of government.

Just as religion is man-made, so nationalism is man-made. Although nationalism was not a new concept, it suddenly took on extra vigor with the French Revolution and the accompanying rise in national consciousness. Besides the decline in religious belief, there was also a related decline in the belief of the divine right of kings, and both of these coincided with the rise of nationalism.

Nationalism in one form or another has been responsible for untold destruction and misery during the past two hundred years, but happily it is now giving way to globalization, the next phase in Western cultural development. But globalization still has a long way to go before it supplants nationalism. And besides, we shouldn't get too excited over globalization, because its outer sheen of respectability hides some rather unpleasant features, corporate greed being one of them.[7]

There are other beliefs, in addition to religious beliefs, both secular and regular, which are related to culture. As traditional religious beliefs have receded, these have tended to become more manifest. Some of them have a quasi-religious nature nonetheless. These are beliefs in the various "establishments" of society: the president, the parliament, the law and the military. They are the "institutions of leadership," whose authority and integrity the people must accept if the community is to function properly. Faith in government is essential to a smoothly running state. But the modern press has brought things to light that have heretofore been hidden from the people's eyes and ears. As a result of this, the corruption that has always existed in these institutions has begun to be exposed for all to see. Again, the emperor has been found to have no clothes. This loss of faith in governmental institutions can have a destabilizing effect on the society as a whole. The human animal always feels better if he has something nice and solid to believe in. Take it away, and his world starts to slip from under him.

Ironically, the West may be suffering from this institutional lack of faith to a greater degree than the rest of the world. Outside of the West, these bodies have never had much of a reputation for honesty or integrity. Apart from the overall corruption of politics and government, courts of law have been seen as woefully lacking in the most elementary protections of prisoners' rights, and justice has been conspicuous by its absence. So the people's opinion of their institutions has always been low. An exception is the case of Japan, whose citizens have traditionally held their leaders in high regard. In fact, until quite recently, the Emperor was worshiped as a god. Even after the catastrophic defeat of World War II, the Japanese did not abandon their leaders. But now, due to problems with the economy and corruption in high places, the Japanese have largely lost faith in their government. If this had been the case in the 1930's, much bloodshed might have been prevented.

Actually, the West is on shaky ground when criticizing the institutions of other nations, for its own institutions have never been free from corruption. However, because they operated in a more efficient manner, and the corruption was well hidden behind closed doors, these facts were concealed from the populace at large. So as a more realistic picture of their own institutions has emerged, the people of the West have had to come to grips with some unpleasant facts.

It's true that the French, the Italians and the Spanish have traditionally displayed a good deal of healthy skepticism with regard to their institutions, but the Americans and the British have traditionally prided themselves in the honesty and integrity of their governments and their leaders. At least, they have done so up until quite recently.

British institutions lost a lot of their luster when the Empire ceased to exist. So Britain has had to adjust to a world where the monarchy is no longer the pinnacle of authority, and where the traditional hierarchical system has effectively been disbanded.

The Americans have an unfortunate tendency to criticize other countries' institutions, while ignoring the faults in their own. This has understandably caused resentment in foreign lands. But in recent years, even the Americans themselves have begun to lose faith in their institutions. The Federal Bureau of Investigation (FBI) and the Central Intelligence Agency (CIA) have never enjoyed very high marks from the public, due to the "spooky" nature of their activities. But even the sacred game of baseball has been tarnished by scandal. And, heaven forbid, the Supreme Court has been suspected of political bias. Since the justices are all political appointees, it's hard to see how anyone in the United States could think that the Supreme Court would *not* have a political bias. But in some ways the Americans are extremely naïve.

In America a capitalist is considered to be a paradigm of human virtue—whereas a communist is (or was) the lowest form of animal life. So the institutions of the American capitalist society are (or were) assumed to be beyond reproach. But now these American exemplars of probity are beginning to be sullied by suspicions of impropriety. Yet another emperor is in danger of losing his clothes.[8]

Recent scandals have seriously eroded the reputation of corporate America, and faith in the free market to solve all economic and social ills has been severely shaken by the excessive greed of company executives. A primary cause of this is the involvement of business with politics. Just as religion and politics don't mix, so business and politics should be kept as far apart as possible. In America there has been little attempt to do this, and so corruption is widespread. Even though such abuses occur elsewhere, the amount of money involved is greater in America, and so the resulting temptations are harder to resist. Since involvement with politics is the chief cause of the problem, it's hardly reasonable to expect that the politicians will be able to clear up the mess. Politics and corruption, like love and marriage, are inextricably entwined.

IN SEARCH OF VALUES

All of the world's cultures have now reached a point where the old certainties have faded and everything seems to have lost its foundation. People in past centuries probably felt this way as well. But previous sources of support, such as religion, no longer provide the same reassurance.

The quest cannot be for new myths to replace the old, for all myths are now seen as fairy tales. Only when the myths were part of the belief system could they fulfill their function of easing the strain of cultural adjustment. Now we must somehow learn to live in a different kind of intellectual framework.

For some, this prospect is bleak indeed. They feel that the scientists have destroyed their world of beauty and romance, replacing it with mere chemical reactions. The physicists are accused of *reductionism*—that they have reduced the world to a mass of tiny interacting particles, obeying laws that only they can understand. Since all emotions can now be reduced to chemistry, what has happened to our erstwhile concepts of value? Brian Greene, in *The Elegant Universe*, states the dilemma thus:

> The reductionist philosophy easily ignites heated debate. Many find it fatuous and downright repugnant to claim that the wonders of life and the universe are mere reflections of microscopic particles engaged in a pointless dance fully choreographed by the laws of physics. Is it really the case that feelings of joy, sorrow, or boredom are nothing but chemical reactions in the brain?[9]

Steven Weinberg, winner of the Nobel Prize in physics, has his own perspective regarding reductionism:

> At the other end of the spectrum are the opponents of reductionism who are appalled by what they feel to be the bleakness of modern science. To whatever extent they and their world can be reduced to a matter of particles or fields and their interactions, they feel diminished by that knowledge. I would not try to answer these critics with a pep talk about the beauties of modern science. The reductionist world view *is* chilling and impersonal. It has to be accepted as it is, not because we like it, but because that is the way the world works.[10]

Weinberg explains that there is no way of formulating a logically consistent value system, just as Kurt Gödel proved that there is no such thing as a logically consistent set of axioms in Mathematics. Whatever precepts or rules one puts forward, there are always circumstances where they begin to unravel—one constantly has to rationalize one's moral or ethical stance by introducing exceptions to the rule. In other words there is no such thing as a *consistent* moral code. An obvious example is the question of taking human life. If one accepts this as a hard and fast rule, then war is prohibited, as well as many aspects of self-defense. One can say that these are obvious exceptions. But there are many other circumstances where one has to make a moral choice. The idea of absolute morality, just like that of good and evil, eludes our grasp as soon as we try to pin down the foundations of a logically consistent moral law.

A ready-made value system, one laid down by a religion for instance, is constantly in need of interpretation. The rules must be adjusted to fit many different circumstances. This can lead to all sorts of logical inconsistencies. And it parallels what happens in any legal system—it can never be made completely watertight. Weinberg says that we are better off realizing that we are "on our own" with regard to values. There *is* no system that we can call God's law.

This does not mean, however, that one should not try to formulate moral principles. Only that one should be aware of their limitations. Once we lay down black and white principles, we expose ourselves to contradictions, because it turns out that morality does not come in black and white, but only in shades of gray. And to further complicate matters, morality changes over time. This can go in either direction. Something considered morally wrong can become morally acceptable, or a morally permissible practice can become immoral.

Isaiah Berlin, in *The Crooked Timber of Humanity,* explains nicely how the "values" of each society differ, and how they can vary within an individual community.

> What is clear is that values can clash—that is why civilisations are incompatible. They can be incompatible between cultures, or groups in the same culture, or between you and me. You believe in telling the truth, no matter what; I do not, because I believe that it can sometimes be too painful and too destructive.[11]

Like Weinberg, Berlin says that the search for the ultimate set of values that would define the ideal society is fruitless. That is why religions that claim to embody absolute truth inevitably clash with others that make similar claims. In the same way, utopian systems, starting with Plato's *Republic,* and including Thomas More's *Utopia* in the sixteenth century, and communism and fascism in the twentieth, which lay down strict rules of behavior that all must follow, are doomed to failure from the start.

The word "pure" is very important to us. Ideally, everything should be pure, which is somehow associated with good, as opposed to impure, which represents bad or evil. But nothing in nature is pure. Natural substances are never chemically pure. Nature abhors purity! And actually, so do we. Take wine for instance. The wonderful taste of a good wine comes mostly from the impurities in it! So, as in nature, absolute standards are not only impossible, they are not really desirable either.[12]

IS IGNORANCE BLISS?

If ignorance is really bliss, there must be a lot of very happy people around. But this does not appear to be the case. Anyway, I'll vote for knowledge over ignorance every time. Alexander Pope's admonition that "a little learning is a dangerous thing" does not strike me as very persuasive. I think that a little knowledge is a lot better than none, just as a little bread is better than no bread at all. Aristotle thought that the acquisition of knowledge was the only really worthwhile activity. Socrates and Plato thought that knowledge and virtue were synonymous.

Education puts us on the road to enlightenment, and there is no substitute for it. But in spite of the fact that knowledge of all kinds is more available than ever before, the general level of education is still abysmal. And small wonder; people simply do not have the time to educate themselves, even if they wanted to, because they have too many other things to take care of, like earning a living and supporting their families. Bertrand Russell's contention that you have to have leisure time in order to get a real education is probably true for anyone outside of academia. (Incidentally, Russell's *History of Western Philosophy* is an education in itself.) As Russell points out, Plato and many of the Greek philosophers felt that leisure was necessary in order to achieve wisdom. This is the aristocratic view. Pythagoras taught that the study of mathematics was essential for the attainment of wisdom, but he was clearly biased.

Even a little education is surely better than none, and exposure to the world of learning often motivates further study. The trouble with public education is that its aim is not so much to educate, as to prepare the citizen to be a productive member of society, which may not require very much genuine education. This is also true of university education as well, since specialization at an early stage makes getting a broad-based education difficult. In my experience, people with a really good education do not fit the normally accepted definition of productive members of society. This is probably because knowledge is more important to them than making a lot of money. They fit the profile of the absent-minded professor better than that of the businessman or the politician.

Just going to school does not suffice for an education. In fact you can even go to the best universities and come out poorly educated—one sees many of examples of this. To be really educated one has to do a lot of study on one's own. By "really educated" I mean having a broad knowledge of many subjects, rather than being a specialist in just one or two. But it's hard to define what constitutes a good education. A *real* education stems from the thirst for knowledge, and is acquired over the course of a lifetime. It can never be considered finished or complete.

A more serious problem with education involves the fact that many people, who should know better, actually don't want it! For them ignorance *is* bliss. This happens when new discoveries or new knowledge clash with traditional beliefs or customs. We saw this with the Copernican revolution. To the Catholic Church, ignorance *was* bliss—knowledge was just too hard to accept. But having once had their fingers burnt, the Church has continued to play with fire, pointing out "errors" in scientific findings that run contrary to church dogma.

When Darwin first proposed his theory of evolution—one of the great scientific achievements of the nineteenth century—many preferred ignorance to enlightenment, and dismissed it out of hand. And as Darwin's ideas have become more and more accepted, there are still those who prefer ignorance to knowledge. Even today, to someone like a creationist, ignorance *is* bliss, and nothing will shake him out of his blissful fantasy. But this is part of the old conflict between faith and reason. Once this sort of thing gets into the realm of politics, rational debate rapidly becomes impossible, demonstrating again that religion should not be allowed to mix with either science or politics.

New historical facts are seldom accepted if they run counter to a society's self image. Such facts are conveniently buried, so as not to upset the rosy image of the past. Practically all nations are guilty of this kind of thing, and the more unpleasant the skeleton in the closet, the more forcefully its memory is suppressed. Of course this can be looked at as a survival mechanism, because thinking constantly about past mistakes can be bad for one's psychological health. But it certainly plays havoc with history. A country's history is usually better known by foreigners than it is by its own citizens.

LAND OF THE FREE

Since the United States is the most powerful and influential country in the world today, it seems appropriate to wind up with a few words about it from the point of view of an outside observer. Several topics relating to the United States have already come up from time to time, but an overall picture of America might help to put things into better perspective. I'll try and make it as objective as possible.

It has been said that the distinctive character of the American people reflects the fact that they are a nation of immigrants. Immigrants tend to be tougher and more individualistic, willing to suffer hardships in order to get ahead in the game of life. This image seems to fit America fairly well, and may account, at least in part, for America's success as a nation.

It goes without saying that Americans think their country stands out among all others. Indeed, like the Jews, who consider themselves as specially chosen by God, many Americans think of the United States as "God's country," meaning that it is somehow specially favored and protected by the Almighty. This accounts to some extent for the prominence given to religion in America, in spite of the supposed separation of church and state. Politicians take advantage of this by talking about God at almost every opportunity. In spite of this, the average American is not particularly religious, although he will probably profess some sort of belief in God. But the mixing of religion and politics has had a harmful effect on civil discourse, especially in the last hundred years.[13]

Even though the founding fathers thought it necessary to restrain the mob, the average American considers *freedom* to be his most important possession. Americans insist that they must be free to express their own opinions, to do whatever kind of work they wish, to live wherever they want, and to pursue happiness in their own individual way. Every American considers this to be his inalienable right, and he will remind you of it at every opportunity. He is suspicious of the government, which he fears might restrict his freedom in some way. Even though many other countries enjoy similar freedoms to those enjoyed by the citizens of the United States, Americans feel that *their* country is the only one that is truly the land of the free.

Another indicator of America's self-image is the World Series, the annual competition for the "world" championship of baseball. The fact that the rest of the world (except for Japan and a few of America's neighbors) does not play baseball is ignored. As far as the Americans are concerned, they *are* the world. The secular religion of baseball is not just a local cult, it's a *universal* religion.

Interestingly enough, there's a smidgen of truth in this. America, as a multi-ethnic society, does in fact represent the world to a considerable extent, since it is open to immigrants from all nations and cultures. And baseball reflects this same diversity, with players whose backgrounds and roots are equally varied. One should add that this was not always the case. Blacks, Mexicans and other minorities were not permitted to play in major-league baseball until after World War II.

We have already met the American patriot. But the fetish that the Americans have regarding their flag goes well beyond the usual expressions of patriotism.[14] It's true that all countries are proud of their flags, some inordinately so. But the Americans carry this to extremes. School children must pledge allegiance to it, as if it were something sacred. Any occasion of any consequence is used as an excuse to display the flag, and little American flags can be found in lapels, on T-shirts, on automobiles, in store windows, in fact just about anywhere. If one fails to pay sufficient homage to the flag, one's patriotism is immediately considered suspect.

Much of America has a puritanical streak, which is not surprising, since the first settlers in New England—the Pilgrim Fathers—were Puritans. Their modern counterparts are the "religious right." These self-appointed guardians of public virtue insist on censoring anything that they consider remotely pornographic, especially if it could conceivably fall into the hands of the young. Schools, art museums and libraries are examined for offending texts and pictures. But the more rational members of the community point out that many of the great historic masterpieces of art and literature—including the Bible itself—contain material that could easily be grist for the censor. The irony of this is somehow lost on the religious right, who would indeed censor such masterpieces if they could get away with it.

Another feature of America is that it lends itself to caricature. There is nothing much that is ordinary about America. Its basic geography seems to emphasize this fact. The country has a tremendous variety of different geological and climatic regions. Nothing seems to be of average size or significance. The mighty Mississippi river, the Rocky Mountains and the Grand Canyon are just three examples of America's many spectacular natural wonders.

The scale of the landscape seems to be reflected in many aspects of American life. Americans like big bouncy cars that use lots of fuel. They like tall buildings, the taller the better. Their newspapers come in one size only—huge. They even tend to overdo personal cleanliness, washing themselves and their clothes at every available opportunity.

The desire for cleanliness does not extend to the environment, however, which is used as a dumping ground for all kinds of rubbish. This is partly because almost nothing is built to last. Planned obsolescence was invented in America. As a result of this, every garbage can and every garbage dump is filled to overflowing, and the problem of where to put the mountains of garbage is one of America's most persistent problems. Naturally, air pollution is another major problem, given America's attachment to the automobile. But one must add that America's abuse of the environment is just about on a par with most other industrial nations, and is a good deal less than some of the worst offenders, such as Russia and China.

Unfortunately, some of the more unpalatable features of the modern world have originated in America. Junk food of all kinds, as well as "soft drinks," which consist of various kinds of chemically treated water—or something resembling water—have all seeped outward from the American heartland to pollute the world at large. Most of this stuff is fattening, so Americans spend much of their time looking for ways to lose weight. Abominations such as *diet* soda and *skimmed* milk have been created to fill this need. "Fast food," a quintessential American invention, ensures that eating will not interfere with more important things, such as making money.

The unfortunate habit of chewing gum—and disposing of the residue in the path of unwary pedestrians—is another American pastime that has found its way overseas. (One place that it has *not* reached is Singapore, where one can be caned for chewing gum in public!) America is also largely responsible for the plague of tasteless advertising and commercialism that has proliferated throughout the planet. She can also be blamed for the abysmal quality of television programs in general. I could continue, but you get the picture. In fairness, one can also fault the rest of the world for enthusiastically embracing many of America's bad habits.

America is a land of contrasts; it has incredible strengths and glaring weaknesses. In its foreign policy it can be generous and open hearted, and also mean-spirited and intolerant; sometimes reaching out the hand of friendship and succor, and at other times acting with a lack of sensitivity typical of the worst authoritarian regimes. Its attitude and policies towards the neighboring countries of Central and South America have been abysmal for the most part.

The image that other countries have of America does not reflect her true character. This distorted image, when compounded with America's frequent foreign policy blunders, has contributed to the poor reputation from which America suffers in many parts of the world. Unfortunately the world sees the worst side of America, rather than her true self.

The industrial might of America is a reflection of its capitalist system, and is something of which all Americans are proud. Although too much has been wasted on needless military expenditures, America has made important contributions to science and scientific research in many areas. Perhaps her most important contribution has been in the exploration of space. The sending of men to the moon; the creation and placing of the Hubble telescope in orbit; as well as the initiation of many interplanetary probes to the outer regions of the solar system, have all made enormous contributions to our understanding of the universe as well as to science in general. These are among the finest achievements of any nation in history, and America can be justly proud of them.

America's governmental institutions, established more than two hundred years ago, are now showing signs of old age, although they were originally ahead of their time. The founding fathers were admirers of Thomas Hobbes. But rather than create a Leviathan, they decided to have a democracy, but with certain limitations, so that the worst impulses of the common people would be restrained. They also created a system of "checks and balances" between the executive, legislative and judicial branches, so that abuses in one area could be corrected before they became too widespread.

The system has worked quite well up until now. But there are definite signs that the checks and balances are no longer working as intended; that the system is being corrupted by the undue influence of money and special interests. From Hobbes' point of view, this was probably to be expected. Rather than being the impersonal state that the Leviathan represented, the American government is exposed to all the frailties of human nature that Hobbes most feared. The president's policies tend to be based on opinion polls, rather than sound judgment. All this, together with the alliance of big business with the military, is turning America into not only an *illiberal* democracy, but also a dysfunctional one. The press, which was intended to keep watch on the government, has largely lost its independence through control by the corporate structure. It no longer protects the interests of the people.

In truth, America's very economic success has tended to increase the amount of corruption in many of her institutions, and corporate greed has had a harmful effect in many areas, especially politics and the environment. The excessive amount of violence in the society, due in no small measure to the inordinate number of guns in private hands, has also had a corrosive effect. "Violence is as American as cherry pie" is a saying that comes uncomfortably close to the truth.[15] The fact that America still retains the death penalty, despite convincing evidence that it cannot be administered fairly, and when almost all other countries have abolished it, only tends to reinforce this impression.

But things are not really as gloomy as they seem. Because of her position as a world leader, America's faults tend to be exposed for all to see, whereas the faults of others are mostly overlooked. America, like any other country, is a mixture of the good and the bad, the generous and the selfish, the farsighted and the myopic, those who believe in fairy tales and those who prefer logic to nonsense. So the struggle between those with a more progressive outlook and those who resist change is messy and noisy, and leaves the rest of the world wondering if the last superpower has lost its way. But if all were quiet and peaceful, then it really would be time to worry. For peace and quiet usually indicate a lack of vitality, and one cannot accuse America of a lack of vitality.

America is untidy because it's free. But of course freedom demands responsibility. It has taken far too long to erase the legacy of slavery, and more still needs to be done in the field of human rights. But a lot of progress *has* been made, in spite of the diehard resistance to change that is typical of human nature in such circumstances.

One danger is that the current war on terrorism will end up repeating the same mistakes of the cold war. Although it started positively, America now shows signs of compromising its basic principles, especially in the field of human rights. Innocent civilians find themselves caught in the crossfire, and as before, expediency is being placed ahead of sound policy, by courting and supporting unsavory regimes that brutalize their own people. America is seen as the defender of the indefensible. The search for terrorists among its own citizens, leading to the detention of suspects without due process of law, bodes ill for American democracy. Worse still, the torture of terrorist suspects, many of whom are completely innocent, can only be described as barbaric. This sort of thing undermines America more than any terrorist is capable of doing.

The ousting of Saddam Hussein was universally cheered, but lack of honesty concerning the reasons for the war, together with lack of foresight about what victory would bring, has left Iraq in virtual chaos and the United States with its credibility severely shaken. Far from winning friends for America, the Iraq adventure has increased anti-Americanism to a dangerous degree.[16]

American generosity, especially to its fallen enemies after World War II, has been the true measure of its spirit. Wherever disaster strikes in any corner of the world, America is in the vanguard of those who would lend aid and comfort to the afflicted. Unfortunately, as so often happens with the performance of good deeds, this generosity is not fully appreciated, and complaints are made that more should have been done.

America's most obvious fault is probably hubris. But this has been the failing of countless states and empires, ever since the days of Mesopotamia and Egypt. Much more serious, and much more insidious, is the military-industrial complex, whose vice-like grip on the political system seems almost impossible to break.

But we must be optimistic about the America. The truth is, we have no other choice. And the optimism would seem justified if we look around and see how many of the world's people would like nothing better than to come to the United States, with its freedom of opportunity and many other advantages. They may criticize her, but they come nonetheless. Even more important than America's economic and industrial strength is her diversity. And the constant flow of immigrants to her shores makes it likely that it will be maintained for many years to come.

The principal attraction of the United States for the oppressed minorities of the developing world is the "American dream" of rags to riches, achievable by anyone who is willing to work hard in the pursuit of his ambitions, however lofty. The American dream epitomizes the United States as the land of opportunity. It allows the extreme disparity of rich and poor to be tolerated by those at the bottom of the ladder, because they believe that it is within their power to rise to the top.

AFTERTHOUGHTS

When I think of earth's place in the cosmos, I sometimes recall the 1951 science fiction movie *The Earth Stood Still*, with Michael Rennie and Patricia Neal. It did not have all the fancy special effects that the latest ones have, but its message came across very well.

Rennie, the man from space, landed his space ship in Washington D.C., near the White House. He had been sent by a cosmic police force to warn the earthlings that their aggressive behavior and proclivity for war were endangering the stability of the galaxy. The wider space community had been watching their tendencies towards violence with increasing dismay. A cosmic force—a galactic "Leviathan" made up of highly intelligent robots—had been formed after all the space communities had agreed to disarm, and entrust all peacekeeping duties to it exclusively. Any disturbance of the peace by any one of them would be met with instant annihilation. The cancer of violence was to be quickly removed before it had a chance to spread.

Rennie was here to tell the inhabitants of earth that their behavior was getting close to the unacceptable level, and that they risked annihilation if they did not mend their ways. He was killed by the military before he could deliver his message. But his body was retrieved and revived by a robot from the space ship; and he was finally able to deliver his message before taking off again.

It does not look as if we will mend our ways without such a warning from outer space, and maybe not even then. But another kind of wake-up call may come when our degradation of the environment becomes so excessive that we will be in danger of causing our own extinction. This may finally be enough to knock some sense into us.

It's possible that an asteroid, or some other type of natural disaster could destroy our planet. But man could also destroy it. Our despoliation of the earth is already far advanced, so let's hope that our intelligence, which has made us supreme among our fellow creatures, will also save us from self-destruction. Actually, during the past fifty years or so, there has been a much greater awareness of our damage to the environment, and some small steps have been taken to remedy the situation. A lot more needs to be done, but at least the problems are no longer completely ignored. It would be a sad epitaph for the human race if the most successful species that ever lived, the crown jewel of nature's kingdom, were to be the one that destroyed all life on planet earth.

The human family, having spread out from its roots in Africa, now encompasses most of the earth. 10,000 generations have passed since the original dispersion began. Over the years the different parts of the human family have become estranged from one another, like any family whose members have left to seek fame and fortune elsewhere, and put down roots in foreign lands. So much time has passed that we do not recognize those we left so long ago as being part of the same family as ourselves. We do not think of them as our own kith and kin, but as foreigners and strangers.

As in any family, one tends to like some members better than others. But one can at least respect them as relatives and fellow human beings, who all belong to the same basic community that started out in Africa so many years ago. Of course the trouble is that our family has got too big for us to be familiar with all its members—and to remember their names and the dates of their birthdays. But we should nonetheless keep in mind that we are still one family, and that we now need to come together again for our mutual protection.

The purpose of this book was to try to make some sense out of the seemingly irrational behavior of the human species. That this was a tall order should be amply evident by now. I thought that by expanding the horizon, so that life on earth could be viewed in a wider context, some of the strange features of human society and its history would become more comprehensible. Towards this end I have tried to present a more realistic portrait of human nature, one that fits into the physical context in a more natural way. I just hope that this effort has succeeded in shining some light into a few dark corners. You may at least have learnt a little history along the way, or perhaps some new ways of looking at history. You may also have learnt a few things about science—perhaps some that you would have been happier not knowing.

The opening of the mind to new ideas and new knowledge is essential to a balanced view of the world. But new concepts must be critically examined as to their validity. Those who are willing to swallow every half-baked idea that comes along will continue to drift aimlessly on a sea of ignorance. How many of these hapless souls do we encounter every day? Our collective capacity to believe in rubbish is truly amazing.

During the past 150,000 years or so man has slowly emerged from his primitive origins, and his consciousness has gradually become more focused on the total context in which he exists. To understand the present it is necessary to investigate the past, and the disciplines of archaeology, anthropology and geology have paid increasing dividends since their rather haphazard beginnings in the nineteenth century. Not that ancient civilizations like the Greeks were not interested in their past. It was just that their science was too primitive for them to gain anything beyond a vague idea of what their ancient ancestors had been like. So any genuine attempt to examine the past was swallowed up in the world of myth.

Although the last few hundred years have seen an accelerating advance in all kinds of knowledge, this knowledge has mostly been confined to a comparative few. The vast majority of the world's population remains largely ignorant of these advances. Only the main features of the Copernican revolution, that the sun rather than the earth is at the center of the solar system, and that the planets move in ellipses, is now generally known. Most of Newton's laws, promulgated in the seventeenth century, are known only in a vague manner, if they are known at all. The law of gravity is one of the few pieces of this priceless legacy that is familiar to almost everyone.

Nevertheless, all is not as gloomy as one might think. The general level of knowledge about such things has begun to rise significantly in the past few decades, due to the increasing availability and more efficient dissemination of all kinds of information. Until relatively recently the average person was almost totally ignorant of the origin of the human species, having only been exposed to some kind of creation myth. But this cloud of ignorance is finally beginning to lift, as schools, museums and the various media are able to disseminate more and more accurate information regarding the latest discoveries. And even though many people are reluctant to abandon traditional beliefs, the light of reason is slowly dispersing the fog of superstition.

The process of enlightenment has been slow and difficult, and has really only just begun. In order to make any real progress we will have to raise the general standard of education to a considerable degree. Those with even a basic education are still in the minority, so until this situation is markedly improved, we cannot expect that things will progress very much from our present state. But something like the Internet has already had a positive effect on the general level of knowledge, even though it has the ability to spread rubbish as well.

It goes without saying that a rise in the level of education must be accompanied by a lowering of the incidence of poverty and disease. But, as with the environment, people are finally beginning to take notice of these things.

Unfortunately education does not guarantee civilized behavior. In recent times, many of those who have been responsible for major outbreaks of death and destruction have been reasonably well educated, or at least have attended schools or universities of good quality. Those in positions of leadership have been driven mainly by personal ambition and the lust for power. Their followers are more often motivated by some kind of ideology, regardless of their level of education.

Knowledge does not seem to cure unsociable behavior, but it does not necessarily encourage it either. Ideology of one kind or another seems to be the most common culprit. The recent plague of terrorism shows this quite clearly. Many of these people are fairly well educated. But an extreme ideology or religion can distort their thinking to such an extent that education becomes irrelevant as far as behavior is concerned. What knowledge they may have is poisoned by ideology.

Just as Gutenberg's press was instrumental in disseminating knowledge to a larger segment of the populace, so now the Internet and other modern media are spreading it to an even wider audience. And the knowledge that is becoming available is of far greater significance than in those early days. A *real* Age of Enlightenment may be just around the corner. The advance of both democracy and information technology means that more and more people are able to share in the knowledge and cultural advantages that were previously confined to a select few. Knowledge is no longer the luxury and privilege that it once was. The book of knowledge is now open to all who wish to read it. And this precious store of information is getting bigger all the time.

Every now and then one hears someone in the academic world say that we have just about reached the boundaries of human knowledge, especially scientific knowledge. They say that we know all the laws of physics that we need, and that any further discoveries will not turn up anything fundamentally new. I'm amazed when I hear this, for I think that we have barely begun to scratch the surface of scientific knowledge. The largest fraction of what is "knowable" is yet to be discovered. Like an iceberg, the unseen part below the surface is much larger than that which is visible. The accelerating pace of research into almost every conceivable field of study is bound to pay bigger and bigger dividends as time goes on. In biology alone the prospects are almost unlimited. We are now beginning to understand the incredible microscopic universe, which exists in all its wondrous complexity within our own bodies and in all matter. Undreamed of in previous millennia, it is now being revealed in all its staggering detail, as more and more powerful probes delve into the very essence and fiber of the material universe.

Is the fundamental building block of matter an infinitesimal one-dimensional vibrating string, whose overall length is of the order of 10^{-35} meters? It seems that this may very well be the case, if string theory lives up to the hopes of its proponents. But you can be sure of one thing. We will eventually know the answer to this question with reasonable certainty.

It's possible that the Theory of Everything is just a will-o'-the-wisp. Our desire to wrap things up in neat packages, and to explain everything precisely, may have propelled us down a path that has no end. From what was said about the laws of nature in chapter 14 (*Does God Know About Lie groups?*), it's conceivable that the laws of physics, which we have been working on so diligently, may not lead us to the totality of understanding that we seek. Even though our physical "laws" may become more and more insightful, and provide us with more and more information about our world, they may be fated to fall short of the ultimate goal, because, *au fond,* they are just descriptions of the phenomena that we observe through our senses. So our quest for the laws of nature may not lead to any final triumph.

As Astronomer John Barrow says of our present search:

> We are working towards some ultimate unified 'theory of everything,' which contains no superfluous elements: the ultimate in logical and conceptual economy. Laws now regarded as distinct and unrelated would be synthesized within a single unique description. This is what most physicists working on such fundamental questions believe. But it maybe that our undoing of the catalogue of Nature's laws will take us down a different road, which will lead us to the recognition that there is no theory of everything: no law at all.[1]

Although we have been able to find rules that make it seem as though nature behaves in an orderly manner, things may not actually be as orderly as we think. Barrow continues:

> Our confidence in the charming 'simplicity' of Nature may be misplaced. Nature may look simple only because we have unlocked so few of its secrets. As we dig deeper into the microscopic structure of matter and space-time, we may strike a seam of great complexity created by the interplay of an enormous number of factors. Such a situation might appear as lawless as pure chaos.[2]

But wherever the quest may lead us, it's clear that we are not in the evening of science, but rather at the dawn. As Brian Greene explains in *The Elegant Universe*, even if we do discover the final Theory of Everything, this does not mean the end of science. He says, "Its discovery would be a beginning not an end." In any case, what lies ahead will undoubtedly cause us much astonishment and wonder, and it will surely alter our understanding of reality once again.

Religion, like myth, provides us with answers to certain "unanswerable" questions. In *The Society of Mind,* Marvin Minsky lists some of these:

> What caused the universe and why?
> What is the purpose of life?
> How can you tell which beliefs are true?
> How can you tell what is good?

So the "authorities" are beholden to come up with answers to these troublesome questions. This is because the answers make people *feel* better about their relationship to the world of culture, just as the myths that Levi Strauss talked about eased the strain of man's accommodation to the restrictions and rules of community life. Minsky calls these questions logically *circular,* because all one can do is argue in circles—*unless*—one has some "authority" who can answer them definitively:

> All human cultures evolve institutions of law, religion, and philosophy, and these institutions both adopt specific answers to circular questions and establish authority-schemes to indoctrinate people with those beliefs. One might complain that such establishments substitute dogma for reason and truth. But in exchange, they spare whole populations from wasting time in fruitless reason loops. Minds can lead more productive lives when working on problems that can be solved.[3]

If you accept the answers to the unanswerable questions, not only will you feel better, but you will also be saved from a lifetime of trying to answer them. However, you may not enjoy complete peace of mind. Minsky continues:

> One can acquire certainty only by amputating inquiry.... To offer hospitality to paradox is like leaning towards a precipice. You can find out what it is like by falling in, but you may not be able to fall out again. Once contradiction

finds a home, few minds can spurn the sense-destroying force of slogans such as "all is one."[4]

So once you have accepted the answers to the unanswerable questions, there's no telling what other kinds of rubbish you may swallow. In other words, your reasoning powers may become seriously impaired.

Our society is based on assumptions about human nature that are nothing more than fantasy. You might say that we live by a series of convenient fictions. Other animals appear to have a much more realistic idea about their place in the world, but then their imagination is not so highly developed as ours. There is no nonsense about it, no pretense. With the human being, almost *everything* is pretense. But at least the great scientific discoveries are not pretense. However, some of these discoveries make a lot of people uneasy, because they tend to call into question the tenets of their fantasy world. When this happens, they try to discredit science! They *pretend* that these things just aren't so. But the structure of belief becomes more and more difficult to sustain, as advances in knowledge and scientific discoveries continue to erode it. Its foundations are constantly being undermined. Like the little Dutch boy with his finger in the dyke, the believers are trying to hold back the ever-rising flood of knowledge, which is threatening to inundate their cozy world of certainties.

As an example of this refusal to accept reality, a recent survey taken in the United States found that over 60% of respondents believed in creationism, while less than 40% accepted the theory of evolution! This is both tragic and ironic, because those who reject evolution on religious grounds are blissfully unaware that religion and evolution are intimately connected!

Looking on the brighter side. In spite of all the violence that is still with us, there are signs that the curse of war is finally beginning to lose its grip. All the mighty empires of the past have crumbled to dust. (Only the American neo-colonial global empire remains, which becomes more unpopular by the minute, even in America.) Colonialism is seen as being responsible for endless conflict among nations. Modern warfare, following the dictates of Clausewitz, has been tried and found wanting. It only led to militarism, which in turn led to suffering and destruction on a horrendous scale—all to no purpose.

So war, in both its holy and unholy varieties, seems to have just about run its course. It's still possible that we *could* see a titanic struggle of "civilizations," one that Samuel Huntington warns us about, such as that between China and the

West. But this looks more and more unlikely as China rapidly joins the global network of trade, and its communist system simply withers away.

The principle that "might makes right" is gradually losing its hold on the human psyche. Now the chief danger is from the fanatic or terrorist, armed with some terrible weapon of mass destruction. The civilized nations of the world will have to come together to meet this menace. And in the process the international institutions may very well become strengthened as never before. The genie of the atomic bomb is out of the bottle and this means that mankind must shed its irresponsible past and behave in a more mature manner. It can be argued, with some merit, that the threat of nuclear catastrophe has actually helped to prevent war—for example between Russia and the United States during the cold war. But this is a dangerous tightrope on which to walk, so some way of controlling these weapons will have to be found. Something like Hobbes' global Leviathan will ultimately be necessary.

But things do seem to be moving in the right direction. Who would have dreamt, fifty years ago, that Europe, having been convulsed by the two most destructive wars in history, would have formed a community of economic and political partnership by the end of the twentieth century? This is a tremendous step forward, and marks significant progress in the transition from confrontation to cooperation. Although the parliament in Brussels falls far short of Hobbes' idea of the Leviathan, these nations will surely never again go to war with one another, whereas for centuries war, or preparation for war, was the normal state of affairs. Just as the Thirty Years War convinced Europe that religious wars must be avoided, so the Second World War finally convinced her that *all* wars should be avoided. And this kind of thing is likely to spread to other parts of the world. So although there is much work still to be done, the general trend seems to be moving in the right direction. Once the true nature of the military-industrial complex is recognized—that it actually tends to foster violence and war rather than prevent it—we may indeed begin to see a new dawn.

As human society has become more complex, the gap between the haves and the have-nots has become wider. So we must also find some way of reversing this trend. But as far as culture is concerned, it looks as if we have passed the point of no return, and excepting a nuclear holocaust or some other such catastrophe, civilization is not likely to collapse any time soon. This is a good thing, because we have now got to the stage where we cannot do without it. Even though our true nature rebels against the world of culture, we cannot return to our former state, we must go forward, forward to a better and more enlightened future.

As Rodney Brooks puts it in *Flesh and Machines:*

> The world is changing, and our humanity within our world is changing with it. The forces of change are irresistible, as they have been for the last five hundred years. Wishing they were not so will do us no more good than such wishing has done in past generations.
>
> The future is best approached with an open mind, with an understanding of our deeply held prejudices, and with a willingness to reexamine the nature of our humanity. Questions about it are going to be forced on us. Blind allegiance to deeply held beliefs will serve us no better than ignorant whining has in the past.[5]

How can we set ourselves free so that we can enjoy both our animal nature and the fruits of our cultural achievements? Our basic nature may have to be changed somewhat, in order to shed the bestial tendencies of our primordial past. Selfishness was necessary for survival in those pre-cultural times; now we have to learn to be unselfish in order to survive in a new world of our own making. To do this we must somehow defeat the scourge of war, and learn to live with each other as equals. Our superior intelligence must be used to free us from the bondage of our primitive and violent past. Then we can begin to build a world that has *real* values, which are accepted and respected by all.

NOTES AND REFERENCES

PART I

1
CULTURAL ORIGINS

1. For an account of the evolution of the universe see Rees, *Just Six Numbers,* Ch. 4.

2. "Complexity" is described by Stuart Kauffman in *At Home in the Universe.* For a discussion of the drawbacks to this approach see John Horgan's article, *From Complexity to Perplexity,* in Scientific American, June 1995. Kauffman has another book called *Investigations,* in which he looks at autonomous systems and other ideas in relation to the origin of life. He has new ways of looking at things like biospheres and their interaction with the life forms within them.

3. For further information about this see Wright, *Nonzero,* p. 244.

4. A recent book by Evelyn Keller, *Making Sense of Life,* examines both the definition of life and the various ways that scientists go about modeling life forms and their development. Interestingly enough, the question of what life is has been stimulated by the attempt to produce it artificially. Claus Emmeche's *The Garden in the Machine* (pp. 33-46) examines the question of whether a-life really is life. He lists five different definitions of life and examines how much a-life resembles the real thing and how it differs from it. Then there is Erwin Schrödinger's classic *What is Life?* Another approach is taken by Frank Vertosick in his fascinating book, *The Genius Within,* which considers life as a network.

5. McFadden, *Quantum Evolution,* p. 16.

6. For an excellent account of just how life has developed during the past four billion years, Richard Fortey's book *Life* is highly recommended.

7. This story is told by Walter Alvarez, one of the scientists who discovered evidence of the impact, in *T.rex and the Crater of Doom*.

8. See Wells, *The Journey of Man,* p. 119

9. See ibid., p. 123.

10. Fortey, *Life,* p. 307.

11. See articles by Nicholas Wade in the *New York Times*, Science Section, 05/02/00 and 11/12/02. The term "Mitochondrial Eve," although frequently used, is really a misnomer. As Richard Fortey explains in *Life*, p. 306, the name is misleading, for it connotes descent from a single "parent," as in the biblical account. It would be more accurate to say that "Eve's" genes survived through several thousand generations, via the female line, by a succession of lucky chances. There must have been many other Eves, but their lines died out through lack of female progeny. There were, successively, many "Adams." The recent book, *The Journey of Man,* by the geneticist Spencer Wells, explains just how this genealogy has been traced throughout the different continents.

12. Premack, *Original Intelligence,* p. 176. This book is highly informative, and looks at the difference in mental capacity between chimpanzees and humans.

13. See McNeill & McNeill, *The Human Web,* pp. 22-3.

14. Ibid., p. 39

15. Patterson, *Archaeology, The Evolution of Ancient Societies,* p. 148.

16. Finegan, *Archaeological History of the Ancient Middle East,* p. 39.

17. Recent archaeological finds at Gebel Tjauti, near Luxor, indicate that the first writing may actually have occurred in Egypt, rather than in Mesopotamia. See article in the *New York Times* Science Section by John Noble Wilford, 04/16/02.

18. See Wheeler, *Civilizations of the Indus Valley and Beyond,* Ch. 2.

19. Yap & Cotterell, *The Early Civilization of China*, p. 22.

20. For details see Gernet, *A History of Chinese Civilization*, pp. 117-169.

21. Information taken from Patterson, *Archaeology*, Ch. 15.

22. The cruelty of the Mayans is featured in an article by Erik Eckholm in the New York Times, (Science), 05/13/86. See also Schele & Freidel, *A Forest of Kings*.

23. See Patterson, *Archaeology*, Ch. 16.

24. Thomson, *The White Rock*, p. 85.

25. The fascinating story of the conquest of the Incas, achieved by Pizarro and his band of conquistadors, including his two brothers and a half brother, is told by William Prescott in *The Conquest of Peru*.

26. The Inca road system was designed for the llama, which likes heights. Roads went straight up the mountainsides, rather than zigzagging back and forth. Tribes that had been conquered by the Incas were forced to maintain the roads, but were not permitted to use them. For details, and other fascinating facts about the Incas, see Thomson, *The White Rock*.

27. According to Diamond, *Guns, Germs, and Steel*, p.39: "The earliest definite signs of that leap came from East African sites with standardized stone tools and the first preserved jewelry (ostrich-shell beads). Similar developments soon appear in the Near East and in southeastern Europe, then (some 40,000 years ago) in southwestern Europe, where abundant artifacts are associated with fully modern skeletons of people termed Cro-Magnons." This points to a major change in human behavior, which may have been caused by subtle DNA changes. But this only had to do with the *wiring* of the brain; the "big brain" had been in existence for millions of years.

28. The conquest of the Aztecs by the Spanish, the death of their king, Montezuma, and the battle for Tenochtitlan, are all recorded by one of the conquistadors, Bernal Diaz, in *The Conquest of New Spain*.

29. McNeill & McNeill, *The Human Web*, p. 115.

30. Lissner, *The Living Past*, p. 172.

2
RITUALS OF SACRIFICE

1. Just how the brain creates these worlds is now beginning to be understood by neuroscientists. For the latest thinking on this, see *Synaptic Self,* by Joseph LeDoux.

2. When I refer to God as "he" I am merely following convention. Obviously it makes no sense to ascribe a sex to God, as if the entity "God" were a *person.* The only sort of God that makes any sense is some kind of motivating force, which was (presumably) in existence before the big bang. The idea that God can think like we do makes no sense at all.

3. There are other explanations for these kinds of paranormal phenomena. One theory, which involves holograms, has been pioneered by two physicists: David Brohm and Karl Pribram. This is explained in Michael Talbot's intriguing 1991 book, *The Holographic Universe.* It ties into the latest research being done by the particle physicists, who are trying to reconcile gravity with quantum mechanics. The work involves something called the *holographic principle* (see Smolin, *Three Roads to Quantum Gravity*). This has many similarities to the ideas contained in the *Holographic Universe.*

4. Minsky, *The Society of Mind,* p. 314.

5. Ferm, *Living Schools of Religion,* p.9

6. Kaufmann, *The Portable Nietzsche (Thus Spoke Zarathustra),* p. 52.

7. Ehrenreich, *Blood Rites,* p. 83.

8. Ibid., p. 73.

9. Both the Neanderthals and Homo erectus moved out of Africa long before modern man. But their limited intellectual capacity may have made them unable to survive the severe climatic conditions of the last ice age. Homo sapiens, however, was able to overcome such difficulties due to his superior adaptive ability.

10. Darwin, *The Descent of Man,* p. 150.

11. See Levi-Strauss, *The Savage Mind*, pp. 25-30.

12. Hedges, *War is a Force That Gives Us Meaning*, p. 23.

13. Gernet, *A History of Chinese Civilization*, p. 45.

14. See Freud, *Moses and Monotheism*.

15. The Greeks were probably the first to produce real literature in any culture.

16. Ferm, *Living Schools of Religion*, p. 68.

17. Yap & Cotterell, *The Early Civilization of China*, p. 128.

18. Strictly speaking, only the indigenous part of Hinduism was native to the Indian sub-continent. The Aryans brought the major portion when they invaded c.1500 B.C. It is not known where the Aryans originally came from, although their language belongs to the Indo-European language group. Their invasion of India probably originated in Russia or Turkistan. The indigenous population of India goes back more than 50,000 years, when the first migrants out of Africa took the coastal route to India and beyond. Others followed much later via Afghanistan. See Wells, *The Journey of Man*.

19. See Shermer, *The Science of Good and Evil*, p. 160.

20. According to Thomas Cleary, the translator of *The Art of War*, who wrote a lengthy introduction, which explained how Taoist thought is incorporated into Tzu's classic.

21. From the introduction to Sun Tzu's *The Art of War*, p. 13.

22. Braudel, *A History of Civilizations*, p. 184.

23. Levi-Strauss, *The Savage Mind*, p.16.

3
EMPIRE AND WAR

1. Two of the best references for this very important subject are: Barbara Ehrenreich's *Blood Rites* and John Keegan's *A History of Warfare*. Both of

these works examine the origins of war going back to the earliest human societies.

2. Hedges, *War is a Force That Gives Us Meaning,* p. 73.

3. Finegan, *Archaeological History of the Ancient Middle East,* p. 41.

4. McNeill, *The Pursuit of Power,* p. 3.

5. Wright, *Nonzero,* p. 4.

6. The fire temples of the Persians were mysterious structures, where an "eternal flame" dedicated to the fire god was kept lighted. But little is known of any ceremonies conducted in these temples.

7. McNeill, *The Pursuit of Power,* p. 9.

8. Ibid., p. 18.

9. Tarn, *Alexander the Great,* p.16.

10. See Bury, *A History of Greece,* p. 744.

11. Ibid., pp. 745.

12. Tarn, *Alexander the Great,* p. 70.

13. Ibid., p. 25

14. Kaplan, *Warrior Politics,* p. 119. The quote within the quote is from *The Iliad* [translated by Robert Dagles (New York: Penguin, 1990)], Book 19, lines 254-65.

15. Kepel, *Jihad,* p. 43.

16. Lewis, *What Went Wrong,* p. 84.

17. Bridge, *The Crusades,* p. 44.

18. Ibid. p. 45.

19. The cultural conflict between Islam and the West is described in detail in Bernard Lewis' book, *What Went Wrong?*

20. Lynn, *Battle,* p. 85.

21. Churchill, *A History of the English Speaking Peoples* (vol. I), p. 328.

22. See Seward, *The Hundred Years War,* p. 213.

23. McNeill, *The Pursuit of Power,* p. 16.

24. Ibid., p. 11.

25. Gernet, *A History of Chinese Civilization,* p. 351.

26. Yap & Cotterell, *The Early Civilization of China,* p. 13.

27. Morton, *Japan, Its History and Culture,* p. 58.

28. Buruma, *Inventing Japan,* p. 179.

29. Morton, *Japan, Its History and Culture,* p.62.

30. Ibid., p. 63.

31. Diamond, *Guns, Germs, and Steel,* p. 257.

32. A fine account of how the Emperor was restored to power after Perry's visit can be found in Ian Buruma's excellent little book, *Inventing Japan: 1853-1964.*

4
ROOTS OF WESTERN CULTURE

1. Bury, *A History of Greece,* p. 80.

2. For the Greek and Roman idea of community, see McNeill & McNeill, p. 68-78.

3. See Russell, *The History of Western Philosophy,* p. 94.

4. Lee Harris, in his book *Civilization and Its Enemies,* has some interesting things to say about Sparta. He says that Sparta represented the institutionalization of the "boy's gang." In our Western society, youth gangs are a form

of association in competition with the family, the traditional means of association. But the gang tends to break up when its members get married and the family reasserts itself. In the case of Sparta, the gang was perpetuated as a *substitute* for the family! "The system of Sparta was designed to keep the ruthlessness of the gang available to be used against its enemies, while controlling it in such a way that it would pose no danger to the society itself. The mechanism by which this was done was the invention of the team." Ibid., p. 87.

5.   Russell, *The History of Western Philosophy*, p. 94.

6.   Cary, *A History of the Greek World, 323 to 146 B.C.*, p. xvi.

7.   The Eastern Empire really had three major cities: Constantinople, Antioch and Alexandria. This reflected the cultural diversity of the eastern Mediterranean, and accounts in some measure for the inability of the East to withstand the inroads of the Moslems and the Turks in later years. Constantinople, in its position astride the dividing line between Europe and Asia, was unable to exert the necessary central control, which was required in order to hold such a diverse domain together.

8.   The history regarding the Roman Republic and founding of the Empire is taken from Hadas, *Imperial Rome*, Ch. 2.

9.   Gibbon, *The Decline and Fall of the Roman Empire*, p. 2.

10. Machiavelli, *The Prince* (XIX), p. 62.

11. Ibid.

12. McNeill, *The Pursuit of Power*, p. 70.

13. Ibid. p. 66.

14. McEvedy, *The Penguin Atlas of Medieval History*, p. 80.

15. Kinross, *The Ottoman Centuries*, p. 191.

16. Ibid., p. 268.

5
RELIGION AND WAR

1. Cipolla, *Guns, Sails and Empires,* p. 39.

2. McNeill, *The Pursuit of Power,* p. 99.

3. Cipolla, *Guns, Sails and Empires,* p. 107.

4. Ibid., p. 108.

5. Ibid., p. 114.

6. Information about the Italian testing ground can be found in McNeill, *The Pursuit of Power,* Ch. 3.

7. Cipolla, *Guns, Sails and Empires,* p. 74.

8. McNeill, *The Pursuit of Power,* p. 117.

9. In *A History of Warfare,* (p.74), the military historian John Keegan asserts that "it was the urge to extend the frontiers of the House of Submission, rather than a base material motive, that drove them to their extraordinary exploits." But as we saw in chapter 3, it was a mixture of motives, both religious and secular, which made the Moslem armies so formidable. And besides, there was no proscription against the accumulation of riches in Islam as there was with Christianity, since Mohammed was a merchant and had no objection to the acquisition of worldly goods. The idea of brotherhood, which Islam imparted, created cohesion and inspiration for the Moslem armies.

10. New Columbia Encyclopedia, p. 1343.

11. Anthony Marx, in his book *Faith in Nation: Exclusionary origins of Nationalism,* maintains that religion has been used to foster nationalism, especially in European states such as Spain, France and England. The Protestant Reformation created the opportunity to define nationality in terms of religion, and this had the effect of consolidating the power of the state. However, this type of nationalism is hardly the all-inclusive kind that sprung from the French Revolution.

12. Hedges, *War is a Force That Gives Us Meaning*, p. 21.

13. Wolpert, *A New History of India*, p. 72.

14. Ibid., p. 89. It is rumored that the horse sacrifice is still practiced in certain areas. "The *ashva medha* was performed to enhance a raja's domain and further prove his prowess. A great white stallion was turned loose and left to wander for a year, followed by a troop of royal horsemen, who staked their king's claim to all the territory within boundaries surveyed by his stallion. At year's end the horse was driven home; first it was ritually mated with the king's wives, then killed and carved into quarters, symbolizing his universality and that of his monarch." Ibid. p. 38.

15. Ibid., p. 90.

16. Ibid., p. 92.

17. Ibid., p. 98.

18. Ibid., p. 109.

6
TRADING EMPIRES AND THE RISE OF NATIONALISM

1. Quoted in Meyer, *The Dust of Empire*, p. 32.

2. See McNeill & McNeill, *The Human Web*, pp. 82-88.

3. Berend, *History Derailed*, p. 240.

4. The rise of the banking system in Europe and how it allowed monarchs to maintain their armies is explained in McNeill, *The Pursuit of Power*, pp. 102-116.

5. Wolpert, *A New History of India*, p. 144.

6. The Fronde was a series of outbreaks of civil unrest, starting in 1648 and continuing for about five years, which occurred during the minority of king Louis XIV. They were caused by the financial exactions of cardinals Riche-

lieu and Mazarin, and also because of efforts by the Parliament of Paris to limit the power of the monarchy. These disturbances had a marked effect on the young king and impressed upon him the necessity to strengthen the power of the military forces against any further challenges to his authority.

7. McNeill, *The Pursuit of Power*, p. 167.

8. Lynn, *Battle*, p. 33. Lynn says that war and the soldiers that fought it were mostly on the northern periphery, while the bureaucracy occupied the center of government and culture. "Highest status belonged not to a violent military elite but to a scholarly bureaucratic elite."

9. McNeill, *The Pursuit of Power*, p. 152.

10. McEvedy, *The Penguin Atlas of Modern History*, p. 64.

11. Tocqueville, *The Old Regime and the French Revolution*, p. 98.

12. Ibid. p. 147

13. Lynn, *Battle*, p. 207.

14. Ehreinreich, *Blood Rites*, p. 194.

15. Berlin, *The Crooked Timber of Humanity*, p. 176.

16. Buruma, *Inventing Japan*, p. 52.

17. Ibid.

18. A good discussion of nationalism, and how it changed from the idea of brotherhood to a narrower association of ethnic identity, or national destiny, can be found in Berend, *History Derailed*, pp. 114-133, also in chapter 6.

19. Certain colonies of insects, such as ants or bees, do exhibit many of the features of an organism. But they are at best borderline cases, and cannot really be considered as organisms in the conventional sense. Frank Vertosick, in his book *The Genius Within*, considers these as super-organisms, and even the entire biosphere can be treated in the same way—as in James Lovelock's Gaia hypothesis. Vertosick maintains that these super-organisms can be considered as possessing life and also intelligence, because of the way they func-

tion as networks that are capable of learning. He sees life and intelligence as basically synonymous.

20. Braudel, *A History of Civilizations*, p. 323.

21. See Ehrenreich, *Blood Rites*, p. 203.

7
THE INDUSTRIALIZATION OF VIOLENCE

1. The manufacture of cotton, in combination with Britain's leadership in shipping, soon produced a monopoly of the cotton trade worldwide. The profits from this, and they were huge, allowed Britain to expand the range and quality of the goods that she produced for the world market. After cotton, iron and steel products became the most successful of Britain's manufactured goods in the nineteenth century. For more about this see Braudel, *A History of Civilizations*, pp. 381-3.

2. Wolpert, *A New History of India*, p. 188.

3. Roy, *An Ordinary Person's Guide to Empire*, p.108.

4. See Cannadine, *Ornamentalism*, p. 44.

5. Ibid., p. 48.

6. A good description of the "sins of partition" is given in Karl Meyer's *The Dust of Empire*, chapter 3. See also Roy, *An Ordinary Person's Guide to Empire*, for a description of the present state of India's democracy.

7. McNeill, *The Pursuit of Power*, p. 220

8. The second Opium War (1856-1860), and the Crimean War were other early instances of the use of photography. But since only long exposures were possible, no direct pictures of the action could be taken.

9. See Bobbitt, *The Heel of Achilles*, p. 539.

10. Barraclough, *The Origins of Modern Germany*, p. 410.

11. Fisher, *A History of Europe*, p. 1007.

12. Ibid., p. 1012.

13. Cobban, *A History of Modern France, Vol 2,* p. 134.

14. Morton, *Japan,* p. 154.

15. Ibid., p. 158.

16. Emperor Hirohito bore ultimate responsibility for the conduct of the Japanese military, and his failure to restrain them places the blame for Japan's aggressions squarely upon him. For political reasons, the United States did not try the Emperor for war crimes. But many, even in Japan, knew that he was indeed guilty. See Daikichi Irokawa, *The Age of Hirohito,* pp. 80-7.

17. McNeill, *The Pursuit of Power,* p. 275.

8
THE WINDS OF WAR

1. Fisher, *A History of Europe,* p. 1043.

2. Ibid., p. 1044.

3. Zakaria, *The Future of Freedom,* p. 47.

4. Fisher, *A History of Europe,* p. 1048.

5. It was called the February Revolution because it occurred in February according to the old Russian calendar. But it actually took place in March according to the Western calendar.

6. Barraclough, *The Origins of Modern Germany,* p. 423.

7. Fisher, *A History of Europe,* p. 1138.

8. See McNeill and McNeill, *The Human Web,* pp. 288-294.

9. Morton, *Japan,* p. 190.

10. For a detailed description of this epic battle, the terrible conditions under which it was fought, and the appalling cost in human lives, see Beevor, *Stalingrad*.

11. The final battles of World War II, culminating in the taking of Berlin by the Red Army, together with the frightful suffering inflicted on the civilian populations of East Prussia, Poland and East Germany are described in Antony Beevor's other book about the war, *Berlin, The Downfall 1945*.

12. See Overy, *Russia's War*, which describes the renewal of the purges by Stalin and the travail of an exhausted Russian people who were afflicted with yet more suffering and deprivation.

13. See Braudel, *A History of Civilizations*, p. 501.

14. During the twentieth century, far more civilians were killed than military personnel—62 million civilians and 43 million military.

15. The important book by W. G. Sebald, *On the Natural History of Destruction*, describes the bombing of German cities during World War II. It examines both the reasons for the bombing and its effect on the German people.

16. See article by Olivier Roy in the *New York Times* op-ed page, 07/22/05.

17. Harris, *Civilization and Its Enemies*, p.13.

PART II

PRELIMINARY THOUGHTS

1. Keegan, *A History of Warfare*, p. 354.

2. Dawkins explains just what he means by a gene: "I am using the word gene to mean a genetic unit that is small enough to last for a large number of generations and to be distributed around in the form of many copies.... What I am doing is emphasizing the potential near-immortality of a gene, in the form of copies, as its defining property. To define a gene as a single cistron is good for some purposes, but for the purposes of evolutionary theory it needs to be enlarged. The extent of the enlargement is determined by the purpose

of the definition. We want to find the practical unit of natural selection. To do this we begin by identifying the properties that a successful unit of natural selection must have...these are longevity, fecundity, and copying-fidelity. We then define a 'gene' as the largest entity which, at least potentially, has these properties." *The Selfish Gene*, p. 33.

3. Premack, *Original Intelligence,* p. 235.

4. Kaufman, *The Portable Nietzsche,* p. 568.

9
SCIENTIFIC MILESTONES

1. Stillwell, *Mathematics and Its History,* p. 3.

2. Anglin & Lambek, *The Heritage of Thales,* p. 29.

3. See Stillwell, *Mathematics and Its History,* p. 9.

4. A good text explaining the basic physics and mathematics of Newton's world is: Frautschi, Olenick, Apostol and Goodstein, *The Mechanical Universe.*

5. Dennet, *Darwin's Dangerous Idea,* p. 42.

6. Edelman, *Bright Air, Brilliant Fire,* p. 46.

7. One of the major scientific breakthroughs of the twentieth century is described in James Watson's *The Double Helix.* Watson relates the story behind this major discovery, and the personalities involved, in his own inimitable style.

8. Darwin, *The Origin of Species,* p. 393.

9. Darwin, *The Descent of Man,* p. 151.

10. For those with some background in group theory a good text is D. H. Sattinger & O. L. Weaver, *Lie Groups and Algebras with Applications to Physics, Geometry, and Mechanics.*

11. For an informative text, giving an account of the various attempts to assess the age of the earth, and on geology in general see Cloud, *Oasis in Space.*

12. Greene, *The Elegant Universe,* p. 87. This book gives a solid introduction for someone trying to get a grasp of the basics of superstring theory. The weird and wonderful world of warped multi-dimensional space loses a lot of its fearsome aura in this elegant exposition.

13. This refers to Max Planck's solution to the so-called Ultra-violet Catastrophe. The classical Rayleigh-Jeans law for radiation energy emitted from an "ideal black body" agreed with observations at low frequencies, but contrary to observation, became infinite at high frequencies. Planck solved the problem by postulating that the energy corresponding to each frequency v must be an integer times the quantity hv, where h is Planck's constant. This meant that only a limited number of energy states could exist at a given frequency, and the higher the frequency the lower the number of such states. Energy was thus seen to come in little discrete packets. By this insightful proposal Planck had given birth to quantum mechanics.

14. See Feynman, *QED.* This book explains the brilliant concept of Quantum Electrodynamics in layman's terms, as only Feynman could.

15. See Glashow, *Interactions.* This book strikes a nice balance between the overly technical and the totally non-technical. Another excellent book about the Standard Model is Barnett, Mühry & Quinn, *The Charm of Strange Quarks.*

16. Watson, *The Double Helix,* p. 202.

17. Ibid. pp. 194-196.

18. See Barabási, *Linked,* p. 180-96.

19. The degree to which the DNA code is predetermined by the structure of the various molecules involved—amino acids, bases, etc.—is difficult to estimate. But it seems extremely unlikely that the same code would be used if life originated more than once. The chances for this are discussed in Christian de Duve, *Vital Dust,* pp. 71-73.

20. In *The Origin of Species,* Darwin goes into a detailed discussion, taking up several chapters, of how varieties eventually lead to new species. He gives numerous examples to illustrate his contention that no outside intervention is necessary to account for the origin and distribution of the different species.

21. See Nagel & Newman, Gödel's Proof. This gives the essential structure of the proof without too much mathematical detail.

22. This relation between unemployment and inflation was used by the International Monetary Fund (IMF). See Stiglitz, *Globalization and Its Discontents*, p. 34.

23. There are now some more realistic economic models available. Joseph Stiglitz, a professor of Economics at Columbia University, received the 2001 Nobel Prize for "analysis of markets with asymmetric information." Stiglitz explained that: "Market economics are characterized by a high degree of imperfections. Older models assumed perfect information, but even small degrees of information imperfections can have large economic consequences. Our models took into account asymmetries of information, which is another way of saying, 'Some people know more than others.'" This sounds like real progress.

24. The theory of networks is being used to model quite a few other things besides the economy. These include society itself, the Internet and the living cell. For details see *Links: The New Science of Networks*, by Albert-László Barabási.

25. In a similar manner, the particle physicists talk about "point particles," which occupy no space. This causes problems with forces that are inversely proportional to distance, because, as the distance tends to zero, the force becomes infinite. But clearly, any elementary particle, an electron for instance, must have a definite size, however small. Similar problems with infinities arise in field theories, such as Feynman's QED.

26. There are an infinite number of points on a mathematical line of finite length, because the line is "continuous," which means that it can be divided up indefinitely. In the real world one cannot go on dividing up things ad infinitum. And it turns out that this is true of *space* as well. Physicists working on the reconciliation of quantum mechanics and gravity have found, by studying the theory of black holes, that space itself is actually discrete, rather than continuous, although the "pieces" are extremely small. In the old Newtonian world, space and time were continuous. But in our new quantum

world, they are discrete. For further details see Smolin, *Three Roads to Quantum Gravity.*

Stephen Wolfram, in his book, *A New Kind of Science* (chapter 9), also discusses this question of the continuum. He takes space to be the fundamental entity, which actually consists of a network of nodes. The position of the nodes is unimportant. What is important is how they are connected to other nodes. This is actually similar to Roger Penrose's *Twistor* theory.

27. Number theory is one of the oldest branches of mathematics. What we are discussing here is what's called *The Theory of Algebraic Integers,* pioneered by Richard Dedekind in a book of that title in 1877. A good introduction to number theory in general is Georges Andrews' *Number Theory.*

10
THE PHYSICAL CONTEXT

1. For more details see Weinberg, *The First Three Minutes.*

2. W. & K. Tucker, *The Dark Matter,* p. 22.

3. A good explanation of the dark energy, or quantum fluctuations, can be found in Smolin, *Three Roads to Quantum Gravity,* p. 83. He relates this phenomenon to Heisenberg's uncertainty principle, and also to the famous Einstein-Podolsky-Rosen (EPR) experiment. The latter concerns the correlation of two photons that have been created together, and travel in opposite directions. When one is measured, the properties of the other are immediately determined, even before it is measured, no matter how far the photons have moved apart. This experiment has actually been performed and the results are as predicted. It means that information, seemingly inaccessible to the second photon, is actually communicated to it because their quantum states are correlated. Believe it or not, this is all related to the dark energy, but only Smolin can explain it properly.

4. Barrow, *The World Within the World,* p. 206

5. For further thoughts along these lines, see for example Strong, *Flight to the Stars.* Another informative book on this subject is Stuart Clark's *Life on Other Worlds and How to Find It.*

6. A fine account of just how these elements and molecules probably came together to produce life can be found in *Vital Dust,* by Christian de Duve. The role that quantum mechanics played in this process is examined by JohnJoe McFadden in *Quantum Evolution.*

7. Fortey, *Life,* p. 36.

8. The details behind this idea of complexity can be found in Kauffman, *At Home in the Universe.*

9. The Anthropic Principle states that since we are here, and intelligent life *has* arisen, one need not argue about the probability of life occurring, because it *did* occur, otherwise we would not be here. The emergence of life may have been a bizarre accident and may never have happened anywhere else, even in another universe, but this does not matter, because the conditions in our universe *did* produce it. Another way of looking at the Anthropic Principle is that the whole cosmos was created just so that man could eventually emerge and perceive it. However, if life were found elsewhere in the universe this version of the Anthropic Principle would seem to fall apart. The Anthropic Principle comes in several flavors (like the quarks!). But the above description gives a rough idea of what it's about. John Barrow objects to it because: "The Anthropic Principle takes a parochial view of life, and assumes that all life-forms in the Universe resemble ours." Also: "The Anthropic Principle is not testable, therefore it is not scientific. It is a quasi-religious principle"—*The World Within the World* (p. 369). Though much discussed in scholarly circles, the Anthropic Principle seems to be of little scientific or philosophical value.

10. de Duve, *Vital Dust,* p. 292.

11. Ibid., p. 297.

12. The Neanderthals were not the only hominids to become extinct. There was also Homo Erectus, or Peking man. But we do not know much about their level of culture, or their precise relationship to modern humans.

13. Ornstein, *The Evolution of Consciousness,* p. 56.

14. Ridley, *Genome,* p. 116.

15. Just how this process takes place, and why it is more beneficial during adolescence is discussed by Jeffrey Satinover in *The Quantum Brain,* Ch. 5. As the title suggests, this book also explores the role of quantum mechanics in the brain. But many other interesting topics relating to brain function, such as the mechanics of memory, are also covered.

16. Darwin, *The Descent of Man,* p. 8.

17. See David & Ann Premack, *Original Intelligence,* p. 4.

18. Darwin, *The Descent of Man,* p. 90.

19. Ibid., p. 130.

20. The ability to construct complex language is a distinctly human trait. The part of the brain that controls language is missing in man's nearest relative, the chimpanzee. The linguist Noam Chomsky discovered in the 1950's that the grammatical structures of all human languages are similar, and that we have an innate ability to learn languages—which becomes weaker as we grow older. Thus, although chimpanzees can be taught a few elements of language, they can never reach the proficiency of a human being. According to Gerald Edelman (*Bright Air, Brilliant Fire,* pp. 126-31), there are "no innate rules for a universal grammar" so this ability is not genetic. But it is not present in other animals. The "language instinct" must have developed after the human line branched off from that of the chimpanzees about seven million years ago. For further details see Ridley, *Genome,* pp. 92-106.

21. Dennett, *Consciousness Explained,* p. 29.

22. Ibid., p. 35.

23. Schrödinger, *What is Life,* p. 99.

24. A good "layman's guide" to this whole question of mind, consciousness and memory can be found in Gerald Edelman's *Bright Air, Brilliant Fire.*

25. Daniel Dennett, *Consciousness Explained,* p. 34.

26. McFadden, *Quantum Evolution,* p. 286.

27. Quantum events are based on probability rather than determinism, but they occur on the micro-scale of the quantum world. On the ordinary scale of our everyday world things are deterministic.

28. Ibid., p. 265. There is also a growing belief that adaptive mutations may perhaps be caused by the effects of quantum mechanical measurement, or decoherence. McFadden cites several scientific papers that claim this to be a fact.

29. Seigfried, *The Bit and the Pendulum*, p. 120. This book explains how the advent of the Information Age has given us a new way of looking at the fundamental entity in the world of physics. In the days of Newton we had "force" as the fundamental building block in the realm of dynamics. With Einstein it was "energy." Now, following an idea originating with the physicist John Wheeler, "information" is also seen as being fundamental. Everything in the world can be thought of as consisting of "bits" of information. So information is connected to existence itself.

30. I know this sounds like a naïve oversimplification, but it's literally true. And sometimes the simplest description is the best one. The important point is that the mind is not a separate entity from the brain. Steven Pinker discusses its actual operation in *How the Mind Works*. Then there is Marvin Minsky's classic, *The Society of Mind*. Another excellent source is Gerald Edelman's *Bright Air, Brilliant Fire*, also *Synaptic Self*, by Joseph LeDoux. For some recent ideas about how one would go about *building* a mind, *Artificial Minds*, by Stan Franklin is recommended.

31. For further details see Edelman, *Bright Air, Brilliant Fire*, pp. 111-146.

32. Grand, *Creation*, p. 93.

33. A good exposition of how neural networks can be modeled by computers can be found in *Emergence*, by John Holland. Another excellent source of information for the general reader is William Allman's *Apprentices of Wonder: Inside the Neural Network Revolution*.

34. Satinover, *The Quantum Brain*, p. 97.

35. Some scientists think that computers will eventually become more intelligent than human beings. A discussion of this can be found in Ray Kurzweil's *The Age of Spiritual Machines*. A few people have voiced fears that such "superior"

creatures might turn humans into slaves, or eliminate them altogether. But Steve Grand, in *Creation* (pp. 96-99), does not think that this is likely to be a problem. After all, these machines are designed by human beings, and so will presumably serve the interests of their creators.

36. Rodney Brooks, one of the leaders in the field of robotics, discusses just how robots will change our lives in *Flesh and Machines.*

37. Gerald Edelman doesn't think that machines can have consciousness, because consciousness arises from the neural circuits in the brain, which do not operate the way a computer does. "Furthermore, the development of a rich syntax and grammar is highly improbable without the prior evolution of a neural means for concepts. If this turns out to be true, it will be obvious why computers are unable to deal with semantic situations. Their embodiment is wrong; it does not lead to consciousness." (*Bright Air, Brilliant Fire,* p. 126.) Edelman does not think that modeling neural networks on computers is productive, because a human programmer sets them up, whereas the brain has no designer or programmer, it is the result of natural selection.

38. Hoffmann, *The Same and Not the Same,* p. 104.

39. John Holland's book *Emergence* goes into this in detail. The gist of it is that a simple process, with simple rules, can generate more complex phenomena. For example, in biological systems, certain molecules, when brought together, can spontaneously create something that is capable of reproducing itself. Thus a step higher on the hierarchy of complexity is achieved.

40. Grand, *Creation,* p. 78.

41. Ibid., p. 146.

42. Emmeche, *The Garden in the Machine,* p. 72.

43. This is excerpted from the article, *A Brief History of the Multiverse,* by Paul Davies, in the New York Times, Op-Ed page, 04/12/03. Davies' most recent book is *How to Build a Time Machine.*

11
LAWS OF MAN AND NATURE

1. Finegan, *Archaeological History of the Ancient Middle East,* p. 65.

2. Wright, *Nonzero,* p. 81.

3. See Plato's *Republic,* Book III. It's interesting that Plato should consider that *philosophers* were the people best qualified for this kind of job. He also says that these wise men should be permitted to lie to the people if they consider this to be in the public interest!

4. See Harris, *Civilization and Its Enemies,* pp. 88-98.

5. Vertosick, *The Genius Within,* p. 196.

6. How these games can be programmed, and their relation to things like neural nets, is discussed by John Holland in his book *Emergence.*

7. Darwin, *The Descent of Man,* p. 634.

8. The Netherlands Institute of Ecology has recently conducted studies that show definite personality traits in wild birds. Source: article by Carl Zimmer, New York Times Science Section, 03/01/05.

9. We do not know if space really *is* curved, as general relativity says it is. It just acts "as if" it's curved. Besides, the equations of the theory have several different solutions, and we are not sure which of them really fits our universe—it depends on the "initial conditions." Could there be other universes where the redundant solutions that don't fit ours are valid? These considerations raise questions as to just how closely general relativity approximates a *real* law of Nature.

10. For the derivation of this equation, see Einstein, *The Meaning of Relativity,* p. 44.

12
POLITICS AND POWER

1. Ortega y Gasset, *Invertebrate Spain,* Chapter 4.

2. See McMillan, *Reinventing the Bazaar,* pp. 94-101.

3. See ibid., pp. 148-66. This explains what kind of government action is beneficial to the market, and what hampers it. But the market cannot operate properly without appropriate regulation.

4. Quoted by Steven Strogatz in his book *Sync,* p. 273. Scientists have recently discovered that there may be a reason for this kind of behavior. It has to do with a process called synchronization, which occurs widely in nature. Details can be found in Strogatz's book, chapter 10.

5. I'm not sure of the origin of this quote. I read it in an op-ed article in the *New York Times* by Paul Klugman.

6. Stiglitz, *Globalization and Its Discontents,* p. 12.

7. Roy, *An Ordinary Person's Guide to Empire,* p. 105.

8. Chua, *World on Fire,* p. 230.

9. Ibid., p. 270.

13
PURPOSEFUL PURSUITS

1. Premack, *Original Intelligence,* p. 9.

2. Nietzsche, *Twilight of the Idols,* (in *The Portable Nietzsche*) p. 502.

3. The work ethic derives from the "Protestant ethic," which was made popular by Max Weber's book, *The Protestant Ethic and the Spirit of Capitalism* (1920). This connects capitalism with the Calvinistic ethos regarding the accumulation of wealth. But Weber was not as optimistic about capitalism as the capitalists. A complex and rather pessimistic character, he tried to explain the fact that most work is not rewarding by asserting that it was in any case an ennobling activity. His voluminous writings on sociology and economics are difficult to digest, but his prediction that capitalism does not necessarily lead to happiness has proved to be accurate.

4. Aristotle, *Metaphysics*, Book I. From *The Philosophy of Aristotle* (tr. by Creed and Wardman), p. 41.

5. Kauffman, *Interactions*, p. 229. This book goes beyond Kauffman's previous book about complexity, *At Home in the Universe.*

6. Darwin, *The Descent of Man*, p. 142.

7. Huntington, *The Clash of Civilizations*, p. 51.

8. For an account of some of these differences see Scott, *Seeing Like a State*, p. 132.

9. For a perspective of various utopian schemes and why they failed, see ibid., pp. 89-90, 114-16.

10. Dawkins, *The Selfish Gene*, p. 117.

11. See Wells, *The Journey of Man*, p. 191.

12. Darwin, *The Descent of Man*, p. 145.

13. Ibid., p. 614.

14. Lissner, *The Living Past*, p. 20.

15. Darwin, *The Descent of Man*, p. 140.

16. See Ibid., pp. 21-23.

17. McNeill & McNeill, *The Human Web*, p. 253.

14
PHILOSOPHICAL VIEWPOINTS

1. Spin is an elusive concept, part mathematical part physical. It has to do with the idea of "intrinsic angular momentum." There are a lot of books that explain spin to a certain degree, but most of them are overly technical. If you are interested in learning more about it, I recommend Feynman, *Lectures in Physics, Vol 3*, or, for the origins of the concept of spin, Tomonaga, *The Story of Spin.*

2. A representation of a group is a specific realization of the group elements by matrices. A Lie Group is actually represented on its own "tangent space," which can be considered as a vector space with a special type of multiplication, constituting the "Lie Algebra." For more information about these things you can consult Sternberg, *Group Theory and Physics;* also Gottfried & Weisskoph, *Concepts of Particle Physics.*

3. For an account of this see Gell-Mann, *The Quark and the Jaguar.* Another excellent reference, also very accessible to the layman, is Glashow, *Interactions.*

4. A very clear and informative account of the background of the Standard Model is Barnett, Murhy & Quinn, *The Charm of Strange Quarks.*

5. You might say that Sophus Lie did not actually *create* Lie groups, that he merely discovered them. They existed in embryo until he came upon them in the nineteenth century, because they are part of the "logical imperative" of the physical world. You can say the same thing about other physical laws as well. But you are only speculating.

6. Roger Penrose has a chapter called Mathematics and Reality in *The Emperor's New Mind,* which goes into this question in some detail. Like Russell, he is firmly of the opinion that the great mathematical formulae describing the physical world reflect the basic essence of things. He considers them to be "God's equations," and that the great scientific theories are "discovered" rather than invented by their creators. This seems to me doubtful at best, because, as we have seen, mathematics has no independent existence outside of the human mind.

7. A book that explains this concept very elegantly is Icke, *The Force of Symmetry.*

8. Our perception of the world has of course evolved as part of biological evolution, like that of every other living creature, anywhere in the universe. So one could say that this picture has gradually emerged with the evolution of complex life forms.

9. Barrow, *The World Within the World,* p. 293.

10. Gaddis, *The Landscape of History,* p. 10.

11. An article in the *New York Times,* Science Section, 09/08/00, by Erica Goode, states that these differences went far beyond the normal cultural differences regarding what people thought *about.* It was found that people actually think *differently* in different cultures. In other words, their manner of thinking about the material world is colored by the culture in which they live.

12. According to the theory of networks, it is not your closest friends that are the most valuable as far as making connections to the rest of the world. Rather it is the weaker links, the mere acquaintances that can really expand your horizons and make the important connections for you. Of course the Internet has provided all sorts of other links that never existed before. For more information about this and other aspects of networks see Barabási, *Linked: The New Science of Networks.*

13. According to Gerald Edelman, there are two types of consciousness: primary consciousness and higher order consciousness. Many animals have primary consciousness, which relates mainly to the environment, involves limited memory, and is not "introspective." It deals mainly with the present, unlike the higher order consciousness of human beings, which can correlate past experiences to form a far more sophisticated picture of the world. A concept of self is the main characteristic of higher order consciousness. This provides for more complex social relationships between individuals. See *Bright Air, Brilliant Fire,* pp. 111-136.

14. For more information on this subject see Ornstein, *The Evolution of Consciousness.*

15. See LeDoux, *Synaptic Self,* pp. 65-96.

16. Smolin, *Three Roads to Quantum Gravity,* p. 64.

17. Russell, *A History of Western Philosophy,* p. 834.

18. Nietzsche, *Beyond Good and Evil,* quoted in Beardsley, *The European Philosophers from Descartes to Nietzsche,* p. 805.

19. Ibid., p. 813.

20. Russell, *A History of Western Philosophy,* p. 765.

21. In *On the Genealogy of Morals (First Essay)*, Nietzsche presents the history of how good and bad have come to be used in this way.

22. Kaufmann, *Nietzsche*, p. 12.

23. Lynn, *Battle*, p. 132.

24. Shermer, *The Science of Good and Evil*, p. 56.

15
THE PATHOLOGY OF WAR

1. See Shermer, *The Science of Good and Evil*, pp. 97-104.

2. Keegan, *A History of Warfare*, p. 5.

3. Ibid, p. 46.

4. In chapter 1 of *Battle*, John Lynn explains at length why there is no historical continuity between the Greek phalanx and modern Western warfare. He also shows that there is no inherent difference Western and the Asian "ways of war."

5. Farewell radio and television address to the American people, January 17, 1961.

6. Ehrenreich, *Blood Rites*, p. 216.

7. Keegan, *War: Great Military Writings*, p. 4.

8. Ibid., p. 5.

9. It has lately come to light that in 1940 Churchill's cabinet debated whether talks with the Nazis were perhaps a prudent alternative to the coming battle. See article by Benjamin Schwarz in the *New York Times*, 11/25/00.

10. What Sherman, the famous Union general, actually said was: "War is at best barbarism…. Its glory is all moonshine. It is only those who have never fired a shot nor heard the shrieks and groans of the wounded who cry aloud for blood, more vengeance, more desolation. War is hell."

11. Ferm, *Living Schools of Religion,* p. 5.

12. Harris, *Civilization and Its Enemies,* p. 65.

13. Hedges, *War is a Force That Gives Us Meaning,* p. 20.

14. The "facade of disavowal" is quite common when dreadful deeds are done by one's countrymen or kinfolk. An example is Saudi Arabia, when 15 of the 19 hijackers in the 9/11 terrorist attacks were revealed to have come from there. The average Saudi simply refused to believe this, in spite of irrefutable evidence that Saudi citizens were indeed involved. Another example is the amnesia of the Turks regarding the genocide afflicted on the Armenians (1894-1915).

15. Even though individual personalities vary, it seems that just about all human beings are capable of committing atrocities, given the right circumstances. Michael Shermer's well-researched book, *The Science of Good and Evil* (chapter 3), describes how those Nazis who carried out the Holocaust were not criminals, but found themselves in situations where they were forced to commit acts that they would normally have considered to be totally immoral. Once the "authority" for such acts is accepted, and the fear of punishment or reprimand is sufficiently strong, no moral scruples can prevent them from being carried out.

16. Hedges, *War is a Force That Gives Us Meaning,* p. 145.

17. Clausewitz, *On War,* p. 119.

18. In *War, Politics and Power,* pp. 145-59, Clausewitz gives an insightful analysis of how the forms of government of the European nations gradually became more centralized and their ability to make war developed accordingly. This development culminated in Napoleon's ability to put vast armies into the field. The result, however, was Napoleon's ultimate defeat, when the rest of Europe rose against him.

    In *Battle,* John Lynn maintains that the methods of warfare throughout history have varied with the different cultures.

19. The instances of rape, and the reasons for it, vary widely under different circumstances, whether or not it is within the confines of war. In *Berlin, The Downfall 1945,* Antony Beevor provides a revealing account of the wide-

spread occurrence of rape by the Soviet Army in World War II. He maintains that the reasons for rape varied widely according to the nationality of the victims and the circumstances of the actual fighting. They varied all the way from the desire for revenge against the Germans, to the basic imperative of procreation.

20. Buruma, *Inventing Japan*, p. 105.

21. Haslam, *No Virtue Like Necessity*, p.250.

22. For a more thorough account of the relations between nation states, and an analysis of several important treaties and peace conferences, such as Augsburg, Westphalia, Utrecht, Vienna and Versailles, see Philip Bobbitt's book *The Shield of Achilles*. The problem with all these "agreements" was the lack of any effective means of enforcement.

23. Kaplan, *Warrior Politics*, p. 63.

24. Machiavelli, *The Prince*, (XVIII), p. 56

25. Kaplan, *Warrior Politics*, p. 56

26. Ibid., p. 55.

27. Fareed Zakaria discusses this at length in *The Future of Freedom*, pp. 199-256.

16
CULTURAL VISTAS

1. Yergin, *The Commanding Heights*, p. 15.

2. For a discussion of why neither the art nor the "values" of one culture is necessarily superior to that of any other, see Berlin, *The Crooked Timber of Humanity*, pp. 1-91.

3. Mikel Dufrenne, in *European Intellectual History Since Darwin and Marx* (ed. W. Warren Wager), explains these different strains of existentialism (see pp. 220-236).

4. Vertosick, *The Genius Within,* p.293. The "bead" here refers to Herman Hesse's *Das Glasperlenspiel* (The Glass Bead Game), where ornate glass beads represent the building blocks of the various branches of human knowledge—each branch having its own distinctive pattern.

5. The Farnsworth House, set on 58 acres of prairie land, 60 miles southwest of Chicago, was sold at auction to the National Trust and the Landmarks Preservation Council of Illinois in December, 2003 for $7.5 million.

6. For the history of this phenomenon see Gilles Kepel, *Jihad.* This brings together the story of the various "Islamist" movements that arose subsequent to World War I. The author explains why he thinks that this extreme form of Islam is now on the decline.

7. For a lucid discussion of globalization and its likely consequences see Stiglitz, *Globalization and Its Discontents.*

8. For further information about Americans' loss of faith in their government, see Fareed Zakaria's *The Future of Freedom,* chapter 4.

9. Greene, *The Elegant Universe,* p. 16.

10. Weinberg, *Dreams of a Final Theory,* p. 52, quoted ibid.

11. Berlin, *The Crooked Timber of Humanity,* p. 12.

12. See Hoffmann, *The Same and Not the Same,* p. 7.

13. A fine account of the mixing of politics with religion in America can be found in Thomas Frank's wise and witty book, *What's the Matter with Kansas?*

14. For further observations regarding the fetish of the American flag see Ehrenreich, *Blood Rites,* p. 218.

15. This is part of a quote from the Black Panther leader, H. (Rap) Brown in 1966. The whole quote is: "Violence is necessary; it is as American as cherry pie."

16. For an eloquent critique of America's misbegotten pursuit of a "neo-liberal" global empire see *An Ordinary Person's Guide to Empire,* by Amundhati Roy.

AFTERTHOUGHTS

1. Barrow, *The World Within the World,* p. 297.

2. Ibid., p. 300.

3. Minsky, *The Society of Mind,* p.49.

4. Ibid., p. 65.

5. Brooks, *Flesh and Machines,* p. 238

GENERAL BIBLIOGRAPHY

✦

(Non-Science)

Alvarez, Walter. *T.rex and the Crater of Doom.* Princeton: Princeton University Press, 1997.

Ardrey, Robert. *African Genesis.* New York: Dell, 1961.

——————*The Territorial Imperative.* New York: Atheneum, 1966.

Aristotle. *The Philosophy of Aristotle.* Translated by A. E. Wardman and J. L. Creed. New York: Mentor Books, 1963

Barraclough, Geoffrey. *The Origins of Modern Germany.* New York: Capricorn Books, 1963.

Bataille, Georges. *Theory of Religion.* New York: Zone Books, 1989.

Beardsley, Monroe C. (editor). *The European Philosophers from Descartes to Nietzsche.* New York: The Modern Library, 1960.

Beevor, Antony. *Stalingrad, The Fateful Siege: 1942-1943.* New York: Penguin Books, 1999.

——————*Berlin, The Downfall 1945.* London: Viking, 2002.

Berend, Ivan T. *History Derailed: Central and Eastern Europe in the Long Nineteenth Century.* Berkley: University of California Press, 2003.

Berlin, Isaiah. *The Crooked Timber of Humanity* (ed. Henry Hardy). New York: Vintage Books, 1992.

Berman, Morris. *Coming to Our Senses.* New York: Simon & Schuster, 1989.

Bierman, John. *Napoleon III and His Carnival Empire.* New York: St. Martin's Press, 1988.

Bobbitt, Philip. *The Shield of Achilles: War, Peace, and the Course of History.* New York: Alfred A. Knopf, 2002.

Bowersock, G. W. *Hellenism in Late Antiquity.* Ann Arbor: University of Michigan Press, 1993.

Braudel, Fernand. *A History of Civilizations* (tr. Richard Mayne). New York: Penguin Books, 1995.

Breasted, James H. *A History of Egypt.* New York: Scribner, 1937.

Bridge, Antony. *The Crusades.* New York: Franklin Watts, 1982.

Brinton, Crane. *Nietzsche. New* York: Harper & Row, 1965.

Brown, Norman O. *Life Against Death: The Psychoanalytical Meaning of History.* New York: Random House, 1959.

Buruma, Ian. *Inventing Japan: 1853-1964.* New York: Modern Library, 2003.

Bury, J. B. *A History of Greece.* New York: Modern Library.

——————The Invasion of Europe by the Barbarians. New York: W. W. Norton, 1967.

Campbell, Joseph. *The Masks of God, 4 vols.* New York: Penguin Books, 1968.

Carman, Harry J. and Syrett, Harold C. *A History of the American People, vol 2.* New York: Alfred A. Knopf, 1957.

Cannadine, David. *Ornamentalism: How the British Saw Their Empire.* New York: Oxford University Press, 2001.

Cavan, Brian. *The Punic Wars.* London: Weidenfeld and Nicolson, 1980.

Cary, M. *A History of the Greek World: 323-146 B.C.* London: Methuen, 1978.

Cassirer, Ernst. *The Myth of the State.* New Haven: Yale University Press, 1963.

Chamberlain, Niel W. *The West in a World Without War.* New York: McGraw-Hill, 1963.

Chambers, James. *The Devil's Horsemen: The Mongol Invasion of Europe.* New York: Atheneum, 1979.

Charques, R. D. *A Short History of Russia.* New York: E. P. Dutton, 1956.

Cheilik, Michael. *Ancient History.* New York: Barnes & Noble Books, 1969.

Chua, Amy. *World on Fire: How Exporting Free Market Democracy Breeds Ethnic Hatred and Global Instability.* New York: Anchor Books, 2004.

Churchill, Winston S. *A History of the English Speaking Peoples, 4 vols.* New York: Dodd, Mead & Company, Inc., 1958.

Cipolla, Carlo M. *Guns, Sails, and Empires: Technological Innovation and the Early Phases of European Expansion 1400-1700.* New York: Minerva Press, 1965.

Clausewitz, Carl von. *On War* (tr. M. Howard & P. Paret). Princeton: Princeton University Press, 1976.

——————*War, Politics, and Power* (tr. E. M. Collins). Washington D.C.: Regnery Publishing Inc., 1997.

Cobban, Alfred. *A History of Modern France, 3 vols.* Middlesex: Penguin Books, 1985.

Coe, Michael D. *Mexico.* New York: Thames and Hudson, 1984.

Conquest, Robert. *The Dragons of Expectation.* New York: W. W. Norton, 2005.

Diamond, Jared. *Guns, Germs, and Steel.* New York: W. W. Norton, 1997.

Diaz, Bernal. *The Conquest of New Spain.* Middlesex: Penguin Books, 1983.

Ehrenreich, Barbara. *Blood Rites: Origins and History of the Passions of War.* New York: Metropolitan Books, 1997.

Fagan, Brian M. *The Great Journey: The Peopling of Ancient America.* London: Thames & Hudson, 1987.

Ferm, Vergilius. ed. *Living Schools of Religion.* Ames, Iowa: Littlefield, Adams, 1956.

Fernández-Armesto, Felipe. *Millennium: A History of the Last Thousand Years.* New York: Charles Scribner's Sons, 1995.

Field, Henry. *The Track of Man.* New York: Dell, 1967.

Figes, Orlando & Kolonitskii, Boris. *Interpreting the Russian Revolution: The Language and Symbols of 1917.* Newhaven: Yale University Press, 1999.

Finegan, Jack. *Archaeological History of the Ancient Middle East.* New York: Dorset Press, 1986.

Fisher, H. A. L. *A History of Europe, 3 vols.* Cambridge Mass.: The Riverside Press, 1937.

Fletcher, Banister. *A History of Architecture on the Comparative Method.* New York: Charles Scribner, 1967.

Frank, Thomas. *What's the Matter with Kansas?: How Conservatives Won the Heart of America. New York:* Metropolitan Books, 2004.

Freud, Sigmund. *Moses and Monotheism.* New York: Alfred A. Knopf, Inc., 1939.

——————*The Future of an Illusion.* Garden City, New York: Doubleday, 1964.

——————*Totem and Taboo.* New York: W. W. Norton, 1950.

Fromkin, David. *A Peace to End All Peace: The Fall of the Ottoman Empire and the Creation of the Modern Middle East.* New York: Avon Books, 1989.

Frost, David and Jay, Antony. *The English.* New York: Stein and Day, 1968.

Garraty, John A. and Gay, Peter (eds.). *The Columbia History of the World.* New York: Harper & Row, 1984.

Gaddis, John Lewis. *The Landscape of History: How Historians Map the Past.* New York: Oxford University Press, 2002.

Gernet, Jacques, (tr. by J. R. Foster). *A History of Chinese Civilization.* Cambridge: Cambridge University Press, 1982.

Ghirshman, Roman. *The Art of Ancient Iran.* New York: Golden Press, 1964.

Gibbon, Edward. *The Decline and Fall of the Roman Empire.* (1 vol. abbr. D. M. Low.) New York: Harcourt, Brace and Company, 1960.

Glover, Michael. *The Napoleonic Wars: An Illustrated History 1792-1815.* New York: Hippocrene Books, 1978.

Glubb, Sir John. *A Short History of the Arab Peoples.* New York: Stein and Day, 1970.

Grant, Michael. *The History of Ancient Israel.* New York: Charles Scribner, 1984.

Gurney, O. R. *The Hittites.* Baltimore: Penguin Books, 1964.

Hadas, Moses. *Imperial Rome.* New York: Time Inc., 1965.

Hahn, Emily. *China Only Yesterday: 1850-1950.* London: Weidenfeld and Nicolson, 1963.

Hale, John R. *Renaissance.* New York: Time Inc., 1965.

Hammond, Norman. *Ancient Maya Ciuvilization.* New Brunswick: Rutgers University Press, 1982.

Harris, Lee. *Civilization and Its Enemies: The Next Stage of History.* New York: Free Press, 2004.

Hart, Roger. *Battle of the Spanish Armada.* Hove, England: Wayland, 1987.

Haslam, Jonathon. *No Virtue Like Necessity: Realist Thought in International Relations Since Machiavelli.* New Haven: Yale University Press, 2002.

Hedges, Chris. *War is a Force That Gives Us Meaning.* Cambridge, Mass.: Perseus Books, 2002.

Heyer, Paul. *Architects on Architecture.* New York: Walker & Co.,1966.

Hodges, Richard and Whitehouse, David. *Mohammed, Charlemagne & the Origins of Europe.* Ithaca, New York: Cornell University Press, 1983.

Hook, Sidney. *Marx and the Marxists.* New York: Van Nostrand, 1955.

Horne, Alistair. *How Far from Austerlitz?: Napoleon 1805-1815.* New York: St. Martin's Press, 1996.

Horney, Karen. *The Neurotic Personality of Our Time.* New York: W. W. Norton, 1964.

Hourani, Albert. *A History of the Arab Peoples.* Cambridge Mass.: Harvard University Press, 1991.

Humphreys, Christmas. *Buddhism.* Reading: Wyman and Sons, 1952.

Huizinga, J. *The Waning of the Middle Ages.* New York: Doubleday, 1954.

Huntington, Samuel P. *The Clash of Civilizations and the Remaking of World Order.* New York: Simon & Schuster, 1997.

Irokawa, Daikichi. *The Age of Hirohito: In Search of Modern Japan.* New York: Simon & Schuster, 1995.

Jacobs, Jane. *The Death and life of Great American Cities.* New York: Vintage Books, 1992.

Jaspers, Karl. *The Future of Mankind.* Chicago: University of Chicago Press, 1963.

——————and Bultmann, Rudolf. *Myth and Christianity.* New York: Noonday Press, 1964.

Joedicke, Jurgen. *A History of Modern Architecture.* London: Architectural Press, 1961.

Judd, Denis. *The Lion and the Tiger: The Rise and Fall of the British Raj.* Oxford: Oxford University Press, 2004.

Kann, Robert A. *A History of the Habsburg Empire 1526-1918.* Berkeley: University of California Press, 1974.

Kaplan, Robert D. *Warrior Politics: Why Leadership Demands a Pagan Ethos.* New York: Vintage Books, 2002.

Kaufmann, Walter. *Nietzsche: Philosopher Psychologist Antichrist.* Cleveland: Meridian Books, 1966.

Keegan, John. *War: Great Military Writings.* New York: Penguin Books, 1999.

——————*A History of Warfare.* London: Pimlico, 1993.

Kenyon, J. P. *The Civil Wars of England.* New York: Alfred A. Knopf, 1988.

Kepel, Gilles (tr. by A. F. Roberts). *Jihad: The Trail of Political Islam.* Cambridge, Mass.: Harvard University Press, 2002.

Kinross, Lord. *The Ottoman Centuries: The Rise and Fall of the Turkish Empire.* New York: Morrow Quill, 1977.

Levi-Strauss, Claude. *The Savage Mind.* Chicago: University of Chicago Press, 1967.

——————*The Jealous Potter.* Chicago: University of Chicago Press, 1988.

Lewis, Bernard. *The Middle East: A Brief History of the Last 2,000 Years.* New York: Scribner, 1995.

——————*What Went Wrong?: Western Impact and Middle Eastern Response.* New York: Oxford University Press, 2002

Lissner, Ivar. *The Living Past: 7,000 Years of Civilization.* New York: Capricorn Books, 1961.

Lorenz, Konrad. *On Aggression.* New York: Harcourt, Brace & World, 1966.

Lukas, John. *Democracy and Populism: Fear and Hatred.* New Haven: Yale University Press, 2005.

Lynn, John A. *Battle: A History of Combat and Culture.* Boulder, Colorado: Westview Press, 2003.

Marcuse, Herbert. *Eros and Civilization.* New York: Vintage Books, 1955.

Marx, Anthony W. *Faith in Nation: Exclusionary Origins of Nationalism.* Oxford: Oxford University Press, 2003.

McEvedy, Colin. *The Penguin Atlas of Ancient, Medieval, and Modern History, 3 vols.* New York: Penguin Books, 1978.

MacDonald, Lyn. *The Roses of No Man's Land.* London: Penguin Books, 1980.

Machiavelli, Niccolò. *The Prince* (tr. by George Bull). New York: Penguin Books, 1999.

MacKendrick, Paul. *The Greek Stones Speak.* New York: Mentor Books, 1966.

McLuhan, Marshall. *Understanding Media: The Extensions of Man.* New York: McGraw-Hill, 1965.

——————and Fiore, Quentin. *The Medium is the Massage.* New York: Bantam Books, 1967

McMillan, John. *Reinventing the Bazaar: A Natural History of Markets.* New York: W. W. Norton & Company, 2002.

McNeill, William H. *The Rise of the West: A History of the Human Community.* Chicago: University of Chicago Press, 1964.

——————*The Pursuit of Power.* Chicago: University of Chicago Press, 1982.

——————*Plagues and Peoples.* New York: Anchor Books, 1976.

——————& J. R. McNeill. *The Human Web: A Bird's-Eye View of World History.* New York: W. W. Norton & Company, 2003.

McPherson, James M. *Battle Cry of Freedom: The Civil War Era.* New York: Oxford University Press, 1988.

Mencken, H. L. *Treatise on the Gods.* New York: Vintage Books, 1963.

Meyer, Karl E. *The Dust of Empire: The Race for Mastery in the Asian Heartland.* New York: Public Affairs, 2003.

Michelet, Jules. *History of the French Revolution* (ed. Gordon Wright). Chicago: University of Chicago Press, 1967.

Morris, Desmond. *The Naked Ape: A Zoologist's Study of the Human Animal.* New York: McGraw-Hill, 1967.

Morton, W. Scott. *Japan: Its History and Culture.* New York: McGraw-Hill, 1984.

Moscati, Sabatino. *The Face of the Ancient Orient.* New York: Doubleday, 1962.

Monk, Roy. *Ludwig Wittgenstein: Duty of Genius.* New York: Penguin Books, 1990.

Muller, Herbert J. *The Uses of the Past.* New York: Schocken Books, 1985.

Mumford, Lewis. *The Highway and the City.* New York: Harcourt, Brace & World, 1963.

Nietzsche, Friedrich. *On the Genealogy of Morals* (tr. by Walter Kaufmann & R.J. Hollingdale). New York: Vintage Books, 1989.

——————*The Portable Nietzsche,* (tr. by Walter Kaufmann). Princeton: Princeton University Press, 1954.

Northrop, F. S. C. *The Meeting of East and West.* New York: Macmillan, 1966.

Norwich, John Julius. *Byzantium: The Early Centuries.* New York: Alfred A. Knopf, 1989

Olmstead, A. T. *History of the Persian Empire.* Chicago: University Press, 1948.

Overy, Richard. *Russia's War.* London: Penguin Books, 1998.

Parker, Geoffrey. *Philip II.* Boston: Little, Brown & Co., 1978.

Parrot, André. *Sumer: The Dawn of Art.* New York: Golden Press, 1961.

Patten, Chris. *East and West.* London: Macmillan, 1998.

Patterson, Thomas C. *Archaeology: The Evolution of Ancient Societies.* Englewood Cliffs, N.J.: Prentice-Hall, 1981.

Pendle, George. *A History of Latin America.* Middlesex, England: Penguin Books, 1983.

Pirenne, Henri. *Economic and Social History of Medieval Europe.* New York: Harcourt, Brace & World, 1937.

Plato. *Great Dialogues of Plato* (tr. W. H. D. Rouse). New York: Mentor Books, 1964.

Prescott, William H. *The Conquest of Peru.* New York: Mentor Books, 1961.

Rashid, Ahmed. *Taliban: Militant Islam, Oil and Fundamentalism in Central Asia.* New Haven: Yale University Press, 2000.

Roy, Arundhati. *An Ordinary Person's Guide to Empire.* Cambridge, Mass.: South End Press, 2004.

Russell, Bertrand. *Human Knowledge: Its Scope and Limits.* New York: Simon & Schuster, 1967.

——————*Unpopular Essays.* New York: Simon & Schuster, 1966.

——————*A History of Western Philosophy.* New York: Simon & Schuster, 1965.

Sartre, Jean-Paul. *The Psychology of Imagination.* New York: Citadel Press, 1965.

Schele, Linda and Freidel, David. *A Forest of Kings: The Untold Story of the Ancient Maya.* New York: William Morrow, 1990.

Schlesinger, Arthur M. *The Bitter Heritage: Vietnam and American Democracy 1941-1996.* Boston: Houghton Mifflin, 1967.

Schram, Stuart. *Mao Tse-tung.* New York: Simon & Schuster, 1966.

Scott, James C. *Seeing Like a State.* New Haven: Yale University Press, 1998.

Sebald, W. G. *On the Natural History of Destruction.* New York: Modern Library 2004.

Seward, Desmond. *The Hundred Years War.* New York: Atheneum, 1978.

Sitwell, N. H. H. *The World the Romans Knew*. London: Hamish Hamilton, 1984.

Spengler, Oswald. *The Decline of the West, 2 vols.* (tr. C. F. Atkinson). New York: Alfred A. Knopf, 1961.

Stiglitz, Joseph E. *Globalization and Its Discontents*. New York: W. W. Norton, 2002.

Stromberg, Roland N. *A History of Western Civilization*. Homewood, Illinois: Dorsey Press, 1963.

Sun Tzu. *The Art of War* (tr. by Thomas Cleary). Boston: Shambala, 1988.

Tarn, W. W. *Alexander the Great*. Boston: Beacon Press, 1964.

Taylor, A. J. P. *The Habsburg Monarchy, 1809-1918*. New York: Harper & Row, 1965.

Thomson, Hugh. *The White Rock: An Exploration of the Inca Heartland*. New York: Overlook Press, 2003.

Tocqueville, Alexis, de. *The Old Régime and the French Revolution*. Garden City, NY: Anchor Books, 1955.

——————*Democracy in America, vol. 2*. New York: Vintage Books, 1990.

Toynbee, Arnold. *A Study of History, 11 vols.* Oxford: Oxford University Press, 1979.

——————*Mankind and Mother Earth*. New York: Oxford University Press, 1976.

Tuchman, Barbara W. *A Distant Mirror: The Calamitous 14th Century*. New York: Alfred A. Knopf, 1978.

Vaillant, G. C. *Aztecs of Mexico*. New York: Penguin Books, 1979.

Versényi, Lazlo. *Heidegger, Being, and Truth*. New Haven, Conn.: Yale University Press, 1965.

Wagar, Warren, W., (ed.). *European Intellectual History Since Darwin and Marx.* New York: Harper & Row, 1966.

Wedgwood, C. V. *The Thirty Years War.* Garden City, N.Y.: Doubleday, 1961.

Wheeler, Sir Mortimer. *Civilizations of the Indus Valley and Beyond.* New York: McGraw-Hill, 1966.

Wilson, David Sloan. *Darwin's Cathedral: Evolution, Religion and the Nature of Society.* Chicago: University of Chicago Press, 2002.

Wolpert, Stanley. *A New History of India.* New York: Oxford University Press, 1982.

Wright, Robert. *Nonzero.* New York: Pantheon Books, 2000.

Yap, Yong and Cotterell, Arthur. *The Early Civilization of China.* London: Weidenfeld & Nicolson, 1975.

Yergin, Daniel and Stanislaw, Joseph. *The Commanding Heights.* New York: Simon & Schuster, 1998.

Zakaria, Fareed. *The Future of Freedom: Illiberal Democracy at Home and Abroad.* New York: W. W. Norton & Company, 2003.

SCIENCE BIBLIOGRAPHY

Allman, William F. *Apprentices of Wonder: Inside the Neural Network Revolution.* New York: Bantam Books, 1989.

Andrews, George E. *Number Theory.* New York: Dover, 1994.

Anglin, W. S. and Lambek, J. *The Heritage of Thales.* New York: Springer-Verlag, 1995.

Bailey, James. *After Thought.* New York: Basic Books, 1996.

Barabási, Albert-László. *Linked: The New Science of Networks.* Cambridge, Mass.: Perseus Publishing, 2002.

Barbour, Julian. *The End of Time; The Next Revolution in Physics.* New York: Oxford University Press, 1999.

Barnett, R. Michael, Mühry, Henry & Quinn, Helen R. *The Charm of Strange Quarks: Mysteries and Revolutions of Particle Physics.* New York: Springer, 2001.

Barrow, John D. *The World Within the World.* Oxford: Oxford University Press, 1988.

Brooks, Rodney, A. *Flesh and Machines: How Robots Will Change Us.* New York: Pantheon Books, 2002.

Calvin, William H. *How Brains Think.* New York: Basic Books, 1996.

——————and Ojemann, George A. *Conversations with Neil's Brain.* New York: Addison-Wesley, 1994.

Casti, John L. *Searching for Certainty: What Scientists Can Know About the Future.* New York: William Morrow & Co. Inc., 1990.

419

Christian de Duve. *Vital Dust: Life as a Cosmic Imperative.* New York: Basic books, 1995.

Clark, Stuart. *Life on Other Worlds and How to Find It.* Chichester, U.K.: Springer-Praxis, 2000.

Cloud, Preston. *Oasis in Space: Earth History from the Beginning.* New York: W. W. Norton, 1988.

Coughlan, G. D. and Dodd, J. E. *The Ideas of Particle Physics.* Cambridge: Cambridge University Press, 1991.

Darwin, Charles. *The Origin of Species (1859).* London: Penguin Books, 1982.

—————————*The Descent of Man; and Selection in Relation to Sex (1874).* Amherst, NY: Prometheus Books, 1998.

Davies, P. C. W. *Quantum Mechanics.* New York: Routledge & Kegan Paul Ltd., 1987.

—————————and Gribbin, John. *The Matter Myth.* New York: Simon & Schuster, 1992.

Dawkins, Richard. *The Selfish Gene.* Oxford: Oxford University Press, 1989.

—————————*The Blind Watchmaker.* London: Longmans, 1986.

Dedekind, Richard. *Theory of Algebraic Integers.* Cambridge: Cambridge University Press, 1996.

Dennet, Daniel C. *Consciousness Explained.* Boston: Little, Brown & Company, 1991.

—————————*Kinds of Minds.* New York: Basic Books, 1996.

—————————*Darwin's Dangerous Idea.* New York: Simon & Schuster, 1995.

Edelman, Gerald M. *Neural Darwinism: The Theory of Neuronal Group Selection.* New York: Basic Books, 1987.

—————————*Bright Air, Brilliant Fire: On the Matter of the Mind.* New York: Basic Books, 1992.

Einstein, Albert. *The Meaning of Relativity.* London: Methuen, 1950.

Emmeche, Claus (tr. by S. Sampson). *The Garden in the Machine.* Princeton, New Jersey: Princeton University Press, 1994.

Epstein, Lewis Carroll. *Relativity Visualized.* San Francisco: Insight Press, 1988.

Feynman, Richard P. *QED.* Princeton: Princeton University Press, 1983.

——————*Lectures on Physics, 3 vols.* Reading, Mass.: Addison-Wesley, 1977.

Fortey, Richard. *Life: A Natural History of the First Four Billion Years on Earth.* New York: Alfred A. Knopf, 1998.

Franklin, Jon. *Molecules of the Mind: The Brave New Science of Molecular Psychology.* New York: Atheneum, 1987.

Franklin, Stan. *Artificial Minds.* Cambridge Mass.: MIT Press, 2001.

Frautschi, Olenick, Apostol & Goodstein. *The Mechanical Universe.* New York: Cambridge University Press, 1986.

Gardner, Howard. *The Quest for Mind.* New York: Alfred A. Knopf, 1973.

Gell-Mann, Murray. *The Quark and the Jaguar: Adventures in the Simple and the Complex.* New York: W. H. Freeman and Company, 1994.

Gelernter, David. *Mirror Worlds.* New York: Oxford University Press, 1991.

Gleik, James. *Chaos: Making a New Science.* New York: Viking Press, 1987.

Glashow, Sheldon L. *Interactions.* New York: Warner Books, 1988.

Goodsell, David S. *The Machinery of Life.* New York: Springer-Verlag, 1993.

Gottfried, Kurt and Weisskopf, Victor F. *Concepts of Particle Physics, 2 vols.* New York: Oxford University Press, 1986.

Grand, Steve. *Creation: Life and How to Make It.* Cambridge, Mass.: Harvard University Press, 2001.

Gregory, R. L. *Eye and Brain: The Psychology of Seeing*. New York: McGraw Book Company, 1966.

Hawking, Stephen. *A Brief History of Time*. New York: Bantam Books, 1988.

——————and Penrose, Roger. *The Nature of Space and Time*. Princeton: Princeton University Press, 1996.

Hoffmann, Raold. *The Same and Not the Same*. New York: Columbia University Press, 1995.

Holland, John H. *Emergence: From Chaos to Order*. Cambridge, Mass.: Perseus Books, 1998.

Icke, Vincent. *The Force of Symmetry*. Cambridge: Cambridge University Press, 1995.

Johnson, George. *Fire in the Mind: Science, Faith, and the Search for Order*. New York: Alfred A. Knopf, 1995.

Jordan, Thomas E. *Quantum Mechanics in Simple Matrix Form*. New York: John Wiley & Sons, 1986.

Kasner, Edward & Newman, James R. *Mathematics and the Imagination*. New York: Simon and Schuster, 1963.

Kauffman, Stuart. *At Home in the Universe: The Search for the Laws of Self-Organization and Complexity*. New York: Oxford University Press, 1995.

——————*Investigations*. New York: Oxford University Press, 2000.

Keller, Evelyn Fox. *Making Sense of Life: Explaining Biological Development With Models, Metaphors, and Machines*. Cambridge, Mass.: Harvard University Press, 2002.

Kurzweil, Ray. *The Age of Spiritual Machines*. New York: Viking Press, 1999.

LeDoux, Joseph. *Synaptic Self: How Our Brains Become Who We Are*. New York: Viking, 2002.

McFadden, JohnJoe. *Quantum Evolution: The New Science of Life*. New York: W. W. Norton, 2001.

Minsky, Marvin. *The Society of Mind.* New York: Simon & Schuster, 1982.

Nagel, Ernest and Newman, James R. *Gödel's Proof.* New York: New York University Press, 1964.

Peat, F. David. *Superstrings and the Search for the Theory of Everything.* Chicago: Contemporary Books, 1988.

Penrose, Roger. *The Emperor's New Mind.* New York: Oxford University Press, 1989.

Pinker, Steven. *How the Mind Works.* New York: W. W. Norton, 1997.

Pollan, Michael. *The Botany of Desire: A Plant's-Eye View of the World.* New York: Random House, 2001.

Premack, David & Ann. *Original Intelligence: Unlocking the Mystery of Who We Are.* New York: McGraw-Hill, 2003.

Rees, Martin. *Just Six Numbers.* New York: Basic Books, 2000.

Rensberger, Boyce. *Life Itself: Exploring the Realm of the Living Cell.* New York: Oxford University Press, 1996.

Ridley, Matt. *Genome: The Autobiography of a Species in 23 Chapters.* New York: HarperCollins, 1999.

Rigden, John S. *Hydrogen: The Essential Element.* Cambridge, Mass.: Harvard University Press, 2002.

Satinover, Jeffrey. *The Quantum Brain: The Search for Freedom and the Next Generation of Man.* New York: John Wiley & Sons, 2001.

Schrödinger, Erwin. *What is Life?* Cambridge: Cambridge University Press, 1992.

Seielstad, George, A. *At the Heart of the Web: The Inevitable Genesis of Intelligent Life.* New York: Harcourt Brace Jovanovich, 1989.

Schermer, Michael. *The Science of Good and Evil.* New York: Times Books, 1004.

Siegfried, Tom. *The Bit and the Pendulum.* New York: John Wiley & Sons, 2001.

——————————*Strange Matters: Undiscovered Ideas at the Frontiers of Space and Time.* Washington, D.C.: Joseph Henry Press, 2002.

Smolin, Lee. *Three Roads to Quantum Gravity.* New York: Basic Books, 2001.

Sternberg, S. *Group Theory and Physics.* Cambridge: Cambridge University Press, 1995.

Stillwell, John. *Mathematics and Its History.* New York: Springer-Verlag, 1989.

Strogatz, Steven. *Sync: The Emerging Science of Spontaneous Order.* New York: Hyperion, 2003.

Strong, James. *Flight to the Stars.* New York: Hart Publishing, 1965.

Sutton, Christine. *The Particle Connection.* New York: Simon & Schuster, 1984.

Talbot, Michael. *The Holographic Universe.* New York: HarperCollins, 1991.

Tomonaga, Sin-itiro. *The Story of Spin.* Translated by Takeshi Oka. Chicago: University of Chicago Press, 1997.

Tucker, Wallace and Karen. *The Dark Matter.* New York: William Morrow & Co.,1988.

Vertosick, Frank T. *The Genius Within: Discovering the Intelligence of Every Living Thing.* New York: Harcourt Inc., 2002.

Ward, P. and Brownlee, D. *Rare Earth: Why Complex Life is Uncommon in the Universe.* New York: Springer-Verlag, 2000.

Watson, James. *The Double Helix.* New York: Simon & Schuster, 1968.

Weeks, Jeffrey, R. *The Shape of Space.* New York: Marcel Dekker, 1985.

Weinberg, Steven. *Dreams of a Final Theory.* New York: Vintage Books, 1993. & Nicolson, 1975.

Wells, Spencer. *The Journey of Man: A Genetic Odyssey.* Princeton, NJ: Princeton University Press, 2003.

Wilczek, Frank and Devine, Betsy. *Longing for the Harmonies: Themes and Variations from Modern Physics.* New York: W. W. Norton & Company, 1988.

Wolfram, Stephen. *A New Kind of Science.* Champaign, Ill.: Wolfram Media, 2002.

Reference Books:

The New Columbia University Encyclopedia. New York: Columbia University Press, 1975.

The Flammarion Book of Astronomy. New York: Simon & Schuster, 1964.

Index

978-0-595-67356-8
0-595-67356-2

Printed in the United Kingdom
by Lightning Source UK Ltd.
109252UKS00002B/37-39